Conducting Social Work Research

An Experiential Approach

Reginald O. York
East Carolina University

Allyn and Bacon
Boston • London • Toronto • Sydney • Tokyo • Singapore

Editor-in-Chief, Social Sciences: Karen Hanson
Series Editor, Social Work: Judy Fifer
Editorial Assistant: Jennifer Muroff
Marketing Manager: Quinn Perkson
Production Coordinator: Christopher H. Rawlings
Editorial-Production Service: Omegatype Typography, Inc.
Composition and Prepress Buyer: Linda Cox
Manufacturing Buyer: Megan Cochran
Cover Administrator: Suzanne Harbison

Copyright © 1998 by Allyn & Bacon
A Viacom Company
160 Gould Street
Needham Heights, MA 02194

Internet: www.abacon.com
America Online: Keyword: College Online

Library of Congress Cataloging-in-Publication Data
York, Reginald O.
   Conducting social work research : an experiential approach /
Reginald O. York.
     p.   cm.
   Includes bibliographical references and index.
   ISBN 0-205-26891-9 (pbk.)
   1. Social service—Research—Methodology.   I. Title.
HV11.Y57   1997
361.3'072—dc21   96-50102
                                     CIP

Printed in the United States of America
10 9 8 7 6 5 4 3 2   03 02 01 00 99 98

Contents

9   Writing Study Purposes, Questions, Hypotheses, and Titles   219

Preface

This is a book that will help the reader to develop skill in conducting social work research. In the pursuit of this goal, you will be given information on specific tasks in research and exercises in which you will be called upon to evaluate alternative ways to complete each task in the research process. These exercises, placed throughout the chapters, ask you to stop, reflect upon what you have learned, and put it into practice. These exercises are designed to facilitate class discussion and give you the opportunity to test your understanding of the material and your ability to use it in research studies. After completing this text, you should be able to complete some research studies on your own, and offer leadership in the completion of most research projects that social workers would be called upon to undertake.

After the introductory chapter you will encounter the first major section of this book, which challenges you to consider the tasks associated with each of the four major purposes of social work research—exploration, description, explanation, and evaluation. Each chapter in this section is devoted to one purpose and provides an example in which you consider each of the major tasks in conducting the particular study exemplified. In five of the six chapters in this section, you will examine how to conduct (a) an exploratory study on stress among social work students, (b) a descriptive study on the qualities of the good manager, (c) an explanatory study on the qualities of the good manager, (d) an evaluative study of a parent skills program using a group research design, and (e) an evaluative study of this same program using a single-subject design. In the final chapter in this section, you will examine program evaluations of various kinds.

In this first section, you will examine both qualitative and quantitative methods of measurement. The example in chapter 2, the first chapter in this section, employs qualitative methods. The example in chapter 3 employs both qualitative and quantitative measurement in the pursuit of the same research question, as does the last chapter in this section, chapter 7. Chapters 4, 5, and 6 employ quantitative examples.

In Unit II, you will be given principles for guiding some of the key tasks in the research process. These tasks include writing the literature review, developing statements of hypotheses and study purpose, selecting scales for measurement, conducting a mailed survey, and writing the methods and results sections of the research report. Each of the chapters in Unit II is organized around practical guiding principles for these tasks.

Unit III takes you on a unique journey in the statistical analysis of research data. You will be given a review of the critical concepts for the data analysis task, a set of decision trees for selecting a statistical measure for your study, a description of sixteen statistical measures included in the decision trees (plus various descriptive statistics), and a guide for using one particular statistical software package for data analysis (SPSS for Windows) with each of these sixteen measures. The final chapter in this section focuses on data analysis for evaluative research. In this chapter, you will encounter additional decision trees for approaching data analysis of both group and single-subject research designs.

This final section is predicated on the assumption that it is not critical that you understand the formula for any particular statistical measure. Instead, you must be given a set of decision trees for finding a measure that fits your particular study, and you must be able to answer the key questions for selecting a statistic. There are, of course, many statistical measures beyond the selected sixteen presented here. But an effort was made to identify statistical measures that fit most situations in which social workers are likely to find themselves. In this final section, you can find a statistic for your study (or most of the studies you are likely to conduct), you can review a description of that statistic, and you can find instructions on how to use the computer for analyzing your data, including how to read the printout from the computer.

This approach is taken instead of presenting information on a few selected statistical measures that you might someday need. I do not expect you to become conversant with any particular measure for statistical analysis. Instead, I want you to have a guide you can use when you need it.

You are likely to find this book different from anything you have seen in social work research. Some of its unique features were discussed in my beginning text on social work research, *Building Basic Competencies in Social Work Research,* published by Allyn and Bacon in 1997.

A major distinction is that this text is predicated on the model of adult learning, in which the reader is actively engaged in the research process and is constantly called upon to make decisions or demonstrate an understanding of why things were done the way they were. It is based on the assumption that the teacher can gain little meaningful ground by saying "Learn this because I say it is something you need to know." Adult learners are mature people who need to be able to make use of knowledge in a way that is meaningful to them.

It has been my experience that social work students appreciate frequent opportunities for reinforcement when they study research methods because much of this content is new to them and requires different ways of thinking. In some ways, it is like learning a new language. Thus, you will find that lessons reinforce and build on information previously presented. I have found that concepts such as sampling, statistical significance, or validity are difficult to assimilate unless lessons are reinforced through new examples.

A major feature of the first section of this text is its organization around the purposes of research, with examples that each cover the entire research process. This differs from the traditional text that presents the various tasks in the research process with a chapter devoted to each. In that type of presentation, I have found students typically have difficulty getting the total picture and seeing how the parts fit together.

The Principles of Adult Learning

The adult learner is unique from the child learner in several important respects. For one thing, the adult learner is problem-focused (task-focused) rather than subject-focused. Most research texts are subject-focused. In other words, the reader is introduced to subjects such as measurement, sampling, research design, and so forth. In this way, the learning is segmented and the learner is assumed to be prepared to delay the gratification of task completion until some time in the future. The present text, however, uses research case examples which deal with the entire process of research in a single chapter. These cases are related to specific purposes of research. Some chapters provide practical guidance on research tasks, while others allow you to find a way to analyze your data.

Adult learners develop a motivation to learn when they have a need to know something. Research instructors, of course, can threaten the student with course failure if they do not learn certain things, and this approach will usually work in motivating the student to work on recalling the content that will be on the exam. But this type of learning is not likely to last, or be meaningful to the student. In contrast to this approach, the present text employs research examples thought to be of interest to the typical social work student.

The adult learner needs to be self-directed. In the typical research text, the reader is viewed as a passive receptacle of knowledge. Many concepts are defined and illustrated and the learner is expected to be motivated to retain such knowledge. Seldom is the learner given any choices of what to do or how to analyze a given situation. The present text employs assignments in which students are asked to apply knowledge gained and to articulate certain concepts in their own terms. In many instances, students are engaged in exercises in which they analyze data or develop items for a questionnaire, or become the subjects of research themselves.

The writing of the beginning text on research, followed by this intermediate one, emerged from my search for ways to make the traditional research text material meaningful to social work students. The product of these efforts over a number of years has been two books on this subject. My students' responses to these books have been overwhelmingly favorable. They have consistently valued my material higher than that in various traditional texts. They have praised the tendency of these material to interactively engage them in research. They would much prefer to practice a skill than merely think about it. I hope this book meets your needs as well as it met the needs of the hundreds of students who encountered the material in it at various stages of readiness. I am indebted to those students for many suggestions, and for allowing me to observe their efforts at learning social work research so I could better address their needs through the learning experiences contained in this text.

R.O.Y.

Acknowledgments

The author would like to thank these reviewers for their comments: Jaak Rakfeldt, Southern Connecticut State University; Lois Millner, Temple University; and Christine A. Hyduk, Wayne State University.

C h a p t e r *1*

Introduction

This is a book on conducting social work research. It is based on the assumption that the reader has completed a beginning course on social work research at either the undergraduate or the beginning graduate level. It is assumed, for example, that the reader can distinguish between research statements of purpose that are and are not consistent with the spirit of scientific inquiry, and can identify some of the most prominent human errors in observation that are addressed by the methods of science. It is assumed that the reader can distinguish between a good and poor statement of a study hypothesis, and can distinguish between the dependent and independent variables in the hypothesis. Among other concepts which one should know from a beginning course would be the concepts of theory, qualitative and quantitative measurement, reliability and validity, study sample and study population, study variable, statistical significance and practical significance, maturation as a threat to internal validity in research designs, and so forth. If these concepts are not familiar to you, you would be well advised to consult a basic text on social work research, including one by the author of this book (York, 1997).

If you are unsure as to your level of familiarity with these basic concepts, you will be particularly interested in the latter part of this chapter in which you will be given a test representing a small sample of questions taken from an exam designed to test the beginning level of understanding of social work research. It is designed only for an overall gauge of your understanding of research, not as an inventory to aid you in pinpointing your particular deficits. Before you encounter this test, however, you will have the opportunity to review some broad concepts that serve as the foundation of this text.

This chapter begins with an overview of the nature of social work research and the nature of scientific inquiry. Scientific inquiry serves as the foundation for various forms of social research, but social work research has some unique qualities that distinguish it. The purposes of research in social work draw your attention to information that help enhance the profession's mission. Research for the purpose of satisfying intellectual curiosity takes a back seat to research that can improve social work practice. In this text, the purposes of social work research are categorized as descriptive, exploratory, explanatory, and evaluative. These purposes will be briefly examined in this chapter.

Following the examination of the nature of scientific inquiry and the purposes of social work research, you will briefly review the process of research, from problem formulation, to study methodology, to data analysis, to study conclusions. Then you will encounter a test which should help you assess your need for reviewing a basic text in research or for reviewing the basic concepts that conclude this chapter. This succinct review is designed to address the needs of students whose level of understanding is nearly adequate. Those with less understanding of the basic concepts will be advised to review a basic text.

The Nature of Social Work Research

Social work research is a means of gaining relevant knowledge through the use of the principles of scientific inquiry. The scientific method is orderly and systematic, and designed to reduce human error in observation. It moves in a logical sequence of steps from examining what is known from others' work, to articulating a question that is insufficiently answered by those works, to developing a means of collecting information that will enhance our ability to grasp reality, to carefully collecting information, and, finally, to drawing conclusions about the question or issue under investigation.

The scientific method is not the only means whereby social workers acquire understanding. Most of what social workers have come to believe as the truth has been acquired by other means. Most of these understandings probably are accurate to a degree, some more than others. The scientific method is a vehicle whereby understandings can be either acquired or tested. Much of what we understand about life has probably been supported to some degree by scientific evidence even though we may not have reviewed such evidence. Most of the reminder of these understandings probably will withstand the test of scientific scrutiny at some future date. However, there are other understandings held by social workers that are substantially flawed, and still others that are only partially supported by scientific evidence. The role of science is to subject these understandings to a special kind of analysis or to generate new understandings where such is lacking. Knowledge that has not been scientifically tested is not assumed to be incorrect, but the rational social worker will place more confidence in that knowledge that has been so tested.

Social workers are required by ethics to employ practice methods that are effective. How will we know what is effective unless we examine the research of others who have tested various approaches to a problem? How will we know the answer to this question if we do not take a research stance with our own work and apply the principles of science to our practice?

Social workers are also called upon to face the challenge of accountability. Increasingly, social workers will be required to provide evidence of the effect of their practice in order to survive. How can this be done in the absence of emphasis upon social work research?

Alternatives to Scientific Research

How do we know what we know? Much (if not most) of our understanding about the world in which we live has come from alternatives to scientific research as a way of knowing. You have learned much from lessons taught by your parents, from your personal experience, or from what has been described to you as common knowledge. Many pieces of your knowledge remain untested by the research method. This does not mean they are incorrect. It simply means that they are untested and lacking in scientific evidence. Knowledge that has passed the test of the scientific method can be better relied upon. You should have more confidence in the validity of knowledge that has passed this test.

There are many ways of acquiring understanding about the social world that are not based on scientific research. Many texts on research list such alternatives to science as authority, tradition, common sense, and personal experience (see, for example, Neuman, 1994).

Authority as a basis of knowing is founded upon the words or lessons of persons in positions of authority such as our parents, teachers, and so forth. We believe something is true because our mother told us it was true. Tradition is something that is handed down from one generation to another as being the truth. Perhaps we acquire some of our prejudices in this manner.

Common sense is something that seems logically to be true to you. One may assume, for example, that the death penalty is a deterrent to murder because it makes sense that people are less likely to commit murder if they know that they could face the death penalty.

Knowledge that comes from personal experience arrives because of our own experiences with life. A popular topic of conversation over the dinner table is how men and women are different. Our perceptions about this question are based primarily on our own life experiences.

Neuman (1994) provides examples of these alternatives to research as a way of knowing. The errors that can come from authority as a basis for knowing can be easily illustrated:

> *History is full of past experts whom we now see as being misinformed. For example, some "experts" of the past measured intelligence by counting bumps on the skull; other "experts" used bloodletting to try to cure diseases. Their errors seem obvious now, but can you be certain that today's experts will not become tomorrow's fools? (Neuman, 1994, p. 3)*

Tradition as a way of knowing can also be easily criticized through examples. Neuman (1994), for example, reports that his father-in-law believes a shot of whiskey will cure a cold. How did he determine this cure? Apparently, it was a piece of "wisdom" that had been passed down from past generations.

An example of error in common sense as a way of knowing is the gambler's fallacy. Do you believe that your poker hand will be better the next round if the past five rounds have left you with poor cards? Neuman explains:

> *Common sense is valuable in daily living, but it can let logical fallacies slip into thinking. For example, the "gambler's fallacy" says: If I have a long string of losses playing a lottery, the next time I play, my chances of winning are better. In terms of probability and the facts, this is false. (Neuman, 1994, p. 3)*

Personal experience as a way of knowing is vulnerable to *selective observation*, as illustrated in the discussion of the myths that opposites attract and that the full moon makes people act weird. We often notice events only when they confirm our theories, and ignore the events that fail to confirm them. If we want to know whether the full moon makes people behave in strange ways, we should compare the incidences of strange behavior during the full moon with the incidences of strange behavior when the moon is not full. To record information only during the full moon is an incomplete examination of the question.

Another common error that comes from personal experience is *overgeneralization.* If the first three homeless people I encounter in my social work practice are obviously mentally ill, I may conclude that the vast majority of homeless people are mentally ill. But my personal experience may not be representative of the total population of homeless people.

The Nature of Scientific Inquiry

Science is a special means for acquiring knowledge. It is founded on a number of principles. Its purpose is to enhance our ability to discover the truth rather than to confirm any particular idea as being the truth. The scientific method, for example, takes no stance on the existence of God, the evil of racism, or anything else. Instead, it makes the assumption that truth is better discovered through certain means of inquiry than other such means. Thus, **the scientific method is designed to help us to understand what *is* rather than what *should be.*** The latter question is philosophical in nature, and the social worker is often required to wear the philosophical hat in order to pursue the mission of the profession. But this hat is different from the research hat, and while one never is completely able to separate these two functions, it is important that the social worker make efforts not to confuse the two. For example, it would be appropriate for the social worker to report data that supports a particular conclusion about what society should do to solve a given social problem, but it would be inappropriate to simply say that scientific data proves that society should do certain things without honest reference to the nature of the data itself.

The scientific stance makes the assumption that **knowledge is tentative.** What is supported by scientific research today can be modified by new research tomorrow. The scientific practitioner will maintain an open mind about the truth and will constantly seek new knowledge about it. For example, it seems that new models of practice produce more evidence of effectiveness at the onset of their discovery than at later times. Perhaps one reason for the evidence of effectiveness in the early stages has to do with the special enthusiasm with which we tend to embrace new ideas. Maybe enthusiasm influences our effectiveness regardless of the practice model. If this is true, it would be detrimental for us to cease our research efforts whenever we have evidence that something works. Maybe it works *here,* but not *there.* Maybe it works for some people but not for others. Maybe it works only when used by enthusiastic practitioners.

With the scientific approach, **we are seeking knowledge that can be generalized from one context to another.** What has been discovered by one researcher should be subject to replication by others. Knowledge gained from one experiment should produce wisdom for many who were not involved in that experiment. The scientific approach to inquiry places emphasis on social patterns which, if understood, will enhance our ability to predict behavior or to respond appropriately to behavior. There are usually many individual exceptions to social patterns because human behavior is very complex. We may learn, for example, that persons who were sexually abused as children are more likely than others to become sexual abusers. But we may also learn that the majority of abused persons do *not* become sexual abusers; thus, we would be very unwise to assume that someone is a sexual abuser simply because he or she was abused as a child. What our data would tell us is that victims of abuse are more at risk for becoming abusers. We know there are many exceptions to the rule because there are other factors that cause a person to become an abuser. The fact that there are exceptions to the rule does not invalidate our understanding of the connection between being a victim and becoming an abuser. It simply tells us about the limitations inherent in our conclusions about this phenomenon.

Theory and Observation in Research

Two of the building blocks of social research are *theory* and *observation.* In a general sense, *theory* refers to our attempts to explain the world in which we live. Any attempt to explain why things are the way they are could be viewed as theory, but certain theories, of course, are far more sophisticated than others. We can theorize about the social world based on our own experience, but, in research, we normally speak of *theory* when it has been formalized in publications and is based on a body of knowledge derived from persons recognized as experts in a particular field. Formal theory typically has been subjected to some testing through research. It helps us answer questions such as "Why do people become depressed?" or "Why do some abused women remain with their abusive partners?" or "Why do certain adolescents turn to drugs?"

Observation refers to our attempts to collect information about the world in which we live. We can use observation to test a theory. For example, if we encounter a theory that abused women return to their partners because of economic dependence, we could measure economic dependence for a group of abused women served by a women's domestic violence shelter and examine whether those who return to their partners are more economically dependent than those who do not. A good study of this theory would measure other variables that might explain a woman's return to her partner to see if economic dependence explains this behavior better than the other variables.

The process of social research can begin with theory or with observation. As you saw above, you can obtain a theory from the literature and test it through observation. You can also begin with observation in order to develop a theory. For example, you could observe homeless people over a period of time and develop a theory about why some people remain homeless while others do not.

The interplay of theory and observation can be illustrated with the example of the full moon and strange behavior. Do some people come to the conclusion that the full moon affects behavior through the observation of behavior during the full moon, or through a theory about how the moon effects behavior? It is typically the former. Some people have observed what they believe is a relationship between the presence of the full moon and strange behavior because they noticed strange behavior during the full moon. This observation process is incomplete, however, if these people fail to collect data on behavior when the moon is not full, so these phases of the moon's cycle could be compared. If full observation did occur and if the data supported the conclusion that behavior is stranger during the full moon, a person with a research approach to knowledge building would next seek a theory to explain why this behavior occurs. What is it about the full moon that makes people act differently?

The process of studying the full moon and behavior could also begin with *theory*. For example, a scientist could study the moon's effect on gravity and the gravity's effect on brain chemistry, then the effect of brain chemistry on behavior. These studies could lead to a theory that would explain why the full moon makes people act differently. This theory could then be tested by studies that examine data on strange behavior during various phases of the moon. Thus, the researcher would have begun with theory and moved to observation, the reverse of what was described above.

The scientific approach makes the assumption that humans are capable of error in their observations of their environment as they probe for answers to their questions and for meaning in their lives. One may be biased, for example, because of self interest, and tend to focus exclusive attention on information that supports a preconception of the truth. Such a person would be viewed as lacking in objectivity, and would have problems developing credibility with others. A person may have a limited view of an issue because of limited personal experiences that may not have provided a good perspective upon the problem. Thus, **the scientific method attempts to control human error in observation.** As much as possible, we seek objective means of measurement when we acquire data about the phenomenon under study. This does not mean that measurement can only come from established scales published in the literature. There are many forms of measurement that are more subjective but are scientific in the sense that attempts were made to reduce bias or other errors in observation.

A good example of how human error sometimes works is the myth that "opposites attract." There is a common belief among many people that men and women who are opposites are attracted to one another for the purpose of mating and that this factor contributes to the continued viability of the relationship. The facts from research, however, support the idea that the more similar two people are, the more likely they will marry and stay married. How did the myth come about? It likely came about because a mating between highly different people tends to stand out in our minds. When we see these exceptions to the rule, we take notice. However, when we see similar people married, we do not notice the fact that they are similar because it is so commonplace. Thus, because we know a few exceptions to the rule, we make the mistake of believing that it is the rule.

How do we know that this generalization about opposites is not true? We can test this theory by measuring similarities among people and determining if people who get married are more similar to one another than they are to people they did not marry. We could examine, for example, whether Catholics are more likely to marry other Catholics than to marry Protestants or people of other faiths. We could examine whether conservatives are more likely to marry other conservatives than to marry liberals. We could do the same for personality traits or social values.

We would, of course, find that most people differ from their mates on some things, perhaps even on many things. But the question would be whether they tend to be more similar than different overall when they are compared to the total population. For example, if we find that 25 percent of the population is Catholic and that 50 percent of Catholics marry other Catholics, we have evidence that people are attracted to others who are similar rather than different. In this case, only one person in four is a Catholic; thus, there is one chance in four that anyone would marry a Catholic if there were no connection between religion and mating. If two persons in four who are Catholic marry other Catholics, we can see that being a Catholic seems to make a difference, and that there is a greater tendency for one to marry someone else who is similar than different. If only one Catholic in ten married another Catholic, we would have evidence that opposites attract. In the pursuit of our research question, we would, of course, examine many variables other than religion in order to determine if the evidence supported the notion that opposites attract.

Another example is the myth that the full moon makes people act differently, especially when it comes to mental health problems or human crises of various kinds. Believe it or not, many studies have been conducted of this question. A review of the literature by the author of this text revealed dozens of studies which failed to find that emergencies or crisis calls or aggressive behavior are any different during the full moon than other periods of time. Only one study (out of many dozens of studies) could be found which supported this theory about the full moon, but the extent to which the study had adhered to the principles of scientific inquiry was questionable (see York, 1997).

So, how did this myth come about? Perhaps it emerged for the same reason as mentioned above. When people see an upturn in emergencies and notice that the moon is full, they take note because they have heard that the full moon effects these behaviors. But have you ever heard anyone say, "Well, we had a large number of emergencies tonight and the moon was *not* full." It is unlikely that we will make such a note because it fails to support the theory.

Before we leave this topic, we should take note of the neverending thrust of scientific research. The scientific stance is that knowledge is never complete. Even if dozens of studies have been undertaken on a topic with similar results, there may be other ways to ask the question and measure relevant variables. There are other populations who may not have been tested on the research question. Thus, we tend to speak of evidence in support of a given conclusion rather than final proof of the truth about the matter at hand. Perhaps there are some kinds of behavior that the full moon affects which have not yet been studied. Perhaps there is a human variable on which difference between mates enhances the durability of the relationship.

If our question is a general one about the full moon or about opposites, we may conclude from the literature that the question has been substantially answered by the research of others. For us to probe further for information on the general question would constitute something akin to reinventing the wheel. In social work research, there are too many important questions to be answered that are lacking in such information for us to justify expending resources in pursuit of such matters.

The Purposes of Social Work Research

In this text, research studies will be classified into four general categories according to the purpose of the study. One purpose is description. Sometimes we want to describe something with precision so that we can understand it better. This will be referred to as *descriptive research.* Examples include the description of the clients of your agency with regard to age, gender, number of children, presenting problem, and so forth. Normally when we conduct descriptive research, we are examining only the nature of certain variables rather than relationships between variables.

Usually when we examine relationships between variables, we are engaging in *explanatory research.* The purpose of explanatory research is to explain rather than merely to describe. When we seek to explain something, we usually examine its relationships with other variables. The more sophisticated our study methodology is in controlling the variables under study, the more we can claim that our study is truly explanatory in nature. For example, we may ask if gender is related to salary when position level is taken into consideration. In other words, we are asking whether gender explains salary. In our examination, we have decided that position level should be taken into consideration because it is another variable that might explain salary. We examine our question by collecting data on salary, position, and gender for a sample of persons. We could find that women receive lower salaries than men but that male managers and female managers receive approximately the same salaries, while male non-managers and female non-managers receive comparable salaries. How could this possibly be true? We might have more females in our sample and we might find that males are more likely to be in management positions and that persons in management positions tend to receive higher salaries. Thus, the reason that males receive higher mean salaries than females is that they are more likely to be employed in management positions. While this scenario is theoretically possible, it was not supported by the facts in at least two studies of salaries among social workers. In more than one study, it was found that male managers made higher salaries than female managers and that male non-managers made higher salaries than female non-managers (see York, 1997).

When you examine data regarding the effectiveness of a social work intervention or program, you are conducting *evaluative research.* In this type of research, you are attempting to determine the extent to which an intervention achieved its objectives. This type of research might be categorized as one type of explanatory research because you are trying to determine if your treatment explains the client's progress. If your clients improve, was it because of your intervention or something else? This type of research will be treated as a separate category from other explanatory studies because of its central importance in social work. A key distinction between the evaluative study and the explanatory study is the presence of an intervention in the evaluative study.

The fourth type of research is *exploratory* research. The exploratory study has the purpose of either developing a theory or describing a phenomenon in ways that cannot be easily quantified. It is especially useful when you have limited knowledge about a given subject or you want to develop a new perspective on it. Exploratory studies might ask what it is like to experience being adopted as an older child, or what are the stages of homelessness, or how does one move from one level of stress to another until they achieve what has been termed "burnout." Such questions cannot easily be understood through quantitative means of observation, wherein variables are measured in discrete form such as a concrete category (e.g., male or female) or scores on a test. Thus, exploratory studies tend to employ qualitative means of observation in which behavior is recorded in a more flexible format. Exploratory studies often employ open-ended questions in interviews or the direct observation of behavior in its natural setting.

While descriptive research will usually employ quantitative means of measurement, it is easy to see how qualitative methods can also be employed to describe a phenomenon. Evaluative research also normally employs quantitative methods, but qualitative means can be employed, especially in the evaluation of service process.

The Research Process

There are many ways one could divide the research process into steps. In this text, the process will be separated into four major phases—problem formulation, study methodology, data collection and analysis, and study conclusions. In the first phase, you articulate the study subject or theme and examine what is known about it from the work of others. Among the information sought in this phase are (a) the nature of the study subject, (b) the reasons that this subject is important, (c) theories about this study subject (d) how variables have been defined and measured in previous research, (e) the results of previous research, and (f) the questions that have been left substantially unanswered by the work of others.

The second major phase of research is the development of the study methodology. This provides the blueprint for action. It indicates how you will conduct your investigation of your research question. At the completion of the problem formulation phase, you should have articulated the research question and should know whether your purpose calls for a qualitative means of measurement (observation) or a quantitative method. Qualitative methods are better suited for the description of social processes where little is known and for the development of theories where such are deficient. Quantitative methods are better suited for the precise description of social phenomena, the testing of theories already developed, or the evaluation of whether social work interventions are achieving their objectives.

The study methodology phase will direct your attention to such tasks as (1) the development of the study hypothesis, where appropriate, (2) the development of the means of measuring study variables, (3) the definition of the study population and the selection of the study sample, and (4) how data will be collected.

The third major phase of research entails the analysis of data. In qualitative research, this will typically involve recording information in narrative form and the coding of this information into themes and drawing connections among the various themes that arise from the data. For quantitative data, analysis typically entails the calculation of both descriptive and inferential statistics. Descriptive statistics are normally used to describe the study sample and the data that are employed to answer the research questions. Testing of hypotheses is aided by inferential statistics which give us an estimate of the likelihood that data can be explained by chance.

In the final major phase of research, you draw conclusions about your study subject and discuss the limitations of your study methodology as a means of providing an answer to your questions. You also discuss the implications of your data and provide suggestions for future research.

A Sample of Questions to Test Basic Knowledge of Social Work Research

The following is a set of questions designed to measure your basic understanding of fundamental research concepts that you should have acquired in a beginning course in social work research. The present book is written for the intermediate student of social work research. If you have much difficulty with the questions in this test, you are advised to review a basic text in social work research. Each of the following questions has one best answer. You should respond with only one answer. It is imperative that you make a commitment for the answer for each question before consulting the answers which follow. In this way, you can receive a valid indication of your level of knowledge. These questions were drawn from a list of approximately 100 questions that were designed to measure basic knowledge. Thus, this is only a small sample of the many questions which could be posed in a comprehensive test of your knowledge. It is not designed to provide feedback to you on your areas of weakness, but only to give you an overall idea of your level of competence. You would need a more extensive test if you wished feedback on the areas of your strengths and weaknesses in basic knowledge about research.

1. Which of the following statements of the purpose of a research study is NOT consistent with the spirit of scientific inquiry?

not justification

____ ✗ ____   **a.** To demonstrate that social work services are meeting client need.

_____   **b.** To identify the needs of the clients of a given program.

_____   **c.** To examine whether the abused wife's economic dependence on the husband is more or less important than the length of the marriage as a determinant of whether the abused wife returns to the abusing husband after treatment from a Women's Shelter.

_____   **d.** None of the above—i.e., all are acceptable statements of the purpose of social work research according to the spirit of scientific inquiry.

2. Suppose you wish to identify the most important needs of your clients. In this endeavor, you ask a group of your clients to rank order a set of needs. Which category of research does this study best fit into?

_____   **a.** explanatory   _____   **c.** evaluative

____ ✗ ____   **b.** descriptive   _____   **d.** variable

3. Which one of the following statements is true?

_____   **a.** The scientific method assumes that people are not prone to error in observation; therefore, we can discover reality by using human observation.

_____   **b.** Human error in observation is something we simply have to live with rather than control.

_____   **c.** Human error is not likely to influence our basic findings from a research study.

____ ✗ ____   **d.** The scientific method assumes that people do err in observation; thus, methods are employed to reduce this error when information is collected.

4. Suppose you wished to conduct a student satisfaction study in a typical school of social work containing approximately 100 students. You will use a questionnaire that asks all students to indicate their gender, age, level of satisfaction with field instruction, and level of satisfaction with classroom instruction. Which of the following concepts would NOT be a variable in this study?

_____   **a.** Level of satisfaction with classroom instruction.

____ ✗ ____   **b.** Student (i.e., whether one is a student). — *all are already students*

_____   **c.** Gender (i.e., whether one is male or female).

_____   **d.** None of the above. In other words, all of these would be variables.

5. If you asked a group of social work students at Middle State University to <u>indicate their level of satisfaction with</u> their social work education, a good way to state the purpose of this study would be:

_____ X _____ **a.** To examine the extent to which social work students at Middle State University are satisfied with their social work education.

_____ **b.** To determine how well Middle State University is achieving its mission of preparing social work students for the realities of social work practice.

_____ **c.** To <u>produce evidence of</u> the effectiveness of the social work program at Middle State University.   *not scientific inquiry*

_____ **d.** All of the above.

6. A theoretical model of stress depicts the relationships between stress (defined as psychological tension), stressors (defined as environmental conditions thought to influence stress), and burnout (a syndrome evidenced by cynicism and emotional exhaustion). This model suggests that stress is caused by stressors. It also suggests that stress can lead to burnout and minor health problems. Which of these variables is presented as serving as a dependent variable in one bivariate relationship (i.e., between two variables) and as an independent variable in another bivariate relationship?

_____ **a.** burnout   _____ X _____ **c.** stress   *dependent – acted upon*
                                                    independent – causation

_____ **b.** stressors   _____ **d.** health problems

7. What is wrong with the following item for a questionnaire?

> What is your political party affiliation or identity?
>
> _____ Democrat   _____ Republican ___ *Other*

_____ **a.** The response categories are not mutually exclusive. *affiliation = one*
                                                                (likes policies)
                                                                but listed as other
_____ **b.** The response categories are not exhaustive.
_____ X _____ **c.** Both of the above.   *Independent, Green ...*

_____ **d.** None of the above.

8. Consider the following two statements:

> 1. Theory refers to our attempts to explain the world in which we live.
>
> 2. Theory always precedes observation in research.

_____ X _____ **a.** Statement 1 is true but statement 2 is false.

_____ **b.** Statement 1 is false but statement 2 is true.

_____ **c.** Neither statement is true.

_____ **d.** Both statements are true.

9. In evaluative research, the statement of the treatment objectives helps the social worker to:

___✗___   **a.** Determine what methods or tools will be used to measure client progress.

_____   **b.** Determine whether to employ parametric or nonparametric statistics.

_____   **c.** Determine how the problem shall be analyzed.

_____   **d.** None of the above.

10. Which part of the problem formulation phase of evaluative research is most relevant to the determination of how the treatment will be designed?

_____   **a.** Information on the importance of the problem to society.

___✗___   **b.** Information on theories about causation of the problem.

_____   **c.** The treatment objectives.

_____   **d.** Information on the size of the sample.

11. In the study of the New Hope Treatment Program (an inpatient mental health treatment program for depression), the mean depression score at pretest was 34.9 while the mean posttest score was 13.8. When these data were subjected to statistical analysis, a t value of 9.02 was derived along with a p value less than .001 (t = 9.02; p < .001). In the determination of practical significance, what information would be most useful?

_____   **a.** The p value derived from the statistical analysis of the data.

_____   **b.** The t score derived from the statistical analysis of the data.

_____   **c.** The mean posttest score.

___✗___   **d.** The difference between the mean pretest score and the mean posttest score, assuming that statistical significance has been established.

12. The results of the evaluation of the effectiveness of the New Hope Center program (see question 11) in the treatment of depression indicated that:

_____   **a.** Statistical significance was achieved (according to the normal standard in the social sciences).

_____   **b.** The differences in the pretest and posttest scores for this group of clients could not easily be explained by chance.

___✗___   **c.** Both of the above.

_____   **d.** None of the above.

13. Quantitative measurement in research is normally more appropriate than qualitative measurement under which of the following circumstances?

_____   **a.** You are seeking to develop theories or hypotheses rather than testing existing ones.

_____   **b.** You are seeking an understanding of the subjective meaning of behaviors rather than their precise description.

_____ **c.** Both of the above.

___X___ **d.** None of the above.

14. Consider the following two questions to be posed to study subjects, then select a statement below that describes your evaluation of them. (*Note: These are the questions in their entirety.*)

> 1. What are your most important unmet needs as a client of this agency?
>
> 2. How many children are living in your home who are under the age of 6?

___X___ **a.** Statement 1 is an example of qualitative measurement, and statement 2 is an example of quantitative measurement.

_____ **b.** Statement 1 is an example of quantitative measurement, and statement 2 is an example of qualitative measurement.

_____ **c.** Both statements are examples of qualitative measurement.

_____ **d.** Both statements are examples of quantitative measurement.

15. Which of the following are tips for conducting the research interview?

_____ **a.** Write up the interview ~~a day or two after~~ *right away* it has taken place rather than right away so your subconscious memory will have had time to synthesize the information and provide you with a holistic pattern of ideas.

___X___ **b.** Engage the interviewee in validating your notes so you can be sure you correctly heard what he or she said.

_____ **c.** ~~Emphasize information~~ *be objective* that confirms your initial impressions so that information can be aggregated in a manner that will achieve a threshold of understanding.

_____ **d.** All of the above.

16. Evaluate the following two statements:

> 1. The interviewer should freely express his or her opinions about the study topic to the interviewee because the interviewee may be curious about this topic and such a dialogue can help to build rapport between the interviewer and the interviewee.
>
> 2. Because of the qualitative nature of the semi-structured interview, no counting takes place in such a study; counting is strictly for the quantitative type of study.

_____ **a.** Statement 1 is true but statement 2 is false.

_____ **b.** Statement 2 is true but statement 1 is false.

_____ **c.** Both statements are true.

___X___ **d.** Both statements are false.

17. Evaluate the following two statements:

> 1. The process of descriptive research begins with the development of the instrument to collect relevant data. *– begin i problem formulation*
>
> 2. In a descriptive study of the students of Collins High School, one of the most important variables would be students. *– not variables since all are students*

_____ **a.** Statement 1 is true but statement 2 is false.

_____ **b.** Statement 1 is false but statement 2 is true.

_____ **c.** Both statements are true.

~~/~~ **d.** Both statements are false.

18. In the descriptive study of the social work program of the neonatal intensive care unit, the variable of "adjustment reaction" was measured by whether or not a given client had been referred to the social work program because they had an adjustment reaction to having a premature baby. In other words, they were classified as either "yes" or "no" for this variable. At what level is this variable measured?

_____ **a.** ordinal *ranked*   _____ **c.** interval *– grouped*

~~/~~ **b.** nominal   _____ **d.** qualitative *–*

19. Which of the following would NOT be evidence that supports either the reliability or validity of the Beck Depression Scale?

_____ **a.** A finding that scores on this scale have a positive correlation with the level of depression that was recorded by clinicians who are working with the persons being tested.

~~*~~ **b.** A finding that scores on this scale are lower after treatment than before.

_____ **c.** A finding that scores on this scale at one point in time have a positive correlation with scores on this scale two weeks later for a group of people who did not have treatment during this period of time. *reliability ?*

_____ **d.** A finding that scores on this scale have a positive correlation with scores on another depression scale given at the same time. *validity ?*

20. Consider the following data on the relationship between school grades and self-esteem. What kind of empirical relationship is illustrated by these data?

	SELF-ESTEEM		
SCHOOL GRADES	High	Low	Total
High	50	25	75
Low	50	25	75
Total	100	50	150

_____ **a.** A positive relationship   _____ **c.** A significant relationship

_____ **b.** A negative relationship   __✗__ **d.** No relationship

21. In evaluative research, whether one uses a superior or inferior research design will be most helpful in determining:

__✗__ **a.** The extent to which one can attribute the client's progress to the intervention rather than something else, such as maturation, testing, etc.

_____ **b.** The extent to which statistical significance can be achieved.

_____ **c.** The extent to which an important problem has been selected.

_____ **d.** How to measure the independent variable.

22. In the one group pretest–posttest design, a set of clients is measured on their behavior before treatment begins and again after treatment is finished. Which of the following threats to internal validity is/are addressed by this design?

_____ **a.** Maturation   _____ **c.** Both of the above

_____ **b.** History   __✗__ **d.** None of the above.

23. In the basic experimental design, a sample of persons is divided into a control group and an experimental group on a random basis. The experimental group is given treatment while the control group is not given treatment. The gains in functioning for these two groups are compared. Which of the following threats to internal validity is/are addressed by this design?

_____ **a.** Maturation   __✗__ **c.** Both of the above

_____ **b.** History   _____ **d.** None of the above.

24. In evaluative research, the sampling methods employed will be most useful in determining:

__✗__ **a.** Whether the results can be generalized to persons not included in the study.

_____ **b.** Whether statistical significance can be achieved.

_____ **c.** Whether practical significance can be achieved.

_____ **d.** What intervention to employ.

Answers to Questions

No.	Answer	Note
1.	a.	Research is a process of discovery, not justification. We do not engage in research for the purpose of proving a point, no matter how noble the point might be.
2.	b.	This study only calls for the description of client needs.
3.	d.	
4.	b.	The concept of student does not vary. All persons in the study are students.

No.	Answer	Note
5.	a.	(a) is more specific to the thing being measured; thus, it is superior to (b) which is more remote from that which is being directly measured. Item (c) is not consistent with the spirit of scientific inquiry.
6.	c.	Stressors are hypothesized to influence stress; thus, stress is the dependent variable in this relationship. Stress is hypothesized to influence health problems; thus, stress is the independent variable in this relationship.
7.	b. c	These response categories are not exhaustive. There is no place for someone who is not either Democrat or Republican. These categories are mutually exclusive because one cannot be both Democrat and Republican.
8.	a.	Statement 1 is true: theory attempts to explain. But statement 2 is false: theory does not always precede observation in research. Some studies are done for the purpose of developing a theory through observation; thus, observation precedes theory. Some studies are done for the purpose of testing a theory; thus, theory precedes observation.
9.	a.	We will measure client progress using tools that are appropriate to the objectives of the treatment.
10.	b.	The choice of treatment model A or treatment model B for the client's problem is guided by our beliefs about the causes of the problem. If depression is theorized to be caused by distorted thinking, our treatment of depression would logically be guided by this idea, and our intervention would focus upon thinking patterns.
11.	d.	Practical significance directs our attention to the question of whether our data provide noteworthy information. For evaluative research, we ask the question whether the client's gain is big enough to be noteworthy.
12.	c.	Statistical significance was achieved because the p value was less than .05. This means that the differences between pretest and posttest scores could not easily be explained by chance.
13.	d.	Quantitative measurement is more useful for studies that attempt to test theories rather than develop them, and it is also more useful for studies which attempt to achieve a precise description. Both (a) and (b) are more suited to the qualitative methodology than the quantitative one.
14.	a.	Question 2 asks for a number, while question 1 asks for words.
15.	b.	Notes should be written up as soon as possible after the interview rather than a day or two later, because our memories can play tricks on us. To be objective, we need to give equal emphasis to information that contradicts initial impressions as we give to information that confirms it.
16.	d.	Both of these statements are false. The interviewer does not want to bias the person being interviewed by expressing opinions about the topic at hand. While numbers are not the central focus in data analysis in qualitative measurement, they are an important tool. It is useful to indicate how many persons mentioned certain themes, or how many times a theme was mentioned by a given person. This is useful information in the development of understanding about the theme.
17.	d.	We begin research with problem formulation, not the means used to measure our study variables. Students would not vary in a study of high school students.
18.	b.	
19.	b.	

No.	Answer	Note
20.	d.	The proportion of students with high grades who have high self-esteem is 50 percent which is the same percentage of those with low self-esteem; thus, there is no relationship between these two variables.
21.	a.	
22.	d.	Neither maturation nor history is addressed by this design.
23.	c.	Both maturation and history are addressed by this design. If groups are composed on a random basis, it is safe to assume that they are equal in the effects of maturation or history on their behaviors; thus, any measured differences between the experimental and control groups can be attributed to the intervention rather than to maturation or history.
24.	a.	Sampling helps us with the issue of generalization.

References

Neuman, L. L. (1994). *Social research methods.* Boston: Allyn & Bacon.

York, R. O. (1997). *Building basic competencies in social work research.* Boston: Allyn & Bacon.

Unit *I*

Conducting Each Type of Social Work Research

Chapter 2
Conducting Exploratory Research on Stress Using Qualitative Methods

Chapter 3
Conducting Descriptive Research on the Qualities of the Good Manager

Chapter 4
Conducting Explanatory Research on the Qualities of the Good Manager

Chapter 5
Conducting Evaluative Research Using a Group Design: Is Project PARENTING Effective?

Chapter 6
Conducting Evaluative Research Using the Single-Subject Design

Chapter 7
Conducting Program Evaluations Using Qualitative and Quantitative Methods

In this section of the book, you will examine each of the four major types of social work research using examples in the categories of both qualitative and quantitative measurement. You will find a review of concepts learned in previous courses as well as a few new concepts. You will also notice that there is a good deal of reinforcement of learning through the review of certain concepts with new examples. A key to this section is that you are asked to participate in the research process. In some cases, you are asked to offer your own decisions about key study questions and in other situations you are asked to be a study subject as well as a researcher. In the latter case, you will collect your own data and analyze it.

Conducting Exploratory Research on Stress Using Qualitative Methods

In this chapter, you will examine exploratory research when qualitative methods of inquiry are employed. The example of the study of stress among social work students will serve as the vehicle for this learning process. In chapter 1, you were reminded of the purposes and process of scientific inquiry. The process of research follows a path which goes from problem formulation to study methodology to data collection and analysis to study conclusions. The four main purposes of social work research were characterized as description, exploration, explanation, and evaluation. While qualitative means of inquiry can serve more than one of these purposes, it is especially well suited to the exploratory type of research.

In this chapter, you will first examine some of the similarities and differences between qualitative and quantitative methods. The focus will then shift to qualitative means of inquiry. Various approaches to qualitative observation will be discussed, but the greater focus will be upon the interview as a vehicle for data collection. This approach to research will be illustrated with the example of the study of stress among social work students. You will examine a literature review and a report on a study conducted by two social work students. Throughout this experience, you will be called on to make decisions about what to study and how to do so. Your final tasks will be to (1) critique the coding of information from one interview of a qualitative data matrix, and (2) critique the basic conclusions drawn by two students based on this data matrix.

This chapter should provide you with the knowledge to conduct a rudimentary inquiry into stress among your own classmates if you should choose to do so. This experience could serve as the foundation for the development of more advanced skills in qualitative research using your own topic of concern.

Qualitative and Quantitative Research

When you have completed the *quantitative* measurement of a study variable with your study subjects, you will have either a category or number to assign to each study participant for each variable. For example, each study subject may be classified as male or female for the variable of gender. The age for each person may be recorded in its basic form or by reference to a category of age (e.g., 0–19; 20–29; etc.). You may have each person in a category according to whether they checked "agree" or "undecided" or "disagree" in response to a particular statement about political ideology.

When you have completed the *qualitative* measurement of social phenomena, you will have words rather than numbers or uniform categories. These words may come from your observations of people in action or from the direct quotes from your study participants. These words will be examined for themes and will be coded accordingly. Thus, qualitative measurement is more flexible, and characterizes each study subject in a more unique format. Persons are not placed into preconceived categories but are given the opportunity to express themselves in their own words or actions.

Purposes of Social Work Research

In the first chapter, you were given a means of categorizing social work research according to the purpose of the study. One of these purposes is *description.* You may need to describe a social phenomenon. In many texts, the concept of descriptive research refers to the precise description of social phenomena utilizing quantitative methods of measurement. An example would include the characterization of an agency's clients in regard to age, gender, race, type of service received, and so forth. Each of these variables can easily be measured in quantitative terms such as categories or numbers.

A second purpose of social work research is *explanation.* This type of research seeks to explain social phenomena by testing theories or hypotheses about it. For example, do abused women remain with their abusive husbands because of economic dependence or because of low self-esteem? Do men receive higher salaries than women because they are employed in higher positions in the organizational hierarchy? This type of research focuses on the testing of theories or hypotheses which emanate from an established knowledge base. In this text, explanatory research will be illustrated with examples using quantitative measurement devices, because such methods are better suited to testing a theory than developing one.

A third purpose of social work research is *evaluation.* With this type of research, you evaluate a social work intervention to determine the extent to which the objectives were achieved. The focus of evaluative research, as this label will be used in this text, is upon outcome. Did the client get better? Did the organization improve its performance? When we focus evaluative research upon outcome, quantitative means of measurement are normally employed because there is more objectivity in such measurement and accountability can be better achieved. For these reasons, evaluative research in this text will be illustrated with quantitative methods of observation.

Some evaluative research, however, focuses upon processes. A question may be raised about why certain types of clients improved more than others, or whether certain standards of service were implemented. A researcher might want to better understand the processes of recovery for a typical client with a given problem. When the focus of evaluative research is upon process, qualitative means of measurement are appropriate.

Another of the four major purposes of social work research is *exploration*. By this, we refer to the examination of phenomena that are less well known. In such cases, we normally seek to describe the social processes or characteristics illustrated by the subject of study, or develop theories about it. In these cases, a flexible means of observation is needed. Thus, exploratory research will be discussed with examples of qualitative measurement.

When to Use Each Approach to Measurement

The choice of a qualitative or quantitative means of observation (measurement) should be guided by the nature of the research question and the existing knowledge about it. Thus, one should not begin the research experience with the idea of conducting a quantitative study or a qualitative study. Methods of observation spring from the nature of the study subject, not the other way around. While either qualitative or quantitative methods can be applied to a wide variety of purposes and circumstances, there are a few guides which can assist the beginning research student in the choice of an observation mode. For example, a qualitative method is typically more appropriate to the extent that each of the following conditions exist:

1. You are seeking to develop theories or hypotheses rather than testing existing ones;
2. You are seeking an understanding of the subjective meaning of behaviors or social processes rather than the precise description of social phenomena;
3. The concepts of interest are not easily reduced to categories or numbers;
4. There is relatively little that is known about the subject of study from the existing literature, or this knowledge base has important missing links.

Unfortunately, there is no clearcut means of employing the above criteria. We cannot say, for example, that if any two of these conditions exist, a qualitative method is clearly superior to a quantitative one. Furthermore, some may argue with any one of these guides. Thus, the researcher should use these ideas only as a general guide, not as a prescription.

Two of the Major Types of Qualitative Research

Characterizing qualitative research into categories is no easy chore. Books that claim to cover the territory of this method have a diversity of labels for various approaches. For example, the *Handbook of Qualitative Research* (Denzin & Lincoln, 1994), provides chapters on case studies, grounded theory, ethnography, historical methods, biographical methods, and clinical research, among others. On the other hand, *Qualitative Research in Social Work* (Sherman & Reid, 1994) divides qualitative research into the categories of ethnographic methods, heuristic methods, grounded theory methods, narrative methods, discourse analysis, and clinical case evaluations. One of the problems with classification is that there is much overlap among the techniques and objectives used by these various types of qualitative research.

Two of the major types of qualitative research are ethnography and grounded theory. These two will be described in more detail because they are widely used. One of these types is well-suited to description, while the other is better suited to the development of theory. Another distinction between these two lies in their methodologies.

Ethnography

Ethnography refers to the study of a culture in its natural setting. The purpose is to describe the way of life of a group from within. This is accomplished by researchers gaining entry into the field through methods designed to gain acceptance and to open their own minds to messages of the group as meanings are held internally. The question focuses on the meanings of things to the culture; thus, preconceived ideas and biases held by the researcher should be dealt with to the extent that this is feasible (Fortune, 1994).

A distinguishing feature of ethnography is that the process of inquiry begins with the selection of a culture to study rather than the articulation of a research problem to solve or a research question to answer. Problems and questions may emanate from the data analyzed; thus, problem analysis and data analysis are not lined up in the same manner as is typical of quantitative research. While some inquiry into the culture and its problems may precede data collection and analysis, the ethnographic researcher is advised to avoid entering the field with a restricted view. One writer offers the following warning: "Because the intent of ethnography is to comprehend, without judgment, alien ideology, ritual, behavior, and social structure, one of the most important aspects of such fieldwork is that the investigator's attitude not be 'loaded' before entering the field" (Goodson-Lawes, 1994, p. 26).

The ethnographic researcher immerses himself or herself in the culture being studied. Methods of observation include participant observation and interviewing. The participant observer interacts with the persons being studied as they go about their daily activities. Observations are made and recorded for analysis. Interviews are more structured interactions between the researcher and the study participant.

Data is collected in ethnographic research through the observations of the investigator, which are recorded in carefully detailed journals. These observations may be organized according to such phenomena as a particular aspect of the culture (e.g., social relations, material culture, religious activities), the autobiographies of individuals, the intensive study of a particular event, detailed observations of a typical day, and so forth (Goodson-Lawes, 1994). Some of the data analysis techniques of grounded theory are employed in reducing the volumes of narrative information into themes.

Grounded Theory

Grounded theory is a second major type of qualitative research. The person using grounded theory will have a more focused study at the beginning of data collection than will the ethnographic researcher. A research topic or theme will be developed from the existing knowledge base. The purpose of this method is to develop explanations, hypotheses, or theories that are grounded in observations of social behavior. Some researchers will avoid exploring the existing literature before collecting data, out of fear of being restricted to it. But most researchers employ the literature review to achieve a focus for the beginning of their inquiry.

The methodology of grounded theory is somewhat more structured than that of ethnography, although, as previously mentioned, some ethnographic researchers borrow from these grounded theory methods. In a nutshell, this methodology entails carefully recording observations or quotes from study subjects, coding this information in several stages of analysis, and drawing connections between themes, which serve as the basis for the theory that is developed.

An illustration can be taken from the work of Belcher (1994) and his colleagues who studied the homeless in the city of Baltimore in the summer of 1989. The study was conducted over a three-month period during which the researchers immersed themselves in the homeless community, becoming familiar with the providers of services to the homeless and focusing attention on a particular health care facility. A group of homeless people was identified for a series of informal interviews that took place in surroundings familiar to the study participants.

The researchers used an eight-step process for study as follows:

1. Ask open-ended questions that emanated from the literature review.
2. Record responses from these questions into a case file for each respondent after each interview.
3. Review the files using the constant comparative method. This method entails comparing files on respondents over and over again until the researcher feels that all possible themes have emerged.
4. Note themes and develop a second set of questions.
5. Pose these questions to the same respondents in a second set of interviews.
6. Record responses in the individual case files and employ the constant comparative method once again.
7. Develop a set of working hypotheses.
8. Discuss the working hypotheses with the respondents to test their accuracy. (Belcher, 1994)

In quantitative research, methods of observation are submitted to the tests of reliability and validity to establish the credibility of the observations. For the qualitative study reported by Belcher, this basic issue was addressed in three ways: prolonged engagement, persistent observation, and triangulation. The first strategy was achieved by the fact that the interviews took place over a three-month period of time, a period considered sufficient to obtain entry into the lives of the study subjects and overcome the normal barriers to understanding the full meaning of behavior. The second strategy was achieved by the extensive eight-step process of observation.

The third strategy for establishing credibility was *triangulation*. This term refers to the use of multiple sources of data collection. For example, if respondents in this study stated that they had been thrown out of a shelter, the researchers would verify this information with the shelter operators.

From this study, the phases of drift among the homeless were enumerated. Phase 1 is the beginning phase of homelessness and is characterized by movement in and out of the homeless status as friends and relatives help out. At this phase, the study participants did not typically classify themselves as homeless. They generally maintain good contacts with sources of support and service providers. After several months of homelessness, people tend to drift into Phase 2, in which an identity as a homeless person is not very strong, but persistent problems such as substance abuse seem to prevent their emergence from the status of the homeless. At the third phase, persons have come to accept themselves as being homeless and have lost hope of a different style of life. These persons typically have been homeless for a year or more and have a great deal of social distance from the mainstream of society.

This characterization of the phases of homelessness led to ideas about the importance of prevention in view of the fact that the longer one is homeless, the greater the problem of achieving a change. Drift from one phase to another was found to be accompanied by an increase in substance abuse, loss of relationships, loss of income, and loss of hope (Belcher, 1994).

What follows is the first assignment in this book. These assignments are designed to be completed in the book for class discussion. In other words, you should provide your answers to the questions and be prepared to share your answers in class. Your instructor may or may not wish to use them for this purpose and he or she may or may not want you to turn them in for a response or grade. If you are using this book for a research text, check with your instructor about these expectations.

ASSIGNMENT 2-A

1. Which of the following situations would call for a qualitative methodology rather than a quantitative one? (You may select more than one alternative)

_____   **a.** You are conducting a study in which you will describe the characteristics of the students in the school of social work in regard to age, gender, race, and chosen specialization in graduate school.

___✓___   **b.** You are conducting a study in which you will attempt to identify the phases by which a student moves through stages of stress, from a state of nonstress to a state which might be called "stress" to a more extreme state that might be called "burnout." You want to discover the elements that might contribute to this progression and how some students find ways to prevent it.

_____   **c.** You are conducting a study in which you will test the following hypothesis: Females receive lower salaries than males even when position level is controlled.

_____   **d.** You are conducting a study in which you will evaluate whether your treatment program for depression is effective in reducing stress for a sample of clients.

___✓___   **e.** You are conducting a study in which you will attempt to characterize the experience of being a client of your agency, from initial contact to termination of service.

Notes: _____

_____

_____

2. Determine whether each of the following statements best fits the quantitative methodology, the qualitative methodology, equally fits each methodology, or fits neither methodology. For your response, write either "qual," "quan," or "both," or "neither" next to each statement.

both qual ?   **a.** Can be helpful in our understanding of social and psychological phenomena.

quant   **b.** Is usually more useful than the other methodology in testing a theory that has been well conceptualized in the literature.

neither *quant*   **c.** Is appropriate for generating information with the purpose of <u>demonstrating</u> that a social work intervention is effective in meeting human need.

qual   **d.** Is usually more appropriate than the other methodology in generating information about a relatively unknown topic.

neither   **e.** Is quite superior to the other method in generating information that is useful to the social work profession.

both *neither*   **f.** Is the approach to take when you are trying to prove a point.

Notes: _____

_____

_____

3. Which of the following questions are better characterized as <u>qualitative measurement</u> than quantitative measurement? (You may select more than one.)

_____   **a.** How many of your children are living in your home at the present time?

___✓___   **b.** What are your most important unmet needs as a social work student in this educational program?

___✓___   **c.** How would you describe your feelings when you experience what you would call "stress"?

_____   **d.** What is the population of the county in which you are employed?

Notes: _____

_____

_____

4. John Powell utilized a qualitative methodology that has been labelled "analytic induction." The procedures for this methodology were described as follows:

1. Formulate a rough definition of the phenomenon to be explained.

2. Formulate a hypothetical explanation of that phenomenon.

3. Study one case in light of the hypothesis with the object of determining whether the hypothesis fits the facts in that case.

4. If the hypothesis does not fit the facts, either reformulate the hypothesis or redefine the phenomenon to be explained.

5. Practical certainty may be attained after a small number of cases has been examined, but the discovery by the investigator of a single negative case disproves the explanation and requires a reformulation.

6. Continue the procedure of examining cases and then redefining the phenomenon or reformulating the hypothesis until a universal relationship is established; each negative case calls for a redefinition or reformulation.

7. For the purposes of proof, examine cases outside the area circumscribed by the definition to determine whether or not the final hypothesis applies to them (Powell, 1984, p. 25).

Would you say the methodology of analytic induction comes closer to characterizing ethnography, or grounded theory? Explain.

grounded theory

Problem Formulation in Qualitative Research

The problem formulation phase of research begins with a topic of concern. This topic may arise from professional practice or personal life experiences or from what we have learned from the literature. A text on qualitative research presented the background for the initiation of a study of abused women who had sought safety in a women's emergency shelter and had decided not to return to their partners:

> *This specific problem did not come to us in a dream, or in the mail, or as a serendipitous insight. It emerged out of our professional work and our experiences as social work researchers and practitioners with an interest in family violence. From our own observations and from what colleagues in the field told us, these women are at a critical juncture in their lives. Few, if any, research studies have identified their experiences and needs at this point in their lives. Thus, there is little reliable information to help us understand how we, as professional social workers, can best help them as they decide to live new lives away from their abusive ex-partners. (Tutty, Rothery, & Grinnel, 1996, pp. 26–27)*

A study of persons who had been adopted as older children was undertaken by John Powell (1984) because of his own experience in this field and his recognition of several developments as well as his own review of the literature over the years of his practice. He recognized that (1) there was a growing emphasis on placing older children for adoption rather than allowing certain children to drift from one foster home to another until adulthood; (2) some research had suggested that adopted children experienced slightly more problems in life than non-adopted children, and that older adopted children had more problems than the younger ones; and (3) there was little published research on the experience of being adopted. He reasoned that a study of persons who had been placed for adoption at an older age would yield rich information on the nature of this experience and provide insight for suggestions on how the placement process could be improved. Consequently, he undertook a study in which he interviewed 17 persons who had been placed for adoption, and developed a number of suggestions for practice.

The problem formulation phase of research provides guidance on whether qualitative or quantitative methods of observation should be employed. A literature review should provide information on ways of conceptualizing the relevant content, the reasons the study subject is important, and theories about the relationships among the variables which are relevant.

In this chapter, you will be given a literature review on stress among social work students (see Exhibit 2.1) so the experience of qualitative research can be accelerated. You can explore the development of your own focus for a study of this topic and examine the data collected by two social work students on this topic.

Your next step is to review Exhibit 2.1 before responding to the questions in the next assignment.

EXHIBIT 2.1   A Literature Review on Stress

In contrast to some fields of business and industry that have often confronted a lack of job challenge as a barrier to work motivation, the human service field has encountered the opposite—the idea that too much challenge in the presence of meager resources can hamper work performance. The term "burnout," which has been used prominently for about two decades (see, for example, Maslach, 1976, & Patrick, 1979), has emerged as the concept of greatest concern because it is viewed as being of immediate influence upon work performance. Persons who are burned out on the job experience emotional exhaustion and lack the energy to perform optimally.

The basic idea behind this line of thinking is that human service jobs contain stressful conditions (stressors) such as work overload which lead to psychological symptoms which have come to be called "stress." Stress can lead to health problems such as insomnia, headaches, and an increase in vulnerability to colds and flu. In the presence of long-term stress, some persons develop burnout. Burnout hampers work performance because it causes social workers to become cynical about their clients, to lack energy for meeting the daily demands of work, and to acquire a desire to leave the job.

(Continued)

EXHIBIT 2.1   *Continued*

Intervening in the relationship of stressors and stress, however, are certain stress buffers, the most prominently mentioned one being social support (Maguire, 1991). For example, some people with high work demands do not develop the symptoms of psychological stress because they have superior support systems. The basic model is depicted below.

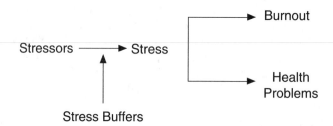

This theoretical model suggests that certain conditions (stressors) lead to certain feelings associated with psychological tension (stress). In other words, persons with a higher level of stressors in their lives will normally have a higher level of stress. But this will not always be the case. There will be exceptions to this rule, and that is why you would not expect to find a perfect empirical relationship between stressors and stress. A perfect relationship would mean that every single person with higher stressors than another person will have higher stress than that other person. The more exceptions to this rule, the lower is the strength of the relationship between stressors and stress.

Why would there be exceptions? One reason is that people are not all equal in regard to the stress buffers in their lives, such as social support. Perhaps if John has higher stressors than Jim but has lower stress, it is because John has more social support. Under these circumstances, you would expect to find a negative relationship between support and stress, meaning that persons with high support would be likely to have lower stress than would those with low support. But if support serves as a buffer between stressors and stress, you would probably find the importance of support grows with increases in stressors. For example, if you studied only persons with low levels of stressors, you would expect to find only a modest relationship between support and stress, because these persons would have little reason to have much stress. For these persons, support would have less influence. But for persons with a high degree of stressors, you would expect to find a strong relationship between support and stress, meaning that those with high support would be much less likely to have high stress. Thus, you can see how stress buffers intervene in the relationship between stressors and stress.

This theoretical model also suggests that stress (psychological tension) leads to certain health symptoms. Health symptoms associated with stress include headaches, insomnia, and illnesses. Thus, you would expect to find that persons with higher stress would be more likely than others to experience these symptoms. You also can see a line drawn between stress and burnout in the model. This suggest that persons with high stress are more likely than others to experience burnout.

You do not see a line drawn between stressors and burnout or between stressors and health symptoms. This is because it is theorized that stressors only lead to health symptoms or burnout if they lead to stress. For some persons, stress buffers will prevent the latter from happening.

Graduate school can be viewed as an environment in which students experience stressors that can lead to stress and burnout, but which can be lessened by the effects of stress buffers

EXHIBIT 2.1   *Continued*

such as social support. While there is an extensive literature on stressors and stress and burnout for persons in general, there is a rather limited body of knowledge on this topic for social work students. Perhaps this is a population for which more research is warranted.

What is Stress?

When people use the word "stress" they have a general idea of what they are talking about, but definitions will vary. Most people think of stress as an uncomfortable condition caused by demands that are made on their lives by work and family responsibilities. Descriptions such as tense, up-tight, and anxious are often associated with the concept we label stress. People usually recognize certain physical symptoms as being associated with stress, such as sleeplessness, headaches, and an increase in minor illnesses such as colds and the flu. Some writers define stress as environmental conditions rather than psychological feelings (see, for example, Shinn, et al., 1984).

For the present study, stress will be defined as a condition of psychological tension that is exemplified by such feelings and moods as apprehension, uneasiness, and nervousness. Stress stands in opposition to feelings and moods such as cheerfulness, relaxation, and contentment. Thus, we are focusing on the psychological dimension of this concept rather than environmental conditions such as job demands, parental responsibilities, or life events such as divorce or the death of a close family member. These environmental conditions can influence stress, but they are considered to be separate conceptually. You could refer to these conditions as stressors rather than stress.

Thus, stress is a condition of the individual rather than the environment. But the environment can cause stress to occur. For example, high caseloads of abused children to serve can cause social workers to be stressed. If most people with high caseloads are found to have high stress while most people with low caseloads are found to have low stress, you could say that there is a relationship between stress and caseloads. But not everyone with high caseloads will necessarily have high stress and not everyone with low caseloads will necessarily have low stress. Other factors can potentially influence stress and explain the exceptions to the rule.

Many studies of stress among social work students have measured stress by asking students to identify the extent to which certain conditions have led them to experience stress (see, for example, Munson, 1984). An example would be a question asking respondents to indicate the extent to which their field supervisor caused them stress, or the extent to which their research course caused them stress. These researchers have chosen to measure stress as a perception of the individual's response to certain potential stressors. Fortune (1987), however, chose to measure stress as a psychological condition by asking students to respond to a stress scale that measured their present psychological condition. Instead of asking students to identify the things they believe caused them stress, Fortune measured stress directly as a psychological condition and then examined the relationship between this condition and certain variables thought to serve as stressors. This research is more consistent with the definition of terms used in the present literature review. You should be careful to define your terms in research because many people define them differently, and you want others to understand what you mean when you say something like "Students who engaged in regular aerobic exercise were found to suffer from lower levels of stress than students who did not."

(Continued)

EXHIBIT 2.1   *Continued*

To What Extent Do Social Work Students Experience Stress?

Moderate levels of stress were found in studies of social work students conducted by Munson (1984) and by Kramer, Mathews, and Endias (1987). However, how one interprets the distribution of scores on such tests is subject to differences of opinion. For example, Munson found a pattern of mean scores at or slightly below the mid-point on his various scales, and he found that one-third or less of his respondents indicated physical symptoms of stress associated with various school factors. He interpreted these data as indicating that students experienced low levels of stress. While this may be a reasonable interpretation of the general pattern, one might also interpret these data as showing a cause for concern because as many as one in three students reported physical symptoms of stress.

What Causes Stress?

In the theoretical model in this review, stress is depicted as being caused by *stressors*. One of the pioneers in the study of stressors is Hans Selye (1980). Selye brought to our attention the effect of stressors upon health. Much of his work focused on traumatic life events such as the death of a spouse or losing a job. Selye found that stressors such as traumatic life events were associated with diminished health.

Munson (1984) found that first-year MSW students had slightly more stress than second-year students, but Tait (1991) found the opposite. General demographic characteristics of students do not seem to be associated with stress. Koeske and Koeske (1989), for example, found no relationship between stress and variables such as age, marital status, and number of children. However, Tait (1991) found a nearly significant positive relationship between stress and the number of children below the age of six. Kramer, Mathews, and Endias (1987) found that part-time students had more stress than full-time ones, while Koeske and Koeske (1989) found that full-time students with part-time jobs had more stress than employed part-time students.

One of the main stress complaints offered by social work students is that they face excessive demands on their time (Kramer, Mathews, and Endias, 1987). However, the demands of graduate school are rather uniform from one student to another; thus, the demands themselves do not serve as a useful variable in the study of stress. But how students combine these demands with other demands in their lives is a potentially fruitful subject of inquiry. Fortune used the students of one graduate school of social work to test the hypothesis that the number of roles occupied by students was negatively related to stress. The roles identified were marriage partner, parent, and employee. Thus, it was expected that the more roles one played, the higher one's stress. But the opposite was found. A negative correlation was found between number of roles occupied and level of stress, meaning that those who occupied more roles had less stress. Potts (1992), however, found no relationship between number of roles occupied and psychological adjustment to the educational process, a concept somewhat different from stress as we have defined it here.

Another finding from the Potts study may be quite instructive to our inquiry. This researcher found that full-time students with full-time jobs had lower psychological adjustment levels than others, but she failed to find any other correlates of psychological adjustment that were especially noteworthy. This finding would suggest that stress is a special problem only for those with excessive demands. Perhaps those with moderately low role demands do not differ in stress from those with very low demands or moderately high role demands. But perhaps those with very high role demands differ in stress from all those at lower levels of demand.

EXHIBIT 2.1   *Continued*

What Reduces Stress?

Stress buffers are variables that might reduce the effects of stressors. The most prominently mentioned stress buffer is social support. Social support is often defined as comfort, assistance, and/ or information one receives through formal or informal contacts with individuals or groups. When people talk of social support, they usually refer to sets of people with whom an individual has an enduring relationship who provide encouragement, caring, and guidance (Maguire, 1991).

Troits (1982) identified several ways to classify social support. Tait employed these classifications in a study of support among social work students (Tait, 1991). These classifications are types of support, sources of support, and structures of support. Types of support include emotional support (esteem building interactions) and instrumental support (aid with tangible tasks). Common sources of support are family, friends, and co-workers. The structure of support entails variables such as the size of the support network, the intensity of the relationships of giver and receiver, and the durability of the network, among others. With this conceptualization, support would be measured by items seeking information on the number of close relationships one has, as well as the intensity of those relationships—in addition to the question of how long they have lasted. The more relationships, the higher the score. The higher the intensity of the relationship, the higher the score. The longer the relationships have lasted, the higher the score.

Another approach to measurement of support is exemplified by the Provisions of Social Relations scale (see Fischer & Corcoran, 1994). On this scale, respondents are asked to indicate their perceptions of how much they can rely on their family and friends when they are in need.

In the general literature, Cohen and Syme (1985) make the case that social support buffers the effects of stressors on stress and illness for the population at large. Lechner (1993) found that support reduced stress for caregivers of dependent parents.

But what about social work students? Is it logical to think that support would reduce stress for them as well? Tait (1991) failed to find a significant correlation between social support and stress for one sample of graduate social work students. But such a relationship was found between support and stress in a study of social work students by Koeske and Koeske (1989). The difference in the methodologies between these studies is quite instructive in our analysis of support as a stress buffer. Tait found that, in general, students with higher support did not have lower stress. Koeske and Koeske undertook a separate analysis of the relationship between support and stress for students with higher levels of stressors. In their study, full-time students with part-time jobs were compared to part-time students with full-time jobs, as well as full-time students with no jobs. Among full-time students with part-time jobs, the stress score for those with high support was significantly lower than for those with low support. This relationship between support and stress, however, was not found for the other two groups of students. Thus, it appears that support makes a difference only for those with higher levels of stressors in their lives.

Another potential stress buffer is locus of control. Locus of control refers to whether one perceives actions as being determined by external forces over which one has little control, or internal forces over which one has extensive control. Persons with an internal locus of control perceive that personal events and their consequences depend on their own actions, while those with an external locus of control perceive that such events are dependent on external factors such as chance or fate. In her study of graduate social work students, Fortune (1987) found that locus of control had a stronger relationship with stress than did such variables as marital status, employment, age, parenthood, years of social work experience, or total number of roles

(Continued)

EXHIBIT 2.1 *Continued*

occupied. She found that students with an internal locus of control had lower stress than did those with an external locus of control.

One of the limitations in the study of stress buffers is that the relationships between stress and other variables tend to be rather low even when they are found to be statistically significant. Fortune (1987), for example, found that the cumulative effects of locus of control and several other variables on stress was rather modest. In her multivariate analysis, she found that the total amount of variance in student stress that was explained by locus of control and several other variables was only 24 percent, meaning that 76 percent of the variance was left unexplained. This means one needs to look further to find a more complete explanation of what causes stress.

What Are the Consequences of Stress?

Two main consequences of stress have been identified in our model. These are health problems and burnout. Burnout is a condition resulting from prolonged or intense stress and characterized by emotional exhaustion, cynicism about the clients and the nature of the work being performed, and a desire to terminate employment. These conditions logically can be considered to have a negative effect on work performance (see Maslach and Jackson, 1981).

The work of Maslach is among the most definitive of those in the field of burnout (see, for example, Maslack, 1978, and Maslack & Jackson, 1981). Among the indicators of burnout identified by Maslack and others are emotional exhaustion, cynicism, and a sense of failure. Emotional exhaustion refers to the tendency to feel overwhelmed by demands and emotionally depleted and physically exhausted from the work day. Cynicism is reflected in the depersonalization of clients. Feelings of failure are also manifestations of burnout, according to these writers. In the human services, professionals often work with difficult clients and with minimal resources which lead to few indicators of success in their work.

Of the three dimensions of burnout, emotional exhaustion was the only one that emerged as clearly a reliable and valid dimension of burnout, according to a study by Wallace and Brinkerhoff (1991). In their study, they identified several potential correlates of burnout. Some of these were role conflict, role ambiguity, work autonomy, and workload.

Health problems such as insomnia, headaches, and minor illnesses have been used by some as direct measures of the concept of stress. But in the model presented in this review, stress is conceived as a psychological condition rather than a physical one, even though it is realized that psychological conditions may lead to physical symptoms. These symptoms are viewed as the consequence of stress rather than as a manifestation of it.

Summary

From the literature, you can draw a conceptual picture of the relationships among the variables of stressors, stress buffers, stress, and burnout. Among the potential stressors identified were traumatic life events in the recent past, multiple role demands, and place in the educational program (e.g., first year versus second year). Little research appears to have been published on life events as a stressor among social work students. Some of the events found to have had the most effect upon the general population include death of a spouse, divorce, death of a close family member, loss of a job, and so forth. Do such events serve as stressors for social work students?

The picture from the literature regarding multiple role demands is mixed. Some research suggests that more roles are better. If so, why would this be the case? Some research suggests that heavier demands lead to more stress. How can this picture be clarified?

EXHIBIT 2.1 *Continued*

Support has mixed reviews as a stress buffer. There is certainly a popular belief that support alleviates stress. Why has the empirical research been mixed in support of this idea? Does support only make a difference for those with the higher levels of stressors, as suggested by one set of study results?

Locus of control is another candidate for the alleviation of stress. One study found that persons with an internal locus of control had less stress. Why might this be the case? Can further insight into this relationship be discovered from further research?

What are other stress buffers? Surely, there are many more that have not yet been published. If we find many more, can we eventually be in a better position to more fully explain stress in the face of stressors?

References

Cohen, S., & Syme, S. L. (1985). *Social support and health.* New York: Academic Press.

Corcoran, K. and Fischer, J. (1994). *Measures for clinical practice: A sourcebook* (2nd ed.). New York: The Free Press.

Fortune, A. E. (1987). Multiple roles, stress and well-being among MSW students. *Journal of Social Work Education, 23* (3), 81–90.

Koeske, R. D., and Koeske, G. F. (1989). Working and non-working students: roles, support, and well-being. *Journal of Social Work Education, 25* (3), 244–256.

Kramer, H., Mathews, G., and Endias, R. (1987). Comparative stress levels in part-time and full-time social work programs. *Journal of Social Work Education, 23* (3), 74–80.

Lechner, V. M. (1993). Support systems and stress reduction among workers caring for dependent parents. *Social Work, 38* (4), 461–469.

Maguire, L. (1991). *Social Support Systems in Practice.* Silver Springs, MD: NASW Press.

Maslach, C. (1978). Burned out. *Human Behavior, 5,* 99–113.

Maslack, C, & Jackson, S. E. (1981). The Measurement of Experienced Burnout. *Journal of Occupational Behavior, 2,* 99–113.

Munson, C. E. (1984). Stress among graduate social work students: An empirical study. *Journal of Education for Social Work, 20* (3), 20–29.

Patrick, P. K. S. (1979). Burnout: Job hazard for health workers. *Hospitals,* November, 87–89.

Potts, M. K. (1992). Adjustment of graduate students to the educational process: Effects of part-time enrollment and extracurricular roles. *Journal of Social Work Education, 28* (1), 61–76.

Schilling, R. F. (1987). Limitations of social support. *Social Service Review,* March, 19–31.

Selye, H. (1980). *Selye's guide to stress research.* New York: Van Nostrand Reinhold Company.

Shinn, M., Rosario, M., Morch, H., and Chestnut, D. E. (1984). Coping with stress and burnout in the human services. *Journal of Personality and Social Psychology, 40,* 864–976.

Tait, D. (1991). Effects of social support on stress for MSW students: An empirical examination. Professional Paper submitted in partial fulfillment of the requirements of the degree, Master of Social Work, to the faculty of East Carolina University.

Troits, P. (1982). Conceptual, methodological, and theoretical problems in studying social support as a buffer against life stress. *Journal of Health and Social Behavior, 23,* 145–159.

Turner, R. J., Frankel, B. G, and Levin, D. M. (1983). Social support: Conceptualization, measurement, and implications for mental health. *Research in Community Mental Health, 3,* 67–111.

Wallace, J. E., and Brinkerhoff, M. B. (1991). The measurement of burnout revisited. *Journal of Social Services Research, 14* (½), 85–111.

ASSIGNMENT 2-B

1. In the literature review, stress was defined as:

____ *al*   **a.** Excessive demands of the environment on the individual.

_____   **b.** Such health symptoms as insomnia, headaches, and colds.

_____   **c.** Emotional exhaustion and cynicism.

____ ✓   **d.** Feelings associated with psychological tension.

_____   **e.** All of the above.

2. How was the concept of "stressor" defined?

conditions that lead to psychological tension

3. How was "burnout" defined?

emotional exhaustion + lack of energy to perform optimally

4. Indicate whether each of the following statements are true or false, given our literature review.

T   (F)   **a.** Burnout causes stress.

(T)   F   **b.** Stress buffers reduce the impact of stressors upon stress.

T   (F)   **c.** The causes of stress among social work students are well known.

(T)   F   **d.** One of the potential consequences of stress is an increase in physical symptoms such as headaches and insomnia.

(T)   F   **e.** According to the conceptual model, one of the explanations for why two persons with similar levels of stressors would have different levels of stress is that one of these persons may have a higher level of social support.

T   (F)   **f.** Among the main causes of stress for social work students are demographic variables such as age, gender, and marital status.

Notes: _____

_____

_____

5. For each pair of questions below, select the one that lends itself to the qualitative method of measurement better than the quantitative one.

Pair 1

_____✓_____ **a.** What things do social work students view as most stressful?

_____ **b.** Does being employed affect stress levels for full-time social work students?

Pair 2

_____✓_____ **a.** What are the ways that social work students cope with stress?

_____ **b.** To what extent do social work students experience stress?

Pair 3

_____✓_____ **a.** What are the stages of stress and burnout for social work students?

_____ **b.** Is there a relationship between stress and social support?

Pair 4

_____✓_____ **a.** What important variables have been left out of the conceptual framework?

_____ **b.** Is there a relationship between stress and burnout?

Pair 5

_____ **a.** To what extent do social work students experience stress?

_____✓_____ **b.** How do social work students experience stress (e.g., What does stress mean in subjective terms? How is it characterized?)

Pair 6

_____✓_____ **a.** How does social support serve as a stress buffer? What might be some of the theoretical explanations for the effect of support upon stress?

_____ **b.** To what extent do social work students experience social support?

Pair 7

_____✓_____ **a.** How are the experiences of African American students different from those of white students with regard to stress?

_____ **b.** Is there a relationship between the number of stressful life events and stress when social support is controlled?

Notes: _____

_____

_____

_____

Methodology in Qualitative Research

The literature review given in Exhibit 2.1 provides potential guidance for either a quantitative methodology or a qualitative one. For example, let's take the question of whether there is a negative relationship between social support and stress. The literature suggests that social support serves as a buffer between stressors and stress; thus, those with higher support would likely have lower stress. Both stress and support can be easily quantified. There are published scales for measuring both variables. Thus, we have a theory and an easy means for quantitative measurement. A survey of persons could be conducted in which their levels of stress and support were measured. These two variables could be subjected to statistical analysis and the conclusions drawn would be generalizable to a much larger population than would normally be the case of a qualitative study. One of the advantages of the survey is that a large number of persons can be included in the study with a minor amount of resources. In other words, this is a very efficient way to collect information for a research study.

But what if we wanted to know more about the process whereby one moves from nonstress to stress to burnout and the kinds of reactions to this progression? There was no information reported on this question in the literature review given. Perhaps this is an area in which there has been little research. This question poses a description of a subjective process rather than the testing of a concrete theory with easily quantifiable variables. Thus, a qualitative methodology is warranted.

What if we wanted to expand the conceptual model? After all, much of the quantitative research has presented rather weak empirical relationships among the identified stressors and stress. Studies that included many variables have found a good deal of the variance in the dependent variable is left unexplained. These findings suggest that the present conceptual model has left out some important variables. What are these variables? A qualitative methodology is well suited to this task.

The focus of the present study is tighter than is often typical of qualitative studies. The most pioneering of qualitative studies have entered a field that is not well understood and the results have provided the foundation for better understanding and future research on the topic. This type of qualitative research requires much training and many resources, neither of which are feasible for the beginning research student. In keeping with the developmental framework for learning that this text espouses, a limited entry into qualitative research will be undertaken.

In their book on qualitative data analysis, Miles and Huberman (1984) offer the following observations:

> *Suggesting that the qualitative researcher use a standardized instrument or lay out a conceptual framework to orient the data collection effort is likely to raise the hackles of some people who, up to now, have done the most qualitative research: social anthropologists and social phenomenologists. From their perspectives, social realities are usually too complex, too relative, or too exotic to be approached with conventional conceptual maps or standardized instruments. They advocated a more loosely structured, emergent, inductively "grounded" approach to gathering data. The conceptual framework should emerge empirically from the field in*

the course of the study; the most important research questions will become clear only later on; the most meaningful settings and actors cannot be predicted prior to fieldwork; instruments, if any, should derive from the properties of the setting, and from the ways its actors construe them.

We go along with this vision—up to a point. Highly inductive and loosely designed studies make good sense when researchers have plenty of time and are exploring exotic cultures, understudied phenomena, or very complex social realities. But when one is interested in some better-understood social phenomena within a familiar culture or subculture, a loose, highly inductive design is a waste of time. Months of fieldwork and voluminous case studies will yield a few banalities (p. 27).

Modes of Gathering Information in Qualitative Research

The literature on qualitative research lists many ways to gather information. We have referred to modes of gathering information by the terms "means of observation" and "measurement" in our previous discussions. We can classify modes of gathering information in qualitative research into three main categories: interviews, direct observation, and indirect observation.

With interviews, researchers are posing questions to study subjects in either a structured or unstructured format. Study subjects know they are being observed and that someone wishes to know something about their opinions or ideas or experiences. With direct observation, researchers are observing behaviors of the study subjects rather than asking them questions about their behaviors. This requires more interpretation on the part of the researcher. With indirect observation, researchers are examining records or art work or literature, or other products which represent something about the subjects of the study.

The Interview in Qualitative Research

In this book, an interview is defined as a personal encounter between persons in which one person (or persons) is seeking information from another person (or other persons). It can take place face-to-face or by way of another mode of personal interaction such as the telephone. It is distinguished from the social survey in which researchers are asking respondents to answer questions by way of a written instrument such as a questionnaire.

By its very nature, the interview is purposive interaction. It goes beyond informal conversation. It suggests that different persons play different roles in the encounter. The main purpose of the encounter is for one or more persons to obtain information from another person (or persons).

We can conceptualize different types of interviews according to structure. A highly structured interview is one in which there is a precise set of questions that are to be asked in a given sequence with some pre-established categories for response. The more structured the interview, the more that the method of observation may be categorized as quantitative rather than qualitative. In this chapter, we will focus on interviews that are qualitative in nature, which means there is a minimum of openness in the structure in which the study subjects can respond in their own words to the questions.

The extent of the structure is exemplified by the number and specificity of questions posed, and the existence of pre-constructed categories into which respondents may fall. The extent of the structure is determined by the specificity of the study question and the clarity of the study subject, which are apparent from the knowledge base undergirding the research question.

Fontana and Frey (1994) provide the following guidelines for the highly structured interview:

> *Never get involved in long explanations of the study; use standard explanations provided by supervisor;*
>
> *Never deviate from the study introduction, sequence of questions, or question wording;*
>
> *Never let another person interrupt the interview; do not let another person answer for the respondent or offer his or her opinions on the question;*
>
> *Never suggest an answer or agree or disagree with an answer. Do not give the respondent any idea of your personal views on the topic of the question or survey.*
>
> *Never interpret the meaning of a question; just repeat the question and give instructions or clarifications that are provided in training or by supervisors.*
>
> *Never improvise, such as by adding answer categories, or make wording changes (p. 364).*

This level of structure may not be appropriate for the typical interview for a qualitative research study in social work because of the imprecise nature of the concepts under exploration in such studies. Yet, these guidelines assist us in gaining an understanding of the means used in qualitative research to reduce human error in observation. In particular, it is important that the interviewer not express opinions on the topic because it is likely that such expressions will influence the response of the study subject.

Semi-Structured Interview

The semi-structured interview is one with predetermined questions with an open-ended format that are asked of all respondents in the same manner. Examples include the following:

> *What does stress mean to you?*
>
> *How do you experience stress?*
>
> *What are the three things you are most likely to do when you are under stress?*
>
> *What do you find has been the best way to cope with stress?*

Each of these questions would be asked of each respondent and would be asked in the same sequence.

With the semi-structured interview, you should follow several guides. First, *be aware of your own predispositions* about the subject under study. You should, of course, avoid revealing these predispositions to the person being interviewed. It is also important that you engage mechanisms to avoid allowing these predispositions to influence your observations. Reflect upon what kinds of responses support or refute your own predispositions, and force yourself to pay attention to all that is said, not just those statements that are congruent with your own views.

A second recommendation is that you *engage the interviewee in the validation of your notes.* You might repeat what you have heard to the persons being interviewed and provide them with the opportunity to correct it or place it more appropriately in their own words if you have inaccurately re-worded their thoughts. When recording statements from the interviewee, you should use the interviewee's words as much as possible. You can re-examine these words later and decide on the broader concepts that may have been expressed. You might want to say something like "Are you saying that you are more likely to use exercise to relieve stress, or relaxation techniques?" By presenting options, you relieve the interviewee of the temptation to agree with you even though there may be some reservations about how you are perceiving these thoughts.

A third recommendation is to *seek disconfirming evidence of your initial impressions.* If you believe that the person being interviewed is focusing the most attention upon spirituality as a means of relieving stress, you might want to count the times that this theme was mentioned and compare it to the times that other themes were mentioned. You might want to ask the interviewee to recount the number of times that spirituality was used in the last two weeks as compared to the number of times that something else was used.

A fourth recommendation is to *engage in note-taking methods that place minimal burden upon your memory.* There is a lot of information that might be portrayed in an interview. Our long-term memories can be in error. You might want to take notes in stages, with the first stage being the interview and the second stage taking place immediately after the interview. During the interview, you will not be able to record every word spoken by the interviewee. Instead, you will want to quote things that seem to be especially poignant and take rather sketchy notes otherwise. The sketchy notes will contain words or phrases that represent certain responses by the interviewee. However, a few days later, you may not remember what these words mean. Therefore, you should undertake the second stage right after the interview. In this stage, the unwritten words are filled in so that you will be able to return to these notes at any later date and fully understand them.

Phases of the Interview Process

After the questions have been determined and a prospective interview subject has been identified, there are several natural phases of the interview. First, we must introduce the purpose of the interview and ourselves, and seek permission for the interview. In this phase it is important that the purpose of the interview be stated, but not any conclusions that might have been drawn from the literature about any aspect of the research question. In other words, you do not want to influence the interviewee's thinking about the questions under study. You should introduce yourself and indicate how the information from the interview will be used, including assurances that their identities will not be revealed in any report on the interview.

In this first phase of the interview process, the researcher should be sensitive to gender or cultural differences between the interviewer and the interviewee which might influence the responses of the interviewee. How open and honest will this study subject be with this particular interviewer? Sometimes women will express themselves differently to another woman than to a man. The key outcome of this first phase of the interview process is the development of trust and rapport between the interviewer and the interviewee.

The next phase is the presentation of the questions and the recording of the information. You should ask the questions in the same way to each person you interview. You should consider beforehand how to define key terms so that you can use a uniform definition to your study subjects.

The third phase is the analysis of the results. You must make sense of your notes. You do this by looking for themes that are common between persons being interviewed. You need to be attentive to the different terms that can be used to express the same thought. And you should be clear on the level of generality of your conceptions of the subject. Are you looking only for rather broad themes, or more specific themes?

In the analysis of data in qualitative research, numbers often get ignored because they are associated with quantitative research. But numbers are an essential component of the qualitative analysis of information. Qualitative researchers count such things as the number of references to a given theme or the number of study subjects who mentioned a given theme.

Sampling in Qualitative Research

Two key tasks in the development of our research methodology are (1) sampling, and (2) instrumentation. While these tasks are addressed in both qualitative and quantitative research, they take on rather different forms. For the typical study using quantitative methods, researchers tend to draw a sample of persons at random from a broader population, if possible. In the attempt to test the hypothesis, they are interested in generating data from a large sample of study subjects so they can generalize the conclusions to others. In qualitative research, you are more likely to employ a purposive sample. In other words, you will select persons who are especially suited to give you the information that you need.

Miles and Huberman (1984) propose that you can consider a wide array of things to sample in qualitative research. For example, they suggested settings, actors, events, and processes as the focus of sampling efforts. If you applied that idea to your study situation, you might think of settings as being classes, field placements, or employment agencies. The actors who might be sampled include students, faculty, and social workers in practice. Processes might include acquiring stress, responding to stress, evolving into a state of burnout, and so forth.

For each of these areas, you must make choices. Do you collect information only from social work students, or do you ask your questions of faculty and professionals in the field? Do you further restrict your field to those in mental health? Do you include students (faculty, professionals) who are pursuing both clinical practice and macro practice, or do you restrict it to those in clinical practice? Do you focus on the acquisition of stress or another process?

You might also want to consider the student's work-study status. Do you focus only on full-time students or do you include part-time students? What about full-time students who are working at least half-time? Wouldn't you tend to see these persons with higher stressors than others? Is this relevant to your study? A graphic depiction of only a few slices of the choice matrix you could confront is presented in Exhibit 2.2. The chart in Exhibit 2.2 has 16 cells and is only a portion of the potential choices available for the sampling task. The choice of a sampling strategy will depend on the nature of the question that has been selected.

EXHIBIT 2.2   An Example of a Choice Matrix for Sampling

	Health	Mental Health	Family & Child	Other
First Year Students				
Second Year Students				
Faculty				
Professionals in Field				

Developing Instruments for Collecting Information

Qualitative studies will vary greatly on the extent to which instruments are developed prior to data collection. The most inductive of studies will have little prior instrumentation. This lack of instrumentation is suitable for studies in which little is already known and the researcher wishes to avoid limiting the observations by prior instrumentation. In such situations, the research will enter the field armed only with a general theme and some ideas regarding where to find information on the chosen study subject. It is only after field notes have been collected that any major type of data organization is undertaken.

When a study is more focused and specific questions have been articulated, additional prior instrumentation is warranted. Miles and Huberman (1984) point out that, if you know what you are after, prior instrumentation will prevent the collection of too much superfluous information. Such information can get in the way of analysis for the specific topic of inquiry, and will reduce the efficiency of information collection. Prior instrumentation will provide the researcher with consistent questions to ask of different study subjects (or different study sites) so that key questions are not overlooked. This development of questions beforehand can also prevent the biased collection of information from the researcher. It is normal for different persons to focus attention on different information based on their own life experiences, interests, biases, and so forth. If you have not asked the same questions of each study subject, you have limited your ability to identify general themes that are relevant to more than one person.

ASSIGNMENT 2-C

1. Are there any modes of gathering information in qualitative research besides the interview? Explain.

pg39   observation – direct & indirect

2. In an interview study, how might interviewers assure themselves that they have interpreted the respondents' answers correctly?

pg41   check notes with interviewee

3. What is one thing you would do as an interviewer that would help to keep your own biases about the subject in check (i.e., prevent it from influencing the respondent)?

either state question exactly same each time or have clear questions formulated ahead of time

4. Which of the following situations would seem to require the MOST structure in the mode of gathering information?

_____   **a.** An examination of the process whereby people become homeless and remain that way as opposed to moving out of this condition.

_____   **b.** An examination of the feelings associated with the experience of being adopted as an older child.

___✓___   **c.** The identification of (a) how students define stress, (b) the most common techniques for coping with stress, and (c) the extent to which students have experienced each of four symptoms of burnout.

Notes: _____

_____

_____

5. Respond to the following statements by circling T for True or F for False.

(T)   F   **a.** In the structured or semi-structured interview, the interviewer should not discuss with the interviewee any theories from the literature about the study subject.

T   (F)   **b.** Because of the qualitative nature of the semi-structured interview, no counting takes place in such a study; counting is strictly for the quantitative type of study.

T   (F)   **c.** The interviewer should freely express his or her opinions about the study subject to the interviewee because the latter may be curious about this and such a dialogue can help to build rapport between the two.

Notes: _____

_____

_____

6. Which of the following are tips for conducting the research interview?

_____   **a.** Write up the interview a day or two after it has taken place rather than right away so that your subconscious memory will have had time to synthesize the information and provide you with a holistic pattern of ideas.

___✓___   **b.** Engage the interviewee in validating your notes so you can be sure that you correctly heard what he or she said.

_____   **c.** Emphasize information that confirms your initial impressions so that information can be aggregated in a manner that will achieve a threshold of understanding.

_____   **d.** All of the above.

Notes: _____

_____

_____

Data Analysis in Qualitative Research

There are many techniques for data analysis in qualitative research, depending on the nature of the study and the specificity of the questions being asked. A key distinction in data analysis between quantitative and qualitative methods is that the structure of analysis is determined before data collection when quantitative methods are employed. For example, the decision to undertake a correlation between self-esteem and depression would be made before data were collected. When you employ qualitative methods, the structure of your analysis is mostly determined after data is collected. You will not know what themes will emerge until you have examined the information that is pertinent to your study subject. Three major approaches that facilitate data analysis in qualitative research will be the subject of the remainder of this examination of data analysis. These are (a) content analysis, (b) levels of coding, and (c) analytic comparison.

Content Analysis

In content analysis, researchers examine artifacts of social communication to make inferences about the messages inherent in that information. Attempts are made systematically to identify the special characteristics of the messages (Berg, 1994). Content analysis can be undertaken with any written form of communication. This can include newspaper articles, public records, transcripts of interviews, and so forth.

The basic task of content analysis is to reduce words to themes or concepts that have meaning to the observation of the phenomenon under study. In this endeavor, the researcher must take precautions to avoid the selective recording of information according to some preconceived hypothesis. All the information available should be objectively analyzed for relevance.

Berg (1994) refers to two types of content analysis—manifest and latent. Manifest content analysis is restricted to the primary terms being used in the source, whereas latent content refers to the broader themes or issues underlying the manifest content. For example, an entire speech may be classified as "radical," or a novel could be characterized by the level of violence it depicts. As one moves from manifest to latent analysis, it is important that the original data not be dropped. One way of verifying a manifest analysis is for it to be tested by others using the same data.

Qualitative studies collect data of a more subjective type than is the case of quantitative studies. Words or concepts are collected as a means of aiding our understanding of our subject. But counting takes place in both qualitative and quantitative observation. The qualitative researcher will often note how many times a certain word or concept was expressed by the sources of information being examined. Certain words will be portrayed by the researcher as being indicative of a certain theme. Words such as "up-tight" or "tense" may both be classified as representing stress. Manifest and latent analysis of content is a form of coding of data from qualitative research. In the next section, you will view a similar conceptualization of this theme.

Coding in Qualitative Research

According to Miles and Huberman (1984),

> *A code is an abbreviation or symbol applied to a segment of words—most often a sentence or paragraph of transcribed field notes—in order to classify the words.*

> _Codes are_ **categories.** _They usually derive from research questions, hypotheses, key concepts, or important themes. They are_ **retrieval and organizing devices** _that allow the analyst to spot quickly, pull out, then cluster all the segments relating to the particular question, hypothesis, concept, or theme [emphasis in original] (p. 56)._

Strauss (1987) describes three main types of coding in qualitative research—open, axial, and selective. A discussion of these types of coding can be found in Neuman (1994). According to Neuman, open coding takes place in the researcher's first pass through the data being examined (e.g., a first review of the transcript of a recorded interview). The task of this type of coding is to locate themes or key concepts that bind certain words together. As illustrated above, such words as "up-tight" and "tense" might be coded as evidence of "stress." In this phase of coding, the researcher might write the word "stress" next to each line of data that contains such words as "up-tight" or "tense."

Axial coding takes place in a second pass through the data. During this phase of coding, the researcher "asks about causes and consequences, conditions and interactions, strategies and processes" (Neuman, 1994, p. 408). Can concepts be divided into smaller divisions, or enlarged into larger categories? Can concepts be organized into a sequence?

Selective coding is the final phase of the coding process. In this phase, the researcher looks selectively for cases that illustrate themes and makes comparisons and contrasts to identify further causal connections in the data or patterns that are broader than those identified in the previous phase. Neuman (1994) uses the example of a study of working class life in the tavern, where marriage was noticed as a theme in many conversations. In the previous phases of coding, marriage was identified as a theme and was divided into major stages such as engagement, weddings, extramarital affairs, and so forth. In the selective phase of coding, a focus turns to differences in the views of men and women. This analysis compares men and women on their ideas about each of these phases of marriage.

Analytic Comparison

Another helpful tool in qualitative research can be drawn from the work of early philosophers on the nature of logic. Neuman (1994) discusses the method of agreement and the method of difference in logical inquiry and refers to this as _analytic comparison_. The method of agreement draws the researcher's attention to what is common across cases so that cause-effect relations can be explored. If several different cases have a common outcome (e.g., high stress) the researcher looks for other commonalities that might be candidates for the cause of the outcome. For example, suppose your study of stress among graduate social work students revealed that each of your first four interviewees had a high level of stress and they all mentioned having an extra distance to drive from home to class and field placement. Each person has both high stress and a long commute. This provides the beginnings of an exploration of the causal connection between commuting distance and stress. But you might find that those with low stress also had a long commute. This is where the method of difference comes into play. With the method of difference, the researcher seeks information on cases with a different outcome from the initial cases, and different causes. If four persons have high stress and a long commute and another four persons have low stress and no long commute, you have more evidence for hypothesizing a relationship between commuting and stress. But if you find that persons with low stress are about as likely to have a long commute as persons with high stress, you have little evidence of a connection between these two variables.

An Example of Data Analysis

The information in Exhibits 2.3 and 2.4 was taken from a team of two students who interviewed six fellow graduate students. Exhibit 2.3 is the transcript of one of the recorded interviews. Exhibit 2.4 is a theme table which the two students developed after reviewing the transcripts of the six interviews. This table helped them visualize the extent to which certain themes emerged and see the potential relationships between causes and consequences. Their sampling method was informed by the interviews as they transpired. The first two persons, selected through convenience, had experienced the death of a person close to them. This was intriguing, so they intentionally sought persons for the next two interviews who were known to them to have had this experience. The final two persons were students who had not had this experience.

Each person was told the purpose of the interview and that their names would not be used in their reports of the interviews. The following questions were posed:

1. In the last six months, what events have caused you stress?
2. How does stress impact your mood?
3. How does stress impact your body?
4. What type of thoughts do you have when you are under stress?
5. How have you attempted to prevent the stress?
6. How have you attempted to relieve the stress?
7. Do you feel you are adequately able to prevent and reduce your stress?
8. How would you describe your stress level compared to that of your classmates? Why?
9. Is there anything else you think I should know about your experience with stress as an MSW student?

EXHIBIT 2.3   Transcript of a Selected Interview* (Interview E in Exhibit 2.4)

Note: The interviewee's responses are indented.

In the last six months, what events have caused you stress?

    Wow, that's quite a few. Moving to the area, being a new resident in _____ was stressful to start with, was stressful because I don't know anybody or have any family here.

You moved in from outside this region?

    I came from New York, so I moved into the area not knowing anyone. So I didn't have any support system. So that was stressful in trying to connect with people. Of course then starting the graduate program was another stressful thing. I have not been in school full time in quite a few years. When I had gone before, I did part-time-type things. Leaving a job where I was autonomous and becoming a student where I felt it was more a parental atmosphere. It was an adjustment as well.

EXHIBIT 2.3 *Continued*

Was there anything else about leaving the job that caused stress other than the loss of autonomy?

> *I left friends, we really had a super work environment. We had good supervision and a good group of people to work for. They were friends. So it was different leaving that type of support at work as well.*

Anything else?

> *Oh yeah! The list is pretty long [laughs]. And probably the next thing that happened was my best friend in New York, has been my best friend for a while, we lived together for the last year or so. He had double by-pass surgery while I was down here and he is up there in New York. So it was difficult to be away and then he ended up being in the hospital between the beginning of October and Christmas four times. Twice for blood clots, once for the surgery and then right before Christmas they thought something was wrong with his heart and put him in again. So those things have been very stressful. I've made, let's see, I'm thinking about the number of trips I did make it back. One in September and October. One at Christmas time. Traveling you know is stressful as well. Going I-95, you really got to be alert, especially during the winter. Traffic is really bad around DC.*

Yeah. The beltway is really horrible.

> *Then when I came back after Christmas, there was my grandmother's death. Seeing her at Christmas time knowing that she was not going to be lasting much more was another thing that was a stressful time. And I'm not done yet! My field placement has just been frustrating for me. I'm not sure what to do about that. It's not the type of experience I had hoped for. I'm not sure what to do about that. Plus, on top of all of that I had an accident with my car. So that was stressful. I have not gotten my car back. I had to rent a car to get around. The last thing is my cholesterol is borderline high. I have lost weight and my cholesterol has gone up. I don't understand that at all. I have been doing a low fat diet and trying to lose weight, but I anticipated my cholesterol coming down.*

Any other stressors?

> *The work load is stressful. The papers and reading.*

How does stress impact your mood?

> *Feeling overwhelmed and anxious, some anxiety. I feel like I get into my own little world I'm concentrating on so focused on trying to stay on top of things.*

Would isolated be the best description of withdrawn?

> *Maybe.*

Preoccupied?

> *Yeah, that's a good word. Cause I feel pressure to get this stuff done. To do what I have to do.*

How does stress impact your body?

> *Headaches and I can't sleep. I fall asleep and then get awake early in the morning. I'll lay there 2 or 3 hours. I study sometimes and then try to take a nap before school. Sometimes I feel nervous too.*

So you feel tense and shaky.

> *Yeah, I feel tension in my back neck and shoulders.*

(Continued)

EXHIBIT 2.3 *Continued*

What type of thoughts do you have when you have experienced stress?

I'm not sure what you mean.

What do you say to yourself?

I got to get this work done. Then sometimes, I tell myself, just relax, do what you can. I think basically, I just plug away at a steady speed.

What do you do to attempt to prevent stress?

Well, I don't know about anything I've done to prevent it. I can tell you what I've done to cope with it.

Okay, that's my next question, what have you done to cope with stress?

Well, when it comes to preventing stress there are a number of those things I have no control over. You know grandmother's death, his surgery, I can't prevent it, they are going to happen. At times a good cry helps. I think I do well with my exercising. I walk to the University to and from or go to the mall. I have a couple of books that a friend has given to me. They're kind of personal growth kind of books. I can read this for my own enjoyment. Sometime, I'll just pick those up. As kind of an inspirational thing. The other week I went and got a massage. I thought, I've just been under so much stress, I'm gonna get myself a treat. I do a lot of, I don't know if I would say praying, at least beseeching my higher power. I guess awareness of a power beyond myself. I've connected somewhat with one girl from church, so from time to time we'll do something together like breakfast. I just do it now and feel more free. The first semester, I would say no, but now I've been more open. I'll call friends and family and my phone bill gets to be pretty high. Also, during the first semester, I had some therapy with a counselor and that helped. My upcoming stress reliever is a trip to Florida during the break.

Do you feel that you are adequately able to prevent and reduce the stress?

Well, I have a problem with that prevention piece because I'm not sure that it's possible to prevent, particularly the outside things that we don't have any control over. Certainly to cope with it, to deal with it, I can, I haven't lost it yet [laughs].

How would you describe your stress level compared to your classmates, and why?

I probably feel like I've had a greater stress load. Because of all the outside things that have taken place in my life in the last six months. I'm not sure anyone has had that combination. As I listen to my field seminar class, I feel my field placement has been more stressful. Other people have had a better experience.

What is it about the placement that makes it stressful?

That's a good question. I'm not sure that I want to say that right now.

Okay. Is there anything else you want to tell me about stress in your experience as an MSW student?

I think I felt a bit disappointed after I got in the program. It was not what I had anticipated. When I went home on my fall break, I was not sure that I was coming back. I had talked to a number of people at home and talked about my unhappiness and debating about not coming back.

How did you resolve it and end up coming back?

I decided I would come back and at least finish the semester. I would at least finish the semester and then check out some other options. So I felt okay to come back. While I was in New York, I look at other programs but the cost was too high. I figured I'm here. I can

EXHIBIT 2.3   *Continued*

get the degree. It is not quite the direction I want to go but at least I will have the degree. So I'm here.

Is there anything else?

   No, that's it.

Thank you for participating.

*Taken from the following paper submitted for a research course at East Carolina University: Drum, David. (1995). "The Significance of Therapy as a Stress Buffer in MSW Students." Used with permission.

EXHIBIT 2.4   Theme Matrix from Six Interviews of Social Work Students*

STRESSORS					
Person A	**Person B**	**Person C**	**Person D**	**Person E**	**Person F**
School work	School work	School work	School work	School work	School work
Internship Travel		Internship Travel		Internship content	
		Poor communication from school		Lack autonomy in school + disappointed with program	
	Lack of time for former routine		Lack of time for former routine	Lack of time for former routine	
Relocated-Loss of support		Relocated with husband in other city		Relocated-loss of support	Relocated-loss of support
Death of mother	Death of a close friend			Death of grandmother	Death of father
Liquidating mother's estate	Reduction of money			Commute to NY to visit family in crisis	Broke up with boyfriend
Dad having emotional difficulties with grief		Maintaining 3 residences	Personal health problems		
Suicides of 2 friends	Husband had major surgery			Close friend with serious health problem	

(Continued)

EXHIBIT 2.4 *Continued*

STRESS BUFFERS					
Person A	**Person B**	**Person C**	**Person D**	**Person E**	**Person F**
Exercise	Exercise	Exercise	Exercise	Exercise	Exercise
Praying	Praying		Church	Praying	
	Time out		Time out	Time out	Time out
	Support from family & friends	Support from friends	Support from family	Support	Support
	Budget time	Budget time			Budget time
Self hypnosis	Positive thinking			Self help books + massage	Positive thinking
Therapy				Therapy	Therapy
		Drinking	Drinking		
		Sleeping		Crying	Lowering expectation for self

STRESS					
Person A	**Person B**	**Person C**	**Person D**	**Person E**	**Person F**
Mood—sad unenergetic	Mood— irritable	Mood— irritable	Mood— irritable	Mood— anxious preoccupied	Preoccupied anxious irritable
Body— headaches stomach aches	Body— fatigue overeating	Body— fatigue overeating headaches	Body—none	Body— headaches loss of sleep tension	Body— headaches loss of appetite
Thoughts— cynical & pessimistic	Thoughts— negative impression of self	Thoughts— pessimistic	Thoughts— cynical	Thoughts— none negative	Thoughts— pessimistic
Coping all right with high level of stress	Coping all right with high level of stress	Coping adequately with slightly higher stress than others	Coping well	Coping all right with high level of stress	Coping all right with lower stress than others

*Taken from the work of two social work students, David Drum and Veronica Ranck. Used with permission.

ASSIGNMENT 2-D

1. Do you agree with the way Interview E in Exhibit 2.3 was recorded on the theme matrix (Exhibit 2.4)? Explain.

   All major items appear to be clocked in. I'd have thought friend illness could be emphasized more — also car trouble not mentioned lots of school work

2. Do you agree with the organization of the content into themes on this matrix? How would you code each line?

   Types of stressors, types of stress buffers, types of stress

3. Are there any hypotheses or propositions or generalizations that come to mind as you examine Exhibit 2.4? If so, explain.

   outside factors cause stress to be higher

Conclusions

The analysis by these two students first focused on death as a stressor. These researchers noted that all four students who had experienced this stressor reported to be coping okay with their stress. Thus, the researchers' attention turned to stress buffers. A trend was noted. Of the four subjects with the death stressor, three had received some form of therapy. This suggested a relationship between therapy and coping with stress. But an exception to this pattern was noted. Person B had experienced the death stressor and had received no therapy, but was reported to be coping well. Further analysis revealed that this person, unlike the others, had not experienced a relocation in order to go to graduate school. These students concluded that stressors should not be examined outside the context of other stressors. These students hypothesized that therapy would serve as a stress buffer for students who had experienced multiple stressors.

References

Belcher, J. R. (1994). Understanding the process of social drift among the homeless: A qualitative analysis. In E. Sherman & W. J. Reid (Eds.), *Qualitative research in social work* (pp. 126–134). New York: Columbia University Press.

Berg, B. L. (1994) *Qualitative research methods for the social sciences.* Boston: Allyn & Bacon.

Denzin, N. K., & Lincoln, Y. S. (Eds.) (1994). *Handbook of qualitative research.* Thousand Oaks, CA.: Sage Publications.

Fontana, A., & Frey, J. H. (1994). Interviewing: The art of science. In N. K. Denzin & Y. S. Lincoln (Eds.), *Handbook of Qualitative Research* (pp. 361–376). Thousand Oaks, CA.: Sage Publications.

Fortune, A. E. (1994). Commentary: Ethnography in social work. In E. Sherman & W. J. Reid (Eds.), *Qualitative research in social work* (pp. 63–67). New York: Columbia University Press.

Goodon-Lawes, J. (1994). Ethnicity and poverty as research variables: Family studies with Mexican and Vietnamese newcomers. In E. Sherman & W. J. Reid (Eds.), *Qualitative research in social work* (pp. 21–31). New York: Columbia University Press.

Miles, M. B., & Huberman, A. M. (1984). *Qualitative data analysis.* Beverly Hills: Sage Publications.

Neuman, W. L. (1994). *Social research methods, 2nd. Ed.* Boston: Allyn & Bacon.

Powell, J. Y. (1984) *Adults who were adopted as older children.* PhD dissertation, University of North Carolina at Greensboro.

Sherman, E., & Reid, W. J. (1994) *Qualitative research in social work.* New York: Columbia University Press.

Strauss, A. (1987). *Qualitative analysis for social scientists.* New York: Cambridge University Press.

Tutty, L. M., Rothery, M. A., & Grinnell, R. M. (1996) *Qualitative research for social workers.* Boston: Allyn & Bacon.

Chapter *3*

Conducting Descriptive Research on the Qualities of the Good Manager

In this chapter, you will continue your learning by conducting a research study. The major purpose of this study is to identify personal qualities believed to make a good social work manager. This process will begin with your response to a research instrument designed to measure the key variables in this study. Your responses will be combined with the responses of the entire class and these data will be subjected to analysis in the pursuit of the research questions.

The research process, of course, begins with problem formulation. You will examine a literature review on the research topic and examine several research questions that might emanate from this review. You will then examine the research methodology and you will collect and analyze the data from your class. The final phase of research will entail the drawing of conclusions about the research questions.

In this chapter, you will take on the role of study participant and researcher by responding to a questionnaire, along with your classmates, and analyzing the results. Before you consider your next step, you are reminded that your participation in this study is voluntary. Those who participate will be asked to turn in their answers to the questions on the next page or two without their names so that their responses will be anonymous. But you may also choose not to participate by turning in a blank questionnaire. In this way, your decision not to participate will not be revealed to others.

Your next step is to respond to the questions appearing in Exhibits 3.1 or 3.2. Before doing so, you should flip a coin and record whether it landed as heads or tails. If it landed as heads, you should respond to the questionnaire in Exhibit 3.1 (p. 56). If it landed as tails, you should respond to the questionnaire in Exhibit 3.2 (p. 57). *You should not read ahead before responding to the instrument on the following page. It is essential that your responses be independent of the kinds of research questions that might be posed in this study. To violate this rule will render the results invalid.*

EXHIBIT 3.1   Questionnaire for "Heads" Flip

The first 16 questions are ones in which you are asked to indicate your opinion about what it takes to be a good manager in a social work agency. You are asked to examine the following list of traits and select 8 that best characterize a good social work manager. Indicate your choices by drawing circles around the 8 items you have chosen. Be sure to select *exactly* 8 items from among the 16 items given below. If you select more or less than 8, your responses cannot be used in this study. When you have finished your response to these first 16 items on this questionnaire, you will have circled 8 of these items and you will *not* have circled the other 8 of these items.

1. Helpful
2. Ambitious
3. Aware of feelings of others
4. Consistent
5. Modest
6. Well-informed
7. Humanitarian values
8. Objective
9. Creative
10. Analytic
11. Sophisticated
12. Competitive
13. Intuitive
14. Self confident
15. Cheerful
16. Aggressive

17. Examine the description of the manager below and then respond to the question about how much you would like to work for this person as your supervisor or manager.

> *Barbara Thompson is known as a manager who "gets the job done" even if she has to be tough with her staff who are not meeting agency expectations. Ms. Thompson is quicker to point out areas of weakness to her subordinates than areas of strength. Some of her staff like her approach because they always know where she stands and because she is fair with them and does not "play favorites." Others complain that she should be more positive with her staff and show that she cares about them as individuals, not just as employees.*

To what extent would you like to work for this person? Indicate your answer by marking one of the following responses:

_____   I would really like to work for this person.

_____   I would not mind working for this person.

_____   I would prefer not to work for this person.

_____   I would really not want to work for this person and would do what I could to avoid it.

18. What is your gender?   _____ Female   _____ Male

19. What is your age?   _____ under 30   _____ 30 or over

EXHIBIT 3.2   Questionnaire for "Tails" Flip

The first 16 questions are ones in which you are asked to indicate your opinion about what it takes to be a good manager in a social work agency. You are asked to examine the following list of traits and select 8 that best characterize a good social work manager. Indicate your choices by drawing circles around the 8 items you have chosen. Be sure to select *exactly* 8 items from among the 16 items given below. If you select more or less than 8, your responses cannot be used in this study. When you have finished your response to these first 16 items on this questionnaire, you will have circled 8 of these items and you will *not* have circled the other 8 of these items.

1. Helpful	**9.** Creative
2. Ambitious	**10.** Analytic
3. Aware of feelings of others	**11.** Sophisticated
4. Consistent	**12.** Competitive
5. Modest	**13.** Intuitive
6. Well-informed	**14.** Self confident
7. Humanitarian values	**15.** Cheerful
8. Objective	**16.** Aggressive

17. Examine the description of the manager below and then respond to the question about how much you would like to work for this person as your supervisor or manager.

George Thompson is known as a manager who "gets the job done" even if he has to be tough with his staff who are not meeting agency expectations. Mr. Thompson is quicker to point out areas of weakness to his subordinates than areas of strength. Some of his staff like his approach because they always know where he stands and because he is fair with them and does not "play favorites." Others complain that he should be more positive with his staff and show that he cares about them as individuals, not just as employees.

To what extent would you like to work for this person? Indicate your answer by marking one of the following responses:

_____   I would really like to work for this person.

_____   I would not mind working for this person.

_____   I would prefer not to work for this person.

_____   I would really not want to work for this person and would do what I could to avoid it.

18. What is your gender?   _____   Female   _____   Male

19. What is your age?   _____   under 30   _____   30 or over

Ethics in Social Work Research

Before you were asked to complete a questionnaire at the beginning of this chapter, you were told that your participation was being requested for a research study along with the other members of your research class. You were told that your responses to the questions would be collected along with the other members of your class, but that your identity would not be revealed in the study. In fact, your anonymity was being assured by the fact that you were asked not to place your name on your questionnaire. You were told that your participation was voluntary and you were given the opportunity to refrain from participation in a way that would not reveal that you had done so. This procedure assured that your participation would be truly voluntary. You were not told, however, about the research question or provided any guidance about how certain responses to these questions should be interpreted. This procedure was designed to avoid appealing to any biases you might have about the subject under study and tempting you to respond according to these biases rather than your independent judgments about the questions under study.

Voluntary Participation

Voluntary participation is one of the major ethical guidelines for social work research that is given in the Code of Ethics of the National Association of Social Workers. To assure voluntary participation, the researcher should provide the study subject with a means of insuring that there is no penalty for refusal. Social work students in a research class might feel pressured to participate if the instructor had a means of knowing who refrained from participation. Of course, the instructor could give his or her word that there would be no penalty, and this may suffice for the majority of students. But a mechanism that prevents the instructor from knowing who participated would be even better as a means of assuring the voluntary nature of the participation.

In order that this ethical concern is properly treated in a study, the potential study participant must be competent to give voluntary consent. They must know the nature of any potential harm that may arise or the potential that their privacy will be placed in jeopardy. Children, of course, are not considered competent to give consent for themselves, and it is typically necessary that parents or guardians be given this responsibility.

Right to Privacy

The protection of the study subject's **right to privacy** is another ethical guideline in social work research. In the present study, this was done by having students turn in their questionnaires without their names or any information that would readily identify them. When dealing with a small sample, the researcher needs to be sensitive to the possibility that given individuals may be identifiable in the data just from their answers to the questions. For example, if a class of social work students had only one African American male, it would be inappropriate for the questionnaire to ask both for gender and race on the questionnaire because this person could be readily identified by anyone examining the questionnaires. The right to privacy increases in research ethics the more the subjects are asked to reveal potentially damaging information about themselves, such as criminal behavior or highly personal information about sexual behaviors and so forth.

Protection from Harm

Perhaps the most important ethical concern is the **protection of the study subject from harm.** Few social work research participants are subjected to potential harm, but there have been some in famous cases. Consider, for example, the study done in the 1930s, in which 100 Black men with syphilis were told they could receive free treatment from the VA hospital when in fact, they were not treated at all but were being used for a research study on the progression of this disease. Even after penicillin was discovered, they were not told of this treatment nor were they given it (Jones, 1981).

Most ethical concerns that confront the typical social work researcher are not easy to resolve. Is it ethical to withhold treatment for a group of clients so that they may become the control group for a research study? Normally this would not be considered ethical. But what if it is not well known whether the treatment will work, so you do not know that you are refraining from giving necessary help? If you reached this conclusion, would you be engaging in a rationalization for the sake of research so it could be justified? What if you only had the resources to treat 30 persons and you had 60 people who asked for the service? Could you select service recipients on a random basis and use those not served as the control group for your research study on the effectiveness of the treatment?

A guideline offered by Rubin and Babbie (Rubin & Babbie, 1993) is that the long-term gain from research should clearly outweigh the disadvantages to the study participants. Sometimes it is necessary to violate the letter of the ethical guideline for the sake of research. Rubin and Babbie give the example of a study of mental hospitals in which a team of researchers had themselves admitted to the hospital by faking a mental illness and then studied whether the clinical staff could distinguish them from the others who were in the hospital with a mental illness. In this case, the hospital staff did not voluntarily consent to be in this study. But there was no way that such voluntary participation could have been assured without rendering the research design useless. Were the benefits of the study greater than the harm that might have come from the lack of voluntary participation in the study?

An Overview of Descriptive Research

When social work research is classified according to the purpose of the study, you can conceive of four major categories—descriptive, explanatory, evaluative, and exploratory. **Exploratory** research seeks a deeper meaning for a relatively unknown topic with the outcome typically being the development of a new theory or hypothesis about the nature of the thing being studied. The well known stages of death and dying were discovered through exploratory research from interviews with persons facing this reality. While the exploratory study often seeks to develop a new theory, testing an existing theory or hypothesis is the purview of the **explanatory** type of study. For example, do differences in position level between males and females explain the fact that males receive higher salaries than females? The **evaluative** study is used to test the effectiveness of an intervention. The present chapter focuses upon the descriptive type of study.

Descriptive research has the purpose of describing something. When quantitative means of measurement are used in descriptive research, the researcher is seeking a precise description of the nature of the thing being studied. For example, you might want to characterize the clients of your agency with regard to age, gender, and the category of their presenting problem. You may want to know the number of children under the age of 6 who are members of the families you are serving. You may want to know the proportion of your agency's clients who are receiving each of the services given by your agency, or the number of persons who have requested each service.

With qualitative methods of measurement, you are normally seeking a deeper meaning of the nature of the thing being studied. You might want to know how homeless people describe their feelings about being homeless. What is this experience really like for those who are experiencing it? This type of study would be classified as exploratory research in this text, because the outcome would be the development of a theory or hypothesis about the nature of being homeless. Some texts may see descriptive research as utilizing either quantitative or qualitative methods of measurement, provided the outcome is a better description of the phenomenon being studied.

When you describe something, you typically characterize it in relation to size or intensity or similarities with something else. You may want to know, for example, the proportion of your clients who are female, or the proportion who are members of minority groups, or the number who have pre-school age children. This information can aid you in understanding how better to serve these clients.

Descriptive data can help you to put things into perspective. What if you find that 72 percent of your clients say they would recommend your agency to others? Is this good news? If so, how good is it? What is the basis for your conclusion? Perhaps it would be helpful to know that this is approximately the same proportion of clients of other similar agencies who hold the same opinion. Now you can put your results into perspective by realizing that your agency is similar to others.

The descriptive analysis of certain variables for a given sample of subjects can aid in the interpretation of data from an explanatory study. When you conduct explanatory research, you need to be cognizant of the general pattern of responses to items that measure your study variables. For example, suppose you ask a sample of social workers to indicate, on a five-point scale, the extent to which they have family or friends on whom they can rely when they need help. Suppose you wish to use this as a measure of social support. Suppose further that none of these social workers responded at the lower end of the scale and only a handful gave responses in the middle of the scale; thus, the vast majority had responses of 4 or 5 on this 5-point scale. Now suppose you find there was not a significant correlation between responses to this question and scores on a stress scale. Does this mean that support is not related to stress in general? This interpretation would be problematic because of the low level of variance on the item used to measure support. A better interpretation of these data would be that persons at the highest level of support were not different on stress from those at moderately high levels of support. These results might also suggest that you need a different means of measuring support.

Descriptive data can be used to compare a study sample with known data from larger groups to whom you wish to generalize your study findings. The safe generalization of study results from a sample to a population can take place only when you have a probability (random) sample. But you often will wish to speculate on the extent to which you can have confidence that your results would be similar for a larger group when the sample was not drawn on a random basis.

What follows is the first assignment in this chapter. As explained in the previous chapter, these assignments are designed to facilitate class discussion. You should respond to each question in these assignments and be prepared to offer your ideas for class discussion unless instructed to do otherwise.

ASSIGNMENT 3-A

1. Do you see any ethical concerns for each of the following situations?

A. An agency has 30 people who have asked for employment counseling services. The agency has the resources to meet the needs of all clients. In order to conduct a study on the effectiveness of employment counseling services, the agency randomly assigned 15 people to the control group and 15 people to the experimental group. The experimental group will immediately receive employment counseling services, while the people in the control group will not be given the service for a period of three months. At the end of three months, the two groups will be compared on their employment situations to see if the counseling made a difference. The control group will be given the service beginning in three months.

Notes: *Do No Harm — waiting 3 months for employment counseling could be devastating*

B. A researcher fakes a heart attack on a busy street corner in order to study different responses of people to stressful situations. No one on the street, of course, is told about the fact that this is a fake heart attack and is part of a study.

Notes: *Street corner subjects are not voluntary*

C. A social work professor passes out a questionnaire in a social policy class which he will use for a study of attitudes toward the poor. He asks that they not place their name on the questionnaire as he walks around the room collecting each student's questionnaire.

Notes: *right to privacy since he collects papers & may know handwriting*

D. A researcher pretends to be mentally ill in order to be admitted to a mental hospital where he can study the behavior of the mental health staff. He does not, of course, tell the staff what he is up to.

Notes: _not voluntary "staff", however may need to be done so natural behavior can be observed_

E. An agency mails out a client satisfaction questionnaire to its clients and asks if they will anonymously respond to the questions.

Notes: _OK – no harm, voluntary (asked), right to privacy all upheld_

F. A research professor asks students to respond to a questionnaire on which the student is given a list of 16 words that might describe the good social work administrator. The student is asked to circle the 8 words on the list that do the best job of describing a good administrator. One-half of these words have been found to be associated with a male sex-role stereotype and one-half have been associated with a female stereotype; thus, the student can determine the extent to which he or she embraces a sex-role stereotype about what it takes to be a good manager. If all 8 items on a student's selected list are male-stereotyped, the student would have the maximum score for this stereotype. If 4 "male" words and 4 "female" words are selected, there is no preference displayed by the student. The questionnaire does not give any information that indicates that the study is about sex-role stereotypes. The question simply asks the student to indicate what it takes to be a good administrator; thus, they do not know that they are displaying their sex-role stereotypes. Their responses are anonymous and they are given the opportunity to turn in a blank questionnaire if they do not wish to participate.

Notes: _OK – voluntary, privacy, no harm upheld_

2. Consider the last situation above (1-F). Each student has selected 8 words. The number of these words that are male-stereotyped constitute the student's score for sex-role stereotype about management. What is the first piece of data you would secure from this study? What else might you do with the data?

sex-role stereotype
# of each level from class

3. Why would a researcher want to examine the patterns of response, or variance, for a variable to be employed in an explanatory study? For example, suppose you asked the clients of your agency to indicate the extent of their satisfaction and you wanted to examine the relationship between level of satisfaction and age. You find that 80 percent of your clients answered "very satisfied" to the satisfaction question while 15 percent answered "satisfied" and only 5 percent answered as either "unsatisfied" or "very unsatisfied."

You'd want to know how common this type of response was compared z other places —

Dif ages might also have "normal" response patterns that affect it

A Study of the Qualities of the Good Manager

In this chapter, you are participating as a subject for a research study and you will also be called upon to be the researcher for parts of this experience. The topic has already been selected and a knowledge base has been developed for it. The literature review for this study is given in Exhibit 3.3. At the beginning of this chapter, you were asked to flip a coin and to respond to the questions in either Exhibit 3.1 or Exhibit 3.2, depending on the result of your coin flip. These two exhibits provide the means used to measure our study variables. The study sample has been determined. It will be those persons in your research class (and possibly those persons in other sections of this research course as well). Your role as researcher will focus primarily on the third and fourth phases of research—data analysis and study conclusions. You will analyze the data regarding the research questions given and you will draw conclusions accordingly. In the next two sections, you will examine the literature and the study methodology that have been developed for you.

Problem Formulation for the Study of the Good Manager

The first phase of the research process entails articulating the theme of interest and examining the existing knowledge about this theme, usually through a literature review. This phase has been labeled "problem formulation." At the completion of this phase, you should be clear on the definitions of key concepts and information on what is known about their relationships. This should guide your attempt to determine how to engage in research which will extend your knowledge about some aspect of the research theme. One of the key questions in this regard is whether a qualitative or quantitative methodology should be used for making observations in the research study. In other words, the problem formulation phase lays the groundwork for the second phase, study methodology.

The present study deals with sex-role stereotypes about management. You were not informed about this theme beforehand, because it might have influenced the way in which you responded to the questions on the questionnaire. Exhibit 3.3 contains a brief literature review on sex-role stereotypes about management. In that review, you should pay particular attention to the definition of concepts, the reasons for studying them, and what is known from the research of others.

EXHIBIT 3.3   An Examination of the Literature

What does it take to be a good supervisor or manager? Is the good manager (1) a person who is objective and analytic, or (2) a person who is helpful and intuitive? While there is little empirical evidence that one of these pairs of adjectives does a better job than the other in identifying the good manager, numerous studies have demonstrated that employees are more likely to identify words in the first pair than the second when they describe the good administrator (Schein, 1973; Schein, 1975; Massengill & DiMarco, 1979; York, 1987). What is most noteworthy about these findings from research is the fact that the words in the first pair (objective and analytic) have been found to be perceived as more like men than women, while the words in the second pair (helpful and intuitive) have been found to be perceived as more like women than men (Schein, 1973).

The implications of this situation are readily apparent. If managers are viewed in terms which are perceived as being more like men than women, women will be less likely to be considered for management positions. It is even possible that women will avoid applying for such positions because of this sex-role stereotype.

Another manner in which stereotypes serve as barriers to women in management is the fact that some people evaluate women more harshly if they exhibit what are perceived as masculine traits. For example, female managers were found to be evaluated by subordinates more negatively than male managers if they exhibited such traits as being directive (Haccoun, Haccoun, & Sallay, 1978), autocratic (Jago & Broom, 1982), or the behavior known as "initiating structure" (Bartol & Butterfield, 1976). This phenomenon tends to restrict the repertoire of behaviors available to women in the management role and makes it more difficult for them to be perceived as successful.

Sex-Role Stereotypes About Management

A sex-role stereotype is a standardized mental picture of gender differences in socially designated behaviors which represents an oversimplified opinion or uncritical judgment. In other words, it constitutes a generalization with serious inaccuracies.

The sex-role stereotype about management basically defines management qualities in terms of masculine traits. According to this line of thinking, managers are supposed to be logical, aggressive, competitive, analytical and so forth. The problem with this line of thinking is that these are also the traits that people generally perceive to be the qualities that men possess in greater amounts than women. Qualities such as compassion, intuitive understanding, and interpersonal sensitivity are believed to be relatively unimportant for the performance of the management role. Yet, these latter qualities are generally perceived to be the qualities of

EXHIBIT 3.3   *Continued*

women. Furthermore, the superiority of "male" traits over "female" traits remains unsubstantiated in research. They are derived primarily from the tendency of dominant groups to overgeneralize about the reasons for their success.

Because men have dominated the management field, there is a tendency for them to believe that all their traits are necessary for successful performance, not just those traits that are truly instrumental. Thus, there has emerged a sex-role stereotype that describes good managers as being those persons who possess these masculine traits.

Terborg (1977) reviewed the literature on women in management in various fields. He concluded that women describe themselves and are described by others as having self concepts that are not suitable for management. Thus, men are not the only ones who generally embrace this sex-role stereotype. It appears that women have been socialized into believing this stereotype as well. But this does not hold true for women who pursue nontraditional careers. According to Terborg, these women tend to reject these stereotypes.

Much of the work on sex-role stereotypes has analyzed the social desirability of masculine and feminine characteristics. A review of such literature by Broverman and others (1972) led to the conclusion that masculine traits were perceived to be generally more desirable than feminine characteristics. According to this review, women are perceived as relatively less competent, less independent, and less logical than men, whereas men were perceived as relatively less sensitive, warm, and expressive than women. In contrast to the above picture, however, is a study of social work students which revealed no significant difference in the perception of what characterizes a healthy male, a healthy female, and a healthy adult (Harris & Lucas, 1976).

A number of studies have addressed the question of sex-role stereotypes about management. In two studies by Schein (1973; 1975) both male and female middle managers in insurance companies were found to describe successful middle managers more in accordance with the male stereotype than the female stereotype. Brenner and Bromer (1981) found in another study that female managers tended to describe themselves more like the male stereotype than the female stereotype. From such studies emerges a picture that suggests that women who succeed in management roles do so either because they are those few who have many male characteristics or because they adopt male features in order to survive. *– or may describe themselves falsely ?*

When women succeed in securing management positions, they encounter another obstacle. It has been suggested in the literature that female managers are judged more harshly than male managers when they exhibit authoritarian behaviors. Staff may respond to a certain behavior in men as simply characteristic of men and it will be accepted, but if a female manager exhibits the same behavior, she may be given a negative label (Jago & Vroom, 1982).

These stereotypes contradict the available evidence on what it takes to be a good manager. A study of two mental health organizations, for example, revealed no consistent relationship between the gender of the leader and either leader behavior or subordinate satisfaction (Osborn & Vicars, 1976). Overviews of previous research on this issue have been offered by Bartol (1978) and by Reif, Newstrom and Monczka (1975). In both cases, conclusions were reached that sexual segregation in the workplace was not supported by the results of research on gender differences. In fact, there may be more evidence of female superiority than male superiority, even though the results of such studies in general are inconclusive. For example, a study by Jago and Vroom (1982) revealed that both female students and female managers were more participative in leadership style than were male students and male managers. According to participative leadership theory, the results of this study would favor the female stereotype.

(Continued)

EXHIBIT 3.3   *Continued*

Why Is This Issue Important?

The effect of this situation for women is obvious. Many women are screened out of consideration for management positions because they do not possess these "masculine" qualities. Women who do succeed in management are those who either happen to possess an unusual number of masculine qualities or adopt these qualities as a means for advancement. In the social work literature, our attention has been called to this issue by such writers as Rubenstein (1981), Faver, Fox, and Shannon (1983), and Chernesky (1980), among others. They contend that the social work profession, although dominated numerically by women, is by no means immune from the discriminatory effects of these stereotypes which have been observed in other fields.

Sex-Role Stereotypes Among Social Workers

The above observations about social work may surprise many people in this field. It would be easy to assume that social workers are more sensitive to factors such as sex-role stereotypes and would be different from others in this regard. But two studies have indicated a tendency for social workers to describe the good administrator more in male-stereotyped terms than female-stereotyped terms (York, 1987; York, Henley, & Gamble, 1985). In those studies, social workers were given a list of 16 words drawn from the work of Schein (1973, 1975). One half of these words had been found in Schein's work to be associated with a male stereotype while the other half had been found to be associated with a female stereotype. The female stereotyped items were as follows: (1) helpful; (2) aware of feelings of others; (3) modest; (4) humanitarian values; (5) creative; (6) sophisticated; (7) intuitive; (8) cheerful. The male stereotyped items included the following: (1) ambitious; (2) consistent; (3) well informed; (4) objective; (5) analytic; (6) competitive; (7) self confident; (8) aggressive.

The respondents were asked to select the 8 items that best characterized the good manager. The variable of male sex-role stereotype was measured by the number of male items selected. This could range from 0 (if all items had been in the female category) to 8 (if all items had been in the male category). A score of 4 would indicate an equal emphasis upon male and female stereotyped items. For these two studies by York and others, the mean score was significantly above the score of 4, indicating a preference for the male items on the scale.

However, another study revealed that social workers did not evaluate their supervisors more positively if they exhibited behaviors generally considered to be in the masculine than feminine category (York, Moran, & Denton, 1989).

Ironically, two of the above studies also revealed that the males in these two samples of social workers actually favored the female stereotype more than did the females. York, Moran, and Denton (1989) found that males evaluated their supervisors more positively the more they exhibited the female-stereotyped traits. This was not true for the females in the sample. York (1987) found that males were more likely than females to select female-stereotyped traits to describe the good manager (t = 1.65; p = .10).

These latter findings create a mystery for research. Would we not expect males to have more of a male stereotype than females? Perhaps males and females in social work are different.

Summary

Studies of more than one population have supported the conclusion that males and females are perceived as being different on a number of behavioral traits. The view that men and women

EXHIBIT 3.3   *Continued*

are perceived as different should not be surprising to society, nor especially problematic, unless these perceptions influence one's view of what it takes to be in a favored position such as management. Unfortunately, previous research has supported the conclusion that people working in the private sector are more likely to describe the good manager in male-stereotyped traits than female-stereotyped traits. To the surprise of some, this tendency has been found to be true for some samples of social workers. Even more surprising was the discovery that male social workers were less likely than female social workers to favor the male stereotype for the manager.

One of the apparent effects of these discoveries is that females may be discouraged from considering administrative advancement because of the perception that they do not possess the traits of the good manager. Another apparent effect is the discouragement of administrators from considering many women for advancement because of this sex-role stereotype.

Another disturbing discovery is that female managers are evaluated more harshly than males for exhibiting certain behaviors. The apparent effect of this tendency is for the female manager to be restricted in the tools available to achieve managerial ends.

Among the questions for further analysis are:

1. Are male-stereotyped traits favored over female-stereotyped traits in the description of the good manager for various populations? Would this be true for social workers?   *Desc.*

2. Why would some populations be different from others in their tendency to favor the male-stereotyped or female-stereotyped traits for the good manager? If social workers are different, why is this true?   *Explan*

3. What male-stereotyped traits are most favored for the good manager? What female-stereotyped traits are most favored?   *D*

4. What male-stereotyped traits are the ones least likely to be perceived by social work students as being like themselves?   *D*

5. Do these discrepancies between self-perception and the good manager serve as a potential barrier to the social work student's interest in administrative advancement in the future?   *E*

6. What is the effect of heightened awareness of sex-role stereotypes about management upon the social work student's career interests?   *E*

7. Are male and female social workers different on their tendency to embrace a male stereotype about the good manager?   *D*

8. For the management role, is the male task-master favored over the female task-master?   *D*

9. Are female social workers (or social work students) more likely than males in this field to accept as one's manager a female who is described as a task-master? Is gender related to the acceptance of the male as a task-master in the managerial role?   *D E*

10. What might explain gender differences regarding the acceptance of the female and the male as task-masters in the managerial role?   *E*

(Continued)

EXHIBIT 3.3   *Continued*

References

Bartol, K. M. (1978). The sex structuring of organizations: A search for possible causes. *Academy of Management Review, 3,* 805–815.

Bartol, K. M. & Butterfield, D. A. (1976). Sex effects in evaluating leaders. *Journal of Applied Psychology, 61,* 446–454.

Brenner, O. C. & Bromer, J. A. (1981). Sex stereotypes and leaders behavior as measured by the agreement scale for leadership behavior. *Psychological Reports, 48,* 960–962.

Broverman, I. K., Vogel, S. R., Broverman, D. M., Clarkson, F. E., and Rosenkrantz, P. S. (1972). Sex-role stereotypes: A current appraisal. *Journal of Social Issues, 28,* 59–78.

Chernesky, R. H. (1980). Women administrators in social work. In E. Norman and A. Mancuso (Eds.) *Women's Issues and Social Work Practice* (pp. 241–263.) Itasca, IL: F. E. Peacock.

Faver, C. A., Fox, N. F., & Shannon, C. (1983). The educational process and job equity for the sexes in social work. *Journal of Education for Social Work 19* (3), 78–79.

Haccoun, D. M., Haccoun, R. R. & Sallay, G. (1978). Sex differences in the appropriateness of supervisory styles: A nonmanagement view. *Journal of Applied Psychology, 63,* 124–127.

Harris, L. H. & Lucas, M. E. (1976). Sex-role stereotyping. *Social Work, 21,* 390–395.

Jago, A. G. & Vroom, V. H. (1982). Sex differences in the incidence and evaluation of participative leader behavior. *Journal of Applied Psychology, 67,* 776–783.

Massengill, D. & DiMarco, N. (1979). Sex-role stereotypes and requisite management characteristics: A current replication. *Sex Roles, 5* (5), 561–570.

Osborn, R. N. & Vicars, W. M. (1976). Sex stereotypes: An artifact in leader behavior and subordinate satisfaction analysis? *Academy of Management Journal, 19* 439–449.

Rief, W. E., Newstrom, J. W., & Monczka, R. M. (1975). Exploding some myths about women managers. *California Management Review, 17,* 72–78.

Rubinstein, H. (1981). Women in organizations: A review of research and some implications for teaching social work practice. *Journal of Education for Social Work, 17,* 20–27.

Schein, V. E. (1973). The relationship between sex-role stereotypes and requisite management characteristics. *Journal of Applied Psychology, 57* (2), 95–100.

Schein, V. E. (1975). The relationship between sex-role stereotype and requisite management characteristics among female managers. *Journal of Applied Psychology, 60* (3), 340–344.

Terborg, J. R. (1977). Women in management: A research review. *Journal of Applied Psychology, 62* (6), 647–664.

York, R. O. (1987). Sex-role stereotypes about social work administration. *Journal of Sociology and Social Welfare, 14* (3), 87–104.

York, R. O., Henley, C. A., & Gamble, D. N. (1985). Strategies for reducing barriers to female advancement in social work administration. Paper presented at the Annual Program Meeting, Council on Social Work Education, Washington, D.C.

York, R. O., Moran, J. R., & Denton, R. T. (1989). Are social workers sexually biased in their evaluations of supervisors? *Administration in Social Work, 13* (1), 45–57.

Methodology in Descriptive Research

The Definition of Study Variables

The *abstract definition* of study variables is crucial in descriptive research. An abstract definition of a variable provides conceptual guidance of the thing that is being measured. How would you define the concept of political conservatism? Would it include only attitudes or would it also include behaviors? What attitudes or behaviors would place one in the category of being politically conservative? Your definition of this term will guide your determination of the means to be employed in measuring it. If you conclude from a study that 32 percent of social work students are politically conservative, what does that mean? Your abstract definition of this term will provide guidance to the reader of your report because one person's definition of conservative may be another person's definition of reactionary or another word generally thought to be more extreme.

In the study in the previous chapter, stress was defined as a psychological state characterized by such terms as tense, up-tight, uneasy, and so forth. A stressor was defined as a condition in the environment that may lead to stress. However, we found that some researchers on this subject defined stress as a set of environmental conditions. Such persons might say that someone with a recent death in the family who had just lost his job and was in debt was highly stressed. But this would not be a proper statement if we conceptualized stress as a psychological condition. Persons with a large number of stressors in their lives would normally have higher stress than others, but stress and stressors are not the same thing, according to our definitions in chapter 2. Thus, our device for measuring stress would not contain questions about the extent to which we had experienced such things as the death of a friend or losing a job or having to care for an elderly parent with serious needs for daily care, and so forth. These things we have defined as stressors rather than stress.

Your definition of variables will guide your determination of how to measure them. Obviously a psychological state is different from an environmental condition. Being politically conservative is not the same thing as voting Republican, even thought we may find that Democrats and Republicans are different on responses to a scale measuring political ideology. Some Democrats can be just as politically conservative as some Republicans. We might use voting tendency as one item on a scale of behaviors designed to measure political conservatism, but we should not label our variable "conservatism" if our only measure is whether one voted Republican. If the latter is the case, you would be well advised to label your variable as "voting Republican" because that is the only thing you actually measured, and that precisely captures the essence of the data.

Reliability and Validity

Reliability refers to the consistency of an instrument or means of observation. One popular means of testing reliability is known as the **test-retest** method. In this method, you give a scale to a group of persons at two points in time and examine the correlation of scores at the two points in time. If John has a higher score than Mary at time 1, he should have a higher score than Mary at time 2. If this does not turn out to be the typical pattern, you have reason to question the reliability of the scale.

Another popular means of testing reliability is through the examination of internal consistency. The question here is whether the items on the instruments seem to be measuring the same thing. One method for this examination is the **split-half** method. In this test of reliability, you split the instrument into two halves and compose two variables, one representing each half. You administer this scale to a group of persons at one point in time and examine whether the two halves correlate. If Barbara's score for the first half of the instrument is higher than Janet's score for this half, she should also have a higher score than Janet for the second half. If this does not turn out to be the typical pattern, we would have reason to challenge the internal consistency of the instrument. This information would suggest that the second half of the items do not seem to be measuring the same thing as the first half. If that is the case, how can we be confident we know what the instrument is measuring?

In the above discussion of the hypothetical scores of Barbara and Janet, we discussed general patterns of responses. There will, of course, be exceptions to the general pattern. The fact that one pair of persons does not conform to expectations does not mean much by itself. What is important is the general pattern and the extent to which there are exceptions to this pattern. The more exceptions, the lower the correlation and the less confidence you can have that your instrument is reliable.

There are several methods of examining *validity,* which refers to the extent to which an instrument truly measures what it is intended to measure. In other words, validity refers to accuracy. An instrument can be reliable without being valid. It can, for instance, be consistently inaccurate. But it cannot be valid without being reliable. Reliability is one basis of support for validity, but it is not a sufficient basis for determining validity.

The simplest form of validity is **face validity.** This refers to whether the instrument seems to be measuring the thing it is supposed to measure. You can examine the instrument and ask yourself if this is true. Better still, you could ask others to examine your instrument for face validity. You could tell these people what you are trying to measure and ask if they believe this instrument does a reasonably good job of doing so. You might even want to ask these people what they believe this instrument measures without telling them what you designed it to measure, then determine whether their answer is reasonably close to your study concept.

A second form of validity is **content validity.** An instrument has content validity to the extent that it covers the total content of the concept you are trying to measure. If you define depression as including feelings of guilt, you might ask yourself if a given instrument for measuring depression contains items that are designed to measure feelings of guilt. If not, it is limited in its content validity in this manner. The question being asked is "How well do the items on this scale represent the total concepts included in our definition of the variable?"

Both of the above forms of validity rely on the judgments of selected persons. You will typically ask persons with expertise on your topic to judge the level of validity of your instrument. In a sense, you might refer to this approach as qualitative in nature because you have not reduced your questions to discrete items that can be tested using quantitative methods.

Several forms of validity have been categorized as **empirical validity** because they subject the instrument to empirical assessment. You might, for example, undertake an examination of the correlation of scores on your instrument with those on another instrument that is supposed to measure the same thing. If scores do not correlate between these two instruments, the two do not seem to be measuring the same thing. Perhaps one is measuring it accurately and the other is not, but if they do not correlate, you will not know which is the better one. Of course, it is also possible that neither instrument is accurately measuring the variable in question.

There are several forms of empirical validity. The distinctions between them are not given considerable importance in this text. Instead, it is suggested that you become familiar with the nature of empirical validity through several examples of it.

You can examine the relationship of your tool to some external criterion that represents your variable in some way. For example, scores on the Graduate Record Examination are supposed to predict performance in graduate school. Are these scores correlated with graduate school grades? If not, you would have questions about the validity of this test.

We would expect that scores on a marital happiness scale would be a good predictor of whether a person was going to seek a divorce. It is logical to assume that persons who are happily married are not going to get divorced, and that a good number of unhappily married persons will get a divorce. If the scores of persons today is not a good predictor of whether they will get divorced next year, we would have reason to question the validity of our instrument. The key question here is whether our instrument predicts behavior that it should predict if it truly measures the thing it is supposed to measure.

When you endeavor to define your variable, you often find that there are concepts close to the one you are defining but not identical to it. You will also find there are variables that are naturally related to your variable, but distinct from it conceptually. Does your variable measure something different from the other variable? If not, we have reasons to question the validity of the instrument. For example, suppose the instructor for your research course gave you a final exam and also administered an IQ test and a test of research knowledge that had been developed by another research instructor. What if you learned that the correlation between scores on your instructor's exam and IQ was .75, while the correlation between these scores and scores on the other research exam was .24? This would suggest that your instructor's exam is a better test of IQ than of research knowledge. While we would expect a correlation between exam scores and IQ to be moderately high, we would challenge the validity of this exam if it did better at predicting IQ scores than it did at predicting scores on someone else's test of research knowledge.

Levels of Measurement

The four levels by which one can measure a variable in quantitative terms are nominal, ordinal, interval, and ratio. A variable measured at the *nominal* level simply places study subjects into categories such as male and female or Democrat and Republican. A variable measured at the *ordinal* level provides levels to the categories, such as low, medium, and high.

A variable measured at the *interval* level provides an order as well, but the difference between the ordinal and interval levels is that for interval variables, the distance between values is equal. For example, a person who is 14 years old is one year older than someone who is 13, who is one year older than someone who is 12. Thus, if age is measured in terms of years (rather than categories of years), we can say that it is measured at the interval level.

A variable measured at the *ratio* level meets the same qualifications as the interval level, with the addition that the ratio variable is measured from a fixed zero point. An easy way to remember the distinction between the ratio and interval variables is that the ratio variable cannot have a negative value. A person's weight, for example, cannot have a value of minus 45 pounds.

These four levels of measurement form a hierarchy: the nominal level is the lowest, the ordinal level is next, then the interval level, and, finally, the ratio level, as illustrated below.

Level 4: Ratio   *Example: What is your age?*

Level 3: Interval   *Example: What is the predicted high temperature for tomorrow?*

Level 2: Ordinal   *Example: Would you consider yourself to be low, medium, or high on job satisfaction?*

Level 1: Nominal   *Example: Are you male or female?*

An important reason for these distinctions is that a variable measured at a higher level can be treated as though it were measured at a lower level for statistical analysis, if needed.

Thus, a variable measured at the ratio level can be treated as though it were measured at any of the other levels because it is the highest level of measurement. An interval variable can be treated as though it were measured at the ordinal or nominal levels, as well as the interval level. An ordinal level can be treated as being either ordinal or nominal. A nominal variable, however, cannot be treated as though it is ordinal, interval, or ratio in the statistical analysis of data—because it is measured at the lowest level.

A deviation from this strict interpretation of levels of measurement is often seen in published reports when variables measured at the ordinal level are treated as though they were measured at the interval level. This is especially the case of a scale which is composed of one's responses to several questions measured at the ordinal level. For example, you may ask respondents to indicate whether they have experienced each of several emotions (1) none of the time, (2) some of the time, or (3) a good deal of the time. You might have such emotions as "tense" and "uptight" and "anxious" and "apprehensive" on our scale. You have asked respondents to give you four responses because you have four items on your scale, and you have asked them to respond according to this three-point ordinal scale to each item. If you were to select only one of these items for analysis, you would have a variable that was measured at the ordinal level. But if you chose to add their scores for all four items by assigning points to each category, you would be creating a scale that most would consider to be a measurement at the interval level.

Sampling in Descriptive Research

The methods used to draw a sample of study subjects for a descriptive study will determine the extent to which the results can be generalized to those not in the study. In some instances, you collect data on all persons in your study population. For example, you might examine data on all persons currently served by your agency. If you only want to know how to describe your current clients, you have no reason to deal with the issues associated with sampling in research. You would simply say that you are describing all your current clients.

The concept of sampling comes into focus when you draw data from a selected group of persons rather than everyone in your study population. You might select a sample of the clients whose cases have been closed during the past three months because you want to know the level of satisfaction of your clients with the services of your agency. Your reason for asking questions of this group of persons is that you believe that they would constitute a representative sample of persons who have been served by your agency in the past year or two. However, you cannot safely generalize your findings from this sample to a larger population unless your sample was chosen on a random basis. Otherwise, you are speculating when you generalize. But speculation is all that is feasible in many instances, and you may have reason to feel confident that your sample is representative even though it is not random.

Remember, the study **sample** is that group of subjects for whom data were collected. Subjects, incidentally, can be in the form of records or entities other than people. The **study population** is that group of persons from which the sample was selected. The study population legitimately can be defined in a variety of ways, provided that all those in the sample are members of that population. For example, the sample of students in your research class would constitute a sample of (1) all research students in your school, or (2) all students in your school, or (3) all students. For each of these groups, every member of your sample is a member of that group; thus, any of these definitions of the study population would be legitimate. It may be helpful to drawn a graphic picture of this relationship between the study sample and the study population with the illustration below:

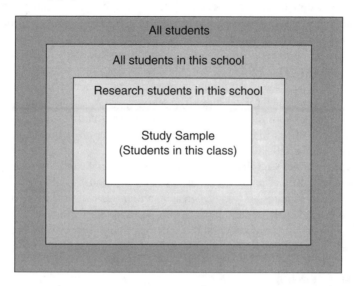

It would not be legitimate to define your study population as female students in your school, assuming that some of the students in your study sample are males, because some of the members in your sample would not be members of that population.

The above discussion is about the various ways one could legitimately define the study population. A legitimate definition of the study population is not necessarily an optimal definition. Logic will tell you that the further you are from the study sample in your definition of the study population, the less optimal is that definition. The less optimal the definition, the less confidence you can have that your results, using the sample, can be generalized from the sample to the population.

In general, you can classify samples into two main categories—probability samples and non-probability samples. A **probability sample** is one in which all persons in the study population have an equal chance of being selected for the sample. You achieve probability samples through random selection. A given probability sample, however, is a probability sample only for the specific group from which it was selected, not for larger groups that encompass this population. When you have a probability sample, you are in the position of estimating the degree of sampling error represented by the sample. You can say, for example, that the percent of persons who would vote for Jane Smith is 45 percent with a margin of error of 3 percentage points. In such a case, you are in a very good position to predict that the percent of persons who plan to vote for Jane Smith falls between 42 percent and 48 percent.

Probability Samples

Perhaps the simplest means of drawing a random sample is know as the **systematic random sampling procedure.** With this method, you first determine the sampling interval by dividing the number of persons in the population by the number to be selected for the sample (e.g., 1000 members of NASW divided by 200 persons to be selected would yield a value of 5, the sampling interval). Once you have secured the sampling interval, you select your first person from among those persons who fall within the first sampling interval. If your sampling interval is 5, you would select the first person at random from among the first 5 persons on your list of persons in your population. Any random procedure will do, such as rolling a set of dice, or using a table of random numbers, or simply saying that the first number between 1 and 5 that you see in the newspaper on your desk will be the first number to be selected for the study. Suppose this number is 3: person number 3 on the population list would be selected for the study. The second person selected would be the person who falls exactly one sampling interval beyond the first person. In the example, that would be person number 8 (3 + 5 = 8). The next person in the example would be person number 13, then person number 18 and so forth.

The **simple random sample** procedure calls for the use of a table of random numbers. You can find such tables in many books on research and statistics. A procedure that uses random sampling techniques but yields a greater sampling error is the **multistage random sampling procedure.** To illustrate, suppose you wished to select a sample of social workers who work in women's shelters throughout the state of Pennsylvania. You could first select a list of all women's shelters in this state, and select a random sample of shelters for your study. Then you could secure a list of social workers from these agencies and select a random sample from this list.

Nonprobability Samples

Nonprobability samples are those that were not drawn on a random basis. Perhaps the most common type of nonprobability sample used by social workers is the **convenience sample.** The convenience sample is the one that is selected out of convenience. For example, you are participating in a study of sex-role stereotypes among social workers. Your class was selected simply out of convenience. The question arises as to whether this sample is representative of a larger group of persons from whom this class was constituted, such as all those social work students in your school who are taking research courses or all those persons who are students in your school, or all persons who are social work students no matter where they are attending school. In these generalizations you would be in a position to speculate, but you would not be in the favorable position of being able to estimate the degree of sampling error, that is, the extent to which the sample might be different from the population.

Sometimes researchers select what is know as a **purposive sample.** This is a sample that is drawn from persons known to have special attributes that are important to the research question. For example, if you wished to examine the reasons why some abused women return to their husbands after receiving the services of a women's shelter, you might select social workers who work for women's shelters as respondents to your survey. These are persons who have special knowledge of the study topic. This would be a better sample than one that sampled social workers in general.

When the members of a study population are difficult to identify, **snowball sampling** will be helpful. With this method, you identify the small number of persons that you know to be members of the study population and you ask them to identify other persons from this population. Then you ask the second group of persons to identify additional persons, and you continue this process until you have a sufficient sample size.

ASSIGNMENT 3-B

1. A sex-role stereotype about management can be defined as a standardized mental picture of gender differences regarding management behaviors which represents an oversimplified opinion or uncritical judgment. Explain what this means in your own terms.

This means that someone has an opinion a generalize or judgement about someone regarding management behaviors that may be inaccurate

2. **a.** Briefly describe, in general, an instrument you might develop for measuring sex-role stereotype about management as you have defined it above.

I would develop a survey to assess if people are judging or stereotyping

b. Give examples of two items that could be on that instrument for measuring sex-role stereotype.

Open-ended questions & closed ended questions
What is your sex?
on a scale from 1 to
Would you consider yourself to be judgemental?   *make this open ended*

c. Select one of the items you listed above. At what level is this variable measured?

___X___ Nominal   __✗✗__ Ordinal   _____ Interval   _____ Ratio

d. Can this variable be treated as though it is measured at one or more different levels for the purposes of statistical analysis? If yes, identify it (or them).

No

3. a. How would you test the reliability of this instrument?

Test-Retest

b. How would this means of testing reliability be classified?

4. Now consider the other item you listed for Question 2b. How would you test the validity of this instrument?

The instrument is measuring what it is supposed to measure. & Ask subjects if they think the instrument does a good job of measuring what it's supposed to measure.

What category of validity is illustrated by the above method of testing validity?

____X____ Face validity   _____ Content validity   _____ Empirical validity

5. Suppose you wished to conduct a study to examine whether social workers or social work students embraced a sex-role stereotype about management.

a. Describe how you would select the persons for this study.

I would go to different schools and pick out classes, that ...

b. What is your definition of the study population?

The group of people that I choose to do my study on.

c. What is your definition of the study sample?

Group of subjects from the study population

d. Will you have a probability sample?

Yes

Methodology for the Study of the Good Manager

Several research questions were posed at the end of the literature review given in Exhibit 3.3. Only a portion of these questions will be addressed in this chapter. They are as follows:

1. What male-stereotyped traits and female-stereotyped traits are most favored in descriptions of the good manager?
2. Are social workers different from other groups in their selections of traits to describe the good manager?
3. Are male-stereotyped traits favored over female-stereotyped traits in the description of the good manager?
4. Are social work students different from other groups in their tendency to favor the male-stereotyped traits?
5. Which male-stereotyped traits that are favored as a description of the good manager are least likely to be included in a self-description by social work students?

   Some of the above questions will be addressed by data from your class, while others will be addressed by data collected by the author of this text. The key variable in this study is sex-role stereotype about management. One's tendency to embrace a management sex-role stereotype could be measured in many ways. Perhaps you can think of a few yourself. A means for measuring this variable has been selected for you and has been presented in the questionnaire you were asked to complete at the beginning of this chapter. It is described below.

The Definition and Measurement of Sex-Role Stereotype

We will employ a definition of sex-role stereotype given in the literature review. A sex-role stereotype is a standardized mental picture of gender differences in socially designated behaviors which represents an oversimplified opinion or uncritical judgment. Thus, a sex-role stereotype exists to the extent that one has a mental picture which oversimplifies gender differences without the benefit of critical examination. Regarding management behaviors, a sex-role stereotype exists to the extent that one has perceived male-stereotyped behaviors as more instrumental in management success than is the case of female-stereotyped behaviors. Furthermore, these perceptions exist in the absence of evidence of the superiority of male-stereotyped behaviors.

To measure sex-role stereotype about management, a list of 16 words, one-half of which were in the female category and one-half of which were in the male category, were placed on a questionnaire with instructions for the respondents to select the 8 items that best characterized the good social work manager (see Exhibits 3.1 and 3.2). Thus, the respondent could receive a male score of 0 to 8 depending upon how many of the 8 selected items were in the male category. The even-numbered items were the male-stereotyped ones. Thus, one's score for sex-role stereotype (SRS) will be computed by adding the number of these items that were selected by the respondent.

For example, if the respondent circled items 1, 4, 5, 7, 8, 13, 14, and 16, the SRS score would be 4. In this case, the student would have selected exactly 4 male items and 4 female items, which would represent no preference for the male stereotype. However, scores above 4 would represent a male preference while scores below 4 would represent a female preference. The following selections would represent a total female preference: 1, 3, 5, 7, 9, 11, 13, 15. In this case, the SRS score would be 0.

Our research question can be examined statistically by determining if the mean SRS score is significantly above the score of 4. The score of 4 would represent no preference by gender. Of course, if the mean SRS score is not above 4, there is no reason to subject our data to statistical analysis. We can examine these data statistically with the one-sample t test. This test will tell us whether our mean score for male traits is significantly greater than a score of 4.

Study Sample

In this analysis of research questions, four samples are employed: (1) a random sample of members of the National Association of Social Workers in one state, (2) a group of 33 graduate social work students from two sections of a research course who participated in a study in the spring of 1993, (3) a class of 23 graduate social work students who participated in a study in the spring of 1994, (4) a class of 48 students in an introductory sociology course, and (4) your class of students. Some data will be analyzed from each of these samples of study subjects for the various research questions examined, but these groups of people do not constitute a common sample of people from which data will be analyzed together.

The sample of professional social workers was drawn from the membership list of the North Carolina Chapter of the National Association of Social Workers in 1986. A random sample of 146 of the 1,400 members of this organization was mailed a questionnaire, of whom 102 responded for a response rate of 70 percent. Of these respondents, 72 percent were female and 92 percent were caucasian. The mean age of these respondents was 41.5, while their mean years of social work experience was 14.5 (for more details, see York, 1987).

The sociology students were given the instrument to measure sex-role stereotype in October of 1989. As far as the instructor could tell, all 48 of the students in this class volunteered to participate. This introductory sociology course was taken by a wide variety of students because it was a required course, or suggested elective, for students in most majors in the social sciences at this university of approximately 15,000 students. The ages of these students ranged from 17 to 40 with a mean of 20 and a standard deviation of 4.5. These students were divided rather evenly by gender, but a slight majority (59%) was female.

The class of 23 social work students was given the same instrument to measure sex-role stereotype as described previously. This was administered to these students in a graduate course in research in the Spring Semester of 1994. Because there were rather few males in this class, information on gender was not collected in order to protect the anonymity of the respondents. For the same reason, these students were asked to indicate their ages by whether they were (1) under 30, or (2) 30 or over. Sixty-five percent of these students indicated that they were age 30 or over. The group of 33 students was administered the same instrument in the spring of 1993.

The last group of study subjects are the students in your class. The instrument for measuring sex-role stereotype was included among the items on the questionnaire given to you at the beginning of this chapter. That instrument will be employed in the study presented in this chapter. Other questions from that questionnaire will be employed in the part of the study to be examined in the next chapter.

ASSIGNMENT 3-C

1. Has a qualitative or a quantitative methodology been chosen for the study of the good manager?

Quant.

Why was this method chosen?

_____

_____

2. Place a check by each of the following which are variables identified in the six study questions presented for the descriptive study of the qualities of the good manager.

_____✓_____ **a.** Type of student (social work or sociology)

_____ **b.** Sex-role stereotype about management

_____ ✓   **c.** Student

_____ ✓   **d.** Female students

_____   **e.** Degree of interest in a management career

_____ ✓   **f.** Self-perception

_____   **g.** Well-informed

3. Is the present study an example of an evaluative study? Explain.

_____

_____

4. What is the operational definition of sex-role stereotype about management?

_____

_____

_____

5. At what level is the variable of sex-role stereotype about management measured in our study?

_____ Nominal   _____ Ordinal   _____ Interval or ratio

6. With regard to that portion of the study which collects data from your class of students, how would you define the study sample?

The study sample is who you will
be the subjects from a population

7. How would you define the study population? (Refer to the previous question.)

pg 12

_____

_____

8. Is this sample an example of a probability sample?

yes

_____

_____

Data Analysis in Descriptive Research

When you analyze data in descriptive research, you want to characterize your study variables in such a way as to better understand the phenomena under study. You want to see what patterns exist for your data. Descriptive analysis of data can focus on dominance, central tendency, and variability, depending on the level of measurement of the variable being studied. *Dominance* refers to the patterns that occur most frequently. For example, what exam grade was received by more students than any other grade? Around what cluster of scores on the exam did the greatest percentage of students' grades fall? *Central tendency* refers to the pattern of values that best represents the middle in an array of data. We often see references to the mean age or the median salary for a group of people. *Variability* refers to the extent to which the values in an array of data are similar or different one from another. The variability of the ages of 21, 23, 24, 25, 25, and 26 is lower than the variability of the ages of 21, 27, 39, 44, 53, and 56. In the latter array of data, the ages of the persons in the sample vary a good deal more than the ones in the first array of ages.

One way to examine variability is the average deviation, which is the average amount that each score deviates from the mean of all scores. The mean for the first set of ages is 24. As you can see, the ages of 21, 23, 24, 25, and 26 do not vary a great deal from this mean. Each one is no more than 3 points away from the mean of all ages. By contrast, the mean of the second set of ages is 40, and the distance between the typical age in this set and the mean is much greater. The deviations from the mean for this latter set of ages are 19, 13, 1, 4, 13, and 16, respectively. The average deviation for this group is 11, compared to an average deviation of 1.16 for the former group.

Descriptive Analysis of Nominal Variables

For variables measured at the nominal level, you can examine frequencies, percentages, and the mode to see what patterns emerge. If you had 6 females and 4 males in your research class, you could say that the **frequency** of females is 6 while the frequency of males is 4 for a total of 10 students. The **percentage** of this total class that is female would be 60 (10 / 6 = .6 × 100 = 60). The **mode** for a variable is the value that occurs the most often. Consider the following set of ages:

  23   25   25   25   29   29   33

The mode for this set of ages is 25 because there are 3 persons with this age and no other age has as many people.

Descriptive Analysis of Ordinal Variables

For variables measured at the ordinal level, you can also examine frequencies, percentages, and the mode, but you can add to our list the median and the range. The **median** is a measure of central tendency. It is the mid-point in the array of data that is examined. The median age for the above set of ages (23, 25, 25, 25, 29, 29, 33) is 25 because it falls exactly at the midpoint of these ages when they are lined up in numerical sequence. As you can see, the first step in computing the median is to arrange the data in numerical sequence. Consider another example in which there is an even number in the set of data as follows: 22, 25, 26, 26, 26, 29, 33, 35, 36, 41. For this set of ages, the median is 27.5, a value which falls midway between the two central values of 26 and 29 when these ages are drawn out in numerical sequences as noted.

The **range** is the distance between the minimum and maximum values. The minimum age in the above example is 22 while the maximum age is 41 with a range of 19 (41 – 22 = 19). The range is calculated by subtracting the minimum score from the maximum score. The range can be classified as a measure of variability.

Descriptive Analysis of Interval Data

For variables measured at the interval or ratio levels, you can add the mean and the standard deviation to the previously mentioned descriptive measures. The **mean** is the average of all values and constitutes a measure of central tendency. The **standard deviation** is a measure of variability. It tells you something about the extent to which the values in an array of data are similar or different from one another. The average deviation tells you the same thing but is calculated somewhat differently and will have a slightly different value than the standard deviation. The average deviation is the average amount that each value deviates from the mean of all values.

An important role for the standard deviation, unlike the average deviation, is that it can be used to estimate the proportion of persons that fall within a certain range of scores, assuming that the scores in the set of data are normally distributed. A normal distribution is depicted by the bell-shaped curve, with which you are probably familiar. As you may recall, human traits have been found typically to be clustered around the mean with lower and lower proportions falling in the extremes at both ends of the continuum. For example, the mean score for IQ is 100 with a standard deviation of 15. The proportion of persons who fall between the mean and one standard deviation above the mean (i.e., an IQ of 115) is approximately 34 percent, but the proportion of persons with an IQ that falls between two standard deviations from the mean (i.e., 130) and three standard deviations from the mean (i.e., 145) is only about 2 percent. The same proportions would hold for deviations from the mean in the opposite direction. For example, the proportion of persons with an IQ from 85 to 100 would be about 34 percent.

When we speak of statistical significance at the .05 (or 5 percent) level, we are making a reference to the normal curve, because 95 percent of all persons in a normal distribution will fall within plus or minus two standard deviations from the mean. Data that falls outside this range will occur less than 5 percent of the time.

Descriptive Analysis for the Study of the Good Manager

What Are the Qualities of the Good Manager?

While the present study focused attention on sex-role stereotypes, the question of which traits are viewed as most useful for management can also be examined. Besides your own class of students, you can review data from the other three samples mentioned previously. In Table 3.1 you can see a rank order of sixteen traits as viewed by professional social workers, sociology students, and graduate social work students. The percent of each group that selected a given trait as being among the eight most characteristic of the good manager is given in parenthesis beside the trait. You can see, for example, that the trait "well informed" was ranked first by the professional social workers and that 97 percent of this group selected this item. This item was ranked second by both the sociology students and the graduate social work students. The items "aware of feelings of others" and "objective" were also selected by a high percentage of each of these three groups.

Some items received rather low ratings by all groups. You might want to consider the implications of these choices, especially as it pertains to the particular sex-role stereotype it represents and whether you would describe yourself with one of these terms. You can also examine differences among these three groups and speculate about the reasons these groups would differ in this way.

TABLE 3.1   Characteristics of the Good Manager as Viewed by Professional Social Workers, Sociology Students, and Graduate Social Work Students (Percent who selected the item given in parentheses)

Professional Social Workers (N = 102)	Sociology Students (N = 49)	Graduate Social Work Students (N = 33)
Well-informed (97%)	Helpful (90%)	Objective (94%)
Aware of feelings of others (91%)	Well-informed (82%)	Well-informed (91%)
Humanitarian values (85%)	Aware of feelings of others (78%)	Helpful (85%)
Creative (85%)	Self confident (76%)	Aware of feelings of others (82%)
Objective (79%)	Objective (74%)	Self confident (73%)
Consistent (76%)	Consistent (57%)	Creative (25%)*
Self confident (69%)	Cheerful (55%)	Consistent (25%)*
Analytic (60%)	Ambitious (53%)	Cheerful (58%)*
Intuitive (53%)	Aggressive (49%)	Humanitarian values (58%)*
Helpful (35%)	Creative (47%)	Intuitive (52%)
Aggressive (17%)	Competitive (37%)	Analytic (24%)
Cheerful (15%)	Analytic (31%)	Ambitious (21%)
Competitive (10%)*	Humanitarian values (29%)	Aggressive (9%)
Ambitious (10%)*	Intuitive (25%)	
Sophisticated (3%)	Sophisticated (14%)	
Modest (2%)	Modest (8%)	

Item was tied with the one before or after.

Are Certain Traits Favored Over Others?

Sex-role stereotype scores were derived from the number of male-stereotyped items selected. One way for you to examine the tendency for persons to embrace a sex-role stereotype would be for you to compute the mean sex-role stereotype score and compare this mean score to a mean of 4.0, a figure that would represent no stereotype (i.e., 4 male items and 4 female items selected). For the statistical analysis of these data, the one-sample t test would be appropriate. It is a statistical measure for determining whether the mean score of a variable measured at the interval level for a sample of people is significantly different from a theoretical score for a population. If you wish to compare a mean to a particular standard score, the one-sample t test would be suitable. This is the situation that is confronted in the pursuit of the present research question.

For the sample of professional social workers described in this chapter, the mean number of male items selected was 4.25 (while the mean number of female traits was 3.75). The standard deviation for the number of male traits was 0.9. This mean of 4.25 was compared to the score of 4.0 with the following statistical results: $t = 2.81$; $p < .01$. For the sample of introductory sociology students, the mean number of male items selected was 4.56 with a standard deviation of 1.1. The mean sex-role stereotype score of 4.56 was compared to the score of 4.0 with the following results: $t = 3.57$; $p < .001$. For the sample of graduate social work students, the mean sex-role stereotype score was 3.91 with the following statistical results: $t = 0.62$; $p > .40$.

ASSIGNMENT 3-D

1. Consider the following set of data on sex-role stereotype (SRS) scores:

Student	SRS Score	Student	SRS Score
#1	3	#6	6
#2	2	#7	5
#3	5	#8	4
#4	4	#9	3
#5	5		

    a. What is the mean for these scores? _____

    b. What is the mode for these scores? _____

    c. What is the median for these scores? _____

    d. What is the range for these scores? _____

2. The standard deviations for sex-role stereotype scores for these three groups of subjects were as follows:

Professional social workers	0.9
Sociology students	1.1
Graduate social work students	0.95

What does this information tell us?

_____

_____

Did these differences in standard deviations surprise you? Explain.

_____

_____

3. Was evidence of the existence of a sex-role stereotype for professional social workers discovered in the data presented?

_____

_____

What about introductory sociology students?

_____

_____

What about graduate social work students?

_____

_____

Examining Data from Your Class

Record your information on Exhibit 3.4 so the instructor can collect data for your analysis. You should turn in a copy of this page to the instructor, who will report the scores for all students. Do not place your name on this form; the information should be anonymous.

EXHIBIT 3.4   My Responses to the Questions on the Qualities of the Good Manager

Examine your responses to either Exhibit 3.1 or 3.2 and display your responses below by drawing a circle around the items you selected. Then, count the number of male-stereotyped items among your list of 8 items. (The male items are the even-number ones.) This is your sex-role stereotype score.

1. Helpful	**9.** Creative
2. Ambitious	**10. Analytic**
3. Aware of feelings of others	**11.** Sophisticated
4. Consistent	**12. Competitive**
5. Modest	**13.** Intuitive
6. Well-informed	**14. Self confident**
7. Humanitarian values	**15.** Cheerful
8. Objective	**16. Aggressive**

My sex-role stereotype score is _____

The name of my manager for question 17 in the exhibit was:

_____ George   _____ Barbara

My level of desire for working for this person was:

_____ I would really like to work for this person.

_____ I would not mind working for this person.

_____ I would prefer not to work for this person.

_____ I would really not want to work for this person and would do what I could to avoid it.

My gender is   _____ Male   _____ Female

My age is   _____ under 30   _____ 30 or over

Turn in this page without your name attached.

Coding of Data for Your Study

There are five variables presented in Exhibit 3.4. These are (1) Sex-role stereotype score, (2) Name of manager examined, (3) Level of desire for working for the manager named, (4) Gender, and (5) Age. To facilitate data analysis, the various response categories for each variable often need to be given a code. The variable of sex-role stereotype score does not need to be coded because it is represented by a number (the number of male-stereotyped traits selected), but each of the four other variables needs a coding scheme because the responses are given in categories. In your study, you will give George the code of *1* and Barbara the code of *0*. You will code the study participants' response to the preference question as follows:

Code   Response

3   I would really like to work for this person.

2   I would not mind working for this person.

1   I would prefer not to work for this person.

0   I would really not want to work for this person and would do what I could to avoid it.

For example, the response "I would prefer not to work for this person" would be coded as 1.

You have two additional variables. You will code male as *1* and female as *0*. You will code "under 30" as *0* and "30 and over" as *1*. With this coding scheme, each study subject's response regarding each variable has been reduced to a number.

A data sheet for all of these five variables is provided in Exhibit 3.5. There are two alternatives for collecting data from the entire class. First, all students could turn in their responses given in Exhibit 3.4, the instructor could convert these responses to the codes given above, place these data in Exhibit 3.5, and give copies to each student for analysis. Second,

---

EXHIBIT 3.5   Data for Your Class Members on Five Study Variables

Student #	Sex-role stereotype score	Manager 1 = George 0 = Barbara	Desire (0, 1, 2, 3)	Gender 1 = male 0 = female	Age 1 = 30 & over 0 = under 30
1					
2					
3					
4					
5					
6					

(Continued)

EXHIBIT 3.5   *Continued*

Student #	Sex-role stereotype score	Manager 1 = George 0 = Barbara	Desire (0, 1, 2, 3)	Gender 1 = male 0 = female	Age 1 = 30 & over 0 = under 30
7					
8					
9					
10					
11					
12					
13					
14					
15					
16					
17					
18					
19					
20					
21					
22					
23					
24					
25					
26					
27					
28					
29					
30					
31					
32					
33					
34					
35					
36					
37					
38					
39					
40					
41					
42					

EXHIBIT 3.5   *Continued*

Student #	Sex-role stereotype score	Manager 1 = George 0 = Barbara	Desire (0, 1, 2, 3)	Gender 1 = male 0 = female	Age 1 = 30 & over 0 = under 30
43					
44					
45					
46					
47					
48					
49					
50					
51					
52					
53					
54					

a copy of Exhibit 3.5 could be passed around the class and each student could place his or her own data on that sheet. In either case, each student will need a copy of Exhibit 3.5 with the data for all class members. Only one of these five variables will be examined in this chapter. The others will be the subject of the data analysis for the next chapter.

Analysis of SRS Scores for Your Class

The first task is to compute the mean sex-role stereotype score for all students in the class. This score will be compared to the score of 4.0 with the one-sample t test through the procedures outlined in this section. Later in this text you will see instructions for using the computer for applying various statistical tests, most of which are not easy to calculate without the computer. The one-sample t test is one exception to this rule. If you have the patience to place your numbers on a page and compute the mean for these data along with the square and square root, you will find you can complete this task in a few minutes.

Simply put, the value of t is derived from the following formula.

t = [(Mean of sample) − (Mean of population)] / Standard Error (of sample)

In your case, the mean of the sample is the mean SRS (sex-role stereotype) score for the members of your class and the mean of the population is 4.0 because this is the mean that constitutes no preference for a gender stereotype, either male of female. To determine the value of t, you will subtract 4.0 from your mean SRS score and divide this figure by the standard error of SRS scores. Instructions for calculating the standard error are given below and illustrated in Exhibit 3.6 with data from another class. The value of t will be used to determine if your class's mean SRS score is significantly different from a score of 4.0.

In Exhibit 3.6, you will find an example of a set of SRS scores with the instructions for computing the value of t. Exhibit 3.7 provides you with a blank worksheet to use in computing the value of t for your class data.

Step One: Sum of Squares

The first step is to calculate the **sum of squares.** On the worksheet (Exhibit 3.7), place each student's SRS score in the second column (*SRS Score*) and calculate the mean of all SRS scores. This figure goes in the third column (*Mean of all SRS scores*), for each student. Next, subtract the score for student number 1 from the mean and place this result in the column labeled *Deviation Score.* Square that figure (i.e., multiply it by itself) and place the result in the last column (*Deviation Score Squared*). Repeat these steps for each student. Add all these squared deviations from the mean together and place this figure in the box at the bottom. This figure is known as the **sum of squares.**

Step Two: Standard Deviation

Next, you compute the **standard deviation** of SRS scores. The standard deviation is the square root of the variance. The variance is the sum of squares divided by N (the number in the sample). Place your sum of squares in the first column for step two and the number of persons in your sample in the third column. Divide the sum of squares by N and place this value in the column labeled *Variance.* Calculate the square root of this figure and place it in the last column. (Most hand-held calculators have a button for the square root.) This is your standard deviation of SRS scores.

Step Three: Standard Error

The third step is to calculate the **standard error** of SRS scores. Place the standard deviation of SRS scores in the first column. Calculate the square root of N and place this value in the third column. Divide the standard deviation by the square root of N and place this value in the last column. This is your standard error of SRS scores.

Step Four: Value of t

Next, you calculate the **value of t.** Place the mean of SRS scores (*Sample Mean*) in the first column and subtract 4 from it and enter this value in the first column. Place the standard error in column three, divide your mean SRS score by this figure, and place this value in the final column. This is the value of t.

Step Five: Statistical Significance

In the final step, you determine the **statistical significance** of your t score. The level of statistical significance for the value of t can be obtained from the tables contained in texts on statistics. For our study, we will use what is referred to as the *one-tailed t test* because we have a directional hypothesis. In this situation, statistical significance at the .05 level is achieved with a t value of 2.0 or higher, provided the size of the sample is 5 or greater. If you need more details than this, consult a table of t in a statistical text. However, this application of the t test (one-tailed) would not be appropriate if your mean SRS score was lower than 4.0 and was found not to be in the direction that you would expect.

EXHIBIT 3.6   An Example of Statistical Analysis of SRS Scores Using the t Test for Paired Data

Step One: Calculate the Sum of Squares

Person	Score	minus	Mean	equals	Deviation Score	Deviation Score Squared
1	4	–	3.74	=	0.26	0.068
2	4	–	3.74	=	0.26	0.068
3	3	–	3.74	=	–0.74	0.55
4	2	–	3.74	=	–1.74	3.03
5	4	–	3.74	=	0.26	0.068
6	4	–	3.74	=	0.26	0.068
7	4	–	3.74	=	0.26	0.068
8	3	–	3.74	=	–0.74	0.55
9	4	–	3.74	=	0.26	0.068
10	3	–	3.74	=	–0.74	0.55
11	4	–	3.74	=	0.26	0.068
12	3	–	3.74	=	–0.74	0.55
13	3	–	3.74	=	–0.74	0.55
14	4	–	3.74	=	0.26	0.068
15	3	–	3.74	=	–0.74	0.55
16	4	–	3.74	=	0.26	0.068
17	4	–	3.74	=	0.26	0.068
18	5	–	3.74	=	1.26	1.59
19	4	–	3.74	=	0.26	0.068
20	4	–	3.74	=	0.26	0.068
21	4	–	3.74	=	0.26	0.068
22	4	–	3.74	=	0.26	0.068
23	5	–	3.74	=	1.26	1.59

Sum of Squares =   10.46

The sum of squares is the sum of all squared deviations from the mean of all scores in the group. It is the last figure in the above chart and will be used in the next procedure.

(Continued)

EXHIBIT 3.6   *Continued*

Step Two: Calculate the Standard Deviation

The standard deviation is the square root of the variance. The variance is the sum of squares divided by N (the number in the sample).

Sum of squares	Divided by	N	equals	Variance	Square root of Variance (Standard Deviation)
10.46	/	23	=	0.45	0.67

Step Three: Calculate the Standard Error for SRS Scores

The standard error for SRS scores is calculated by dividing the standard deviation of SRS scores by the square root of N (the number of students in the class).

Standard deviation	divided by	Square root of N	equals	Standard error
0.67	/	4.80	=	0.14

Step Four: Calculate the Value of t

The value of t is calculated by computing the difference between the mean of the sample (in our case, the mean of SRS scores) and the mean of the population with which the sample mean is being compared (in our case, a mean of 4.0), and dividing that value by the standard error of the SRS scores.

Sample Mean	minus	Population Mean	divided by	Standard error	equals	Value of t
3.74	−	4.0 = −0.26	/	0.14	=	1.86

Step Five: Determine Statistical Significance

In determining the likelihood that your mean SRS score would be different from 4.0 just by chance, you would use the one-tailed t test because you have reason to predict whether the mean score for your data would be expected to be higher or lower than the mean to which it is being compared. In our case, this is true. We expect the mean SRS score to be higher than 4.0. If we find this not to be true, we would stop our analysis because what we expected did not turn out to be true. If we do find a higher SRS score than 4.0, we would examine the likelihood that the difference between it and 4.0 can be explained by chance. A t value of 2.0 (using the one-tailed t test) would be significant at the .05 level if the sample size is 5 or greater. A t value lower than 2.0 might be significant if the sample is larger than 5. You may want to consult a statistical text for more information.

EXHIBIT 3.7   Worksheet for Statistical Analysis of SRS Scores Using the One-Sample t Test

Step One: Calculate the Sum of Squares, Page 1

Person	Score	minus	Mean	equals	Deviation Score	Deviation Score Squared
_____	_____	–	_____	=	_____	_____
_____	_____	–	_____	=	_____	_____
_____	_____	–	_____	=	_____	_____
_____	_____	–	_____	=	_____	_____
_____	_____	–	_____	=	_____	_____
_____	_____	–	_____	=	_____	_____
_____	_____	–	_____	=	_____	_____
_____	_____	–	_____	=	_____	_____
_____	_____	–	_____	=	_____	_____
_____	_____	–	_____	=	_____	_____
_____	_____	–	_____	=	_____	_____
_____	_____	–	_____	=	_____	_____
_____	_____	–	_____	=	_____	_____
_____	_____	–	_____	=	_____	_____
_____	_____	–	_____	=	_____	_____
_____	_____	–	_____	=	_____	_____
_____	_____	–	_____	=	_____	_____
_____	_____	–	_____	=	_____	_____
_____	_____	–	_____	=	_____	_____
_____	_____	–	_____	=	_____	_____
_____	_____	–	_____	=	_____	_____
_____	_____	–	_____	=	_____	_____
_____	_____	–	_____	=	_____	_____
_____	_____	–	_____	=	_____	_____
_____	_____	–	_____	=	_____	_____

Sum of Squares = _____

(Continued)

EXHIBIT 3.7 *Continued*

Calculating the Sum of Squares, Page 2 (if needed)

Person	Score	minus	Mean	equals	Deviation Score	Deviation Score Squared
——	——	−	——	=	——	——
——	——	−	——	=	——	——
——	——	−	——	=	——	——
——	——	−	——	=	——	——
——	——	−	——	=	——	——
——	——	−	——	=	——	——
——	——	−	——	=	——	——
——	——	−	——	=	——	——
——	——	−	——	=	——	——
——	——	−	——	=	——	——
——	——	−	——	=	——	——
——	——	−	——	=	——	——
——	——	−	——	=	——	——
——	——	−	——	=	——	——
——	——	−	——	=	——	——
——	——	−	——	=	——	——
——	——	−	——	=	——	——
——	——	−	——	=	——	——
——	——	−	——	=	——	——
——	——	−	——	=	——	——
——	——	−	——	=	——	——
——	——	−	——	=	——	——
——	——	−	——	=	——	——
——	——	−	——	=	——	——
——	——	−	——	=	——	——
——	——	−	——	=	——	——

Sum of Squares =

EXHIBIT 3.7   *Continued*

Step Two: Calculate the Standard Deviation

The standard deviation is the square root of the variance. The variance is the sum of squares divided by N (the number in the sample).

Sum of squares	Divided by	N	equals	Variance	Square root of Variance (Standard Deviation)
	/		=		

Step Three: Calculate the Standard Error for SRS Scores

The standard error for SRS scores is calculated by dividing the standard deviation of SRS scores by the square root of N (the number of students in the class).

Standard deviation	divided by	Square root of N	equals	Standard error
	/		=	

Step Four: Calculate the Value of t

The value of t is calculated by computing the difference between the mean of the sample (in our case, the mean of SRS scores) and the mean of the population with which the sample mean is being compared (in our case, a mean of 4.0), and dividing that value by the standard error of the scores for the sample (e.g., SRS scores).

Sample Mean	minus	Population Mean	divided by	Standard error	equals	Value of t
–		4.0	=	/		=

Step Five: Determine Statistical Significance

You would use the one-tailed t test if you have reason to predict whether the mean score for your data would be expected to be higher or lower than the mean to which it is being compared. In our case, this is true. We expect the mean SRS score to be higher than 4.0. If we find this not to be true, we would stop our analysis because what we expected did not turn out to be true. If we do find a higher SRS score than 4.0, we would examine the likelihood that the difference between it and 4.0 can be explained by chance. A t value of 2.0 would be significant at the .05 level if the sample size is 5 or greater. A t value lower than 2.0 might be significant if the sample is larger than 5. You may want to consult a statistical text for more information.

ASSIGNMENT 3-E

1. Did you find that the mean SRS score was above 4.0?

2. If yes, was this score significantly above 4.0?

_____ yes _____ no

Explain.

_____

_____

3. Did you find that your class results were similar or different from the results of data presented for professional social workers, sociology students, or graduate social work students?

_____

_____

Does Sex-Role Stereotype Interfere with Perceived Competence?

A major reason for concern about the existence of a sex-role stereotype about management is that social workers, especially female social workers, may perceive that they are not well-suited for the management role because they have been influenced by this stereotype. If a female social worker perceives that the best managers possess the male traits and that she does not possess these traits, it is a logical assumption that she would be less inclined to believe she has what it takes to perform well in the management role. Consequently, she would not apply for such a position. This may explain why fewer females than males express interest in being a manager.

In the spring of 1994, a survey was conducted of a class of 23 graduate social work students to examine this issue. These students were given the same instrument for measuring sex-role stereotype as described in this chapter. They were also asked to describe themselves using the same instrument. In other words, they were asked to select the eight traits (from among the sixteen on the list) that best described themselves. These selections were compared to the ones they had selected to describe the good manager in order to identify the traits that were on their personal list but not on their list which described the good manager (nonmatched traits). A key question was whether they were more likely to have nonmatched traits that were in the category of the male stereotype.

The following data presents the number (and percentage) of students who had a non-match for each of the six traits that were found on one or more of these students lists:

TABLE 3.2   **Number of Students Without a Match Between Self-Description and Description of the Good Manager**

Trait	Number	Percentage
Well-informed	10	43%
Self confident	9	39%
Consistent	7	30%
Objective	4	17%
Ambitious	1	4%
Analytic	1	4%

Do you notice anything especially interesting about this list of traits? Each one is in the category of the male stereotype. What does this suggest to you? Is this variable (incongruence between self-perception and perception of the good manager) a potential barrier to female advancement? The vast majority of the students in this class were female. In fact, there were so few males, gender data were not collected in order to protect the identity of each student in the data. A good question would be whether males and females differed on this variable.

There are any number of new research questions that could arise from your study. *Ideas for Further Research* is one of the topics for the Conclusions section of a research report. But first, a summary of the results of the study should be presented along with the limitations of the methods employed. In the final assignment, you will be asked to develop a statement of study conclusions regarding the data presented in this chapter regarding each of the study questions.

ASSIGNMENT 3-F

Develop a statement that presents the conclusions of your study.

Examining the Characteristics of the Good Manager Using Qualitative Methods

You have examined the extent to which your class embraces a sex-role stereotype about what it takes to be a good social work manager and you have had the opportunity to compare these results to three groups of persons for whom data were supplied in this text (sociology students, professional social workers, and graduate social work students). In this research, quantitative methods of measurement were employed through the use of a list of sixteen descriptors from which the respondents were asked to select eight that best represented the good manager. Among the limitations of quantitative research are the restricted boundaries within which data are collected. The study participants had no opportunity to describe the good manager in any words except the ones on the instrument. Perhaps the truth is that there are twenty ways in which the good manager is like the male stereotype, and twenty ways in which the good manager is like the female stereotype. If this were true, there would be no evidence of a sex-role stereotype. Given a list that contained all forty of these traits, social workers would tend to select an equal number of male and female traits. But, suppose the instrument employed in our present study contained only three of the good female traits and six of the male traits. This would provide a bias in favor of finding a male stereotype.

Perhaps the truth is that there are fifty traits of the good manager but only ten of them are related to a sex-role stereotype. If you found that six of these ten were characteristic of the male stereotype but only four were in the female category, you would have evidence in favor of a male stereotype, but you would be better able to place this information into perspective. Now you could say that 12 percent of the traits of the good manager are in the male stereotype as compared to 8 percent being in the female stereotype. You could further say that 80 percent of the traits of the good manager were unrelated to gender stereotype.

The flexibility of qualitative methods would provide a better opportunity for such a discovery as mentioned above. In a preliminary attempt to pursue this option, I asked a sample of social work students to participate in a study in which one-half (randomly selected) were asked to describe the good social work manager and the other half were asked to describe how males and females were different. The idea was to compare the list of good manager traits to the list of male and female characteristics to see how many matched the descriptors of males, how many matched the descriptors of females, and how many matched with neither.

The first step in the data analysis was the content analysis of the descriptions given to the good manager. Two steps were used. First, a word was placed in the margin to code the idea being presented. For example, one student wrote "gives support, advice, and constructive criticism." Three words were noted—support, advice, and constructive criticism. The second step was the combining of words that were similar. For example, the words "advice" and "constructive criticism" were collapsed under the theme of "feedback" which was viewed as similar to "communication skills," a descriptor given by another student. The question arose as to whether they should all be placed under "communication" or whether there were adequate distinctions among these three variations of communication that warranted separate treatment. This second step led to a list of ten descriptors of the good manager. They were: supportive, gives feedback, teacher, goal-oriented, good communicator, fair, knowledgeable, ethical, participative, open-minded.

The two steps above can be referred to two stages of content analysis. The same procedure was undertaken with the lists of male characteristics and female characteristics. The final male characteristics listed were: assertive, task-oriented, competitive, aggressive, logical, solution-oriented, tunnel-visioned, thinking-oriented, unemotional. The female list contained the following items: expressive, feeling-oriented, emotional, nurturing, compassionate, empathic, and relationship-oriented.

The main concept on the male list that matched with the manager list was "goal-oriented." The female list was matched with the manager list on the concept of "supportive." In addition, the manager trait of good communication skill seemed to align with the female list which had the concept of "expressive." The majority of the manager traits were not clearly matched with either the male or the female list.

ASSIGNMENT 3-G

What are your observations about the relative utility of qualitative and quantitative methods for the study of the major research question pursued in this chapter?

References

Jones, J. (1981). *Bad Blood.* New York: Free Press.
Rubin, A. & Babbie, E. (1993). *Research Methods for Social Work* (2nd ed.). Pacific Grove: Brooks/ Cole.

Chapter *4*

Conducting Explanatory Research on the Qualities of the Good Manager

In the previous chapter, you examined sex-role stereotypes about the qualities of the good manager by determining whether the students in your class had a significant tendency to favor traits stereotypical of males more than those stereotypical of females. When you responded to the questionnaire for that study, you were also asked to indicate the extent to which you would prefer to work for a hypothetical manager. Depending on your coin flip, you had either George or Barbara for your manager. The descriptions for these two hypothetical managers were identical except for the name of the manager. One of the problems faced by female managers, according to the literature review given in the previous chapter, is that they are often evaluated more harshly than men for exhibiting task-master type behaviors. If women are treated more negatively than men for the same behaviors, we have evidence for sexual discrimination in the workplace. The question arises as to whether social work students embrace this stance in which these behaviors are viewed as more acceptable if they come from a man.

In this chapter you will examine this question. You will also examine the relationships among some of the variables in this study, such as between sex-role stereotype score and gender. This chapter will illustrate explanatory research. You will rely on the literature review and the study methodology enumerated in the previous chapter for this illustration. Thus, the focus for the present chapter will be testing the hypothesis that persons with a task-master with a male name will be more favorable in their response than those with a task-master with a female name.

100

Problem Formulation in Explanatory Research

Some of the tasks of problem formulation for explanatory research include identifying the major subject of interest, examining how relevant concepts have been conceptualized and measured by others, and identifying the reasons why the subject is important. These tasks were dealt with in the previous chapter when descriptive research was being illustrated. With regard to these questions, problem formulation for descriptive research is similar to that for explanatory research.

A major distinction between descriptive and explanatory research is that descriptive research seeks to describe, while explanatory research seeks to explain. In the previous chapter, you examined whether social work students embraced a sex-role stereotype about management. In this chapter, you will examine whether the gender of a certain type of manager explains the student's level of preference for working for this manager. If female managers are treated differently from male managers, you could say that the gender of the manager is one of the things that explains the treatment of the manager.

The focus of the explanatory research study is testing a hypothesis. The research hypothesis is a tentative statement of the expected results of an empirical examination of the research question. For example, the hypothesis "Males will report higher salaries than females" identifies the nature of the expected relationship between gender and salary. Thus, the problem formulation phase of explanatory research should provide guidance on the development of the study hypothesis. The study hypothesis should be supported by the literature review or the particular knowledge base that serves as the foundation for the study. This support can be direct or indirect. *Direct support* takes the form of an empirical finding from others which suggests that a certain hypothesis is a true statement. Direct support can also take the form of a theory suggesting that a relationship exists between certain variables. *Indirect support* comes from the researcher's creative use of the existing knowledge base and the drawing of logical inferences from that knowledge.

The literature review given in the previous chapter suggested that people tend to embrace a sex-role stereotype about what it takes to be a good manager. This serves as one barrier to the female who is interested in being a manager. Another obstacle identified in that literature was that females are judged more harshly than males if they exhibit the behaviors of the task-master as manager. A question that arises from this knowledge base is whether social work students would have this same tendency to judge women differently.

Sometimes the manager needs to be a task-master. If women are reluctant to exhibit this behavior because of the sexual stereotype that invades the minds of subordinates and peers, they would be unfairly restricted in the repertoire of management behaviors at their disposal in their primary work role. This could affect their performance and their prospects for advancement.

The social work student is one type of social worker. Social work students undertake internships in which they serve in the role of social worker. Furthermore, a great number of graduate social work students have prior social work experience. Issues relevant to social workers in general would be relevant to social work students. Thus, you could articulate your research question as follows:

> *Do social work students evaluate a female task-master manager more negatively than they evaluate a male task-master manager?*

ASSIGNMENT 4-A

1. Which of the following distinguishes an explanatory study from a descriptive one?

    _____   **a.** The presence of a study sample.

    _____   **b.** The presence of a measurement device.

    ___X___   **c.** The presence of a hypothesis.

    ___Ø___   **d.** The presence of a knowledge base, usually derived from the literature.

2. What is the central research question posed in the present study?

    Whether the gender of a certain type of manager explains the students' level of preference for working w/oe tas for this manager

3. With regard to this research question, what is the *dependent* variable?

    a. Gender of the manager.

    b. Gender of the student in the study.

    (**c.**) Level of preference for working with a task-master type manager.

    d. Task-master type manager.

4. What is the *independent* variable in this question? *Gender of the manager*

5. Why is this research question important?

    It is important to understand one's own stereotypes so that we can change our behaviors to treat people as equals.

Methodology in Explanatory Research

For explanatory research, the study methodology addresses the following topics:

1. The study population and the study sample.
2. The study hypothesis.
3. The means used to measure study variables.
4. The reliability and validity of measurement devices.
5. The method used to collect data.

All of the above items except number 2 have been discussed previously, because they are all relevant to the descriptive study. The study hypothesis is one item that distinguishes the explanatory study from the descriptive one. The hypothesis predicts the study results if these results are consistent with the knowledge base on which the study rests. It is a statement, not a question. It makes reference to the specific items being measured in the study, not others that might be inferred from them. The hypothesis is void of unnecessary words. For guidance, you may see one of the latter chapters which provides practical advice on this task.

If you want to know whether social workers' evaluations of managers are influenced by the gender of the manager, you have two major variables to measure:

1. The gender of the manager being evaluated, and
2. The evaluation of the manager by others.

You could ask social workers to rate the performance of their present managers and to indicate the gender of those managers. You could compare the ratings of male managers with the ratings of female managers. But you would not know whether these managers exhibited the type of behavior in question.

You could ask whether these managers exhibited task-master behavior and restrict your analysis to those managers who were perceived as exhibiting this behavior. You could compare the ratings of male task-masters and female task-masters. This methodology could be argued as being suitable to the research question, but it could be improved.

Control in Explanatory Research

The issue of control in explanatory research is the key to improving the methodology mentioned above. If you want to know if the gender of the manager explains the manager's evaluation, you would want to control for other things that might influence the evaluation of the manager.

To illustrate with a different example, suppose you wanted to know if there was evidence of sexual discrimination in salaries for social workers. A logical first question you could pose is whether the salaries of men and women in social work differ. In an introductory text on social work research (York, 1997), this question was illustrated with data from a survey of social workers in one state. It was found that the mean 1986 salary of male social workers was $32,025 as compared to a mean of $23,754 for females. This difference was statistically significant and most would agree that it was of practical significance as well.

Explanatory research poses the question "Why?" Why do females receive lower salaries than males? Sexual discrimination founded on prejudice would typically be offered as one answer. But does this explain the entire difference in salaries? What if you found that females were more likely than males to be working part-time? If this difference in male and female patterns of work was the only reason that males received higher salaries, you would likely revise your explanation of these differences as being founded on sexual prejudice.

What if you found that males were more likely than females to be employed in management positions? Knowing that position level is related to income, you would naturally want to control for position level in your analysis of the differences in salary between males and females. In that introductory research text just mentioned, the variable of position level was controlled in the examination of male and female salaries. Any number of additional variables could have been controlled in that research, but the focus was on this one variable for the purpose of illustration. The mean salaries of male managers and female managers were compared. If it had been found that male managers and female managers had comparable salaries, evidence for sexual prejudice in the administration of salaries would not have been supported as a reason why females received lower salaries. But these data revealed a mean salary for male managers of $44,044 as compared to a mean salary for female managers of $25,584. Thus, the fact that males were more likely than females to be found in management positions was not found to be an explanation for the wide differences in salary between men and women.

In the study examined in this chapter, you would want to consider if variables other than gender of the manager might explain the evaluation of the manager. To the extent feasible, you would want to control for these variables in your examination of the research question. Of particular importance is the prospect that some of these other variables may explain the relationship between the gender of the manager and the evaluation of that manager by social workers. In one study of social workers, it was found that females were more likely than males to embrace a sex-role stereotype about management (York, 1987). This was a surprising result. What if it is true that female social workers are more likely than male social workers to evaluate a female task-master more harshly than a male task-master? In view of the fact that females tend to dominate samples of social workers, such a reality could explain differences in the evaluation of male and female managers. In this situation, a study that did not control for gender would lead to the conclusion that all social workers held this prejudice against the female manager while, in fact, it was only the females who held this prejudice. The same limitation would hold if it were the males who held this prejudice. However, a female prejudice would have a greater overall influence on the data because there are typically more females than males in samples of social workers.

It could be that the particular form of task-master behavior varied among those being evaluated, and that this variable was the key to the evaluation rather than the gender of the manager being evaluated. Suppose the females being evaluated in this study just happened to be especially harsh in their task-master behavior, and this was the reason that females received lower overall mean ratings of performance. In this case, the evaluation of the manager would be more appropriately attributed to the harsh form of task-master behavior rather than the gender of the manager. Perhaps males and females who exhibit the same level of this behavior are rated similarly.

The social desirability bias is another factor to be taken into consideration in the methodology of an explanatory study. You might expect that social workers would believe that sexual prejudice is not an acceptable social attitude. You would, therefore, expect that some social workers who embraced a sexual prejudice would wish to hide this prejudice from themselves as well as from others. Consequently, if you asked your study subjects to identify the gender of the manager being rated, they may reconsider their evaluation of this person, especially in the case of the rating of female managers. This event could lead to the data being distorted by the need to be socially desirable rather than completely truthful.

Other variables could influence the evaluation of the manager and could explain this relationship between gender of the manager and evaluation of the manager. The more variables you can identify and control in your study, the more confidence you can have in your data as a definitive test of the research question.

Study Design and Measurement of Variables

The questionnaire that collected the data for the present study was given in the previous chapter. In that chapter, you were asked to read a statement describing a hypothetical manager. You were asked to flip a coin to determine whether you would respond to the questions in Exhibit 3.1 or Exhibit 3.2. If your coin flip resulted in your responding to the questions in Exhibit 3.1, you would have had Barbara Thompson as your hypothetical manager. If your coin flip resulted in your responding to the questions in Exhibit 3.2, you would have had George Thompson as your hypothetical manager. You were instructed not to read the questions on the alternative exhibit so you would not become aware of the nature of the methodology. In this way, the members of your class were randomly assigned to respond to either Barbara or George as the hypothetical manager. You were asked to indicate the extent to which you would like to work for this manager on a four-point scale.

You have two major variables in your study:

1. The group a student was in (either *George* or *Barbara*).
2. The degree to which the student wanted to work for the manager.

Thus, data were collected on each of these two variables. The level of preference for working for George can be compared to the level of preference for working for Barbara.

What about the question of control? If you compare these preference levels for George and Barbara, can you have confidence that the results will not be distorted by extraneous variables? The methodology for the present study employs two features that serve to control for these extraneous influences. First, evaluators were divided into two groups on a random basis. When random assignment is employed, the different groups can be assumed to be similar. You would expect to find a roughly equal number of males and females, of persons who like task-master behavior and those who don't, and so forth. Thus, any influence of such variables on the dependent variable would be controlled. If there were an equal number of persons who liked and disliked task-master management, this variable could not influence the outcome of the study. For example, the negative persons in each group would cancel each other out.

Another feature that served this control function was the fact that the only difference in descriptions of the hypothetical managers given to the two groups of persons was the name of the manager, one being male and the other being female. Thus, the only thing that could logically influence differences in the level of the ratings of the two managers is the gender of the manager.

These two features of the present study illustrate one of the major means for achieving control in an explanatory study—the research design. You can design your study in such a way as to control for the extraneous variables that might lead you to misinterpret your data. In the classic experimental design which will be discussed in more detail in the next chapter on evaluative research, persons are randomly assigned to two groups with only one group receiving the social work intervention. The fact that persons were randomly assigned to their group means you can have confidence that the persons in these groups are comparable on variables that might influence their progress on the target behavior that is the subject of treatment. The only difference is that one group received treatment and the other group did not. Therefore, you can be confident that any differences between the groups after the treatment period can be attributed to the treatment rather than something else.

A second major means of control lies in the manner in which you statistically analyze your data. In the salary example, the mean salary of male managers was compared to the mean salary of female managers in order to control for position level in the examination of the relationship between gender and salary. In the chapters on statistical analysis to come later in this book, you will see explanations of more sophisticated means for controlling for an extraneous variable in the examination of the relationship between two key variables.

ASSIGNMENT 4-B

1. What is the hypothesis for this study?

The group of the respondent determined the degree to which the student wanted to work for the manager.

2. For this hypothesis, what is the *dependent* variable?

Degree to which the student wanted to work for the manager

What is the *independent* variable?

The group of the respondent.

3. How is the *dependent* variable being measured in this study? Select one.

  a. Whether the respondent is a male or female.

  b. The group of the respondent (either George or Barbara for the hypothetical manager).

  c. The number of male-stereotyped traits selected to describe the good manager.

  d. The respondent's answer to the question regarding level of preference for working with the hypothetical manager (Question 17 in the exhibit).

  e. Whether the respondent's age is under 30 or 30 or above.

4. How is the *independent* variable being measured in this study? Select one.

  a. Whether the respondent is a male or female.

  b. The group of the respondent (either George or Barbara for the hypothetical manager).

  c. The number of male-stereotyped traits selected to describe the good manager.

  d. The respondent's answer to the question regarding level of preference for working with the hypothetical manager (Question 17 in the exhibit).

  e. Whether the respondent's age is under 30 or 30 or above.

Notes: _____

_____

_____

5. Describe how you would employ the test-retest method of assessing reliability with the question used to measure the dependent variable in this study.

_____

_____

6. Suppose you were undertaking a study of marital satisfaction. If someone were to point out to you that your scale for measuring marital satisfaction had no items which addressed sexual satisfaction, what form of validity or reliability would this question be addressing?

_____   **a.** Content validity

_____   **b.** Empirical validity

_____   **c.** Test-retest reliability

_____   **d.** Internal consistency

7. Suppose the results of the Good Manager study reveals that there is *not* a significant preference for working for George over Barbara. Would you have reason to be concerned that these results could have been influenced by the desire of social workers to avoid expressing a sexual prejudice? Explain.

_____

_____

8. Are there any variables that you believe should be controlled in the statistical analysis of your data for this study? Explain.

_____

_____

9. What is your study sample?

_____

_____

10. What is your study population?

_____

11. Do you have a probability sample?

_____

_____

Data Analysis in Explanatory Research

In most explanatory studies, you will find there are two major phases of data analysis. The first phase deals with the descriptive analysis of the study variables, while the second phase deals with testing the hypothesis. Descriptive data analysis was discussed in the previous chapter, but you also should be concerned with descriptive analysis in the explanatory study. There are two major reasons: (1) to inform the reader of the nature of the study sample that was used, and (2) to examine the distribution of values on the study variables in order to better interpret the data that test the study hypothesis.

When you describe your study sample, you normally report the proportions of males and females, the mean age, and other variables that might be of special interest to the particular study. This provides readers with a basis for drawing their own conclusions about whether the study results are relevant to their situation.

Before you subject the data for the present study to a statistical test of the hypothesis, you should examine the distribution of values on the study variables. If you see that there is very little variance on the study variables, you will know that this variable, as measured in this study, is not a good vehicle for testing the study hypothesis. You may be in danger of misinterpreting your study results. To illustrate, suppose you wished to test the hypothesis that there is a negative relationship between social support and stress for social work students. In other words, you expect to find that those with higher support will have lower levels of stress. Suppose the following were the data from the question "To what extent do you have family or friends that you can count on to help you with important life problems?"

Frequency	Response
23	To a very great extent.
15	To a great extent.
4	To some extent.
0	To a little extent.
0	Not at all.

In this example, you have no students who responded at the bottom two levels and you have only 4 who responded at the middle level. The vast majority of your study subjects had either a "great" deal of support or a "very great" deal of support. What if you employed this variable in a study of the relationship between support and stress and did not find a significant relationship? Does this mean that there is no relationship between support and stress in general? Does this mean that it makes no difference how much support you have? These would be misinterpretations of the data. Instead, you would be on safer ground to conclude that stress is not affected by movement from *high* support to *very high* support. You did not have the data to examine this question in general, because you had no persons at low levels of support in your study sample.

The Empirical Relationship

In the explanatory study, the concept of the **empirical relationship** is a vital tool for analysis. When an empirical relationship exists between two variables, you will find that there is a particular pattern in the measurement of people on these variables. For example, you might find that males have higher salaries than females. This means there is an empirical relationship between gender and salary. You might find that persons with higher levels of social support experienced lower levels of stress than those with lower levels of social support. This means you have found an empirical relationship between social support and stress. A key to the concept of "empirical relationship" is *measurement.*

Two major concepts regarding empirical relationships are:

1. *the direction of the relationship, and*
2. *the strength of the relationship.*

The direction of the relationship can take three basic forms. There can be a positive relationship between two variables, a negative relationship, or no relationship. If you hypothesize that there is a **positive relationship** between self-esteem and job satisfaction, you would expect that those who are higher than others on one of these variables will tend to be higher than others on the other variable. For example, if John's score for self-esteem is higher than Bob's score for self-esteem, you would expect that John's score for job satisfaction would be higher than Bob's score for job satisfaction.

However, if the typical pattern is that a person who is higher than another on one of these variables would tend to be *lower* than the other person on the other variable, you would have an example of a **negative relationship.** For example, you would expect to find a negative relationship between social support and stress, because you would expect that persons with high support would tend to have low stress.

No empirical relationship between two variables would be exhibited by a situation in which there is no pattern to the scores of persons on the two variables. For example, if John is higher than Bob on A and higher than Bob on B, you have one piece of evidence for a positive relationship between these two variables. But what if you found that John is higher on A than Bill but lower on B than Bill and you find that Barbara is higher than Sam on A and higher than Sam on B but she is higher than Janet on A but lower than Janet on B. If you find little consistency in these comparisons, you have evidence of the absence of an empirical relationship between the two variables.

Examining the Strength of the Relationship

The above examples comparing hypothetical people in a study is relevant to the concept of the **strength of the relationship.** A perfect empirical relationship between two variables would mean that everyone who was higher than another person on one variable would be higher than the other person on the other variable. There would be no exceptions to this rule. But, in social research, you almost never find a perfect empirical relationship. In fact, it is *so* unusual, such a finding should lead one to suspect that something is not quite right in the study methodology. A perfect relationship is depicted by a coefficient of 1.0 when data are subjected to analysis with one of many statistical measures. Coefficients can range from 0 to 1.0, with 0 representing absolutely no relationship, and 1.0 representing a perfect relationship. The more exceptions to the pattern in the data, the lower the coefficient. The lower the coefficient, the lower is the strength of the empirical relationship.

Comparison Group

Perhaps the best way to explain the notion of the strength of the relationship is to take examples from evaluative research. Suppose you have a group of clients who were treated for alcoholism and you measured whether they recovered by investigating their condition six months after treatment. If they had remained sober throughout this period of time, they were deemed to be recovered. If they had not, they would be considered to have not recovered.

Suppose you also have a comparison group of persons who were having an alcohol problem at the time that your clients entered treatment but these people did not receive treatment. Thus, you have a treatment group and a comparison group. You will compare the proportion of your treated clients who recovered to the proportion of the comparison group who recovered, as a measure of the effectiveness of your treatment. If 80 percent of your clients recovered but only 20 percent of the persons in the comparison group achieved recovery, you have evidence of the effectiveness of your treatment. The difference in the recovery rates would provide evidence of the effect of treatment. Because 2 persons out of 10 (20%) recovered without treatment (the comparison group), you would expect that 2 out of 10 of your clients would have also recovered without treatment. The difference between this rate (2 out of 10 or 20%) and the rate of recovery for your clients (8 out of 10 or 80%) can be attributed to the treatment rather than the effects of maturation (i.e., the fact that persons mature over time without intervention and some will find a way to recover on their own). Thus, treatment made a difference for 6 persons out of 10, or 60 percent.

Why 60 percent instead of 80 percent? Remember that 20 percent were expected to recover without treatment but 80 percent actually recovered; thus, 60 percent of our clients are believed to have achieved recovery *because* of our treatment (80% − 20% = 60%). Remember that clients can achieve recovery (or improvement) for many reasons. The critical question in evaluative research is whether treatment is the reason for the recovery or improvement.

phi Coefficient

If we take the above example and convert the 60 percent figure to a fraction (i.e., 0.60), we will have a good estimate of the value of the statistical measure known as *phi coefficient*. This is not the way that phi coefficient is calculated, but it is an easy way to estimate it. You will seldom be at great variance from the actual value of phi coefficient if you use this method.

Interpreting Exhibit 4.1

The value of phi coefficient, and similar coefficients derived from other statistical measures, is a means of determining the strength of the relationship. These coefficients typically can range from 0 to 1.0. In Exhibit 4.1, you can see an illustration of a perfect relationship (phi coefficient = 1.0) and no relationship at all (phi coefficient = 0). Example A displays a perfect relationship. In this table, you can see that 100 percent of those in the treatment group recovered, compared to 0 percent in the comparison group. These data suggest that recovery is completely dependent on treatment—you recover if you are treated and you do not recover if you are not treated. Example B illustrates no relationship at all. The proportion of persons in the treatment group who recovered (30%) is exactly the same as the proportion of persons in the comparison group who recovered (30%). It appears that treatment makes no difference at all.

Proportions and Frequencies

You will notice that you were comparing proportions rather than frequencies when you examined the data in Exhibit 4.1. If you had been comparing frequencies, you would have seen that the number of recovered persons in the treatment group was twice the number of persons in the comparison group who recovered, but this would have been misleading because there were twice as many people in the treatment group as there were in the comparison group; thus, this group had an unfair advantage from the standpoint of frequencies. You would also have erred if you had compared the proportion of recovered persons who were in the treatment group as compared to the other group. In this case, you can see that twice as many recovered people were in the treatment group than the comparison group. The error would have been for the same reason: treated people had twice the likelihood of recovering than the comparison group, simply because their frequency was twice as high.

EXHIBIT 4.1   Perfect Relationship and No Relationship

Example A: A Perfect Relationship

	GROUP		
RECOVERY	Treatment	Comparison	Total
Yes	50 (100%)	0 (0%)	50
No	0 (0%)	25 (100%)	25
Total	50 (100%)	25 (100%)	75

Example B: No Relationship

	GROUP		
RECOVERY	Treatment	Comparison	Total
Yes	30 (30%)	15 (30%)	45
No	70 (70%)	35 (70%)	105
Total	100 (100%)	50 (100%)	150

Strong Versus Weak

A perfect relationship between two variables is, of course, the strongest relationship that can exist between two variables. The perfect relationship is hardly ever discovered in social science research. Instead, you will see coefficients of 0.35 or 0.68 and so forth when you view the results of statistical analysis for data that lend themselves to this type of statistical analysis. The higher the coefficient, the stronger the empirical relationship. In Exhibit 4.2, you can see two illustrations of data which display different strengths of relationship. Example A in that exhibit displays a moderately weak relationship, while Example B displays a stronger relationship. Incidentally, there is no pat answer to the question of what coefficient should be labeled as "weak" versus "moderate" versus "strong." Opinions will vary on this question. In this text, you will be given guidance on how to make this decision for yourself, with the idea that what should be labeled strong or weak may vary with the circumstances of the study.

Interpreting Exhibit 4.2

In Example A in Exhibit 4.2, you can see that 60 percent of those in the treated group recovered, as compared to 30 percent of those in the comparison group. Thus, the estimate of the phi coefficient would be 0.30 (0.60 − 0.30 = 0.30). In fact, you can see that the actual phi coefficient was 0.288, a trivial difference from the estimate. (In publishing results, of course, you would report the actual phi coefficient rather than the estimate, the latter being only for convenience when computers are not available for statistical analysis.) You may or may not consider this difference between these two groups as noteworthy. Treatment did seem to make a difference for 3 out of 10 persons (60% − 30% = 30%). Maybe this is noteworthy. The more important point for the present lesson is that the strength of the relationship in Example B is greater than the strength of the relationship displayed in Example A. In Example B, 75 percent of the treated group recovered, contrasted with only 25 percent of the nontreated group. The estimate of the phi coefficient would be 0.50, and, as you can see, the actual phi coefficient is 0.48. Thus, treatment seems to make a difference for 5 persons out of 10 (75% − 25% = 50%) as compared to only 3 persons out of 10 in Example A.

EXHIBIT 4.2   Strength of the Relationship

Example A: A Weak Relationship

	GROUP		
RECOVERY	*Treatment*	*Comparison*	*Total*
Yes	30 (60%)	30 (30%)	60
No	20 (40%)	70 (70%)	90
Total	50 (100%)	100 (100%)	150

[Chi square = 12.5; phi coefficient = 0.288; p < .001]

EXHIBIT 4.2 *Continued*

Example B: A Stronger Relationship

	GROUP		
RECOVERY	Treatment	Comparison	Total
Yes	30 (75%)	5 (25%)	35
No	10 (25%)	15 (75%)	25
Total	40 (100%)	20 (100%)	60

[Chi square = 13.71; phi coefficient = 0.48; p < .001]

ASSIGNMENT 4-C

1. Examine the following data regarding responses to the question about preference for working with the hypothetical manager:

Frequency *Response*

3	I would really like to work for this person.
12	I would not mind working for this person.
11	I would prefer not to work for this person.
5	I would really not want to work for this person and I would do what I could to avoid it.

Because the above sample is small, data of this type typically must be reorganized into fewer categories for statistical analysis. In the present study, you will divide all respondents into only two categories and will label these "Low" and "High." At what point would you divide respondents into only two categories for statistical analysis given the above data? Would you combine the top two categories and the bottom two categories?

_____

_____

2. What if you found the following data from your survey? What problem would this present?

Frequency *Response*

0	I would really like to work for this person.
1	I would not mind working for this person.
3	I would prefer not to work for this person.
22	I would really not want to work for this person and I would do what I could to avoid it.

3. Examine the following hypothetical data for the present study.

PREFERENCE	*George*	*Barbara*	*Total*
High	8	6	14
Low	12	9	21
Total	20	15	35

What kind of empirical relationship is illustrated by these data?

_____ **a.** No relationship

_____ **b.** A positive relationship

_____ **c.** A negative relationship

Notes _____

_____

_____

Statistical Versus Practical Significance

Statistical significance refers to the likelihood that a given set of data results can be explained by chance. It is quantified by the value of p (i.e. $p < .05$). The p value is given in a fraction that indicates the proportion of times this configuration of data would occur by chance. The value .05 means 5 percent of the time, or 5 times out of 100. This figure is the normal standard in the social sciences for the declaration of statistical significance. In other words, if the statistical test for your study hypothesis yields a value less than .05, you would normally declare that statistical significance has been achieved. In this case, the lower the value, the better is the level of statistical significance. A p value of .01 means only 1 time in 100, while a p value of .001 means only 1 time in 1,000.

Setting a standard for statistical significance is an arbitrary decision. The standard of .05 is generally accepted, but there is no special scientific basis for this standard. If you were to select the .10 level, you would simply be saying that your standard was not as high as that which is normally required in published research. The .10 level means that your data would be expected to occur by chance 1 time in 10 (10 times in 100). Perhaps that is sufficient for your purposes.

Once you have established a standard, you are saying that you are not confident you have discovered reality rather than chance if your data fail to achieve that standard. Thus, you would be walking on thin ice if you were to discuss nonsignificant results as though you had discovered reality. Unfortunately, you may find authors of published research making this mistake in their discussions of their findings.

Practical significance refers to the practical implications of the results, or whether the results are noteworthy. If 60 percent of the treatment group recovered and 30 percent of the comparison group recovered, is this of practical, or clinical, significance? In other words, would these results justify a celebration of some kind, or would they be disappointing?

When drawing conclusions about practical significance (sometimes referred to as "substantive significance" or "clinical significance"), you would seek guidance from an examination of the magnitude of the relationship between variables or the differences between the groups being compared. If you found that males received average salaries of $31,450 while females received average salaries of $30, 890, would you have practical significance? What about a difference of $34,500 and $28,900? If the correlation between self-esteem and school grades is 0.25, is this of practical significance? There is no clear basis for this decision. It is a matter of judgement. The critical lesson is that you seek guidance for this decision in the strength of the relationship between the study variables.

Interpreting Exhibit 4.3
Can you have practical significance in the absence of statistical significance, or vice versa? The data in Exhibit 4.3 may help with your investigation of this question. Example A indicates a weak relationship where statistical significance was not achieved. In fact, these data did not even come remotely close to achieving statistical significance. This means you would not have confidence that repeating this experiment with this treatment would achieve any improvement at all over nontreatment. Differences of such slight magnitude with a relatively small sample will very often occur by chance. Thus, you could not take seriously even these small difference between the treatment group and the comparison group. To discuss practical significance in this situation would be silly.

Now, take a look at Example B in this exhibit. The difference in recovery rate between the treatment group and the comparison group is exactly the same as with Example A where statistical significance was not achieved. Of the treated group, 50 percent recovered as compared to 40 percent of the nontreated group. This is a rather small difference, but statistical significance was achieved. Why? The answer lies in the difference in the sample size between Example A and Example B. In Example A, there were 40 persons in the study. In Example B, there were 400 persons in the study. How do you interpret a phi coefficient of .10 when statistical significance has been achieved? You could say you can be confident that there really is a trivial difference between being treated and not being treated. Consequently, this is an example where you might say that statistical significance was achieved but practical significance was not achieved.

EXHIBIT 4.3   Effect of Sample Size on Statistical Significance

Example A: Weak Relationship without Statistical Significance

	GROUP		
RECOVERY	Treatment	Comparison	Total
Yes	10 (50%)	8 (40%)	18
No	10 (50%)	12 (60%)	22
Total	20 (100%)	20 (100%)	40

[Chi square = 0.4; phi coefficient = 0.10; $p > .40$]

(Continued)

EXHIBIT 4.3   *Continued*

Example B: Weak Relationship with Statistical Significance

	GROUP		
RECOVERY	Treatment	Comparison	Total
Yes	100 (50%)	80 (40%)	180
No	100 (50%)	120 (60%)	220
Total	200 (100%)	200 (100%)	400

[Chi square = 4.04; phi coefficient = 0.10; p < .05]

ASSIGNMENT 4-D

1. Examine the following hypothetical results.

PREFERENCE	George	Barbara	Total
High	10	18	28
Low	8	7	15
Total	18	25	43

[Phi coefficient = 0.32; p < .05]

Discuss whether the above data support the following hypothesis: Social work students with a male task-master type manager will express a higher preference for working for this manager than will those social work students who were given a female task-master type manager.

This is false because more people preferred Barbara on the high level

2. Examine the two examples below.

Example A

	GROUP		
RECOVERY	Treatment	Comparison	Total
Yes	10	10	20
No	10	30	40
Total	20	40	60

Example B

	GROUP		
RECOVERY	*Treatment*	*Comparison*	*Total*
Yes	10	10	20
No	10	90	100
Total	20	100	120

Do either of these tables exhibit a stronger empirical relationship than the other? Explain.

_____

_____

3. Suppose two models of treatment were subjected to empirical analysis like the above examples in which a treatment group is compared to a nontreatment group. The phi coefficient for Treatment Model A was 0.65 (N = 100), while the phi coefficient for Treatment Model B was 0.65 (N = 50).

_____ **a.** Was the strength of the relationship between treatment and recovery greater for one of these models than the other? Explain.

_____

_____

_____ **b.** Is either of these models more likely to be supported at a statistically significant level than the other? Explain.

_____

_____

_____

Examining Data for the Present Study

The previous chapter had a data sheet for students to record their responses to the questions posed on the questionnaire (Exhibit 3.4). The data for the entire class is displayed in Exhibit 3.5. You will need to use Exhibit 3.5 as data for the present study.

Two of the questions serve as the means for testing your basic hypothesis: Social work students given a description of a task-master type manager with a male name will express a higher level of preference for working for this person than will social work students given the same description with a female name for the manager.

There are two key variables in this analysis—the manager's name and level of prefer-ence. For the first variable, students are divided into two groups: those with George and those with Barbara. For the second variable, students responded to a question that had a four-point scale. To simplify your analysis, you can divide the members of your class into two categories according to their level of preference. You should calculate the frequencies for each of these four levels of preference before making a determination of where you should draw the dividing line. If responses are generally negative, you might have to place those in the most negative category in one group and all the others in the other group. In this situation, those in the most negative category would be classified as LOW for prefer-ence while all others would be classified as HIGH for this variable.

This grouping might seem strange in view of the fact that persons who said, "I would prefer not to work for this person" would be in the HIGH category along with those who maintained a more positive stance. But this level of preference is higher than the lowest level where people responded, "I would really not want to work for this person and would do what I could to avoid it." Remember that the variable is level of preference, so as long as you have people in categories that vary by level of preference, you have done your job of measuring the variable. Keeping students in their original response categories in the mea-surement of this variable would be a superior way to test your hypothesis, but you are ad-vised to reduce the data for this variable into only two categories to simplify the analysis. It is also advisable to reduce the number of categories of a nominal variable when you have a small sample.

The next assignment carries you through the first few steps in your data analysis.

ASSIGNMENT 4-E

Step 1.   Tally the responses for each class member on the variable dealing with level of preference for working for the hypothetical manager. Use the data from Exhibit 3.5.

Frequency   Level of Preference

_____   I would really like to work for this person (code = 3).

_____   I would not mind working for this person (code = 2).

_____   I would prefer not to work for this person (code = 1).

_____   I would really not want to work for this person and would do what I could to avoid it (code = 0).

Step 2.   Determine where to draw the line in order to dichotomize the members of your class on the variable of level of preference. You should examine the distribution of scores above, and determine where to draw the line to have the best balance of persons in two categories. Pref-erably, you would place those in the top two categories in the category of "High" and those in the bottom two categories in the category of "Low."

Step 3.   Distribute the study subjects into the following table according to their categories for (1) manager, and (2) level of preference. For example, if a student held a high preference for working for George, this person would be one of the frequencies for cell A. The total number of students with a high preference for George would be placed in Cell A while all those with a high preference for Barbara would be placed in Cell B. Those with a low preference for George would be placed in Cell C, while the number of students with a low preference for working with Barbara would be placed in Cell D.

Preference Level	Manager		Total
	George	**Barbara**	
High	Cell A	Cell B	
Low	Cell C	Cell D	
Total			

Step 4. Determine if the proportion of students with a high preference for George is greater than the proportion with a high preference for Barbara. Divide the number with a high preference for George by the total who had George. Do the same for Barbara. Compare these proportions. What do these data tell you?

You have compared the proportion of George's students who were high for preference with the proportion of Barbara's students who were high for preference. Was the proportion for George higher than for Barbara? If not, you can stop your analysis, because your hypothesis is not supported by your data. If the answer is yes, the question becomes whether the proportion for George was *significantly* greater than the proportion for Barbara. This is where statistical significance comes into play.

Interpreting Exhibit 4.4

For data in a 2 by 2 table (i.e., the relationship between two dichotomous variables), the chi square statistic is appropriate. The procedure for calculating the value for chi square is given in Exhibit 4.4. (Note: if the proportion of high scores for Barbara was greater than the proportion of high scores for George, you might want to determine if this difference is statistically significant, but you would no longer be examining your original hypothesis.)

The formula for calculating chi square used in Exhibit 4.4 is taken from Siegel (1956) and it contains a correction for continuity; thus, it is more conservative than the standard formula for chi square, which is not sensitive to problems that exist with small samples. Even when this correction is employed, **you should not use chi square when expected frequencies are less than 5.** The *expected frequency* is the frequency you would expect to find if there was absolutely no relation between the two variables. This situation is illustrated by Example B in Exhibit 4.1. In that table, the proportion of treated persons who recovered (30 percent) was exactly the same as the proportion of nontreated persons who recovered. Thus, there was no relationship between treatment and recovery.

We calculate the expected frequency for a cell in a table by multiplying the row total for that cell by the column total for that cell and dividing that figure by the number in the sample (N). Take, for example, the following data:

	George	Barbara	Total
High	10	8	18
Low	6	7	13
Total	16	15	31

We would calculate the expected frequency for cell A by multiplying the row total for this cell (18) by the column total for this cell (16) and by dividing this figure by the total in the sample (31). In our case the expected frequency for cell A (those who were high for George) would be 9.29 ($16 \times 18 = 288 / 31 = 9.29$). We will find expected frequencies less than 5 in data from small samples: thus, **chi square is not appropriate for small samples (e.g., less than 20).** In many cases with samples above 20, you will find expected frequencies less than 5. You will often find expected frequencies less than 5 if you have actual (observed) frequencies less that 5.

Your next task is to determine if there is a significant preference for a male task-master over a female task-master. The instructions for calculating chi square and phi coefficient are given in Exhibit 4.4. Follow these instructions before responding to the questions in Assignment 4-F.

EXHIBIT 4.4   Calculating Chi Square and Phi Coefficient

EXAMPLE

	MANAGER		
	George	*Barbara*	*Total*
Preference			
High	15 (A)	8 (B)	23 (A+B)
Low	10 (C)	17 (D)	27 (C+D)
Total	25 (A+C)	25 (B+D)	50 (N)

EXHIBIT 4.4 *Continued*

Enter your data below.

MANAGER

	George	*Barbara*	*Total*
Preference			
High	A = _____	B = _____	_____ (A+B)
Low	C = _____	D = _____	_____ (C+D)
Total	_____ (A+C)	_____ (B+D)	_____ (N)

Step 1: Subtract B times C (BC) from A times D (AD).

	$A \times D = AD$	$B \times C = BC$	$AD - BC = \#1$
Example	$15 \times 17 = 255$	$8 \times 10 = 80$	$255 - 80 = 175$ (#1)
Your data →			

Step 2: Compute the square of #1 and multiply this value by N.

	$(\#1)^2$	N	$(\#1)^2 \times N = \#2$
Example	$175^2 = 30{,}625$	50	$30{,}625 \times 50 = 1{,}531{,}250$ (#2)
Your data →			

Step 3: Multiply A+B by C+D by A+C by B+D.

	A+B times C+D times A+C times B+D equals #4
Example	$23 \times 27 \times 25 \times 25 = 388{,}125$
Your data →	

Step 4: Compute the value of chi square by dividing #2 by #4.

	#2	#4	#2 / #4 = chi square
Example	1,531,250	388,125	$1{,}531{,}250 / 388{,}125 = 3.94$
Your data →			

(Continued)

EXHIBIT 4.4   *Continued*

Step 5: Determine statistical significance.

When using chi square for determining statistical significance, you must determine the "degrees of freedom" based on the particular configuration of the table you are using. For data in a 2 by 2 table, the number of degrees of freedom is 1. With 1 degree of freedom, a chi square value of 2.71 is significant at the .10 level, while a chi square value as high as 3.84 is significant at the .05 level, and a chi square as high as 6.64 is significant at the .01 level. Because your data are in a 2 by 2 table, you can use this information to determine statistical significance.

If, on the other hand, you had data in a 2 by 3 table, the number of degrees of freedom would be different from that of a 2 by 2 table and the above information could not be applied to such data. This would also be true for data in a 2 by 4 table or 3 by 4 table, or any type of table other than the 2 by 2 table. In these situations, you would need to consult a text of statistics for a table to be used for such data.

Step 6: Examine the strength of the relationship.

A helpful guide for determining practical significance is the strength of the relationship. The strength of the relationship between variables displayed in a 2 by 2 table can be examined with the use of phi coefficient. One of the ways to calculate the value of phi coefficient is by calculating the square root of the value of chi square divided by N. First, divide chi square by N. Then determine the square root of that value.

	Chi square divided by N = N/X2	Square root of N/X2 = phi coefficient
Example	3. 94 / 50 = 0.0788	Square root of 0.0788 = 0.28
Your data →		

ASSIGNMENT 4-F

Discuss whether the data for your class support the following hypothesis: Social work students given a hypothetical task-master type manager named George will express a higher level of preference for working for this manager than will social work students given a hypothetical task-master type manager named Barbara.

_____

_____

_____

_____

What are your study conclusions?

References

Siegel, S. (1956). *Nonparametric statistics for the behavioral sciences.* New York: McGraw-Hill
York, R. O. (1997). *Building basic competencies in social work research.* Boston: Allyn & Bacon.

Chapter 5

Conducting Evaluative Research Using a Group Design:

Is Project PARENTING Effective?

In this chapter, you will engage in some of the activities of evaluative research when group research designs are employed. You will examine data from an evaluation study that was undertaken by a social work student of a parent development program for adolescent parents in an alternative high school. You will analyze each phase of the evaluative research process, culminating with your own computation of the statistical analysis of the data drawn from that study. At the completion of this chapter, you will be able to:

1. Identify what is missing from the process of evaluative research when given an example;

2. Define the goals and objectives of a given intervention;

3. Describe an intervention in regard to structure, content, and personnel;

4. Articulate the justification for selecting a given intervention for achieving a set of objectives, given a knowledge base regarding the dynamics of the problem being addressed;

5. Identify the strengths and limitations of four dominant research designs in regard to four common threats to internal validity;

6. State the hypothesis for an evaluative research study;

7. Analyze the data for a study using the one-group pretest-posttest design in regard to statistical significance;

8. Articulate the answer to the research question and the limitations of the study results.

Evaluating Social Work Practice: An Overview

In this book, the research process has been organized into four major phases: Problem Formulation, Research Methodology, Data Analysis, and Conclusions.

Problem Formulation Phase of Evaluative Research

In the Problem Formulation phase of evaluative research, you should define and analyze the problem that the intervention addresses. The description of the intervention in this text is incorporated into the problem formulation phase, but it could just as well be presented in the study methodology phase, in view of the fact that it constitutes the independent variable in the analysis of results. However, it is placed in the problem formulation section to highlight the importance of the link between the nature of the problem and the nature of the intervention.

Your definition of the problem being addressed by the intervention will provide guidance in determining how client progress will be measured. How, for example, would you define spouse abuse? Would your definition include both verbal and physical acts of violence, or just physical acts?

Which of the following would you include in a definition of depression: feelings of sadness, feelings of worthlessness, feelings of guilt? All of these were included in a definition of depression given in the literature review of a study presented in a beginning text on social work research (York, 1997). That definition also included disturbances of appetite, sleep, and general activity. However, it is important to consider the fact that depression is a syndrome rather than a set of independent conditions. In other words, sleeplessness alone is a poor basis for determining that one is depressed. It is when a number of the above conditions are present together that one should recognize depression.

Armed with a good definition of the target behavior, the practitioner is prepared to seek or develop a means of measurement. If a certain measurement instrument on spouse abuse only includes physical acts of violence, that instrument would be an inadequate means of measuring this variable if you had included verbal acts of violence in your definition.

The analysis of the problem will serve as a guide for selecting an intervention. If depression is viewed as being caused by distorted thinking patterns, a treatment modality that intervenes in one's thinking patterns would be a logical intervention. If drug education is the solution for drug abuse, it would appear that practitioners are assuming that drug abuse is caused, in part, by some form of ignorance. If you believe that social isolation, ignorance of good parenting techniques, and personal history of poor role models are some of the causes of child abuse, you would be justified in including social support, parent education, and role modeling in your chosen intervention for abusive parents. Some questions, organized by research phase, are presented in Exhibit 5.1.

**EXHIBIT 5.1   Questions to Be Considered in the Phases of Evaluative
Research**

Problem Formulation

1. What is the major problem confronting the client(s)?

2. Why is this problem important?

3. How is this problem defined?

4. What are the causes of this problem or the needs of persons experiencing it?

5. How can the intervention be described?

   a. Objectives

   b. Structure

   c. Content

   d. Personnel

6. How is the intervention justified?

Study Methodology

1. What is the study sample and the study population?

   a. How was the study sample selected?

   b. How is the study population defined?

2. What evaluative research design will be employed?

3. What is the study hypothesis?

4. How will the dependent variables be defined and measured?

   a. What is the abstract definition of each dependent variable?

   b. How will each dependent variable be measured?

   c. What evidence suggests that these measurement devices are reliable or valid?

   d. What means of observation will be employed?

Data Analysis

1. How is the sample described in relation to basic characteristics?

2. What were the scores of the clients on each of the dependent variables at each administration of the tests?

3. Did the application of statistical tests provide evidence of the statistical significance of the
   results?

EXHIBIT 5.1   *Continued*

Conclusions

1. How can the results of this study be best summarized?

2. What are some of the limitations of this study in regard to research design, measurement, or sampling?

3. Was practical significance achieved?

4. What are the implications of these results for social work practice?

Describe the Intervention

The description of the intervention includes reference to goals, objectives, structure, content, and personnel. The goals and objectives specify the purpose of the intervention, while the structure, content, and personnel refer to ways one can explain the nature of the intervention so others will understand just what it was that did or did not work when the data have been analyzed.

A *goal* is a long-range preference statement of what is to be accomplished for the consumer of service. An *objective* is a measured amount of progress toward goal accomplishment. The condition that would represent long-term rehabilitation for the client is typically the focus of the goal. However, the achievement of the goal is often outside the reach of human services, because they are usually time-limited. Therefore, the focus for examining client progress toward the goal is more often the objective of intervention.

In a study of the treatment of sexual offenders, the goal was identified as the reduction of repeat sexual offenses, but this variable was not directly measured. Instead, the researcher focused on changes in the conditions thought to contribute to one's risk for committing these crimes. One of these was the tendency to engage in cognitive distortions of the crime committed. Thus, this served as the focus of one of the treatment objectives (York, 1997, pp. 220–257).

It is important that the intervention be carefully defined. If you do not clearly define the intervention, you will be unclear as to what it was that actually should be credited with client improvement or blamed for lack of progress. It is also important that the implementation of the intervention be carefully monitored so you can be assured that the intended intervention was actually carried out.

Structure of the Intervention.   The intervention can be described with regard to three characteristics: structure, content, and personnel. The *structure* of the intervention provides information on how much service is to be offered and the context in which it will be offered. You might describe the structure of family therapy as a series of five to seven sessions of one hour each which will be offered once a week for five to seven consecutive weeks. You would also define what a therapy session entailed in rather simple terms (e.g., a personal interview which takes place in the office of the mental health center with all members of the target family present along with the therapist). You could describe the structure of a residential treatment program as 24-hour residential care with daily individual therapy sessions of one hour each, daily group therapy sessions of two hours each, and daily recreational therapy which includes an activity chosen by the client from a list of options and which occupies the client for a period of approximately two hours daily.

The structure will provide information on the amount of intervention being provided. Armed with this information, you can better assess whether the accomplishments of treatment justified the costs.

Content of the Intervention.   The *content* of the intervention describes the model employed, the topics of the training, or any other information that will serve as a guide to the theory behind the intervention. If family therapy is employed, what model of therapy is used? If training is the intervention, what are the topics to be covered?

One of the most important reasons to describe the content of the intervention is to inform the observer of the assumptions that underlie what is being done. Any model of treatment makes certain assumptions about human nature. What are the assumptions behind this particular model?

Personnel of the Intervention.   The *personnel* of the intervention is rather simple to describe. It refers to the types of persons who are the practitioners. Are they psychiatrists, certified clinical social workers, psychologists, MSW social workers, BSW social workers, social workers without any social work degrees, or something else? The rationale for this information is that a certain model of intervention may rest on the assumption that trained practitioners are implementing the service. If this assumption is not correct in your situation, you need to know this so that you can better interpret your findings and draw conclusions.

Justify the Intervention

Justifying the intervention is one of the more difficult tasks in evaluative research for the social worker, especially the social work student. Too often, social workers take a position in which it is well established that a certain model of intervention is being employed and little is done to question the wisdom of this intervention. Social workers too often get caught up in the task of deciding what the intervention will look like if they implement it well and do not take the time to stop and analyze whether it is the optimal treatment for the problem being addressed.

Examining Causes.   Analyzing the cause of the problem and stating the objective of the intervention can help you determine the most logical intervention to accomplish the objective. If ignorance is the cause of the problem, the objective might be to improve knowledge; thus, some kind of training may be the logical solution. If a dysfunctional communication pattern is the cause of the problem, one objective might be to improve the communication ability of family members, and the intervention might be family therapy with a special focus on communication patterns among family members.

If you wished, you could delve into this problem even more by asking "Why do people have dysfunctional communication?" Is it because they have not had good role models of communication behavior? If so, perhaps demonstrations of functional communication patterns would be useful. If they cannot communicate well because of psychological needs that inhibit the reception of messages from certain other persons, perhaps the solution would be to identify these needs and to develop a logical strategy for meeting these needs so they would not interfere with communication skills.

Examining Needs.   Sometimes it's more helpful to examine the needs of persons with this problem rather than the causes of the problem. For example, it would do us little good to determine the causes of mental retardation if our goal was to improve the life conditions of persons with this condition. Instead, we might focus on the unmet needs of such persons.

Common Mistakes.   One of the common mistakes made in evaluative research reports by social work students is to justify the intervention based on the belief that it will achieve the objectives. One might say something like "Brief therapy was selected because it is believed that it will have a positive effect on depression." The question that should be addressed is *why*. Why is it believed that this particular intervention will achieve a given objective? What does brief therapy do that has a logical connection to the problem of depression?

Logical and Emperical Support.   The latter example made reference to **logical support** for the selection of an intervention. This support relies on logic. It is logical to assume that training is a good solution to the problem of ignorance. But training is not as likely to affect deep-seated psychological disturbances that are not based on simple ignorance. Another basic approach to the justification of the selection of an intervention is the use of **empirical support.** This form of support relies on the research of others where certain types of interventions have been evaluated as a means for achieving certain objectives. For example, if you found several studies showing that persons treated with cognitive therapy achieved a significant improvement in depression, you would have empirical support for the use of cognitive therapy in the treatment of depression.

ASSIGNMENT 5-A

1. A clear definition of the problem is MOST helpful to the social work researcher in which of the following ways? (Select one.)

   _____   **a.** Selecting the intervention.

   _____   **b.** Selecting the research design.

   _____✓_____   **c.** Selecting the means to measure the dependent variable.

   _____   **d.** Selecting the means to test the validity of the measurement tools.

2. A good problem analysis is MOST helpful to the social work researcher in which of the following ways? (Select one.)

   _____✓_____   **a.** Selecting the intervention.

   _____   **b.** Selecting the research design.

   _____   **c.** Selecting the means to measure the dependent variable.

   _____   **d.** Selecting the means to test the validity of the measurement tools.

3. For each of the following sets of statements, one is best conceptualized as the goal of treatment, one is best conceptualized as the objective of treatment, and one is suitable for *neither* the statement of the goal nor the objective. Separate each set of statements into these categories by placing the word GOAL next to one, the word OBJECTIVE next to a second one, and the word NEITHER next to the third one.

Set Number 1

Objective   To improve family communication for families with an alcoholic member.

Neither   To provide family therapy for families with an alcoholic member.

Goal   To alleviate the negative social consequences of the problematic consumption of alcohol.

Set Number 2

Goal   To reduce the incidence of child abuse.

Objective   To improve the abusive parent's knowledge of the appropriate developmental expectations of children at each age of development.

Neither   To improve the quality of life.

Set Number 3

Neither   To provide social work services to high school students at risk for dropping out of school.

Goal   To reduce the incidence of high school dropouts.

Objective   To improve the self-confidence in school work of high school students at risk for dropping out of school.

4. Briefly describe the structure of a familiar social work intervention.

Family Therapy will last 6-8 sessions

5. Give one statement that fits the description of the content of the intervention described above.

Family therapy will include working on communication between each member of the family, by using ___ Therapy.

6. Give one piece of logical support for this intervention.

Improving communication will help the family to work out their problems better.

Study Methodology Phase of Evaluative Research

The Study Methodology phase of the research process should present information on the study sample and population, the research design, the means used to measure the client's progress (dependent variable), and the study hypothesis. This information will provide details on the nature of the study and how it was executed. **Note:** The description of the intervention was discussed in the previous section on the Problem Formulation phase, but the intervention description could just as well have been incorporated into this section, since the intervention is the independent variable for the study.

The Study Sample and Study Population

The study sample consists of those persons from whom data were collected. This refers to your client group, or the treatment group. A sample, by definition, is a portion of a larger entity. That larger entity is the study population. Whenever you treat a group of clients, they constitute a sample of a larger group of persons. There are many ways to define the study population, but there is only one correct way to define the study sample. Any definition of the study population is legitimate as long as every person in the sample is a member of that population. Your group of clients represents larger groups of persons. This would include all the clients served by your agency, or all persons in your community with a given problem, and so forth.

Probability Sample.   Your sample is not a **probability sample** of a given population unless your sample was drawn at random from that specific population. You can only be safe in generalizing from your sample to a population if it is a probability sample of that population.

If you do not have a probability sample, you should consider information that will improve your speculations about the generalizations of your study results. If you have data on the study population (e.g., mean age, proportion of females, proportion with a given problem, mean income level, etc.), you could compare your study sample to that population to see if there are major differences that would challenge your ability to generalize your findings to that population.

Threats to Internal Validity

When you measure client progress in an evaluative research study, you wish to be able to attribute this progress to the intervention. If the mean depression score for 15 clients is 15.2 at the end of treatment but was 31.5 at the beginning of treatment, you would like to attribute this progress to the treatment program that was implemented. But you know that other things can cause a client to get better (or worse). Sometimes people improve through normal processes of growth and adaptation to their circumstances. Sometimes people improve because something happened to them independent of the treatment. Such things might be conceptualized as alternative explanations for the client's progress. In research language, we are speaking of threats to internal validity.

Internal Validity.   *Internal validity* refers to the ability of a research design to address factors other than the treatment that could be the cause of the client's change as measured by the research instruments. If you only measure clients after treatment, you have no information on their conditions before treatment; thus, you do not have a measure of client progress. You are left to speculate on their pretreatment condition. If you measure client conditions before and after treatment, you have measured client progress. But you do not have information that helps you to rule out normal client growth over time as the basis for the progress rather than the treatment. If you compare your clients to another group who did not receive service, you do have a basis for considering this explanation for client progress. If your clients improved and your comparison group did not, you have information supporting the idea that the treatment should be credited with the improvement rather than normal growth over time. If you have the luxury of assigning clients and nonclients to their groups on a random basis, you have information to elevate your confidence in your treatment's effectiveness another major step.

Maturation.   The above example examined *maturation* as a threat to internal validity. Maturation refers to normal growth and development over time. If you have recently experienced a marital separation, you will likely be somewhat depressed over it. If you do not receive treatment for this depression, you will likely improve on your own over the next six months. In other words, you will likely be less depressed six months from now than at the present time, even in the absence of treatment. But what if you do receive treatment during the next six months? Your improvement is probably not entirely because of treatment.

In order to take maturation into consideration, your research design must have either a comparison group or information on client progress during a period of time before treatment began. A comparison group is a vehicle for measuring the effect of maturation. If the average improvement for the comparison group is 3 points on your depression scale, you will assume that your clients would have improved this much on their own. Thus, your treatment can be credited only with the difference between 3 points improvement and the level of your clients' measured improvement on this scale. Of course, you must address the issue of statistical significance before drawing conclusions.

History.   Another of the most important threats to internal validity to be taken into consideration is *history*. History refers to changes in the client's environment, other than the treatment, that may be the cause of the measured change in behavior. If your unemployed client obtained a job at the mid-point of your treatment period, it may be the job that elevated his or her self-esteem rather than the treatment.

Testing.   A third major threat to internal validity is *testing*. This refers to the effects of the testing experience itself. Does the fact that John was tested on self-esteem last week affect the way he will respond to this same scale this week? Testing is especially important to consider for tests of knowledge. Mary may remember the questions asked on the first exam and be better prepared to respond for that reason alone. Maybe Mary has had time to think about some of these questions and realized her mistake on the previous test.

Other Threats.   Several other threats to internal validity that have been examined in the literature will not be discussed here. Most texts on research will provide further guidance on this question. One of the primary references on this issue is the work of Campbell and Stanley (1963).

A key question to answer for your own study is whether you have reason to be concerned with any of these threats. For example, you would expect new parents to naturally grow (mature) in parenting ability over a six-month period of time, but their growth over a two-week period would probably be minimal. Does your treatment extend over six months or two weeks? In the former case, you will need a research design that addresses maturation.

In the case of *history* as a threat, you can collect information during the treatment period which considers this factor. Did elements in the client's environment change? In selecting a research design, you should try to predict the potential for such changes in determining the type of design you will need to employ.

EXHIBIT 5.2   Additional Threats to Internal Validity

Three threats to internal validity were discussed in the body of this text. Several additional ones will be presented here for your reference.

Instrumentation as a threat to internal validity refers to the validity of the measurement devices employed in the study. If these instruments are not valid measures of the dependent variable, you cannot conclude that the treatment was effective. The instruments can be invalid because of a flaw inherent in the tool itself, a flaw that would have been discovered in a good test of validity. Instruments that have been well tested should cause little concern on this basis. However, we can also have an instrumentation problem if we fail to administer the instrument in a proper way.

Statistical regression refers to the fact that people naturally tend to regress to the mean when they stand at extreme positions from the mean. For example, a person who scored lowest

(Continued)

EXHIBIT 5.2   *Continued*

on IQ is more likely to score higher the next time than would be the case of someone who scored at the mean. Likewise, a person who scored highest would likely score *lower* the next time, because this person would also be regressing to the mean. In other words, both extremes move toward the mean on subsequent measurements. This is a natural phenomenon; thus, if we select the most extreme clients for treatment, we can expect that their scores will be more likely to improve without treatment than would be the case of less extreme clients. If we select extreme persons, we will need for our research design to address this threat to internal validity.

Selection bias is a third threat to internal validity that will be described here. This refers to the fact that the method used to select the clients for the study may be biased in some way that would affect their measured progress. If we intentionally select only the most highly motivated clients for our study, we would be introducing a selection bias into our study. However, if we divide these highly motivated persons into a control group that does not get treatment and an experimental group that receives treatment, we have a means of addressing this potential problem.

The *reactive effects* of the client to being in treatment is another threat to internal validity. Clients sometimes improve simply because they are being included in a study rather than the fact that the specific treatment protocol is effective in achieving progress. Clients may feel special because they are in a study and this factor may influence their progress.

Mortality is the final threat to internal validity to be described here. Some clients drop out of treatment before it is complete and are removed from the study. Are these persons different from those who remained? If so, in what way? Was it because treatment was not working for them? If this is true, then the persons in your study are restricted to certain persons for whom treatment was effective.

Research Designs

There are two major categories of research designs for evaluative research—group designs and single-subject designs. With group designs, you are collecting the same data on a group of clients who are receiving the same service. With single-subject designs, you are collecting data on a single subject. With group designs, you typically will collect data at two points in time—before and after the treatment period. With single-subject designs, you will collect the same data many times for the same client. In this chapter, you will examine group designs. Single-subject designs will be presented in the next chapter.

The previous section discussed threats to internal validity. Research designs vary in the extent to which they address these threats. Some do not address a given threat at all. Others may address a particular threat in a minimal way, while still others may address this threat optimally. A critical question to ask is *What threats to internal validity should I be especially concerned with in my study?* This should serve as a guide to the selection of a research design and to the interpretation of the study results.

In the descriptions of group designs, symbols are used as shorthand for the design. The letter O represents an observation (measurement of client conditions), while the letter X represents a treatment. The letter R represents a random assignment of persons to their group status.

One-Group Pretest-Posttest Design.   The basic before-and-after study is referred to as the **one-group pretest-posttest design.** The designation of this design is as follows:

$$O_1 \quad X \quad O_2$$

The above symbols reveal that the clients had a measurement before treatment (observation at time 1), followed by a treatment, which was followed by another measurement of their condition (observation at time 2). With this design, you have a basis for measuring client progress, but you do not have a basis for addressing maturation as a threat to internal validity. You do not have a basis for taking normal growth and development into consideration. If you compared your clients to a nontreated group, you would have such a basis. You would also have a basis for considering maturation if you had collected data repeatedly over time for your clients before treatment began. Such information would tell you the extent to which clients had progressed on the target condition in the period before treatment.

Two other threats to internal validity were discussed above. The one-group pretest-posttest design does not address either of these two threats. History is not taken into consideration, nor is testing. A comparison group would have provided a basis for measuring the potential effects of these conditions upon the client's progress. You would normally be able to assume that the two groups were comparable on both of these variables. In other words, the growth of the persons in the comparison group would be just as vulnerable to the effects of history or testing as would be the case with the treatment group. If you have information suggesting that these groups are not comparable, you cannot make this assumption.

Your measurement of client behavior before and after treatment will typically employ a scale of behavior that measures client conditions at the interval level. A person's score on a self-esteem scale or a depression scale would be examples. In this situation, your statistical analysis of data would take the form of a computation of a *gain score* for each study subject, and the statistical analysis of the *mean gain score*. The gain score is computed by taking the difference between each person's pretest score and posttest score. The gain score for a scale on depression, assuming that higher scores mean more depression, would be computed by subtracting the posttest score from the pretest score. If Susan's depression score is 30 before treatment and 15 after treatment, her gain score would be 15. This would represent her level of improvement on depression. However, if you are measuring a variable like self-esteem, where higher scores represent better functioning, you would subtract the pretest score from the posttest score to obtain a gain score.

You could submit the gain scores of your clients to statistical analysis using the t test for paired data. The statistical question being posed is whether the mean gain score is significantly greater than a score of 0, which is what you would expect to find if the treatment had no effect at all. You will see how this works later in this chapter.

Comparison Group Design.   In the design presented above, there is only one group, the clients. In the **comparison group design** (also known as the **non-equivalent control group design**), a treated group is compared to another group that did not receive the treatment. In the following designation, there are two groups of persons; one is receiving treatment and the other is not.

$$O_1 \quad X \quad O_2$$
$$O_1 \qquad\;\; O_2$$

Notice that the letter X is in the row for the first group but is absent in the row representing the second group. The letter X refers to the introduction of a treatment. As mentioned above, maturation is addressed in the comparison group design. History is another threat to internal validity that is addressed by this design. You would normally assume that changes in the environment would be common to persons in both groups; thus, differences in growth between the groups can be attributed to the treatment. Naturally, you could not make this assumption if you had contrary information about the environments of the two groups.

The statistical analysis of data for the comparison group design entails comparing the mean gain scores for each group, assuming that the dependent variable is measured at the interval level (or you feel comfortable treating your dependent variable in this way). You would create a variable that represents the client's gain in functioning in the same manner as described above. The mean gain in functioning for the treatment group would be compared to the mean gain in functioning for the comparison group. If the dependent variable were measured at the interval level, the t test for independent samples would be an appropriate statistic for determining significance.

Pretest-Posttest Control Group Design.   There are several variations of the experimental design. The most common one is the **pretest-posttest control group design.** This design is similar to the comparison group design with one important distinction—persons are assigned to their group status on a random basis. This means that a sample of persons needing a certain treatment is divided into two groups on a random basis, and that one of these groups receives the treatment and the other does not. The major feature that all experimental designs have in common is the use of random assignment of persons to groups.

Another symbol in our shorthand for designating research designs that has not yet been employed is the letter R, which represents a random assignment of persons to the different groups. In the comparison group example, there is no letter R. This means these persons were not assigned to their group status on a random basis. Instead, a client group was compared to another group selected on some other basis. In the example of symbols below, the persons in each group are assigned to their group status on a random basis.

$$R \quad O_1 \quad X \quad O_2$$
$$R \quad O_1 \qquad\;\; O_2$$

The random assignment of persons to groups covers a host of threats to internal validity. Furthermore, it addresses these threats in a better manner than designs such as the comparison group design. Practitioners can be more confident that the treatment group and the other group are comparable on such things as environmental changes or maturation or testing, because the only thing that distinguishes them is their random assignment to their group status.

A nonrandom comparison group is more likely to be different from the treatment group than the randomly assigned control group. With the comparison group design, you must ask yourself whether there is reason to believe there is a difference between the two groups that might influence their improvement. How did you select this group as the comparison group? Did you compare clients receiving treatment with a group drawn from people on the waiting list? If so, what determines the waiting list status? If it is severity of problem, then you have discovered a basis on which the two groups are different, and you must consider the possibility that this is the cause of the difference in growth between the comparison group and the treatment group, rather than the treatment itself. If you select the students in Ms. Smith's class as a comparison group for the new technique used by Ms. Jones, you must consider that these two groups of students have different teachers and that Ms. Jones may simply be a better teacher; this fact may be the reason her students do better rather than the new technique she is using. However, if you select 10 teachers at random to be taught the new technique and compare their students with 10 other teachers' students selected at random, you would be in a good position to assume that teaching ability was comparable between the two groups.

Posttest-Only Control Group Design. Another experimental design worthy of special attention is the **posttest-only control group design.** When you are in a position to assign persons on a random basis, you do not have to use a pretest measurement. You can assume that persons in the two groups are similar at the pretest time period. If they are in their groups on a random basis, there is no reason for one group to be significantly different from the other. The symbols for this design are as follows:

$$R \quad X \quad O_2$$
$$R \quad \quad O_2$$

The statistical analysis of data for the posttest-only control group design takes the form of comparing the two groups on the dependent variable at the point in time in which intervention is terminated. If the treatment group (experimental group) has a significantly higher level of functioning than the control group, you would attribute that superiority to the treatment. The statistical test employed would be similar to that for the pretest-posttest control group design except that, with the posttest-only control group design, you would be comparing the two groups on the basis of their level of functioning at one point in time rather than comparing the level of gain between the two groups.

There are many more research designs than those presented here, and there are other threats to internal validity than those discussed in this chapter. The purpose of the present discussion is to cover the most common designs and the threats that are most likely to be of concern to social work research. Other texts on research can be consulted for a more thorough treatment of these concepts.

Interpreting Exhibit 5.3. A summary of these four designs and the three threats to internal validity is given in Exhibit 5.3. As you will see, the one-group pretest-posttest design does not address any of these threats at all. The comparison group design addresses each of these threats on a minimal level; thus, you must consider factors that might challenge the validity of this design, such as known differences between the comparison group and the treatment group. The two experimental designs address each of these three threats to internal validity at an optimal level.

EXHIBIT 5.3   Research Designs and Threats to Internal Validity

Research Design	Threat to Internal Validity		
	Maturation	*History*	*Testing*
One group pretest-posttest	Not at all	Not at all	Not at all
Comparison group	Minimally	Minimally	Minimally
Pretest-posttest control group	Optimally	Optimally	Optimally
Posttest-only control group	Optimally	Optimally	Optimally

The Research Hypothesis

The research hypothesis in evaluative research portrays what the study results will look like if the treatment is effective. Before you are prepared to state the hypothesis, you must have determined how client progress will be measured and what research design will be employed.

A research hypothesis will identify the study variables and the type of relationship that is expected between them. It is presented in the form of a statement rather than a question. It should identify both the dependent and independent variables, and it should be stated in precise terminology. Examples of research hypotheses for evaluative studies are as follows:

1. Scores on the Self-esteem Inventory for clients of the Adolescent Treatment Program will be higher after six months of treatment than before treatment began.
2. The number of confirmed cases of child abuse will be greater in counties that administered the Child Abuse Awareness Campaign than in matched counties which did not administer the Child Abuse Awareness Campaign.
3. Improvement in Scores on the Beck Depression Inventory from the pre-treatment period to the post-treatment period will be better for persons in the experimental group than persons in the control group.

Measuring the Dependent Variable

The dependent variable in evaluative research is the client's target behavior. This behavior is determined by the objective of treatment. There are two types of definitions of the dependent variable: abstract and operational. The *abstract definition* provides guidance on the nature of the entity of concern. It provides conceptual boundaries to the target of intervention. The definition of the client's problem, as described in the Problem Formulation phase discussion, serves as the guide for this task. In fact, that definition will typically suffice for the abstract definition of the target behavior. The *operational definition* provides information on how the behavior is to be measured. A researcher might say, for example, that our operational definition of depression is the client's score on the Beck Depression Inventory.

You can find instruments for measuring client behavior in several reference works on this subject. These are discussed in Chapter 10.

Advantages of Established Instruments.   There is a major advantage of selecting an instrument that has already been developed and published. The development of an instrument takes a good deal of work. Researchers normally go through several drafts of items for a scale before they narrow it down to the items they consider to be most helpful. Then, it is typical that the instrument is tested for reliability and validity. While you will not find that all published scales have been tested thoroughly, you can have confidence that a good deal of work has gone into their development.

Create a New Instrument.   Another alternative is to construct an instrument yourself. The abstract definition of the dependent variable should be your primary guide. You will sometimes find that existing scales miss some important aspect of your dependent variable and that it is necessary to develop your own scale. You might also find that existing scales are too complicated to administer to your clients. In these cases, you might take the existing scale as a guide for the development of one that is simpler.

Assessing Reliability and Validity.   You have reviewed the concepts of reliability and validity several times in previous chapters. *Reliability* refers to the consistency of an instrument or means of observation, and is tested through such methods as the test-retest method and the split-half method. *Validity* refers to accuracy—how well an instrument measures what it was intended to measure. Validity can be assessed by careful and objective review of the instrument with the assistance of key informants who understand the concept being measured. Another (and generally more rigorous) way to examine validity is to subject the instrument to empirical assessment: compare the results of the tool to an external criterion that represents the variable of interest. This external criterion could be the results of another instrument (preferably one with established validity), or "real life" evidence such as good grades corroborating results that predict success in school, or plans to divorce corroborating results that indicate low marital satisfaction.

ASSIGNMENT 5-B

1. Does the one group pretest-posttest research design differ from the comparison group design in regard to maturation as a threat to internal validity? Explain your response.

   Yes, the one group pretest-postest did not address maturation at all because it has no control group to compare maturation with. The comparison group does address maturation.

2. Suppose you wish to reduce the stress levels of social work students through a support group intervention. You will measure stress using an established stress scale (one that has performed well in tests of reliability and validity) at the middle of the first semester immediately before you start the intervention, and you will measure stress with the same scale at the completion of the intervention, which will take place at the end of the second semester of study. Which of the following threats to internal validity should you be more concerned with in your selection of a research design?

_____ **a.** Testing

__✓___ **b.** Maturation

_____ **c.** Instrumentation

Notes: _____

_____

3. Suppose you wish to evaluate the effectiveness of a 20-day inpatient treatment program for depression. You will use an established depression scale for measuring depression before and after treatment. Your clients have come for treatment because of severe depression over a period of months or years. In this situation, would you need to be particularly concerned with maturation as a threat to internal validity? Explain.

Yes, you need to have a control group to compare results to see if the treatment program is actually working and what the gain from the program is.

Would you need to be especially concerned about any of the other threats to internal validity? Explain.

You would need to be concerned with instrumentation, and history to see if those factors affect ~~treatment~~ how the clients will improve or not.

4. Which of the following would be the most appropriate way to state the hypothesis for the study of stress described in question 2?

_____ **a.** Students will appreciate the value of support and this will result in their achieving improvement on stress.

_____ **b.** Students will improve on stress.

__✓___ **c.** The students' level of stress will be lower after treatment than before treatment.

_____ **d.** Will students achieve a gain on stress due to the support group intervention?

5. Which of the following would be *least* useful in confirming the reliability or validity of a depression scale that you wish to use in your study?

✓ _____ **a.** You find that scores for depression on this depression scale have a positive correlation with the level of depression that was rated by clinicians working with the sample of clients in the study.

_____ **b.** You find that depression scores are significantly lower after treatment than before treatment began.

_____ **c.** You find that scores for one-half of this scale have a positive correlation with scores on the other half of this scale.

Notes: _____

_____

_____

_____

Data Analysis

In the presentation of data, you should provide information on the nature of the sample, the distribution of scores on the dependent variable, and the application of tests of statistical significance.

Nature of the Sample

The sample description provides the reader with the ability to speculate on whether your results are relevant to another situation. The reader may want to know the racial, gender, or class distribution of your sample. If your sample has no members of minority groups, your results should be interpreted in this light. If your sample is restricted to low-income persons, a given reader may consider this to be important for his or her purposes. Samples that are heavily weighted to men or women will alert the reader to the potential that your results may not be generalizable to members of the minority gender. A social worker who specializes in work with the aged would be especially interested in knowing that the average age of your study subjects was 33 and that the oldest person in this sample was 61.

The following three pieces of data would normally be included in your report:

1. The number and proportion of males and females.
2. The number and proportion of persons by racial or ethnic group.
3. The minimum, maximum, and mean age.

In addition, you will want to describe your clients in ways that are especially relevant to your study. Income or social class or category of mental status are examples of variables that might be especially relevant to your study.

If you selected persons by asking for volunteers, you will need to report how many persons were asked to volunteer and what proportion of these persons actually did so. If you conducted a mailed survey, you should report the proportion of persons who responded.

Distribution of Scores

The reader of your report will want to know the distribution of scores on the dependent variable. What, for example, was the mean score for depression before treatment and after treatment? What was the range of scores on this variable? How do these scores relate to some perspective on such scores through comparisons to thresholds for clinical significance or by comparison to known data on certain kinds of persons? If you have information on these things, you should report them. If not, you should at least provide complete information on the distribution of scores so others can place your data into perspective.

If you are reporting on the results of a study of the effectiveness of a given intervention for a relatively small group of clients, it would be helpful to display each subject's scores for the dependent variable in a table. This would be done before and after treatment for research studies that collect this information. These data provide the reader with the ability to examine the variance of scores from one subject to another. Perhaps you had several clients with a vary large gain but most subjects had minimal gain. How should we interpret these results? Perhaps you had a noteworthy number of clients who started with high scores on the dependent variable and had little room for growth. A failure to discover statistical significance should be interpreted in this light.

Information on statistical significance should also be included in your data analysis section of the report. You should include the value of the statistic along with the value of p as applied to that statistic. In the social sciences, the generally accepted standard for statistical significance is .05. You will often see data reported with the designation "$p < .05$". This means that the data would occur by chance less than 5 times in 100. The p value can be reported either in the form of "$p < .05$" or by the report of the actual p value (e.g., $p = .02$).

Here are a few examples of ways to present some of the results:

1. The mean pretest score for self-esteem was 32.03, and the mean posttest score was 32.83. The mean gain of .8 was not statistically significant ($t = 1.03$; $p = .31$).
2. A score of 17 on the Beck Depression Scale is considered to be indicative of borderline depression, while a score over 40 indicates extreme depression. Individually, all subjects reduced their level of depression to some extent. The mean pretest score was 34.87, while the mean posttest score for these 15 clients was 13.8. The mean difference of 20.06 indicated a significant improvement in depression ($t = 9.02$; $p = .001$).
3. The results displayed in Table 2 reveal that 70 percent of the persons in the treatment group were abstinent from alcohol six months after discharge, compared to only 40 percent of those in the comparison group. This difference was statistically significant (chi square = 8.2; phi coefficient = .30; $p < .01$).

Statistical Significance

It is important to avoid confusing statistical significance with practical significance. Statistical significance refers to the likelihood that the data would occur by change. It is possible to have data with limited practical significance that achieves statistical significance. Perhaps there is only a small difference between pretest scores and posttest scores, but these differences are determined to be unlikely to occur by chance. This gives you some confidence that your treatment was effective, but you must also conclude that the effectiveness level is very small.

Drawing Conclusions

In the final section of the research report, you should summarize your findings with special attention to practical significance. You should also discuss some of the limitations of your findings. Study limitations can usually be identified after close scrutiny of the study methodology.

Researchers are typically limited in their ability to generalize their findings due to the sample employed. The research design will typically fail to address certain threats to internal validity. What are the implications of this fact? Are there reasons to be especially concerned about these particular threats?

Studies will often be limited by the methods employed to measure study variables. There are typically many client conditions that could serve as the focus of measurement, but we select certain ones for measurement. What about the ones left out?

Perhaps there are limitations regarding the instrument employed for measurement. Has it been tested for reliability and validity? Does it clearly fit the abstract definition of our dependent variable?

While there will always be a myriad of potential limitations for any given study, the researcher is cautioned against being overly conservative. A little common sense will help. The fact that you may be able to identify eight limitations of your study does not necessarily mean that you cannot take your results seriously. All studies have imperfections. A distinction should be made between imperfections and fatal flaws. The latter would be limitations of a study that render the results more or less useless.

ASSIGNMENT 5-C

Suppose you are testing a support group intervention for social work students which is designed to reduce stress. A stress scale has been given before and after treatment. The scale calls upon the study subject to respond in one of three ways to a list of words describing stress feelings such as "tense" and "uptight" and "anxious." The three responses given were (a) Most or all of the time, (b) Some of the time, and (c) Seldom or never. Each person was asked to indicate how much he or she had been experiencing each feeling during the past several weeks. A score of 2 was given for a response of "Most or all of the time," while a score of 1 was given for "Some of the time" and 0 for "Seldom or never." There were 10 items on the scale; thus, scores could range from a low 0 (a response of "seldom or never" to each of the 10 items) to 20 (a response of "Most or all of the time" to each item).

1. Suppose you tested a group of students and found a mean score of 4.8 at the pretest time. What would be the implications of this finding?

The average respondent had stress pretty seldomly.

_____

_____

2. Suppose you had a pretest mean score of 13.3 and a mean posttest score of 9.1 (t = 2.1; p < .05). Would you say that statistical significance had been achieved?

Yes, the p score is less than .05, therefore it is statistically significant

_____

3. In the above example, would you say that practical significance had been achieved? Explain.

Yes, the results are noteworthy. There was little change, but still was effective.

_____

An Examination of Project PARENTING

In this chapter, you will examine evaluative research through an example. The example deals with the evaluation of a project designed to improve the parenting skills and the home environment of teenage mothers who are still in school and whose children are at risk for child neglect and abuse. The information for this exercise is taken from the following source:

> *Doctor, Cynthia L. (1989). Adolescent Parenting. Professional Paper submitted to the faculty of the School of Social Work, East Carolina University.*

Phase 1: Problem Formulation

The Nature of the Problem

The goals and objectives of Project PARENTING are founded on a knowledge base related to the effects of adolescent parenting on the growth and development of the children as well as the psychological health of the parents.

EXHIBIT 5.4 A Brief Literature Review on Adolescent Parenting

The information in this exhibit is drawn from the Professional Paper of Cynthia Doctor (1989). Used with permission.

The United States has one of the highest teenage birth rates among the developed nations (Southern Regional Project on Infant Mortality, 1988). Over one million teenagers become pregnant each year in the United States, and over one-half million of them give birth (Roosa, 1984). These pregnancies impose an enormous cost physically, emotionally, and morally to the teenagers themselves, and to society as a whole.

Among the problems associated with adolescent pregnancy is a higher incidence of child neglect and abuse, shorter gestational ages, lower birth weights, a higher retardation rate, and a higher frequency of deviant behavior (Broman, 1981). Not only must the baby of the teenager pay such a price, but society pays a price for this problem as well. Approximately one-half of all families receiving public assistance under the Aid to Families with Dependent Children program were begun with a teenage pregnancy (Southern Regional Project on Infant Mortality, 1988).

The typical teenage parent is not ready for the parenting task, having not yet completed all stages of childhood themselves. Such parents are placed into the position of being in a giving role when their adolescent needs have not yet been met. Immature parental responses are common. Among the more common parental deficits is verbal interaction (Osofsky & Osofsky, 1970). Among the most severe consequences is child neglect and abuse.

Project PARENTING is one answer to the problem. It provides training in parenting skills to teenage mothers. Participants in this program have been identified as exhibiting high risk for child maltreatment due to socioeconomic deprivation, living in dysfunctional families, and an especially early age at the onset of parenting.

Causes and Consequences of Adolescent Parenting

Adolescence is a distinct state of development that has its own unique needs and concerns. This state is characterized by the development of a clear and continuing sense of who one is and what one's goals are. Often the social-emotional maturity of adolescents does not lead to appropriate problem solving skills. Compounding this situation is the issue of self-esteem. Adolescents struggle with this issue daily. Persons with low self-esteem are often compelled into early sexual activities as a means of enhancing their esteem.

Not only does the adolescent often engage in early sexual activity in order to gain self-esteem and love from a partner, but it is also speculated that the teenage mother often gets pregnant in order to have a child who will love her because no one else seems willing to do so. But having a child for this purpose is dangerous, because infants are in a highly dependent state and not in a position to be benevolent toward others. The expectation that the child will meet the needs of the mother inevitably leads to disappointment and serves as one of the prime causes of child abuse.

Pregnancy complications very common to adolescent mothers are higher levels of toxemia, anemia bleeding, cervical trauma, and premature delivery. In their study of low-income pregnant teenagers, Osofsky and Osofsky (1970) found that poor nutrition was associated with prolonged labor, delivery complications, prematurity, low birth weight, and mental retardation.

Characteristics of Effective Parenting

Good parenting is often described as warm, consistent care which appropriately anticipates the needs of a child at various stages of development. Being responsive to infant emotional signals

(Continued)

EXHIBIT 5.4 *Continued*

is a critical factor in the facilitation of positive parent-child interaction patterns (Kropp & Haynes, 1987).

Essential to effective parenting are attitudes toward parenting, emotional maturity, and knowledge of child development. Thus, knowledge alone is not sufficient. Unfortunately, many adolescent parents do not have the emotional maturity to serve in this critical role.

Adolescence is a stage in which the individual is rather self-absorbed and not in a good position to be giving to an infant and to engage in self-sacrifice. Furthermore, most teenagers have given little thought to the parenting role. Consequently, they respond spontaneously according to role models they have observed or their own personal needs of the moment. Neither are usually sufficient to guarantee a reasonable effort at parenting.

The Intervention

Project PARENTING is designed to alleviate the negative consequences of adolescent parenting. These consequences include child abuse, poor social and emotional development, and public dependency. The acronym PARENTING stands for Proactive Assessment and Regulation of Environmental Nurturing and Teaching Interventions for Normal Growth. It is an educational program for adolescent mothers with children aged 0 to 3 years.

Project PARENTING focuses on increasing knowledge of child development and child management, enhancing parent-child bonding through positive interaction, and improving the social support of teenage mothers. An effort is made to improve parent-child interaction by assisting the mothers in learning to recognize the emotional signals or cues sent by their children. Thus, sensitivity and consistency are key objects of attention. It is believed that poor parenting among adolescents is caused, in part, by inadequate knowledge of child development, inadequate skill in parent-child interaction, and inadequate parental role models.

Three components comprise the Project PARENTING model. Clients of this program receive classroom instruction, supervised training in a day care setting, and in-home modeling. The classroom instruction is provided in an alternative high school once per week for two hours each session for the six months of the treatment period. The supervised training in the day care setting is provided by having the mother attend day care one half day per week and interact with both the child and the day care staff where staff provide specific instructions in child care. The in-home modeling is provided by having a specially trained child care worker visit the mother in the mother's home twice per month for the six months of the treatment period. In the home, the social worker interacts with the mother and child and provides a model for the mother to follow.

References

Broman, S. (1981). Long-term development of children born to teenagers. In K. Scott, T. Field, & E. Robertson (Eds.), *Teenage parents and their offspring.* New York: Grunne & Stratton (195–225).

Kropp, J. P. & Haynes, O. M. (1987). Abusive and nonabusive mothers' ability to identify general and emotion signals of infants. *Child Development, 58,* 187–190.

Osofsky, H. J. & Osofsky, J. D. (1970). Adolescents as mothers: Results of a program for low-income pregnant teachers with some emphasis upon infant development. *American Journal of Orthopsychiatry, 40* (5), 825–834.

Roosa, M. W. (1984). Short-term effects of teenage parenting programs on knowledge and attitudes. *Adolescence, 19* (75), 659–666.

Southern Regional Project on Infant Mortality. (1988) *Adolescent pregnancy in the south.* Washington, DC.

ASSIGNMENT 5-D

1. How would you label and define the problem addressed by Project PARENTING?

Over 1 million children get pregnant and over ½ million have babies. The prob. is that many adoles. parents do not have the em. maturity to serve in this critical role.

2. Why is this condition considered to be a problem in our society?

There are neg. consequences related to adol. parenting such as: child abuse, poor social & emotional dvp, etc.

3. What are some of the most important causes of this problem?

Adolescents are self-absorbed and often engage in sexual behavior to boost self-esteem and feel loved by someone.

4. What is the broad goal of the intervention (Project PARENTING)?

Project PARENTING is designed to alleviate the neg. consequences of adolescent parenting.

5. What are some of the objectives of this intervention?

focuses on increasing knowledge of child development & child management, etc.

6. How would you describe this intervention in regard to structure?

_____

_____

_____

7. How would you describe this intervention in regard to content?

_____

_____

_____

8. How would you describe this intervention in regard to personnel?

_____

_____

_____

9. What is the rationale for this intervention? In other words, how is it justified as a response to the problem it addresses?

_____

_____

_____

Phase 2: Research Methodology for Project PARENTING

The adolescent mothers who participated in this study were all of the agency's clients who met the following criteria:

1. they participated in this program from June 1986 to January 1989;
2. they were 20 years of age or younger at the time of delivery;
3. they had at least one child aged infancy through three years; and
4. they had been administered the HOME Scale and the Teaching Scale at two points in time that were six months apart, once before treatment and once after six months of treatment.

A total of 17 persons met these criteria and were included in the study.

These 17 adolescent mothers were given instruments to measure their progress (the HOME Scale and the Teaching Scale will be described in the next section) at two points in time which were six months apart. The first administration for each client was immediately before the first service from the program. The second administration for each client was after she had received six months of services. This study includes mothers served over a period of time that covered two and one-half years.

Two types of behavior constituted the focus of treatment: (1) positive parent-child interaction, and (2) positive home environment. Positive parent-child interaction was defined as the extent to which the mother of a child aged birth to three years interacted with the child in such a manner that demonstrated (a) sensitivity to the child's cues, (b) responsiveness to the child's distress, (c) fostering of the child's social-emotional growth, and (d) fostering of the child's cognitive growth. In addition, positive parent-child interaction was viewed as being demonstrated by the child's positive response to the parent.

A positive home environment was defined as one which included the following: (a) a mother who demonstrates emotional and verbal responsivity to the child; (b) avoidance of punishment and restriction; (c) organization of daily activities and freedom from hazards; and (d) variety of stimulation.

Parent-child interaction was measured by the Teaching Scale of the Nursing Child Assessment Training Project of the School of Nursing at the University of Washington. This scale contains a total of 73 questions which are posed in a Yes/No format. These questions are answered by the trained observer who observes the mother's interaction with the child. Among the items on this scale are the following:

1. Parent positions child so child is safely supported.
2. Parent praises child's successes or partial successes.
3. Parent does not yell at the child.
4. Parent describes perceptual qualities of the task materials to the child.

The client is given one point for each response of YES. Because there are 73 items on this scale, the client can receive a score that ranges from a minimum of 0 to a maximum of 73.

Positive home environment was measured by the Home Observation for Measurement of the Environment Scale, better known as the HOME Scale. It is also a part of the Nursing Child Assessment Training Project of the School of Nursing at the University of Washington. The HOME Scale has a total of 45 items in the same format as the Training Scale (i.e., each item is answered as either YES or NO). Thus, the total possible score for this scale is 0 to 45. Among the items on this scale are the following:

1. When mother is away, care is provided by one of three regular substitutes.
2. Child has push or pull toy.
3. Mother reads stories at least three times weekly.

At the time these scales were used for Project PARENTING, the social work student responsible had not been able to locate information on the reliability or validity of these scales. It was noted, however, that these scales had been published and widely used.

ASSIGNMENT 5-E

1. How would you describe the study sample and the study population?

_____

_____

_____

2. Is this an example of a probability sample? What are the implications of your answer?

_____

_____

3. What research design was employed here?

_____

_____

4. What threats to internal validity should have been addressed by the design employed? In other words, what threats should have been considered of special importance, given the nature of the situation in which the intervention was being employed?

_____

_____

_____

5. How well were these threats addressed by the chosen research design?

_____

_____

_____

6. There were two dependent variables in this study. Name them.

a. _____

b. _____

7. What was the abstract definition of the first dependent variable?

8. What was the operational definition of this first dependent variable?

9. What was the abstract definition of the second dependent variable?

10. What was the operational definition of this second dependent variable?

11. State one of the research hypotheses for this study.

12. What difference in score for a typical client on the Teaching Scale do you believe would represent practical significance? In other words how much difference do you believe Project PARENTING should make in the lives of these clients to justify what you believe would probably be the costs of this program?

13. How might either the reliability or validity of the Teaching Scale be assessed?

_____

_____

_____

Phase 3: Analyzing the Data for Project PARENTING

Data on the Teaching Scale and the HOME Scale were collected on each client before entering the training program and again six months later. The training program took place in the interim. Data were also collected on the age of the mother, whether the mother was residing with the family of origin, and the age of the child. These data are presented in Table 5.1 for the Teaching Scale. Data were also collected on clients' pretest and posttest scores on the HOME Scale. These data are presented in Table 5.2.

TABLE 5.1 Pretest and Posttest Scores for Clients on the Teaching Scale and Related Data

Case Number	Pretest Score	Posttest Score	Age of Mother	Age of Child (months)	Residing with Family of Origin
1	37	37	16	1	Yes
2	43	63	16	2	No
3	41	51	18	2	No
4	38	48	14	2	No
5	39	42	17	3	Yes
6	52	38	19	4	No
7	30	36	18	5	No
8	39	44	15	6	No
9	34	53	20	6	Yes
10	49	38	21	8	No
11	54	48	16	9	No
12	57	40	23	10	Yes
13	45	36	14	10	Yes
14	41	50	18	10	No
15	38	41	16	11	Yes
16	41	34	18	15	Yes
17	56	36	16	16	Yes
Mean	43.18	43.23			

Above data taken from Cynthia Doctor's Professional Paper, "Adolescent Parenting." School of Social Work, East Carolina University, 1989. Used with permission.

TABLE 5.2   Pretest and Posttest Scores on the HOME Scale and Selected Data

Case Number	Pretest Score	Posttest Score	Age of Mother	Age of Child (months)	Residing with Family of Origin
1	20	27	16	1	Yes
2	29	34	18	2	No
3	22	37	16	2	No
4	19	21	14	2	No
5	23	25	17	3	Yes
6	22	30	19	4	No
7	21	23	18	5	No
8	26	28	15	6	No
9	25	31	20	6	Yes
10	35	36	21	8	No
11	30	27	16	9	No
12	25	28	23	10	Yes
13	20	32	14	10	Yes
14	17	24	18	10	No
15	21	22	16	11	Yes
16	22	21	18	15	Yes
17	17	21	16	16	Yes
Mean	23.17	27.47			

Above data taken from Cynthia Doctor's Professional Paper, "Adolescent Parenting." School of Social Work, East Carolina University, 1989. Used with permission.

When you analyze data with the one-group pretest-posttest design, you determine whether the mean gain in functioning is greater than 0, the score that would represent no gain at all. For example, if Janet's score on the HOME Scale is 24 before she entered the program and 22 after six months in the program, she would have a negative gain, or more appropriately, a loss rather than a gain in functioning on the behaviors measured by this scale. If her case is typical, the mean gain score for all clients would be a negative number, and there would be no reason to examine the data statistically. You would already know the treatment did not work.

Your task includes determining a gain score for each client, and applying the t test for paired data which will tell you the probability that the difference between the mean gain score and a score of 0 would occur by chance. This procedure is less complicated than most statistical tests. Thus, you will actually compute this statistic for your data using a hand calculator.

This procedure is illustrated on the following pages. First, list the Before score and the After score for each person. Next, calculate the means for both the Before scores and the After scores for all persons. Then, examine these means to see if the After score is greater than the Before score. If this is not true, the procedure stops here and you declare that your data did not support the conclusion that the treatment was effective.

Assuming that the mean After score was greater than the mean Before score, the next step is to subtract the Before score from the After score for each individual in order to determine the GAIN score for each study subject. Subtract the Before score from the After score because you are seeking higher scores on the scale as a demonstration of effective treatment. If the dependent variable had been depression, you would have wanted to see lower scores after treatment rather than higher scores. Thus, you would have subtracted the After score from the Before score to obtain a GAIN score.

Next, a standard deviation is calculated from these GAIN scores. This is employed in the calculation of the standard error which, in turn, is employed in the calculation of the value of t. The value of t is derived by dividing the mean GAIN score by the standard error for these scores. The statistical significance of t is determined by reference to a table of t in a text on statistics.

A Before and After study (one-group pretest-posttest design) would employ a different statistical test if the data were measured at a different level, such as nominal or ordinal. Also, a different type of t test would be employed for data measured at the interval level if it had been drawn from independent samples—that is, data on the HOME scale taken from two different groups (e.g., treatment and comparison groups).

These procedures are outlined in Exhibit 5.5. A worksheet for calculating the value of t is given in Exhibit 5.6. You will need to make duplicate copies of this in order to complete the assignments that follow. It is suggested that you reserve Exhibit 5.6 for making copies only, rather than completing any of your work in this exhibit. In this way, you will have a clean copy of this worksheet for future use.

EXHIBIT 5.5   Procedures for Calculating the Value of t When Paired Data are Employed

1. Enter the posttest (AFTER) score for each subject in column 1 and the pretest (BEFORE) score in column 2 and enter the difference (GAIN) in column 3. Note that you will have a negative GAIN score if the pretest score is greater than the posttest score.

2. Calculate the mean for all GAIN scores by, first, adding together all positive GAIN scores and adding together all negative GAIN scores and subtracting the negative total from the positive total to derive a grand total for all GAIN scores. Divide the grand total by N (the total number of persons for whom you have pretest and posttest scores). This is your mean GAIN score.

3. Enter the mean GAIN score in column 4 and subtract the GAIN score from the mean score for each subject. Enter this difference in column 5.

    Remember: if you have a negative GAIN score to subtract from the mean and the mean is a positive score, you will be adding two negative numbers which means that you add the absolute value and assign the negative sign. For example, the difference between a GAIN score of −1 and a mean of +3 would be −4 because −1 is 4 points less than +3. In the example given below, the mean for all gain scores is 4.2.

1 AFTER		2 BEFORE		3 GAIN		4 MEAN		5 DEVIATION
20	−	23	=	−3	−	4.2	=	−7.2
23	−	20	=	3	−	4.2	=	−1.2
27	−	21	=	6	−	4.2	=	1.8

EXHIBIT 5.5 *Continued*

4. Square the deviation score in column 5 and enter this figure in column 6. Remember that a negative score becomes a positive score whenever it is squared. Thus, all values in column 6 will be positive.

5. Sum all scores in column 6. This is your SUM OF SQUARES.

6. Calculate the STANDARD DEVIATION of GAIN scores by dividing the SUM OF SQUARES by N (the number in the sample) and taking the square root of that figure.

7. Calculate the STANDARD ERROR of GAIN scores by dividing the STANDARD DEVIATION by the square root of N.

8. Calculate the value of t by dividing the mean GAIN score by the STANDARD ERROR.

The value of p (probability of chance) can be determined by examining a table in a text on statistics. With the pretest-posttest design, we will use the one-tailed values of t for determining the value of p. With a sample of 5, a t of 2.13 would be significant at the .05 level. A t of 1.83 would be significant with a sample of 10. For our data (N = 17), we need a t of 1.75 or higher in order to achieve significance at this level (.05).

EXHIBIT 5.6 **Worksheet for Calculating the Value of p for Paired Data**

Step 1: Calculate the Sum of Squares

	1 After Score		2 Before Score		3 Gain Score		4 Mean Gain Score		5 Deviation Score		6 Deviation Score Squared
1	_____	–	_____	=	_____	–	_____	=	_____		_____
2	_____	–	_____	=	_____	–	_____	=	_____		_____
3	_____	–	_____	=	_____	–	_____	=	_____		_____
4	_____	–	_____	=	_____	–	_____	=	_____		_____
5	_____	–	_____	=	_____	–	_____	=	_____		_____
6	_____	–	_____	=	_____	–	_____	=	_____		_____
7	_____	–	_____	=	_____	–	_____	=	_____		_____
8	_____	–	_____	=	_____	–	_____	=	_____		_____
9	_____	–	_____	=	_____	–	_____	=	_____		_____
10	_____	–	_____	=	_____	–	_____	=	_____		_____

(Continued)

EXHIBIT 5.6 *Continued*

	1 After Score	2 Before Score	3 Gain Score	4 Mean Gain Score	5 Deviation Score	6 Deviation Score Squared
11	_____	− _____	= _____	− _____	= _____	_____
12	_____	− _____	= _____	− _____	= _____	_____
13	_____	− _____	= _____	− _____	= _____	_____
14	_____	− _____	= _____	− _____	= _____	_____
15	_____	− _____	= _____	− _____	= _____	_____
16	_____	− _____	= _____	− _____	= _____	_____
17	_____	− _____	= _____	− _____	= _____	_____

TOTAL OF ALL GAIN SCORES = _____ / _____(N) = _____   _____   _____
                                                                 (Mean)   (Sum)*

(Enter mean in Column 4)

*The sum of the figures in Column 6 constitutes the Sum of Squares which is used in the next step.

Step 2: Calculate the Standard Deviation for GAIN Scores

The standard deviation is the square root of the sum of squares divided by the total number in the sample (N).

SUM OF SQUARES = _____ / _____ (N) = _____ which has a square root of _____
                                                                    Standard deviation

Step 3: Calculate the Standard Error

The standard error is the standard deviation divided by the square root of N.

Standard Deviation of GAIN Scores = _____ / _____   = _____
                                         (square root of N)   Standard Error

Step 4: Calculate the value of t

The value of t is calculated by dividing the mean GAIN score by the standard error.

Mean GAIN Score   = _____ / _____   = _____
                           (Standard error)   This is t

Step 5: Determine the Statistical Significance of t.

The value of p (probability of chance) can be determined by examination of a table in a text on statistics. With the pretest-posttest design, we will use the one-tailed values of t for determining the value of p because we have a directional hypothesis. With a sample of 5, a t of 2.13 would be significant at the .05 level. A t of 1.83 would be significant with a sample of 10. For our data (N = 17), we need a t of 1.75 or higher in order to achieve significance at this level (.05).

ASSIGNMENT 5-F

1. What was the mean BEFORE score for the Teaching Scale?

   _____

2. What was the mean AFTER score for the Teaching Scale?

   _____

3. What was the mean GAIN score for the Teaching Scale?

   _____

4. Was there a statistically significant gain on the Teaching Scale? Discuss.

   _____

   _____

5. What was the mean BEFORE score for the HOME Scale?

   _____

6. What was the mean AFTER score for the HOME Scale?

   _____

7. What was the mean GAIN score for the HOME Scale?

   _____

8. Was there a statistically significant gain on the HOME Scale? Discuss.

   _____

   _____

Phase 4: Drawing Conclusions About Project PARENTING

Now that you have examined the data, you are ready to draw conclusions about the results. You will recall that several points were made earlier about drawing conclusions in evaluative research studies. Some of the things to consider in the conclusions section of such a report are the following:

1. What was the purpose of the study? What were you attempting to find out?
2. Briefly, how did you attempt to achieve this purpose? In other words, who was included in the study, how were the dependent variables defined and measured, and what research design was employed? (This should be very concise. Don't repeat the entire methodology section.)
3. Did you find a statistically significant gain in functioning in regard to the dependent variables?
4. Can you declare practical significance? In other words, do you conclude that the intervention was effective? What is the basis for this conclusion?
5. What were some of the limitations of the study in regard to issues such as the validity of the means for measuring study variables, the potential that the findings can be generalized to populations of persons not included in the study, and so forth?

A conclusion section of a report of a hypothetical study is presented in Exhibit 5.7. In this study, the effectiveness of a public awareness campaign regarding child abuse is examined. Review this exhibit before addressing the questions in the final assignment.

EXHIBIT 5.7   A Summary Section of a Hypothetical Study

The purpose of the study reported in this paper was to examine the effectiveness of the Child Protection Campaign of Hope County in the enhancement of the number of abused children identified for protection by the protective services system. The Public Awareness Campaign included 12 public service announcements aired on one TV station and 84 such announcements aired on 6 radio stations. It also included the presentation of talks on child abuse to 17 different civic organizations and 5 professional organizations in Hope County. This program lasted for six months. While the short-term objective of this effort was to enhance the number of children identified for protection, the broad goal was to reduce the incidence of child abuse.

The number of children confirmed as abused by the protective services program of the Hope County Department of Social Services served as the measure of success for this program. The number confirmed as abused before the initiation was compared to the number confirmed as abused at the completion of this six-month effort. This gain in number of abused children identified for protection was compared to the same figure for Walker County, a neighboring county with similar demographics. The monthly mean number of confirmed abuse cases in the six months preceding this program for Hope County was 12.4 as compared to a mean of 17.6 during the six months of the campaign. The mean gain of 5.2 additional children identified for protection for Hope County was compared to a mean gain of 1.3 for Walker County, a difference that was found to be statistically significant ($t = 4.3$; $p < .01$).

An improvement from about 12 children identified per month to about 17 identified for protection is considered to be of practical significance. One may even argue that one additional child identified for protection would be of practical significance. But we must consider the allocation of resources when considering practical significance. There are always many alternatives for achieving the goal of a social program. Perhaps these resources could have been better placed elsewhere. But herein lies one of the major strengths of this effort. It achieved its

(Continued)

EXHIBIT 5.7 *Continued*

gain with a minimum of resources because much of the effort was voluntary. The public service announcements cost the agency nothing except for the time of certain staff in overseeing the effort. The public speeches also were of minimal expense.

One of the limitations of this study lies in our ability to generalize these findings to others. The data from these two counties do not constitute a probability sample of a larger population of persons; thus, we must generalize with caution. Perhaps of most importance is the limitation that relates to the measured accomplishments of this study with the overall goal, which was to reduce the incidence of child abuse in Hope County. For this goal to be achieved, the protective service system must provide effective service to those children identified. The present study only dealt with that component of the system which identifies children for protection.

One of the strengths of this study lies in the research design employed. Because the results of the campaign in Hope County were compared to data from a similar county without such a campaign, several of the bases for challenging the validity of the findings were addressed. Perhaps the most important threat to internal validity to be addressed in this study was that of history. It is quite possible for there to be changes in the environment that would have naturally changed the incidence of reports of child abuse independent of the Child Protection Campaign. If data had only been collected in Hope County, we would have had no basis for addressing the possibility that the environment changed in some way that led people to be more likely to report cases of abuse. While this is still a possible explanation for the findings, it is not likely to serve as a solid explanation in view of the fact that data were compared to another community where environmental changes were just as likely to happen.

ASSIGNMENT 5-G

Write your own conclusions section for a report of the study of Project PARENTING.

References

Campbell, D. T. & Stanley, J. C. (1963). *Experimental and quasi-experimental designs for research.* Boston: Houghton Mifflin.

York, R. O. (1997). *Building basic competencies in social work research.* Boston: Allyn and Bacon, 220–257.

C h a p t e r **6**

Conducting Evaluative Research Using the Single-Subject Design

In this chapter, you will examine some hypothetical data from a few clients of Project PARENTING. You will employ the AB single-subject research design in this exercise. There will not be a restatement of the problem, the treatment objectives, the intervention, or the instruments for measuring the dependent variables because they are the same for this exercise as the one in the previous chapter. The research design will be different. Instead of the one-group pretest-posttest design, you will examine the single-subject design.

At the completion of this chapter, you will be able to identify the sequence of steps in the use of the AB single-subject research design, identify the strengths and limitations of this design, and undertake the analysis of data when this design is employed. Given a set of data, you will be able to (1) determine whether the data are appropriate for statistical analysis, (2) determine the method of statistical analysis for the data, if one is appropriate, and (3) apply two simple approaches to statistical analysis.

Overview of Single-Subject Designs

In the previous chapter, you examined various group research designs and applied one of these to a set of data regarding Project PARENTING. The group research design employs data from several clients. In contrast, the single-subject design employs repeated measurements of the dependent variable for a single subject. The single subject can be an individual client, or a community, or an organization, or some other entity, providing that the entity is treated as a single subject for data analysis. For example, you might want to reduce the absenteeism rate for an organization by using a job enrichment program. You could collect data on the absenteeism rate for this one organization at several points in time before and during the program as a means of evaluating the effectiveness of this program.

Most social workers, of course, will employ the single-subject design for evaluating the effectiveness of a chosen treatment for a single client. You could use this design for several clients if you analyzed the data individually. The point is that the data analysis focuses on a single subject where repeated measurements of the dependent variable have been taken.

The first several steps in the use of the single-subject design are similar to the use of the group design. For both types of designs, you must select the client, analyze the client's problem, determine the treatment objective, determine the methods to be used to measure client progress, and select an intervention. A key distinction is the collection of repeated measurements of the dependent variable when you employ the single-subject design.

One of the major advantages of the single-subject design is that the treatment can be altered during the treatment phase of the study. While the basic single-subject design illustrated in this chapter does not call for an alteration of the treatment, there are single-subject designs that provide for this change.

The single-subject design holds much promise for the clinical social worker who is assigned individual cases with varying problems and treatment alternatives. The group design requires that a group of clients receive the same intervention for the same treatment objective with a common means for measuring progress. With the single-subject design, you can tailor the treatment and the objective and the measurement of progress to the individual client.

Interpreting the Nomenclature

There are a variety of single-subject research designs. These include the AB design, the B design, the ABA design, the ABC design, and the ABAB design. With each of the designations, the letter A refers to a baseline period during which the client is repeatedly measured on the dependent variable but is *not* receiving treatment. All other letters refer to treatment periods, with B representing the first treatment, or the only treatment, and C representing a second treatment given after a period of time in which the client was receiving the treatment labeled as B.

The B design means that the client was not measured on the dependent variable before treatment began; thus, there was not a baseline. The AB design means that the client was measured repeatedly before treatment began and received only one type of treatment. The ABC design means that a client was measured during a baseline (Phase A), during the first treatment (the B phase), and was given a second treatment (the C phase). The ABAB design means that the client was measured on the dependent variable during a baseline (A) before treatment began, was offered a given treatment (B), was withdrawn from treatment but measurements continued (the second A phase, or baseline), and had the same treatment reinstated (the second B phase).

The AB single-subject design will serve as the primary focus of this chapter. Information on a set of hypothetical clients of Project PARENTING will be used for analysis. After this exercise, some of the other single-subject designs will be discussed.

ASSIGNMENT 6-A

1. The problem that is being addressed by the intervention employed by Project PARENTING is as follows:

   pg 146

2. One of the components (activities) of the intervention is as follows:

3. One of the objectives of this intervention is as follows:

4. The means for measuring client progress regarding this objective (refer to the question above) is as follows:

5. Regarding this means of measuring client progress, what difference in scores between pretreatment and intervention would you say would constitute practical significance?

6. The ABCD single-subject research design has how many different interventions?

   Three

7. The B single-subject research design has how many baselines?

The AB Single-Subject Research Design

A major limitation of the one-group pretest-posttest design for evaluating social work practice is that there is no attempt to control for maturation as an alternative explanation for the cause of behavior change. People grow over time without social work intervention. Perhaps the growth measured in a study using this design could be explained simply by maturation.

One method of taking maturation into consideration is to employ a comparison group or a control group. The growth measured for the treatment group can be compared to the growth measured for the other group to determine the extent to which one can rule out maturation as the reason the client improved.

AB Single-Subject Design Addresses Maturation

Another method is to employ one of the single-subject designs which include a baseline of measurements of the client's behavior before treatment begins. If the subject has tended not to experience growth during a baseline period prior to treatment, it is easier to make the case that the progress measured during the treatment period was due to the treatment itself rather than maturation. If there is growth during the baseline period, this pattern can be taken into consideration in the analysis of the data. In single-subject data analysis, we are examining whether the client progress, as measured in the study, is superior to the trend that was underway during the baseline period. If maturation is influencing the client's progress, this is taken into consideration.

AB Design Addresses Testing Threat

The AB single-subject design also addresses a number of other threats to internal validity. One of these is known as *testing*, the tendency of persons to change their response to the measurement device because of the effects of repeated measurements. An individual may, for example, remember previous responses and try to be consistent or to look better by giving certain responses which may not be accurate reflections of their conditions. If a person is vulnerable to this tendency, it should be evident from the baseline trend during which they are being tested.

AB Design Does Not Address History

A threat to internal validity (or an alternative explanation for the client's change) that is not addressed by the AB single-subject design is that of *history*. It is possible that something has changed in the client's environment during the treatment period that explains the change, rather than the treatment. With the AB single-subject design, we have no method for considering this explanation for the client's growth. A design that does a better job of dealing with history as a threat to internal validity is the comparison group design, because it is assumed that changes in the environment for two such groups of people during the same time period would be common for the two groups. The ABAB single-subject design would also address this threat because it is highly improbable that instrumental changes in the client's environment would occur only during the two treatment periods yet not influence the client's behavior during either of the two baseline periods.

AB Design Procedure

The procedure for the AB single-subject design is as follows:

1. Select a client for treatment. This constitutes the sample.
2. Define and analyze the problem that the intervention (treatment) should address.
3. Develop the objectives of intervention.
4. Select an intervention.
5. Select a means of measuring the client's progress regarding the treatment objective (i.e., the dependent variable).
6. Collect data on the dependent variable during a baseline period which takes place prior to intervention.
7. Introduce the intervention and continue to measure the dependent variable on a continual basis during the intervention period.
8. Analyze the data by comparing the data during the treatment period to the trend that was displayed during the baseline period. Is the pattern of data during the treatment period significantly better than the pattern that would have been predicted by the baseline trend?

This chapter refers to the previous chapter for the first five steps. The AB single-subject design has already been selected; thus, you will pick up with step 6 in this chapter and examine some hypothetical data regarding clients of Project PARENTING.

Measuring Client Behavior During a Baseline Period

This step in the research process involves the repeated measuring of the client's behavior during a baseline period, the period of time immediately before treatment begins. The purpose of this task is to determine trends in the client's target behavior. This is helpful in interpreting the results of intervention. The trend that is displayed in the baseline period is projected into the treatment period and represents what is believed to be the client's status in the absence of treatment. For example, if a client's score for depression was 30 for each baseline period (an unlikely event), you can easily see that the score of 30 would be projected into the treatment period and the treatment recordings would be compared to this trend to see if they were significantly better.

Baseline Recordings

The baseline recordings of target behavior are placed on a chart such as the one illustrated in the examples in Exhibit 6.1. You can see from Example A that the client's score for self-esteem was 10 for week 1 of the baseline period and moved to 20 at week 2. The scale for the client's behavior is listed on the side of the chart (the vertical axis) while the time periods are presented across the bottom (the horizontal axis). The recordings represent the intersection of a time period and a score on the scale. The time periods can be daily, weekly, monthly, or some other period of time, provided the interval is equal between each time period that is displayed across the bottom. For example, you would not have the client's first three time periods on the chart be daily while the second three were weekly.

Ideally, the baseline recording of target behaviors should take place several times before intervention begins, and the number of baseline recordings should be roughly equal to the number of treatment recordings. While this may be feasible for the experienced researcher who is placing major focus on research, it is not often feasible for the average social worker. The best opportunity for this kind of data for the baseline is the situation in which the social worker is employed in an institution that is routinely collecting data that can serve as a measure of client progress. A school is a good example because it is routine for schools to keep records on absences, number of disciplinary actions, grades, and so forth. If these can be used as measures of client progress regarding the treatment objectives, the social worker could begin the intervention right away and use past data as the baseline. For such lucky persons, the information given later on the more sophisticated means of data analysis will be useful. At the present time in this text, we will examine a simple means for data analysis.

Six recordings of target behavior are recommended in order to obtain a good measure of the trends in target behavior. However, I consider four recordings to be minimally sufficient to consider the data to represent a trend. It is important to employ professional judgment in determining the minimum number of such recordings. The idea is to obtain a reliable trend in client behavior that can be projected into the future. If the client's baseline trend is not a good predictor of future behavior (in the absence of treatment), you have no reason to employ it in the analysis of the treatment effectiveness. If you do not find it feasible to collect as many as four baseline recordings, you may want to employ a modified form of the AB design in which you record behavior before treatment in such as way as to give you confidence that it is a valid means of projecting the client's behavior into the future. I will discuss this alternative in the data analysis section to follow.

Analyzing Baseline Recordings

The trends during baseline should be analyzed. Several questions are considered in this analysis.

1. Are these valid scores of the client's target behavior?
2. Is this pattern of scores a good basis for predicting the client's progress without treatment?
3. Does this pattern suggest that treatment is warranted?

The clinician might give a client a depression scale in which the client's score is clearly not representative of the client's level of depression as observed in the clinical interview. Sometimes clients respond to scales according to what they want to be rather than what they really are. A lack of congruence between scale scores and clinical observation should normally be interpreted as evidence that the score is not valid. It is possible that the clinician is not correct. However, the absence of congruence between clinical observations and scale scores means that one or both of these two means of observation is not valid. Thus, incongruence should cast doubt upon the scale as a valid measure of client conditions.

The purpose of recording behavior during the baseline period is to estimate the likelihood of client progress in the absence of treatment. The client's progress during the treatment phase should be superior to this estimate in order for us to believe that treatment made a difference for the client. Thus, a second question is whether the recordings during the baseline period serve as a good basis for this prediction. Again, you must employ clinical judgment. You may have reason to believe that the client's condition moved at a more rapid pace than it is likely to do in the future.

Problematic Baseline Trends

Two types of trends are not amenable to statistical analysis. One of these is when the measurements of the dependent variable are fluctuating wildly from one measurement to another, as illustrated by Example A in Exhibit 6.1. This client's scores for self-esteem are fluctuating from 10 to 20 to 12 to 24 to 14 to 22. This is a rather unstable trend and is difficult to extend into the treatment period. Thus, you may be well advised to abandon the examination of statistical significance with these data.

Another trend that does not lend itself to statistical analysis is the one in which the client's behavior appears to be progressing at such a pace as to reach the ceiling of the scale

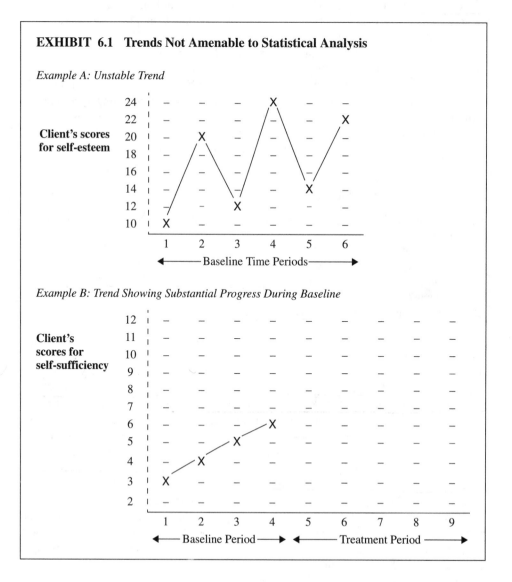

EXHIBIT 6.1   Trends Not Amenable to Statistical Analysis

Example A: Unstable Trend

Client's scores for self-esteem

Example B: Trend Showing Substantial Progress During Baseline

Client's scores for self-sufficiency

before treatment ends. Let's assume that the highest score one could receive for self-sufficiency was 12. In Example B in Exhibit 6.1, the client's scores started at 3 for week 1 but moved to 4 for week 2, then 5, and then 6. We collect these data in order to project a trend into the treatment period. If we extent this trend into the treatment period, we will project a trend of 7 for week 5, a score of 8 for week 6, a score of 9 for week 7, 10 for week 8, and 11 for week 9, the last week of the treatment period. In other words, the client is projected to move to a score within one point of the maximum for this scale by the last week of the treatment period, and this is what we expect to happen in the *absence* of treatment! What difference in this pattern could we reasonably expect treatment to make? Practically none! So, we had better select a different treatment objective, select a different means of measuring client progress, or determine that this client does not need treatment because he or she is making reasonable progress on his or her own.

Baseline Trends

In both of the examples depicted in Exhibit 6.1, the use of statistical analysis of data is problematic. In such instances, it may be advisable to continue the baseline period or abandon the idea of statistical analysis of the data. In the case of the unstable baseline, an extended baseline period may produce a period of stability which can better serve as a predictor of the client's behavior during the treatment period in the absence of treatment. In the second case, the client's growth may stabilize rather than continue to grow toward the maximum level of functioning.

The trends illustrated in Exhibit 6.1 are ascending (i.e., moving upward). In cases where the trend is either ascending or descending, we extend the line that has begun during the baseline period, into the treatment period. The recordings of client behavior during the treatment period are placed on the chart and this pattern is compared to the projected pattern. The treatment is considered effective if it shows a trend that is significantly better than the baseline projection.

Another type of trend during baseline is one that is level, that is, neither ascending nor descending. For example, the number of fights between father and son may be recorded during a baseline period as 7 one week, 8 the next, 7 the next, 9 the next and 8 the final week.

ASSIGNMENT 6-B

1. The AB single-subject research design is superior to the one-group pretest-posttest research design in that the AB design, unlike the one-group pretest-posttest design, addresses which one or ones of the following threat(s) to internal validity?

   a. Maturation   **b.** ~~History~~   **c.** Testing

   Explain how this is so.

   Testing/maturation – baseline testing can set maturation pattern or lack of it. Testing – baseline shows tendency

2. The purpose of charting the baseline data is: *determine trends*

    a. To apply clinical judgment to the validity of the scale used to measure client progress.

    b. To test the suitability of employing the chosen instrument as a measure of client progress.

    c. To determine the extent to which the client appears to need treatment on the chosen behavior.

    d. To develop a basis for predicting the client's behavior during the treatment period.

    e. All of the above.

    f. None of the above.

3. In previous discussions of explanatory research, the definition and analysis of the problem being addressed by the study was the first major step in the research process. After this step came such steps as selecting the sample, determining how variables will be measured, collecting data, and so forth. Is there a difference between this sequence of steps and the sequence when the AB single-subject research is normally used by the social worker? Explain.

Sample exists first. Problem, measurement choice, collection of data

4. Let's suppose the following charts are for self-esteem scores from a scale that can range from 0 to 30. Comment on each of these trends regarding its suitability for statistical analysis.

baselines

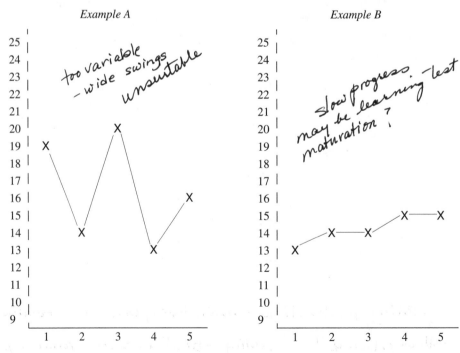

Example A — *too variable – wide swings unsuitable*

Example B — *slow progress – test may be learning? maturation?*

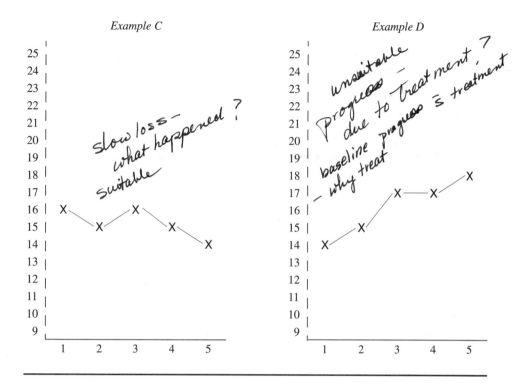

Continued Recording During Treatment Period

The measurement of target behavior continues throughout treatment. If the trend during the baseline period is going up or down, it is important that the measurements during the treatment period are recorded on a graph with the same time periods as the baseline. For example, if you asked your client to record his or her behavior each day for a week as the baseline, you will need to record all behaviors, both baseline and treatment, on a chart that is organized by day rather than week.

You should remember that you are projecting the baseline into the future. If the trend is going either up or down and you have measured this trend by the day rather than by the week, the only valid projection from this baseline would be one in which you projected it into the future by days. It is not imperative, however, that the client's behavior be recorded each day during the treatment period. While it is not optimal, there may be circumstances in which it is acceptable for recordings to be on days 14, 21, 28, and so forth. This may be appropriate if the client had been measured on the dependent variable daily for one week before treatment and received treatment once weekly for a period thereafter. The client's behavior during the treatment period could be recorded once per week. These circumstances, however, are not optimal. It would be imperative for the researcher to have good reason to believe that the daily recordings constituted a valid prediction of the client's behavior for the treatment period if treatment had not been available.

Analyzing the Data

When you analyze data in evaluative research, you must consider both practical significance and statistical significance.

Practical Significance

Practical significance is a matter of professional judgment. The question is whether the amount of client progress is noteworthy. Is it enough for us to feel that our intervention was successful? In the previous chapter, you were asked to consider how much of an improvement in scores on the two instruments would constitute practical significance. You may recall that this question was posed to you before you examined the actual data from the study. In determining how much progress is sufficient, you should not be biased by the actual results of the study. It is natural for us to want to believe that our intervention was successful, but we must not lose our objectivity when examining our data.

If your data fail to pass the test of practical significance, you have less reason to address statistical significance. It is possible to have statistical significance in the absence of practical significance. Such a situation tells us nothing more than the fact that our client's trivial gain in functioning cannot easily be explained by chance. In other words, we can be confident that our treatment really did have a trivial effect upon the client's condition.

Statistical Significance

If you have evidence for practical significance, you should consider statistical significance. This issue is somewhat problematic in the evaluation of single-subject data, because of the small sample of data that are normally collected. The fewer the items of data collected, the less likely you are to achieve statistical significance. Another complication is that such data are drawn from related samples, whereas many of the most useful statistical techniques are designed for data drawn from independent samples. I will discuss this issue later.

Two major statistical measures are prominently used with single-subject research data. One employs the binomial test, while the other uses the standard deviation.

Binomial Test

The **binomial test** is rather simple—it tells us whether a distribution of scores in two categories is significantly different from the distribution that is expected to occur by chance (e.g., a 50–50 split of scores into the two categories). When you draw a line projecting the client's scores from the baseline into the treatment period, you would normally expect half of these treatment scores to be above the line and the other half to be below the line, in the absence of treatment. One of the situations in which the binomial test can be used is when the client's scores during the baseline period are all the same. This score would represent what you would expect the client's scores to be during the period of time that treatment is being offered if the treatment had no effect whatsoever.

In the example below, suppose you wished to enhance the self-esteem of an adolescent in an inpatient treatment program. You have measured the client's self-esteem once each day for six days prior to his entry into treatment. You will continue to measure his self-esteem during the six days of treatment and compare the treatment scores to the baseline scores. The client received a score of 3 each day that the self-esteem scale was administered during the baseline period. Thus, you would expect this trend to continue in the absence of treatment.

Scores for
Self-esteem

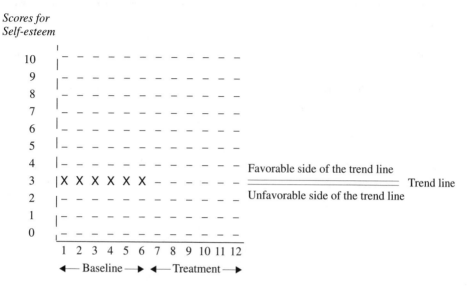

You will measure the client's self-esteem each day during the six-day treatment period. You expect his scores to be better than 3. If one-half of his scores during treatment were 4 and one-half were 2, you would have one-half of his scores above the trend line and one-half below the trend line. This would be clear evidence of the absence of effectiveness because this is the trend you would expect in the absence of treatment. But what if you have 4 scores above the line and 2 below? This is better than 3 above and 3 below, but is it *significantly* better than the 50–50 split? This is where the binomial test comes into play. In this particular situation, all six of the treatment recordings would have to be above the trend line in order for you to declare statistical significance.

In the above example, I used the binomial test where a 50–50 split was assumed to exist in the treatment period in the absence of treatment. This would not likely be true, however, if you recorded the dependent variable as either YES or NO because you would normally be measuring a problematic behavior which the client exhibited a large proportion of the time. For example, you might find that the client's behavior fell into the NO category 4 out of the 5 times it was recorded in the baseline period. In this case, you would expect the same trend in the treatment period in the absence of treatment. This display of baseline recordings would change the number of favorable recordings during the treatment period that would demonstrate statistical significance. More about the details of this later.

Standard Deviation

The **standard deviation** approach is employed when the data during the baseline is rather level, meaning that there is not a notable trend upward or downward. With this approach, you calculate the mean of the baseline recordings and draw a line that represents this score into the treatment period. This is the client's projected trend in the absence of treatment. To achieve statistical significance, your treatment recordings must do more than be better than this mean—they must be *significantly* better than this mean. If they are not significantly better than this baseline mean, you have data that can too easily be explained by chance rather than data that supports the effectiveness of the intervention. To determine if the mean of treatment recordings is significantly better than the baseline mean, you calculate the standard deviation of the baseline data, multiply this by 2, and add this figure to the baseline mean. The result of this computation tells you the treatment mean that you must have in order to achieve statistical significance at the .05 level.

Analyzing Data When the Baseline Trend Is Level

The standard deviation approach is employed in situations where the trend in the baseline period is level rather than ascending or descending. A level trend does not mean the data must form a straight line. (In fact, if the data forms a straight line, you cannot employ this method, because it depends on the analysis of variance within the scores during the baseline period.) A level trend means the measurements during the baseline period are not going gradually up or down. This approach requires that data be measured at the interval level, although ordinal measurement is sometimes considered to be acceptable.

To achieve statistical significance, your treatment mean must be greater than the figure that represents two standard deviations better than the baseline mean. Whether better means higher or lower is determined by whether you are trying to increase the target behavior or reduce it. In the example below, assume we are charting self-esteem scores for a client. Because higher scores on this scale indicate higher self-esteem, we wish to increase these scores. The baseline trend is level. The mean for the baseline is 13.5 (12 + 13 + 14 + 15 = 54 / 4 = 13.5). The standard deviation for these scores is 1.1; thus, the treatment mean must be better than 15.7 in order for the data to be statistically significant (13.5 + 1.1 + 1.1 = 15.7).

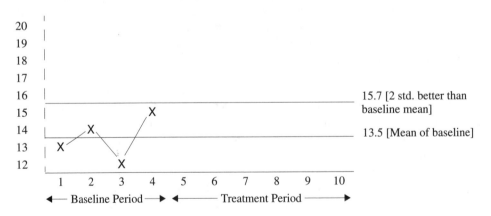

The standard deviation approach requires knowledge of how to calculate the standard deviation. A worksheet for calculating the standard deviation of GAIN scores was used in the previous exercise on the evaluation of the effectiveness of Project PARENTING. For your convenience, the procedures for calculating the standard deviation are given in Exhibit 6.5. Note that there is no BEFORE and AFTER score to be considered. In the previous exercise, the standard deviation was calculated only from the GAIN scores, just as it will be calculated below on the regular scores.

Analyzing Data When the Trend Is Going Up or Down

Behavior sometimes changes without treatment. A client may be improving, or regressing, as a natural course of life events when treatment is not available. When the client's scores on the target behavior are exhibiting a trend that is going up or down, you should use the **celeration line approach** to the statistical analysis of single-subject data. With this approach, you use the baseline recordings of target behavior to draw a slanted line into the treatment period which represents your best estimate of the client's scores during the intervention period in the *absence* of treatment. In other words, this is the trend that represents no treatment. You will compare the actual data in the treatment period to this trend line to see if the intervention was effective.

In the following example, assume that you wish to increase the client's scores for self-esteem on a scale that ranges from a low of 0 to a high of 20. Scores below 10 are considered indicative of a person with a self-esteem problem. In this example, we can see that the client's scores for self-esteem during the baseline went from 3 to 2 to 4 to 4 to 5, and, finally, to a score of 6 for the last baseline recording. If we project this trend into the treatment period, we would draw a line that reaches a score of 10 by the 12th time period (the sixth recording during the treatment period).

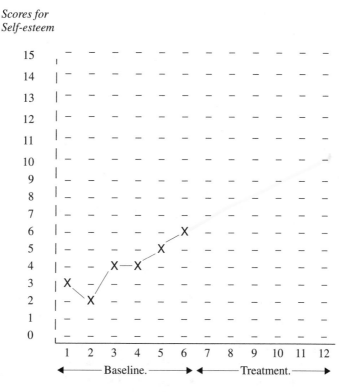

Thus, you would expect the client to reach a score of 10 by the completion of the treatment period without treatment. You would add your treatment period data to the above and determine if those scores represented a significantly better improvement in self-esteem than that which was predicted.

The effectiveness of treatment would be supported to the extent that the scores during the treatment period were superior to the trend line. But how much better must they be in order to be *significantly* better than the trend line? For examining statistical significance, you can employ the binomial test with the data. The binomial test reveals whether the distribution of scores between two categories is significant. In the present example, you would expect an equal distribution of scores above and below the trend line if the treatment makes no difference. This is what you would expect in the absence of treatment. If you have 6 treatment recordings, you would expect 3 to be above the line and 3 to be below the line in the absence of treatment. A distribution of scores during this period that was 4 above the line and 2 below the line would be better than this projected data, but it would not be significantly better because this distribution would occur by chance fairly often. In fact, you would need for all six of your treatment recordings to be superior to the trend line in order to declare statistical significance at the .05 level. If you had measured the client on the dependent variable 8 times during the treatment period, you could declare statistical significance if 7 of the 8 recordings were superior to the trend line. Determining statistical significance with the binomial test for various distributions of scores requires consultation with a statistical table. I will discuss how to determine statistical significance with the binomial test later in this chapter.

Drawing the Trend Line

How do you draw the trend line? There is a very simple method for drawing the trend line. You divide the baseline into two halves and compute the mean of each half and draw a line which connects these two mean scores. First, compute the mean of the first half. Next, place a mark at the midway point of the first half which represents the mean of that half. Do the same for the second half: compute the mean of the second half and place a mark at the midway point of the second half which represents this mean score. Place a ruler on the page so that you connect these two marks and draw a line extending throughout the treatment period.

In the example shown at the top of page 175, the mean of the first half was 3 (3 + 2 + 4 = 9 / 3 = 3) while the mean for the second half was 5 (4 + 5 + 6 = 15 / 3 = 5). A mark was placed at the score of 3 for time period 2 (the midpoint of the first half of the baseline) and at the score of 5 at time period 5 (the midpoint of the second half). These dots were connected with a ruler and a line was drawn into the treatment period.

Time Periods—Warning

Warning! Be sure that the time periods for the baseline and treatment recordings are uniform. If you measure the client daily for the baseline, you must use a set of time periods on your chart that represent days rather than weeks or some other time period. For example, suppose you measure the client's target behavior once daily for a week for the baseline and provide treatment once per week for six weeks, with treatment recordings taken once per week. This is not an optimal approach to data analysis, but it may be the best that you can do under the circumstances. If so, you will need to record both the baseline and treatment scores on a chart that has days at the bottom throughout both the baseline and treatment periods. Your

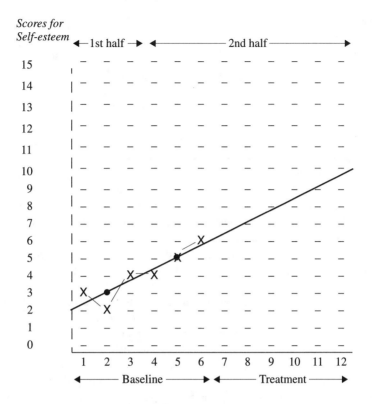

chart will be a little different because it will contain treatment recordings only during every seventh day during the treatment period. In this example, you would have a chart with 49 time periods at the bottom because you have a total of seven weeks between the baseline and treatment periods.

Analyzing Data When Progress Is Measured in Only Two Categories

The standard deviation approach to statistical analysis is appropriate when the dependent variable (the target behavior) is measured at the interval level. The celeration line approach can be employed if the dependent variable is measured at either the interval or ordinal levels. Sometimes, however, the client's target behavior is measured as either Yes or No. For example, you may be measuring a troubled adolescent's behavior at school according to whether there was or was not a citation for disciplinary action in a given week. During the baseline, you may have data which reveals that there was at least one citation for disciplinary action for weeks 1, 2, 4, 5, 7, 8, 9, and 10 but not for weeks 3 and 6. Thus, the answer is "Yes" for 8 of these 10 weeks and "No" for the other 2 weeks. These data are illustrated at the top of p. 176.

Suppose you implement a treatment and wish to know if the number of citations for disciplinary action was significantly lower during the treatment period than the baseline period. You would expect the rate of citations to be the same for the treatment period as the baseline period (8 out of 10 or 80%) if treatment made no difference at all. In this situation,

Citation for
Disciplinary Action

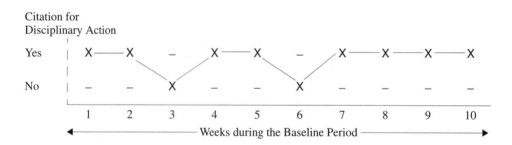

Weeks during the Baseline Period

the number of favorable recordings of behavior during the baseline is 2 out of 10 or 20 percent, because a favorable behavior is depicted by the absence of disciplinary action.

What if you found that there was a citation in only 2 or the 6 weeks of treatment? This would mean that there was a favorable recording in 4 of the 6 treatment weeks (66.6 percent). Favorable recordings in 66.6 percent of the weeks of treatment would be better than the baseline trend of 20 percent favorable recordings, but would it be *significantly* better?

To answer this question, you can turn to the binomial test once again. But instead of assuming there will be a 50 percent rate of favorable recordings in the treatment period in the absence of treatment, you would assume a 20 percent rate because this reflects the baseline data. In the situation where 4 out of 6 treatments recordings are favorable and only 20 percent of the baseline recordings were favorable, statistical significance will be achieved. In other words, the distribution of 4 out of 6 is significantly different from 2 out of 10, and that is the information derived from the binomial test.

This information is contained in Exhibit 6.2. In that exhibit, refer to the first column which depicts various proportions of favorable recordings during the baseline. In our example, that figure was 20 percent. The figure that comes closest to 20 percent but is higher is 25 percent (0.25). Thus, you would use one of the lines that presents a .25 proportion of favorable baseline recordings. In our case, there were 6 treatment recordings. The second column in Exhibit 6.2 depicts various numbers of treatment recordings. One of these figures is "6 or more" which would fit our situation. The next column indicated the number of favorable treatment recordings necessary to achieve statistical significance. In the line from Exhibit 6.2 that reads ".25" in the first column and "6 or more" in the second column, you will see the designation "All but 2" in the third column. This means that you have statistical significance if all but 2 of your treatment recordings are favorable.

EXHIBIT 6.2   Determining Statistical Significance with the Binomial Test

1. Establish a trend line which projects the baseline data into the treatment period.

2. Determine the proportion of baseline recordings that were on the favorable side of the trend line. If you employ the celeration line with ordinal or interval data, you should assume a 50–50 split (i.e., 50 percent).

3. Determine the proportion of treatment recordings that were on the favorable side of the trend line.

(Continued)

EXHIBIT 6.2 *Continued*

4. Examine the data below in order to determine the level of statistical significance (p). For example, if you have a 50–50 split in the baseline and you have 5 treatment recordings and all 5 of these recordings are on the favorable side of the trend line, your p value will be .03 and you will have achieved statistical significance at the normal standard of .05.

If the proportion of favorable recordings in the baseline is this:	AND the number of treatment recordings is this:	You will have statistical significance if the number of favorable treatment recordings is this:
.50 (i.e. a 50–50 split)	4 or less	Not applicable
.50	5 or more	All must be favorable
.50	7	6 (p = .06)
.50	8 or more	All but 1 must be favorable
.50	10 or more	All but 2 must be favorable*
.25	3	Not applicable
.25	4 or more	All
.25	5 or more	All but 1
.25	6 or more	All but 2*
.10	4 or more	All but 1
.10	6 or more	At least one-half

Unless otherwise noted, the statistical significance level for the one-tailed test is .05.

*At higher numbers of treatment recordings, you can achieve statistical significance with a lower number of favorable treatment recordings. Consult a statistical text.

ASSIGNMENT 6-C

1. With the AB single-subject research design, the client's target behavior is measured:

_____ **a.** Once in the baseline period and once in the treatment period.

_____ **b.** Several times in both the baseline and treatment periods.

_____ **c.** Several times in the baseline period and once in the treatment period.

2. The trend line is established from data drawn from:

_____ **a.** The baseline period only.

_____ **b.** The treatment period only.

_____ **c.** Both the baseline and treatment periods.

3. Guidance for practical significance is provided from:

_____ **a.** The extent of the difference between the trend line and the treatment recordings.

_____ **b.** The likelihood that the results could occur by chance.

_____ **c.** The p value from the statistical analysis of the data.

4. If your trend line is drawn at a score of 17 on a 40-point scale measuring self-esteem and your treatment period mean is 19, you will be correct to say which of the following things:

_____ **a.** You have achieved statistical significance.

_____ **b.** You have achieved practical significance.

_____ **c.** Both of the above.

_____ **d.** None of the above.

5. The standard deviation approach is used in which of the following situations?

_____ **a.** The trend during the baseline period is level rather than going up or down.

_____ **b.** The trend during the treatment period is level rather than going up or down.

_____ **c.** The trend during the baseline period is going up or down.

_____ **d.** The trend during the treatment period is going up or down.

6. In which of the following situations would you rely on the binomial test for determining statistical significance?

_____ **a.** The trend for interval level data is going up or down during the baseline period.

_____ **b.** The client's behavior is measured in a dichotomous fashion (e.g., either Yes or No).

_____ **c.** Both of the above.

_____ **d.** None of the above.

Other Single-Subject Research Designs

The previous section described the use of the AB single-subject research design because it is the most common one in use. There are additional single-subject designs to be discussed in this section. The first is the B design, in which there is no baseline set of recordings of target behavior, but only a set of recordings during the intervention period. The second is the BC design, in which the treatment is changed. The B phase represents the first approach to treatment, while the C phase represents the second approach to helping the client with the target behavior. The third is the ABC design, in which a baseline of data is collected prior to the first approach to treatment, which is followed by a second approach to treatment. The fourth is the ABAB design, which is considered to be an example of an experimental design. In this design, there is a baseline (the first A phase), followed by treatment period 1 (the first B phase), followed by a withdrawal of treatment while measurement continues (the second

A phase), followed by a reintroduction of the same treatment (the second B phase). In other words, both A phases are baselines during which treatment is not offered, and both B phases are periods during which the same approach to intervention is implemented.

The B Single-Subject Design

When you use the B design, you record the client's target behavior several times during the treatment period. There is no baseline of recordings. Statistical analysis of these data is problematic because of the absence of the baseline trend. However, there is a statistical measure that can be employed to determine if the slope of the line that represents the treatment period data is significantly different from a horizontal line which would represent no gain at all. Details on this approach are given in Chapter 17.

Modified AB Design

A modified form of the AB design calls for at least one measurement before treatment begins; this score is used as the dividing line in the treatment period in the data analysis. For example, you might have your client take the Beck Depression Inventory at the beginning of the first treatment session before you have engaged in any therapeutic efforts. If this score seems to represent the client's level of depression in recent times, you would use this score in your analysis of the client's scores that you will record during the treatment period. It would be very helpful for you to have two or three measures of a variable such as depression in order to establish a reasonable score for projecting the client's behavior into the treatment period. Only one measurement would be more appropriate for something like a test of one's level of knowledge about something.

With the modified AB design, the binomial test could be applied to the treatment period recordings. The question is whether the number of treatment recordings of target behavior that are superior to the line (representing the single score before treatment began) are significantly greater than the number that are not. For depression, better scores would be below the line. If you were measuring self-esteem, better scores would be above the line.

In this application of the binomial test, you are assuming that one-half of the scores should be on either side of the projected line if the treatment had no effect at all. Thus, you are applying the binomial test, which assumes a 50–50 split in the distribution of scores. Information on this test can be found in Exhibit 6.2. From this exhibit, you can discover the following information:

1. With fewer than 5 treatment recordings, you cannot establish statistical significance. Thus, your data would not lend themselves to statistical analysis and you would be advised to abandon the statistical question.
2. With 5 or more treatment recordings, you will have statistical significance ($p < .05$) if all the treatment recordings are on the favorable side of the trend line.
3. With 7 treatment recordings, you will have data that approaches statistical significance ($p = .06$) if all but 1 of these recordings are on the favorable side of the trend line.
4. With 8 or more treatment recordings, you will have statistical significance ($p < .05$) if all but 1 of these recordings are on the favorable side of the trend line.

These statements do not apply to situations where the dependent variable is measured in a dichotomous fashion (e.g., as either Yes or No) unless you can assume that no more than one-half of the client's pre-treatment behaviors on this variable were favorable. For example, if Yes is the favorable answer and the client had been engaging in this behavior approximately two-thirds of the time, the above statements would not apply to this situation.

To illustrate, suppose you have recorded a client's depression score before treatment as 29. In the illustration below, all 8 of the treatment recordings were better than this score; thus, statistical significance was achieved.

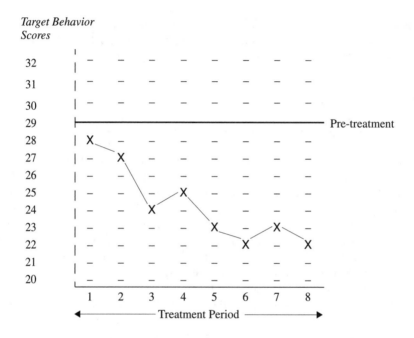

A major advantage of the regular AB design is that the baseline provides a means of addressing maturation and testing as threats to internal validity. With the B design and the modified AB design, this advantage is lost because you do not have a baseline trend. If you have as many as four recordings before treatment, you can normally consider this to be a minimal amount of data to establish a trend that can serve as a measure of the potential effect of maturation.

The BC Design

With the BC design, you implement one approach to treatment without taking a baseline and you change the treatment. You repeatedly record the client's target behavior throughout both periods of time. Your statistical question is whether the client's improvement was significantly better during the second phase of treatment than the first. Without the baseline, you do not have a quantitative basis for determining the client's pre-treatment condition and determining if the first phase of treatment was effective. But you can analyze whether the second treatment was more effective than the first.

For example, suppose you had an assessment period with a client during which you assessed the client's problems and engaged in supportive therapy for a period of five weekly sessions. After the first session, you realized that one the client's problems was depression, so you began to measure the client's depression at the beginning of the second session and you repeated this procedure for each weekly session for the next four weeks of the supportive therapy phase of treatment. This first phase of treatment will be labeled the B phase. You begin the implementation of cognitive therapy with session number 6 and continue this treatment for 6 weekly sessions. You continue to record the client's depression each week for these six weeks of the second phase of treatment. This latter period is the C phase. Thus, you would be examining whether cognitive therapy was significantly more effective than supportive therapy with this client.

The statistical analysis of data with the BC design takes the same form as it does for the AB design. If you pretended that the B phase was the baseline and the C phase was the treatment, you would execute the data analysis procedures exactly the same as with the AB design. In other words, you would examine the B phase to determine the nature of the trend and select either the standard deviation method or one of the approaches that employs the binomial test. If you selected the standard deviation approach, you would calculate the mean and standard deviation for the B phase data, and the mean for the C phase data, and determine if the C phase mean score was at least two standard deviations better than the B phase mean. If you examined your data with the binomial test, you would draw a line that represents the B phase data into the C phase and examine whether the number of scores that were superior to this trend line was significantly greater than the number of scores that were not.

The ABC Design

When you employ the ABC design, you take baseline and treatment recordings just as you do with the AB design, but you add a second treatment and continue to record the client's target behavior. The second treatment is the C phase. Thus, the ABC design simply adds a baseline to the BC design. The statistical questions are twofold: (1) Were the scores in the first treatment period (B phase) significantly better than the baseline trend? and (2) Were the scores for the second treatment significantly better than those for the first treatment? Because the first treatment stands between the second treatment and the baseline, you are not in a good position to compare the C phase data to the baseline, because you cannot easily distinguish the effects of the second treatment from the first. However, you might want to see if the data in the C phase are superior to the baseline and interpret these results with caution.

Two Experimental Designs—ABA and ABAB

Among the single-subject research designs considered to be experimental designs are the ABA design and the ABAB design (Bloom, Fischer, & Orme, 1995).

ABA Design

With the ABA design, you collect data during a follow-up period (the second baseline). Thus, you have a baseline of scores, followed by set of scores for the treatment period, followed by a set of scores after treatment has terminated. If the scores in the B phase are superior to the baseline and if these scores return to the baseline level after treatment, you have stronger evidence for causation than you do for the AB design.

When the ABA design is employed, you have two statistical questions to answer: (1) *A*re the scores during the treatment phase significantly better than the baseline? and (2) Are the scores during the treatment phase better than the scores during the second baseline? You would examine these questions in much the same way you would examine data with the AB design, but you would undertake two separate statistical analyses.

ABAB Design

When you employ the ABAB design, you collect data during the first baseline, during the first introduction of the treatment, during a second baseline period, and, finally, during a second treatment phase. In this situation, there is only one approach to treatment, but it is offered at two different time periods with a baseline period between the two treatment periods. This requires a withdrawal of treatment, and a return to treatment.

With the ABAB design, three statistical questions are posed: (1) Are the scores during the first treatment phase significantly better than the scores during the first baseline? (2) Are the scores during the first treatment phase significantly better than the scores during the second baseline? (3) Are the scores during the second treatment phase significantly better than those in the second baseline period? The statistical analysis for each of these questions takes a similar form to the analysis of data for the AB design.

ABA and ABAB Advantages

Both of these designs address some of the threats to internal validity that are not addressed by the AB design. One of these is history, which refers to the effects of changes in the client's environment independent of treatment. With the AB design, there is the possibility that the client's environment has changed during the treatment phase; thus, changes in the client's scores between the treatment phase and the baseline may be attributed to this event rather than the treatment. If this were true, you would not see the client's scores return to the baseline level when treatment was withdrawn and the second baseline of data recorded. A failure of the client's functioning to return to the first baseline level during the second baseline period would challenge the wisdom of arguing that the client's progress during treatment should be attributed to a change in the environment. Thus, the ABA design would address history as a threat to internal validity.

The same is true for the ABAB design. It is highly unlikely that an instrumental change in the client's environment would occur only during the two treatment phases and would be absent in its effects during the two baseline phases.

The Issue of Autocorrelation

Both the standard deviation and the binomial test are designed for data that are drawn from independent samples rather than related samples. Data that are drawn from independent samples would be illustrated by data taken from different people. When we take several recordings of the same scale from one person, we have what is known as data drawn from related samples. Using such statistical measures as the standard deviation and the binomial test for data drawn from related samples is okay if our data is not autocorrelated. According to Bloom, Fischer, and Orme (1995, p. 499):

> *One of the most troublesome assumptions underlying many statistical tests as applied to the analysis of single-system designs is the assumption that the observations are independent.* Independence *essentially means that one observation can't be predicted from other observations. For example, if a client's behavior at one time predicts other behavior, the observations would not be independent. . . . When observations are not independent, they're said to be dependent, or correlated. Of particular importance to the analysis of single-system design data is the correlation of adjacent observations within a series of observations made over time. This type of dependency is known as* serial dependency, *and is quantified by a type of correlation known as* autocorrelation [emphasis in the original].

The text by Bloom et al. (1995) contains methods for testing for autocorrelation and for transforming autocorrelated data into a form suitable for statistical analysis. However, these authors cite works of others which suggest that autocorrelation is seldom evident in published single-subject research. Thus, it is an issue that would seem to be of special concern only for researchers who are determined to have no possibility of technical shortcomings in their work. This issue, of course, may be especially important for those who wish to publish the results of their evaluations.

ASSIGNMENT 6-D

1. The B single-subject research design addresses which of the following threats to internal validity?

_____ **a.** Maturation

_____ **b.** History

_____ **c.** Testing

_____ **d.** All of the above.

_____ **e.** None of the above.

2. The BC single-subject research design addresses which of the above threats to internal validity?

_____

_____

_____

3. The AB single-subject research design addresses which of the above threats to internal validity?

_____

_____

_____

_____

4. The ABAB single-subject research design addresses which of the above threats to internal validity?

_____

_____

_____

_____

_____

An Exercise Using Hypothetical Data from Clients of Project PARENTING

In this exercise, you will employ hypothetical data relevant to the study of the effectiveness of Project PARENTING, explained in the previous chapter. Data for the HOME scale will be presented for several hypothetical cases. You will examine these results and determine whether the intervention has been effective.

EXHIBIT 6.3   HOME Scores for Three Hypothetical Clients

| | ← *Baseline Recordings* → | | | | | ← *Treatment Period* → | | | | | |
Case	Jan	Feb	Mar	Apr	May	Jun	Jul	Aug	Sep	Oct	Nov	Dec
1	18	17	19	19	18	18	21	23	19	26	26	29
2	18	19	21	20	21	22	21	24	23	26	28	29
3	19	14	21	28	17	21	22	26	19	33	14	28

Enter data from Exhibit 6.3 in the three worksheets which follow, using one worksheet for each client. Designate each HOME score by drawing a small circle around the appropriate dash on these charts. Indicate each of the 12 scores in this fashion.

EXHIBIT 6.4   Worksheet for Plotting Scores for Clients

CLIENT NUMBER 1

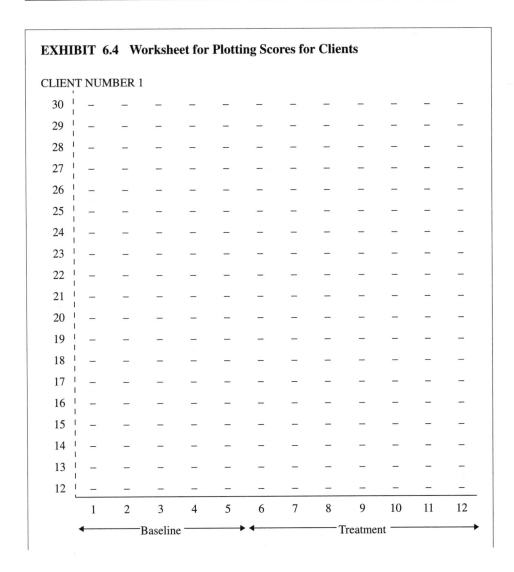

EXHIBIT 6.4 *Continued*

CLIENT NUMBER 2

	1	2	3	4	5	6	7	8	9	10	11	12
30	–	–	–	–	–	–	–	–	–	–	–	–
29	–	–	–	–	–	–	–	–	–	–	–	–
28	–	–	–	–	–	–	–	–	–	–	–	–
27	–	–	–	–	–	–	–	–	–	–	–	–
26	–	–	–	–	–	–	–	–	–	–	–	–
25	–	–	–	–	–	–	–	–	–	–	–	–
24	–	–	–	–	–	–	–	–	–	–	–	–
23	–	–	–	–	–	–	–	–	–	–	–	–
22	–	–	–	–	–	–	–	–	–	–	–	–
21	–	–	–	–	–	–	–	–	–	–	–	–
20	–	–	–	–	–	–	–	–	–	–	–	–
19	–	–	–	–	–	–	–	–	–	–	–	–
18	–	–	–	–	–	–	–	–	–	–	–	–
17	–	–	–	–	–	–	–	–	–	–	–	–
16	–	–	–	–	–	–	–	–	–	–	–	–
15	–	–	–	–	–	–	–	–	–	–	–	–
14	–	–	–	–	–	–	–	–	–	–	–	–
13	–	–	–	–	–	–	–	–	–	–	–	–
12	–	–	–	–	–	–	–	–	–	–	–	–
	1	2	3	4	5	6	7	8	9	10	11	12

◄——————— Baseline ———————► ◄——————— Treatment ———————►

(Continued)

EXHIBIT 6.4 *Continued*

CLIENT NUMBER 3

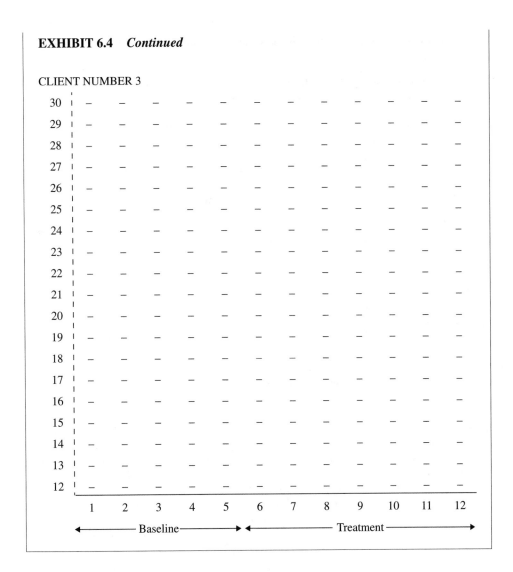

EXHIBIT 6.5   An Illustration of the Calculation of the Standard Deviation

The standard deviation is the square root of the sum of squares divided by the number in the sample. The sum of squares is calculated by subtracting each score from the mean of all scores and calculating the square of that figure, then summing all of these squared deviations from the mean.

Example: Assume that the scores below represent self-esteem. The following is the method for calculating the sum of squares. (Note: A negative number becomes a positive number whenever it is squared.)

Time Period	Score		Mean		Deviation	Deviation Squared
1	11	–	11.83	=	–0.83	0.69
2	10	–	11.83	=	–1.83	3.35
3	14	–	11.83	=	2.17	4.71
4	13	–	11.83	=	1.17	1.37
5	11	–	11.83	=	–0.83	0.69
6	12	–	11.83	=	0.17	0.03

$$71 / 6 = 11.83$$
(mean)

10.84
(sum of squares)

There are 6 scores in our example; thus, N = 6. We will divide 10.84 by 6 and take the square root of this figure as illustrated below.

10.84 / 6 = 1.806, which has a square root of 1.34.

The standard deviation for our example is 1.34. The mean of baseline recordings is 11.83. If we double our standard deviation, we will obtain a score of 2.68, which we will add to the mean of 11.83 for a figure of 14.51. Thus, we will need for the mean of our intervention recordings to be equal to or greater than 14.51 in order for our data to achieve statistical significance. If this set of procedures is not yet fixed in your mind, don't worry! There is a step-by-step guide for these procedures in the next exhibit. Another option is Appendix C, which provides a slightly easier breakdown of the steps in this procedure.

EXHIBIT 6.6 The Standard Deviation Worksheet

	Score	minus	Mean	equals	Deviation	Deviation squared
Recording #1	_____	–	_____	=	_____	_____
Recording #2	_____	–	_____	=	_____	_____
Recording #3	_____	–	_____	=	_____	_____
Recording #4	_____	–	_____	=	_____	_____
Recording #5	_____	–	_____	=	_____	_____
Recording #6	_____	–	_____	=	_____	_____

Total = _____
(SUM OF SQUARES)

SUM OF SQUARES = _____ / _____ (N) = _____ which has a square root of _____

This is the STANDARD DEVIATION

ASSIGNMENT 6-E

1. Which approach to the statistical examination of data was appropriate for each of the three clients?

   Client #1: _____

   Client #2: _____

   Client #3: _____

2. What are your conclusions about statistical significance for each client?

   _____

   _____

   _____

   _____

   _____

   _____

   _____

3. What are your conclusions about practical significance for each of these clients?

_____

_____

_____

_____

_____

_____

_____

_____

References

Bloom, M., Fischer, J., & Orme, J. G. (1995). *Evaluating Practice: Guidelines for the Accountable Professional.* Boston: Allyn and Bacon.

Conducting Program Evaluations Using Qualitative and Quantitative Methods

When you examined Project PARENTING, you were engaging in some of the activities associated with one type of program evaluation. Project PARENTING is a program with the goal of improving the parenting skills of adolescent parents. Objectives included improving the parent-child interaction and improving the home environment for the child. The extent to which these objectives had been achieved was examined through the one-group pretest-posttest research design in which the dependent variables (parent-child interaction and home environment) were measured before and after six months of participation in the program. This was an example of the evaluation of outcome. In this chapter, you will also examine the evaluation of input and the evaluation of process.

What is a program? A program is an organized set of activities designed to achieve a particular goal or a set of objectives. The activities are interdependent in that they depend on one another for the achievement of the objectives. A program has an identity and specified resources. Programs within an agency or system can be conceptualized at various levels. You may be working with a support group for abused women that you would conceptualize as a program within an overall agency effort to meet the needs of women in a given community. The overall effort could also be conceptualized as a program at a broader level.

The provision of family therapy to a given client in a family services program would not be considered an example of a program. Normally, service to a single client is given within the context of a program but is not a program itself.

A program evaluation is an effort to apply the principles of scientific inquiry to program decision making. For example, program managers need to know the character and incidence of the needs associated with target problems. They need to identify the characteristics of effective service so programs can be designed well. And they need to be able to justify their programs by demonstrating that they have been effective in meeting human needs.

The Systems Model for Classifying Evaluation Efforts

In systems terminology, a human system can be conceptualized in regard to its inputs, its process, and its outputs. *Input* represents the energies that come into the system, while *process* refers to the mechanisms for transforming the input into an *output.* In simple terms, a client with a need comes to the agency (input), receives a service (process), and is changed in some way (output). Another simple conceptualization is that the agency hires staff with certain credentials (inputs), designs services and establishes service protocols to guide their delivery (process), and achieves the goals and objectives of the program (output).

In this chapter, program evaluation will be discussed in regard to evaluating need (input), evaluating service process, and evaluating client outcome (output). Previously in this text, evaluative research has been examined only in regard to client outcome. When the concept of evaluation is expanded to the idea of program evaluation, the scope of activities is broadened.

How could Project PARENTING have been evaluated regarding input or process? A need assessment could have been undertaken in which the extent of need for parent training for adolescent mothers would have been measured. How many adolescent mothers does this community have? What is the extent of parenting skills of these mothers? What proportion have a serious deficit in skills? What obstacles to improvement do they tend to face?

Service process could have been evaluated through the monitoring of service activities to obtain information on the extent to which the components of the program were implemented according to design. The characteristics of clients who achieved the most gain or participated most fully could have been identified. Client interactions with others could have been observed, so a portrait of the service process for the typical client could been painted for the purpose of adding insight into how this process might be improved. The cost per client served could be compared to the same costs of other alternatives for achieving the same objectives. Perhaps short-term participation could be compared to long-term participation, to see if long-term intervention, which costs more, achieved significantly more gain than short-term intervention.

The evaluation of output, or outcome, entails the measurement of client gain, or the achievement of the program's objectives in some other way. For Project PARENTING, it involved comparing of client scores on parenting skills after treatment with the same scores before treatment.

Evaluating Need

A need is a gap between what is and what should be. A need assessment is an attempt to identify the community's perceptions of gaps and to measure them. What one identifies as a need, another may not. What is generally recognized as a need in a given community may not be recognized in another community. What is recognized today as a need (or a social problem) may not have been recognized as such fifty years ago.

Needs generate from social problems, the latter being defined as an undesirable condition of the individual or the environment. We normally recognize unemployment as a problem. Society's goal regarding this problem is to reduce it as much as possible. The needs of the unemployed could entail skill development, enhanced motivation, increased self-confidence, improved knowledge about job openings, transportation, and so forth.

Social problems and social needs serve as guides for program goals and objectives. The goal of an employment training program might be to reduce unemployment, or to place certain persons into jobs, while the objectives might be to improve job interviewing skills, or job motivation, or knowledge of job openings, and so forth.

Quantitative Approaches to Needs Assessment

Quantitative approaches to needs assessment include the waiting list for a service, agency records on the types of services requested and utilized, demographic reports such as the census, and the social survey. Some of these sources of information could employ qualitative methods. For example, a social survey could use open-ended questions, and narrative text in agency records could be subjected to content analysis. But these sources normally are used to collect quantitative data.

Service Statistics for Needs Assessment.   Service statistics probably serve as the most prevalent means of needs assessment for the human services. There is no more powerful indicator of need than the extent to which a given service has been requested by people in the community. If people view something as a need, they are likely to express this view through a request. Furthermore, if they make a request, they are more likely to make use of the service. A waiting list is the foremost measure of unmet need for most human services.

This source of information on need has the limitation of missing need that is perceived but not turned into action through a request. One of the reasons a perceived need is not turned into action is that people may not know the service exists; in fact, a service for this need may not exist. In this case, people do not have the opportunity to make their need known.

Social Surveys.   Needs that are not yet served can be assessed through social surveys. The citizens of a given community can be asked to respond to a questionnaire related to a given type of need. The social survey is especially useful in this regard. It is also useful for collecting information on the extent to which a problem (or need) exists in a community. Some people who have a need and know about a service that addresses it do not request that service. How many such people are there in a given community? Why have they not requested the service? These are among the questions that can be answered through a social survey.

Demographic Reports.   Another quantitative approach to needs assessment is the demographic report, best exemplified by the census. From such sources, you can obtain information on the characteristics of the community that are most relevant to a given need. For example, knowing how many children under school age are living in a household under a certain income level in a given county can assist in the assessment of need for day care among low income households in that county. The major limitation of that source of information is that data are not very specific to the agency's need for information.

Qualitative Approaches to Needs Assessment

Among the qualitative approaches to needs assessment are public hearings, interviews of key informants or clients, focus groups, and the nominal group technique. These approaches are better suited for identifying the nature of need and unearthing new needs than for precisely measuring needs, the latter being better served by quantitative methods.

Qualitative approaches to needs assessment include all those means of measurement of need where categories of things are not specified ahead of time. As previously mentioned, a social survey could have open-ended questions, and this would be an example of qualitative measurement. A more common use of qualitative methods is the **public hearing** in which people are invited to say what they wish rather than respond to categories. Interviews with **open-ended questions** would constitute another example of qualitative measurement. The **focus group** is another example. These are small groups of people, usually six to eight individuals, who participate in a structured discussion of a selected theme (for more information, see Krueger, 1993). That theme could be the unmet needs of senior citizens of Hinshaw County, or the needs of the homeless in Cedar City, or the relative need for support, enhanced self-esteem, or legal assistance for abused wives.

The **nominal group** technique is a qualitative approach to collecting information that combines qualitative and quantitative methods. It entails the engagement of a small group of key informants in identifying and prioritizing ideas. It is well suited to questions related to need, and will be illustrated in the second part of this chapter.

Evaluating Service Process

Service process refers to actions taken in behalf of the program in order to achieve the desired results. To achieve the goals of the program, staff with certain credentials are hired (inputs). These credentials are believed to be necessary for effective service. These persons are instructed to administer services as designed (process). This might include restricting services to clients who are eligible for the service according to established policies. The service process might include assuring that each client is informed of his or her rights. It might include referrals of certain clients to certain other services. It might include assuring that each client is served through an established protocol of services so important considerations are not overlooked, as, for example, a protocol for how the emergency room of the hospital will treat each victim of rape.

Quality Assurance

Monitoring variables such as those mentioned above serves as the focus of quality assurance efforts. The term "quality" is used in many ways by human service professionals. It could mean anything from whether the credentials of staff are appropriate (Are the staff *qualified?*) to whether the clients gained in their social functioning. According to Coulton:

> *Quality is an elusive concept that implies value. A service that is of high quality has features that are valued by relevant individuals or groups. Quality assurance*

*programs seek ways to objectify what are essentially subjective phenomena so they
can be examined (Coulton, 1991, p. 253).*

Coulton divides quality into three categories: *structure* (or inputs), *process,* and *outcome.*
Staff qualifications would fit into the first category, while service process fits into the second and client outcome into the third.

It has been my experience that quality assurance is highly focused on input and process variables, rather than outcome. We often refer to these variables (input and process) as *standards.* Standards are developed because they are believed to lead to effective outcomes, but we should not lose sight of the fact that standards are *not* outcomes. The primary reason for the high degree of focus on standards is the lack of good information on client outcome and the difficulties of gathering such information.

Qualitative Evaluation of Service Process

A key question that can be best answered through qualitative methods is "What is it like being a client of this program?" If you were to follow a client through the entire process from calling the agency, to being greeted by the receptionist, to being given the intake interview, to being given the central service, to being discharged, what kinds of insights could you gain about how to make the service better? Perhaps improvement is needed in the recruitment of clients, the intake procedures, the service design, or termination and follow-up. Perhaps there are stages in the therapeutic process for certain types of clients that should be better addressed in treatment. These are the kinds of questions about service process that can be addressed by qualitative methods.

A modest attempt at the evaluation of service process for my research instruction was undertaken in the summer of 1996 when three students volunteered to conduct interviews of their fellow research students of the previous school year. They were in a group of students who had taken two research courses in the night sections of these courses because they were employed and were pursuing graduate education on a part-time basis. Six students, who constituted a convenience sample (for the interviewers), were selected for interviews. These students were asked to describe the process they went through by recalling their earliest experiences, how they reacted to them, and how this experience evolved over the course of the school year in these two courses. They were also asked to indicate the major outcomes of that experience and to identify the most important factors that contributed to those outcomes. They were not to restrict themselves to their interactions with the instructor in their reflections. Each interview was tape-recorded and transcribed, and only the transcripts, without student names, were given to me.

Several themes were evident from these interviews. These student entered the first research course with a good deal of initial anxiety. This anxiety was relieved by several factors. This group of students had been in classes together before and had bonded to a limited degree. However, the anxiety about research tended to place them all in the same boat where they needed each other, the result being that the bond was "cemented" throughout the first part of the first research course. As the instructor, I was credited with relieving some this anxiety through an adult education approach to instruction in which students were engaged in exercises with case examples that involved them in the research process. Such words as "interactive" and "participative" and "open" were used to convey this idea. The second course, however, was not as positively evaluated. There was a common perception that there were too many projects to complete in the time allowed and there were insufficient instructions on how to do them. This second course engaged students in the conducting of research activities in which they played the role of researcher. The review of these transcripts provided more than the above perceptions. When I read them, I obtained several mental pictures of the experience from the standpoint of the student which I used in the development of future experiences for students. This is one of the advantages of qualitative research. (I would like to thank the three volunteers who conducted these interviews. They were Denise Billman, Crystal Griffen, and Patricia Vincitorio.)

Evaluating Efficiency

When we say that a service is delivered more efficiently, we normally are saying that we are getting more for the money. If the Hampton Family Counseling Center delivers family therapy at a cost of $75 per hour, we might say it is operating more efficiently than the Hampton Psychiatric Center that is delivering family therapy at a cost of $125 per hour. If the child abuse investigation program for the Parker County Department of Social Services spent $200,000 this year and completed 200 child abuse investigations, you could say that the cost per child abuse investigation was $1,000 ($200,000 / 200 = $1,000). These figures, of course, would be based on the assumption that all of the $200,000 was devoted only to child abuse investigations. If the Walker County Department of Social Services was spending $1,400 per child abuse investigation, you could say that the Parker County DSS was operating its program more efficiently than the Walker County DSS.

In the above examples, costs were computed in regard to units of service delivered rather than client outcomes. The ultimate study of efficiency would be the computation of costs per client achievement or the benefits to the community. If we could compute the cost per child abuse incident prevented, or the cost per client rehabilitated, we would be in the best place to examine efficiency. However, this is not often feasible in human services; therefore, efficiency will be examined in this chapter in regard to units of service delivered.

Step 1: Define the Unit of Service
The first step in examining service unit cost is defining the unit of service for a given program. The simplest way to define the unit of service is a client served. If your program spent $123,443 and served 890 persons, the cost per client served would be $138.70 ($123,443 / 890 = $138.70). Measuring service by nothing more than clients served is less meaningful than measuring service time or episodes of service. An hour of counseling, or a day of residential care, or a completed child abuse investigation are examples of breaking services down into time or episodes of service.

Step 2: Compute Total Cost
The next step is to compute the total cost of delivering the program's service units. This may be problematic, because agencies often do not break down their costs in ways that the cost per unit of service can easily be computed. When you compute total program costs, you will need to consider indirect as well as direct costs. Direct costs are those that can be easily attributed to the program, such as the costs of salaries for the staff who deliver the service and the supplies they use, the cost of their transportation, and so forth. Indirect costs are those costs the agency incurs in support of the programs. For example, the agency

has an executive with a salary and an office and so forth. These costs have to be assigned to the agency's programs so that the total agency budget is assigned to one or more programs. You might need to compute the indirect costs and arbitrarily assign a portion to your program in the computation of the total cost of delivering the units of service that you are analyzing.

Step 3: Compute Cost Per Unit

Your next step is to compute the cost per unit of service. This entails dividing the total program costs by the number of units of service delivered. The final step is to place that figure into perspective by comparing it to something. You could compare it to your unit costs of last year or the unit costs of another agency that delivers the same service. You might compare it to some idea of what a reasonable cost per unit of service would be.

Evaluating Outcome

In this text, you have examined the evaluation of outcome for Project PARENTING. The goal of this program was to improve parenting skills of adolescent parents, while the objectives were to improve parent-child interaction and to improve the home environment. Parent-child interaction and home environment were measured by established scales. The clients were measured on these variables before and after six months of intervention.

The process for evaluating program outcome begins with the statement of the program's objectives. Before this process begins, however, it is assumed that the client's problems have been analyzed sufficiently to provide the information necessary for establishing of the objectives. The objectives are measured amounts of progress toward goal attainment, the latter being the long-range condition that is deemed desirable. If the goal is readily measurable, it would serve as the focus of attention.

A means of measuring the objectives is developed and a research design is chosen. The intervention is implemented, and data are collected and analyzed in order to determine the extent to which the objectives were achieved. Outcome evaluation focuses on the client's condition. The question is whether the client received a significant gain in functioning. Outcome does *not* focus on the service the client received, or how many sessions were completed and so forth. Such questions are the focus of other types of evaluation mentioned above.

A key to good outcome evaluation is the articulation of the program's goals and objectives. A crisis intervention program once presented the following as the objective: "To deliver crisis intervention to the victims of rape." Is this a useful statement for outcome evaluation? You will notice that it identifies something about the nature of the service, but says nothing about the expected outcome for the client. Thus, you would need to articulate what the client is expected to gain if you were to engage in an outcome evaluation of this program.

The actual measurement of progress is another essential ingredient of outcome evaluation. Client conditions should be measured as directly as is feasible. Normally, a client satisfaction survey is not considered a sufficient mechanism for outcome evaluation, because it does not usually measure client functioning. Measuring depression with a depression scale before and after treatment is an acceptable means of outcome evaluation, but satisfaction with service is a different matter. Client satisfaction can be useful information, but it does not measure progress.

Problems with Outcome Evaluation

The limitations inherent in the evaluation of outcome have placed it lower on the scale of attention to accountability efforts than is the case with some of the other types of program evaluation. One of the major problems with outcome evaluation is the difficulty of stating clear outcome objectives and finding the means and the resources to measure their achievement. Human service leaders have too often given up on this task too quickly and have found themselves in a difficult situation with regard to accountability. As pressures mount, these leaders will find a way to measure outcome or they will suffer the obvious consequences. Because outcome evaluation has been the focus of two previous chapters, it will take a back seat to other evaluation efforts in this chapter.

Client Satisfaction

A common method of evaluating human service programs is through the client satisfaction survey, in which former clients are asked to indicate their level of satisfaction with the services they received. Being able to quote figures on the percent of former clients who were satisfied is useful to the program administrator in the achievement of accountability for the program. Furthermore, if clients are satisfied, staff will feel better about their efforts. If clients are not satisfied, the evidence is available to promote change. The key assumption of the client satisfaction survey is that satisfied clients had their needs met. If a client is satisfied, it is assumed that he or she actually improved in functioning. Thus, the higher the level of satisfaction, the more effective were the services.

But satisfaction is an opinion, not a measure of functioning. A direct measurement of functioning is required to overcome the limitations inherent in this assumption. In the absence of such a direct measure of client conditions, satisfaction is a useful surrogate for treatment effectiveness. Royse and Thyer (1996) report that there is some evidence that client satisfaction is related to symptom relief for mental health clients. But two key problems with client satisfaction studies were identified by these authors—levels of client satisfaction tend to be uniformly very high, and client dropouts tend to be excluded from this analysis.

Uniformity of Client Satisfaction

Royse and Thyer reviewed numerous studies of client satisfaction with different types of human services. They discovered that a typical survey yielded a finding that 70 to 90 percent of clients were satisfied with the services they received. They found this pattern to be present for various types of programs in various countries. The uniformity of such positive results raises questions about this source of information for the determination of treatment effectiveness, because studies of actual client gain have tended not to be so positive. Thus, knowing that 75 percent of your clients are satisfied only tells you that they are similar to the persons who have been treated through a wide range of interventions for a wide range of problems.

If you employ a standardized instrument for measuring client satisfaction that has been administered by programs similar to your own and you have data from the other surveys, you would have a basis of comparison. You would be able to say that client satisfaction for your clients was above or below or similar to that of other clients served by similar programs. But it is difficult to interpret the basic results of such a survey without this kind of information.

Program Dropouts Excluded from Surveys

A second problem identified by Royse and Thyer is that program dropouts tend to be excluded from analysis. Persons who dropped out may have been ineffectively served and may be dissatisfied with the services they received. It stands to reason that dropouts would be less satisfied than those who completed treatment.

A third problem with client satisfaction surveys identified by Royse and Thyer is that response rates to the survey are often very low. They found that response rates typically were in the 25 to 30 percent range, with a 15 percent rate not unusual. How are we to interpret data when 75 to 85 percent of the clients failed to respond? These results would be rather difficult to interpret.

An Example of Needs Assessment Using the Social Survey

In the summer of 1996, the School of Social Work at East Carolina University decided to conduct a survey of need for an Off-Campus Program for graduate study in the area of the state surrounding the city of Wilmington, N.C. This program offers the foundation year of study toward the MSW degree on a part-time basis in localities that are a significant distance from the E.C.U. campus in Greenville, N.C. This alternative had been offered in Wilmington in the late 1980s and in the city of Fayetteville from 1994–96. For several years, employed social workers from the Wilmington area had called and written to the school expressing an interest in another opportunity for this program.

It was decided that a needs assessment would be undertaken for the dual purpose of determining the priority that should be accorded this alternative for graduate social work education, and to acquire information that would aid in the planning of such a program. There were two parts to this assessment. First, a telephone survey was conducted of key informants who were in professional leadership positions. That survey provided open-ended questions regarding the need for this program from the agency's standpoint and the likelihood that the agency would support their employees who enrolled. The response was very positive.

The second part of that assessment was the survey of need among persons who might apply for such a program. A few of the questions to be answered were the following:

1. To what extent is there a need for this program? (How many persons are likely to apply for it?)
2. How should the program be structured to best address the needs of the students? For example, should classes be conducted on the weekends or during the week?

3. To what extent have the prospective students been exposed to social work education in their undergraduate work?
4. What proportion of the prospective students would likely request a field internship in their employing agencies?

When you undertake a needs assessment, you will want to place the results into perspective. How much need is enough need to generate action? What concerns should guide the planning of a response to need? The first question above was motivated by the fact that a minimum of 25 students is needed to constitute a viable class that can be financially supported. Further, the rate of admissions to applications for the particular MSW program was approximately 50 percent, meaning that approximately 50 percent of all applicants were offered admission. Sizable variance in admission rates among various components of the graduate program was considered problematic. Finally, it had been found that approximately 50 percent of interested persons actually apply for off-campus programs. If 100 persons indicated interest, 50 would likely apply and approximately 25 of those would be admitted.

Before you are prepared to construct a survey instrument, you need to be clear on your study purpose and the general research questions that serve that purpose. This information guides the construction of items for the instrument. A common mistake is for the novice researcher to begin the process by brainstorming the questions to place on the survey instrument. This approach leads to two problems: unnecessary items are included that encumber the questionnaire and reduce the response rate, and essential items are overlooked.

Following the articulation of the study questions for the needs assessment survey, a questionnaire was developed. An introduction to the questionnaire explained the purpose of the study and asked respondents to provide their answers to the questions by placing a number in the column that corresponded to their response. The coding of responses was given at the end of each question. Among the questions on that survey instrument were the following:

1. How likely is it that you would apply for admission to this program if it is offered in the fall of 1997?

   [1 = Definitely; 2 = Probably; 3 = Uncertain]
2. Classes may be offered during the week in the evening or on Saturdays during the day. What would be your first preference for the time for classes?

   [1 = Mon; 2 = Tues; 3 = Wed; 4 = Thurs; 5 = Fri; 6 = Sat]
3. What was your undergraduate major?

   [1 = Social Work; 2 = Psychology; 3 = Sociology; 4 = Other social sciences; 5 = Other]
4. One of the requirements of the Off-Campus Program is a practice internship in a social work agency for 24 hours per week for one semester. If you were to enroll in the Off-Campus Program, would you request an internship in your employing agency?

   [1 = Yes; 2 = No; 3 = Uncertain]

Another step in the survey process is the selection of a study sample. The study sample consists of those persons from whom data are collected. The sample is distinguished from the study population in that the latter is the larger group from whom the sample was selected. In the needs survey, a *purposive* sample was selected because the purpose of the study was to document the extent and nature of need for persons interested in becoming students in this program. Thus, it was necessary to locate potential students rather than persons (or social workers) in general. A purposive sample is an example of a nonprobability sample (not selected on a random basis); thus, the results of this needs survey could not be safely generalized to a larger study population. However, this survey was designed to locate persons in need and obtain information on their need rather than to generalize to larger populations of persons. A public opinion survey would have called for a probability sample (where respondents would have been selected randomly from a list of persons in the population), because such a survey would have the intent of generalizing about the community's public opinions.

A mailing list was secured by reviewing the names of persons who had indicated interest and by asking the key informants to distribute copies of the survey to interested individuals. The questionnaire had a statement at the bottom that encouraged the respondent to distribute copies of the instrument to other interested persons. This procedure is indicative of the *snowball sample,* in which selected persons are encouraged to locate others who are also encouraged to locate others for the study. In a sense, the sample snowballs into a bigger and bigger sample of persons.

Three months following the initiation of the survey, a total of 161 questionnaires had been returned. Of these individuals, 102 (63 percent) indicated they would "definitely" apply for this program, 42 (26 percent) said they would "probably" apply, and 17 (11 percent) were "uncertain." Saturday was the first choice of the week for classes for 93 (58 percent) of these individuals while 23 (14 percent) marked Tuesday, 17 (11 percent) selected Monday, 12 (8 percent) favored Thursday, 10 (6.2 percent) preferred Wednesday, and 5 (3 percent) wanted classes on Friday. Of these individuals, 48 (30 percent) had majored in social work in college while 39 (24 percent) were sociology majors, 29 (18 percent) were psychology majors, 25 (15 percent) majored in other areas of the social sciences, and 16 (10 percent) were in the category of "other." Practice internships in the employing agencies of these prospective students was favored by 112 (70 percent) persons, while only 3 (2 percent) were against such an arrangement and 44 (27 percent) were uncertain.

ASSIGNMENT 7-A

Prepare a summary of the above needs assessment survey.

Identifying Need and Setting Priorities Using a Qualitative Method: The Nominal Group Technique (NGT)

Nominal group technique (NGT) is a structured group method of decision making that is designed to maximize participation among a small group of key informants. The outcome of this technique is a prioritized list of ideas around a designated theme or question. It is qualitative in nature because it begins with an open format for the generation of ideas. It lends itself quite well to the identification of need and the establishment of priority among those needs.

Briefly, nominal group technique entails:

1. the silent generation of ideas in writing by each participant,
2. a round-robin recording of all of each participant's ideas on a flip chart,
3. serial discussion of each idea for purposes of clarification,
4. a preliminary vote on item importance,
5. a discussion of the preliminary vote, and
6. a final vote.

The benefits of NGT are numerous. Its greatest contribution to problem solving is that it promotes (a) equality of participation, (b) greater tolerance of nonconformity, and (c) a high level of task motivation. Persons who become engaged in an NGT meeting tend to come away with a heightened feeling of involvement and contribution to the outcome of the meeting. Thus, they tend to be more committed to follow-up efforts. The practice of requiring participation leads not only to higher motivation but also tends to result in a larger quantity and range of ideas for consideration. Dominance of the discussion by a vocal few is minimized by the procedures of NGT.

On the other hand, the nominal group technique is a costly endeavor, especially for large groups, because the process is time consuming and requires that large groups be divided into sub-groups of five to nine members for the NGT procedures. Thus, a group of 90 people would have to be divided into ten groups of nine each which, of course, would require the services of ten group leaders skilled in the NGT procedures.

Preview: Six Steps of the NGT Process

A preview of the six steps in the NGT process will illustrate the spirit of the technique. In step 1, the group facilitator presents the question to be addressed and the time limit for thought (usually 5 minutes). The question is presented both verbally and in writing to insure clarity. The level of abstraction is defined, but the facilitator avoids offering examples that may tend to lead group members in a narrow direction. For example, with the question "What are the chief problems encountered by children in one-parent, low-income households?" the facilitator may go on to define "problem" as a condition, not a lack of a certain service. But the leader would want to avoid offering examples or responding to such examples offered by group members.

In this first step, it is important that one group member not be allowed to disturb another or attempt to influence their ideas. NGT leaders should model such behavior by working quietly themselves.

In the second step, the facilitator asks for one item from each member's list and records it on a flip chart, after which he or she asks for a second item from each member and so on until each member's list has been exhausted. Group members are encouraged to add items to their lists as this step progresses. It is important that the facilitator not allow group members to debate their ideas during this step. All members should be given equal opportunity to offer their ideas in their own words, but they should be encouraged to express them in brief phrases that can be realistically placed on a flip chart. Neither the group facilitator nor other members should suggest the wording for a member's idea unless it is entirely necessary.

In the third step, each idea is discussed in turn for purposes of clarification and to eliminate duplication. Items are not, however, debated or grouped into broad categories. Items that are fundamentally duplicates of others are eliminated, but all group members have the option of having their ideas stand if they so desire.

In step 4, group members select five to nine items of most importance and rank them. (Everyone should select the same number of items.) The votes are tallied by assigning the highest value (e.g. seven points) for a rank of 1, the second highest value for a rank of 2, and so forth. No points are given for items not included in the priority category (e.g. the top seven). These points are totaled for each item and the results are presented to the group.

A certain degree of anonymity is important in this step. The facilitator could ask the group members to write their votes and pass them in. The range of votes should be displayed for each item to illuminate the group's variability and to facilitate a discussion of the preliminary vote.

The discussion of the preliminary vote takes place in step 5 of the NGT procedure. Participants are encouraged to reflect on the vote and share their observations. If, for example, item 14 on the list received ranks of 1,1, 2, 6, 7, 7, from six members and was not ranked at all by three participants, it may be revealed that certain members had information not available to others. The sharing of this information could influence the final vote on item importance which constitutes the last step in the process.

In step 6, participants are asked to rank the items once again. The votes are tallied and the results are reported to group members.

Limitations of NGT

Keep in mind that this procedure is useful for generating ideas in the absence of a convenient list of response categories and for setting priorities among those ideas by a small group of key informants who are given equal power in the decision process. It is not useful for resolving conflict or achieving a negotiated agreement between conflicting parties. It is not useful for routine meetings or coordination of activities.

Preliminary Considerations in the Use of NGT

Your first task is to determine whether NGT is the appropriate tool for your purpose. The product of NGT will be a list of ideas in response to a key question such as "What are the most important unmet needs of the graduate social work students of this university?" If a comprehensive list already exists that you are confident will cover all important needs, you could simply give this list to key persons and ask for a ranking of priorities. The NGT procedures are designed both to generate new ideas and to rank them.

Another consideration is that the persons who participate must have knowledge about the question being posed. In the example above, social work students in this particular university would surely qualify. Further, it must be feasible to divide participants into groups of five to nine persons with a group leader for each. It is also essential that group leaders have given thoughtful consideration to their unique role as facilitators of this process. They must be prepared to embrace the spirit of NGT. Finally, there should be a reasonable likelihood that the results will be taken seriously by those in key positions to make decisions about need.

In your preparation for the actual meeting, your first concern will be the meeting room. It should be arranged with tables for each group which can comfortably seat five to nine group members. There should be sufficient space between groups to prevent them from disturbing one another. You will need a flip chart for each group where ideas can be written, and some tape to place each page on the wall for all to see. You will also need a set of 3 by 5 index cards for participants to record their votes.

Introducing the NGT Process

Many people will not be familiar with the nominal group technique. It is your responsibility as leader to facilitate each participant's understanding of the procedure and the importance of the topic under consideration. But first, you should welcome group members and provide introductions as needed. Then you should explain the procedures to be employed as well as the purpose for the meeting. It is also crucial that you explain the use that will be made of the group's decisions that result from this meeting.

You should explain that the Nominal Group Technique is designed to maximize the contribution of each participant to the thoughtful generation of ideas around an important issue and the establishment of priorities among those ideas. It involves the silent generation of ideas, the recording of each participant's ideas on a flip chart, the clarification of these ideas and a vote on the importance of each item.

Step 1: Silent Generation of Ideas in Writing

Write the question for exploration on a flip chart and read it aloud to the group. Ask if there is any need for clarification of the question. Be careful not to bias the group's process by giving your responses to the question. Also, be sure that others do not do the same. Ask participants to spend five minutes silently writing responses to the question in brief phrases. Remind them that their ideas should be brief enough to be listed on a flip chart.

In this step, be sure to model good group behavior by silently working on the question yourself. If necessary, politely remind participants that they are to work silently throughout the five-minute period.

Step 2: Round-Robin Recording of Ideas on a Flip Chart

Explain that you will go serially around the room asking each group member to report one item from his or her list to be placed on the flip chart. Number each idea starting with number 1. You will repeat this procedure until all items from each member's list are included. Remind the group that no debating is allowed and that all participants should present their ideas in their own words.

Explain that participants should feel free to add additional items to their lists as they go through this step. Items from someone else's list may stimulate further thoughts. Starting at your left, go around the table asking for one item from each participant. Record the item on the flip chart in a brief phrase *in the participant's own words*. If necessary, ask the participant to re-phrase the statement so it is brief enough.

Repeat this procedure until all items are recorded. Group members, however, should be asked not to report items that duplicate others on the flip chart. However, it is not your prerogative to eliminate a participant's idea because you believe it duplicates an idea already on the chart. Each participant must make that decision regarding his or her idea.

Step 3: Serial Discussion for Clarification

Explain that the purpose of this step is to clarify the meaning of each item, not to debate or resolve differences. Starting with the first item, ask if there are any questions anyone would like to raise. Solicit group involvement in the clarification of the items so that members do not feel "put on the spot" to answer questions regarding their items. Go to item 2 and so on until all items are covered.

In this step, it is critical that you pace the group so that relatively equal time is given to each item. There is an unfortunate tendency for groups to spend considerable time on the first items and have little time for the remainder, especially the last items on the list.

During this step of the NGT process, you may wish to have items eliminated that are substantially similar to others or to do some grouping of ideas. It is important, however, that each participant be given the right to keep his or her idea as presented if desired. It is usually wise to avoid the temptation to collapse all items into a few broad categories for the voting procedure which comes next, but it may be useful to place separate items into groups so participants can see how many of their votes are going into one basic category.

Step 4: Preliminary Vote on Item Importance

Each idea will have a number next to it on the flip chart pages, which will probably be spread out on the wall because there are likely to be more ideas than could be written on one page. Ask participants to select the five ideas they believe are most important. Their next step is to rank these items by giving the most important idea five points, the next most important idea four points, and so on until they have given points to each of the five ideas. The fifth idea, of course, will have one point. Items not among the top five will receive no points. (Be sure not to make the mistake of having the participants assign the number 1 to the top choice, the number 2 to the next and so on, using the *lowest* score as the top choice; if they do, items that were not on anyone's list will win because they will have the lowest score.)

Pass around index cards and ask participants to write the item number and the points on the card. They should be sure to distinguish between the item number and the points by using such expressions as "Item #8 = 2 points." On a flip chart, record the vote for each person next to each item number. Suppose you had seven group members for your group. Your tally sheet might appear as follows:

Item #	Points	Total
1	2-4-4-5	15
2		0
3	1-3-3-5-4-3	19
4	5	5
5	5-5-1	11
etc.		

There were seven participants in our hypothetical group. Item number one received two points from one person, four votes from two people, five points from one participant, and no points from the remaining three individuals.

Step 5: Discussion of Preliminary Vote

Give the group members a moment or two to reflect on the votes displayed on the flip chart. Then ask for discussion about the preliminary vote. If there was much variance on an item (e.g. votes of 5, 5, 1, 2, 1, 5, 0), you may want to ask for a discussion of these differences. Do some participants have access to more information than others? Are the differences simply an accurate reflection of differences in judgment among group members? Be sure to avoid allowing participants to pressure one another during the discussion. Also, be sensitive to the potential that too much discussion of an item may distort the group's final vote by bringing that item to a greater level of consciousness.

Step 6: The Final Vote

Repeat the procedures of Step 4. The final vote will serve as the basis for the ranking of the items.

ASSIGNMENT 7-B

Use the NGT procedures to examine need in accordance with a particular question. You will need to select the question, select the key informants, and engage these persons in the identification of need through the NGT procedures. You might want to use your fellow students if another group is not convenient. The question might be "What are the most important unmet needs of the social work students of this university?"

References

Coulton, C. J. (1991). Developing and implementing quality assurance programs. In Edwards, R. L., & Yankey, J. A. (Eds.), *Skills for effective human services management* (pp. 251–266). Washington: NASW Press.

Delbecq, A. L., Van de Ven, A. H., & Gustafson, D. H. (1975). *Group Techniques for Program Planning*. Scott, Foresman and Co.: Glenview, IL.

Krueger, R. A. (1993). *Focus groups: A practical guide for applied research.* Newbury Park, CA: Sage.

Royse, D., & Thyer, B. A. (1996). *Program Evaluation* (2nd ed.) Chicago: Nelson Hall.

Tutty, L. M., Rothery, M. A., & Grinnell, R. M. (1996). *Qualitative research for social workers.* Boston, MA: Allyn and Bacon.

Unit *II*

*Practical Guidelines
for Conducting
Social Work Research*

In this section of the book, you will be given practical guidelines for conducting certain tasks of the research process. While the tasks included here are not exhaustive of all research activities, they are believed to represent the tasks for which social work students tend to need special help. Each of these chapters are organized around principles to guide your action.

Chapter *8*

Developing the Introduction and Literature Review for a Research Study

The literature review for a research report provides the conceptual framework upon which the research study is founded. It lets the reader know about the nature of the topic, why it is important, and what needs to be done about it. It covers many of the same points as the introduction, but the introduction covers them in a very concise manner. Furthermore, the introduction will add a brief explanation of the nature of the study to be done. The basic points to be included in the literature review are the following:

1. What is the problem or issue being addressed?
2. Why is this problem or issue important?
3. What do we presently know about this problem or issue from the existing literature?
4. What research is presently needed regarding this problem or issue?
5. What is the research question or hypothesis to be addressed in the present study?

The introduction to your study will include the above with the addition of a brief description of the nature of the study being undertaken. It should be only a few paragraphs and does not need to be set aside with headings or subheadings. It is often useful to write the literature review first, addressing each of the above points. Then it will be easier to write the introduction. Often, your ideas of major points will shift as you write the literature review and further examine the literature while in the writing phase. Thus, you may not be prepared to write the introduction until the literature review is complete.

The introduction and literature review are the first two parts of a research report. Following the literature review will be a description of the research methodology, which will be followed by the results of the study. The conclusions or discussion section of the report will be last. In this chapter, you will examine tips for writing the introduction and the literature review. First, you will examine some basic considerations.

General Guidelines

Principle 1:   *Select a topic with an accessible knowledge base.*

Some topics simply have not been the subject of much published theoretical or empirical work. Develop a basic bibliography very early in the process to examine this issue before it is too late. While it is true that a subject with little previous research is normally considered to be a rich terrain for new research, it is usually not advisable for beginning researchers to tackle such problems. Selecting such a topic does not excuse the researcher from the necessity of securing a knowledge base for the study. Instead, it requires that the researcher be creative in this endeavor by linking the chosen topic to literature in related areas and articulating the connection between the two.

A common mistake is for the student to do a cursory examination of the literature and erroneously conclude that little or no research has been done on the topic. The literature is vast. Before a student is entitled to comment, he or she must undertake at least one computer search of an appropriate literature database. If a student can legitimately say that an on-line search of the Social Work Abstracts database, which contains more than 40,000 entries, generated only three articles with the keywords "aged," "rural," and "schizophrenia," then he or she is entitled to say that little has been reported in the social work literature on the subject of schizophrenia among the aged in rural areas.

Be mindful of the quality of various sources of information in the literature. Graduate level references are those from scholarly journals such as *Social Work, Social Service Review,* and so forth. While information from newspapers and popular magazines may be necessary in unusual circumstances, they should not be used as major sources of authority on the nature of a problem, how it is defined, or theories about it. These references should only be used as supplementary sources of information. Information from agency policy manuals or reports should be considered in the same way. When you feel you have adequately surveyed the literature, you should examine the number of relevant references from graduate level sources in order to determine the adequacy of your knowledge base.

Avoid references to class lectures or workshops when you present your knowledge base. If something important has been said in either of these, you can bet that it has also appeared in a published source. You should find those published sources and make reference to them.

Principle 2:   *Develop a first draft of an outline of the literature review before you begin writing.*

After you have examined the literature and made notes from it, you should develop a first draft of an outline of your literature review before you begin writing. You will likely change some parts of this outline as you write, because new ideas will emerge regarding this task. Without an outline, you are likely to fall into the trap of moving back and forth between subjects, leaving the reader confused as to where you are going with the topic.

Consider the task of reporting on a study that evaluates a treatment model for the resolution of grief. The following outline illustrates the organization of the content.

Loss and grief.

> *What is loss?*
>
> *Types of loss.*
>
> *Why is loss important?*
>
> > *Loss leads to grief which is painful.*
> >
> > *Grief can interfere with social functioning and happiness.*
>
> *The developmental perspective of Kübler-Ross.*
>
> > *The stages of grief reaction.*
> >
> > *The healthy resolution of grief.*
>
> *Obstacles to healthy resolution of grief.*
>
> > *Pain of loss leads to avoidance.*
> >
> > *Resolving anger is particularly difficult for some.*
> >
> > *A healthy view of the future is impeded.*

How grief can be treated.

> *The special needs of grieving persons.*
>
> *Two forms of therapy that address these special needs.*
>
> > *Supportive therapy.*
> >
> > *Cognitive therapy.*
>
> *Research on treatment has been inconclusive.*

The purpose of the present study.

> *To examine the effectiveness of a combined model of supportive and cognitive therapy in the reduction of grief symptoms for a sample of twelve adults seeking help from a community mental health center.*

The above outline begins with a definition of the problem and moves to a discussion of why it is important. Then it addresses theory and research about the problem which justifies the purpose of the present study. Finally, the purpose is stated very clearly.

The literature review should be organized by theme, not by source. Organize your themes in a logical fashion and present the ideas of various authors around the themes. For example, you should present what various authors have to say about theme A, then what various writers have to say about theme B, and so forth. You should not state what John Smith has to say about themes A, B, and C and then proceed to review what Mary Jones has to say about themes A, B, and C.

Unorganized movement back and forth between topics in a literature review is not an easy thing to avoid for many beginning research students. That is a main reason that you should develop an outline of the literature review. The outline will bring the disorganization to light.

Principle 3: *Divide the literature review into sections with headings.*

The literature review should be separated by headings, but the extensiveness of the headings is a matter of individual judgment. It is also advisable to use different formats for the headings to help readers understand where they are in the paper. For example, you could use all

capitals for the major headings of the major sections of the overall paper (i.e., LITERA-
TURE REVIEW, METHODOLOGY, RESULTS, CONCLUSIONS) with these major
headings centered. Then you could put major headings within these sections in a format that
begins each word with a capital and centers the title. Next, you could place sub-headings
flush with the left margin but set aside from the text as with the other headings. Finally, if
you need sub-headings within sub-headings, place them as the beginning of a new paragraph with the topic underlined, or use italics if you can type or print in that format.

Principle 4:   Use a reference format consistently throughout your paper.

You will need to cite the sources that you employ in your paper. The APA (American Psychological Association) format has been increasingly used by different journals and schools
in the past decade and is employed by most social work journals. Thus, you are encouraged
to employ this format. You should do this consistently. A paper that moves between formats
is not acceptable.

I will present some of the basic guidelines for the use of the APA format. First, the
sources that you employ in your paper are listed at the end of the paper, not at the bottom
of each page. In this reference list, include *only those sources that you actually cited in the
paper.* If you did not refer to a given source in your paper, do not include it in the reference
list. The reference list is organized alphabetically according to the author's last name. Illustrations of specific forms for the different types of references are given in Exhibit 8.1.

EXHIBIT 8.1   Examples for APA Reference List Citations

Book

Pfeffer, J. (1985). *Power in organizations.* Boston: Pitman Publishing.

Edited book

Adams, P. & Nelson, K. (Eds.). (1995). *Reinventing human services.* New York: Aldine de
Gruyter.

Journal article

Jerrel, J. M. & Knight, M. A. (1985). Social work practice in rural mental health systems.
Social Work, 30 (4), 331–337.

Chapter in an edited book

Gruber, M. (1978). Total administration. In Simon Slavin (Ed.), *Social Work Administration*
(pp. 359–374). New York: Haworth Press.

Magazine article

Gleick, E. (1996, July 22). Suicide's Shadow. *Time,* pp. 40–42.

EXHIBIT 8.1 *Continued*

Newspaper article

Study finds free care used more. (1982, April). *APA Monitor,* p. 14.

Report

Birney, A. J. & Hall, M. M. (1981). *Early identification of children with written language disabilities* (Report No. 81-1502). Washington, DC: National Education Association.

Unpublished manuscript

York, R. O. (1996). The assessment of need for an off-campus program. Unpublished manuscript. East Carolina University: School of Social Work.

In the body of the text, identify the author or authors and the year of the publication in parentheses after the reference to the particular work. If the citation is a direct quote, you would add the page number to the reference. See, for example, the following:

> *Johnson (1996) provides an argument in favor of the lipsit theory. An alternative viewpoint, however, is provided by several others (Brickson & Holloway, 1981; Jackson, 1967; Sampson, Barley, & Pivot, 1984). According to one author, however, "neither the proponents nor the opponents of lipsit theory have produced one shred of empirical evidence in support of their positions" (Parker, 1984, p. 73).*

Principle 5: *Use direct quotes sparingly.*

Be careful not to overdo the direct quotation of material from the literature. You should describe the material in your own words with a reference to the source. Direct quotes should be used for a profound statement or eloquent way of saying something. An example of a good quote:

> *Chronic excessive drinking, or addiction to alcoholism, with its compulsive character and devastating effect, has become one of the great public health problems of our world (Block, 1965, p. 19).*

An example of an inappropriate quote is as follows:

> *Several investigators have studied the influence of pretreatment personality.*

The second example above is a rather routine statement that should be in your own words. If you rely too heavily on direct quotes, you are in danger of presenting an image of someone who does not know how to say things in their own words. Try to avoid quoting someone who is quoting someone else. It is tempting to quote Smith who quotes Jones and Bennett and Pearson on a given topic. This is not good form, because you are supposed to do your own library research and interpretation. To do this, you should go to the original source yourself. If this is impossible, yet the quote is essential to your review, you should indicate that you received the quote from the second source rather than the original source. For example, you could say the following in parenthesis after the quote: (Paul V. Jones, as cited in Smith, 1982, p. 23).

Principle 6:   Establish the authority behind what you say.

Be sure any factual statement is backed by a reference to the source of the information. Also, give credit for ideas obtained from your literature sources even when you paraphrase them yourself. Ask yourself, at the end of each paragraph, if you need to give a reference to someone for the idea you are presenting.

The specification of the reference should be at the end of the idea presented or at the end of the paragraph, whichever comes first. You should present this reference information in such a way that you leave the reader with no doubt about what information is being credited to the particular source. Do not go on for several paragraphs regarding information from a single source without making it clear that all this information is credited to this particular source. If you have such a situation, you could begin by saying something like, *According to a theory by Jones (1986), there are two main components of effective treatment for alcoholism....* You could begin the next paragraph by saying *This theory by Jones proposes that the helping person engage in....* In this case, you would not need to enter the year in parenthesis after the name of Jones, because it is clear you are making a further reference to Jones who was referenced fully in the paragraph above. However, if you do not refer to this theory again until several pages later, you would need to repeat the reference information as originally presented with the last name and date.

Throughout your paper, you need to be concerned with the justification of what you say. As noted above, you should give reference information to sources which provide certain information. Do not make statements of fact without such a reference. Also, you should normally avoid making statements of your own opinions. See, for example, the following statement from one student's paper:

> *Unfortunately, the federal government does not comprehend the fact that it takes money to hire workers to meet an ever growing need for help.*

Such a statement would not be appropriate in a research paper, although it may acceptable in other types of papers or documents. It would be quite appropriate, however, to make statements of facts (backed by references) about how much money the government is giving to a program or how it has cut back on funds and so forth. Such statements of fact can do an even better job than your opinion of conveying the message. It would also be okay to refer to opinions of certain writers if they are pertinent to your study and if you provide appropriate reference information.

It is likewise critical that you justify the study you are proposing. It is tempting to present literature about the general theme without providing a clear link between the theme and the study you wish to present. Take, for example, one student's proposal to test the effectiveness of the intervention model developed by Alcoholics Anonymous as a treatment of depression in an outpatient mental health center. This student described depression and the AA model but did nothing to link the two. There was the implicit assumption that if a treatment model works well with one problem, it should work well with any problem. This is faulty thinking, lacking in basic logic. Why would one believe that the AA model would be effective with depression? You might be able to justify this proposal by presenting an analysis of characteristics that alcoholics and depressed people share, and a rationale for why the AA model is especially relevant given this particular similarity.

Principle 7: ***Stay focused and be clear about what you say.***
In the review of the literature, you should try to draw the big picture within which your study is contained. However, it is easy to "lose the trees for the forest" as well as vice versa. You should be careful not to give equal attention—and certainly not more attention—to variables within this broad picture that are not variables in your own study. You don't want the reader to lose sight of your study variables.

You should also avoid interjecting references to *your* study throughout the literature review. The purpose of the literature review is to present a knowledge base supporting your study. You will discuss your own study in the methodology section of your paper. The two, of course, must be related.

Be sure you present your literature in a way that is understandable by the reader. One of the common pitfalls is to refer to an idea or study result before you have adequately explained what the study was all about so the reader can fully understand your reference to it. You should not begin a reference to a study from the literature with a statement such as, *A majority of these persons indicated that they were suffering from a high level of stress.* Instead, you should begin the reference with a statement about the nature of the study. For example, you might say: *One study of stress among social work students indicated that a majority of the 45 students surveyed indicated that they were suffering from a high level of stress (Johnson, 19xx).* Information about the nature of the sample is also helpful. Was this study from the students of only one university or several? Was it a random sample or one selected specifically because these persons had complained of having a stressful situation?

Be sure to provide concise, yet full, information from a given source. If it is a report on an empirical study, say something about the nature of the study (sample, etc.) as well as the findings. It is of little value to the reader to know simply that a certain person studied this problem if you don't tell them the results of that study. And if you tell the reader nothing about the nature of the study, he or she is not in a good position to see how relevant it is to a particular conclusion. Be sure not to expect the reader to get inside your head when he or she is reading your paper. Be clear. Do not, for example, make a vague reference to "this agency" when referring to your study agency in the middle of the literature review, expecting the reader to realize that you are talking about your study agency. Such a reference would normally be out of place anyway. Your review should stick to the literature. You will discuss your own study later. But, of course, your literature review should be relevant to your study.

A common mistake is to say that a given researcher found a relationship between variable X and variable Y, then fail to clarify the direction of the relationship. Don't assume the reader will know that a discovery of a relationship between marital status and recovery means that persons who were married had a better recovery rate.

Another common mistake is to make up acronyms to use throughout the paper to avoid repeating a title many times. Certain acronyms are appropriate because they are well known. For example, we are now quite aware what AIDS means; however, most people would have trouble remembering that PWA refers to "people with AIDS," even if you went to the trouble of spelling this out at the beginning of the paper.

Principle 8:   Demonstrate your contribution.

The knowledge base employed is a critical factor in determining the quality of the literature review. The best knowledge bases are extensive, showing evidence of both depth and breadth. The breadth of your knowledge base is revealed in the number of references you find. The depth of the knowledge base is revealed in the types of references consulted. Sophisticated works on research or theory have greater depth than articles that provide one person's practical suggestions on a theme. While the latter is not an irrelevant source, it is not wise to over-rely on such sources. Furthermore, a dozen works of depth would be considered more "extensive" than perhaps several dozen of the other type.

The breadth of the literature review is evidenced by the range of the types of sources consulted and the range of the perspectives considered. One should not become so over-reliant on one perspective that its weaknesses are overlooked. And one should not become over-reliant upon sources of a "practical" nature which have no theoretical or empirical base. Many models and theories have become popular without any scientific justification. When this is the case, you can normally find articles that criticize the weaknesses inherent in the model or point out that the limited research on the model has proven inconclusive.

The focus of the paper provides evidence of the student's creativity. It should be unique. Thus, over-reliance on one source for guidance is ill-advised. The way you organize the literature is your unique contribution to our understanding of the issue. Needless to say, your focus should be clear to the reader.

Creativity is further indicated by your analysis and criticism of the material explored. Focusing your attention primarily on an uncritical description of a particular program, method, or theory does not show evidence of creativity.

The conclusions section of your literature review is one place where your creativity is best expressed. This section should reveal your conclusions rather than your summary of the conclusions drawn by one of the sources you consulted, even though the latter may be appropriately included in this section. Avoid using direct quotes in this section of the paper—you do not want to give the impression that you cannot say important things in your own words.

Principle 9:   Avoid lengthy paragraphs.

Try to remember what you learned in your English courses about a paragraph, that it should be limited to one idea. Knowing when to make a paragraph break is not the easiest task to master because there are themes and sub-themes and sub-themes of sub-themes within your general subject area. One tactic for addressing this principle is to look at the length of your paragraphs. It is unlikely that you will have an entire page of material that should be contained within one paragraph.

The paragraph break is much like the subject headings that you will employ—both help readers know where they are in your literature review. When the reader sees a new paragraph, he or she is alerted to the fact that a change has taken place.

The Introduction to Your Paper

Because it is usually easier to write a thorough introduction after you have written your literature review, hints about the introduction are discussed at this point. The introduction captures the reader's attention and sets the stage. It does not need to be set aside with a separate heading from the literature review; it simply begins the paper. The heading "Literature Review" can be your first major heading. In the introduction, let the reader know the problem you are addressing, why it is important, and what you intend to do about it in your study.

Principle 1:   The introduction should be brief; full explanation of theories or research findings should be reserved for the literature review.

The introduction to a research study should be no longer than one page. Details from the literature should be reserved for the literature review section. Quotes from the literature and references to sources should be rather limited, because you will provide such information in the literature review. You should avoid redundancy. Assertions made about the theme of the paper in the introduction, however, should be backed by information in the literature review.

Principle 2:   Begin the introduction with a description of the problem and the reasons for its importance.

The first thing the reader wants to know is, "What is this paper about?" The next thing is, "Why should I be concerned about it?" Consider the following statement:

> *Among young people in this nation, there are approximately 500,000 suicide attempts each year, about 5,000 of which actually result in death. These statistics highlight the fact that suicide is the third leading cause of death for persons between the age of 15 and 24 (Morrison, 1987).*

What did you learn from this brief sentence? First, you can see that the topic is suicide, but not suicide in general. It is about suicide among the young people of our nation. Next, you learned that there are a large number of suicide attempts each year among our youth and that it is the third major cause of death.

If you were to begin the introduction with the above statement, it should be followed by brief statements which reveal the major themes of the study, such as, for example, the treatment of suicide, or the prevention of it. Then, state the purpose of the study.

Principle 3:   Clarify the purpose of the study after the description of the problem.

The purpose statement should be placed early in the paper, but not until you have given the reader a reason to believe that this purpose is worthwhile. Do not begin the paper with a statement of the purpose of the study being described. You should entice the reader into the subject before laying out the purpose of the study you are presenting. The following is one example:

Recent studies indicate that many first marriages end in divorce, and the average duration of matrimony is quickly declining. Thus, divorce appears to have become a more acceptable alternative for coping with dissatisfaction in marriages. In light of the short duration of so many marriages, it can be speculated that many of these relationships contained the seeds of their own destruction from the pre-marital period of the relationship.

Premarital counseling has long been considered an effective means for preventing marital disharmony and keeping marriages together for the duration of life. The effectiveness of premarital counseling, however, has not been clearly established. While some researchers have reported success, others have produced conflicting results.

The purpose of the study reported in this paper is to examine the effectiveness of one premarital counseling program in the enhancement of marital satisfaction. Several variables considered to be related to marital satisfaction will also be examined to determine if premarital counseling is related to marital satisfaction when other variables are controlled.

In this example, the problem was presented succinctly and the purpose was stated in the third paragraph. The literature review which follows this introduction will elaborate on various forms of marital counseling, the objectives of such counseling, and the results of studies that have examined the effectiveness of this form of counseling.

Make sure your purpose (or objective) is consistent with what you intend to study. Don't say that your objective is to define the role of social work in working with people who have AIDS when you are proposing to study the relationship between knowledge and attitudes about AIDS. Don't say that your objective is to examine the relationship between drug abuse and school performance when you are really going to test the effectiveness of an intervention designed to improve the school performance of adolescents at high risk for substance abuse.

Chapter 9

Writing Study Purposes, Questions, Hypotheses, and Titles

When you state the purpose of your study or your research question, you are informing the reader of the primary contribution of your research. You provide guidance on the direction you will take the reader and the kinds of information that he or she can expect to find in your study.

Neither the exploratory study nor the descriptive study typically has a hypothesis, but they will have purposes or questions to be answered. You might, for example, be conducting an exploratory study for the purpose of developing hypotheses about variables that buffer the effects of stressors for social workers. In this case, you are not testing a hypothesis, you are developing hypotheses. Thus, you do not have a research hypothesis at the beginning of your collection of data. In another example, you might be conducting a descriptive study about the characteristics of your agency's clients, with the purpose of describing your clients in such a manner as to contribute to the identification of need. In this case, you also are lacking a hypothesis to be tested.

Both the explanatory and the evaluative types of studies will have hypotheses to be tested. An explanatory study might be conducted to determine if gender explains salaries for social workers when position level is taken into consideration. This purpose statement can easily be turned into a research question: *Does gender explain the salaries of social workers when position level is taken into consideration?* The hypothesis could be stated as follows: *Among social workers, males will report higher salaries than females even when position level is controlled.*

An evaluative study might be conducted to determine if Project PARENTING improves the parenting skills of adolescent mothers. The research question could be, *Does Project PARENTING improve the parenting skills of adolescent mothers?* The research hypothesis related to this study could be stated as follows: *The parenting skills of adolescent mothers will be higher at the completion of Project PARENTING than at the beginning.* If this is beginning to sound redundant, don't worry. It is not necessary to make all three statements for an evaluative or explanatory research study. **The only essential statement for these two types of studies is the hypothesis.**

In this chapter, you will be given a number of principles to guide your development of statements of your study purpose, research question, research hypothesis, and the title of your report. An excellent source of help with these statements is the book entitled *Writing Empirical Research Reports* by Pyrczak and Bruce (1992). Some of the suggestions which follow are aided by that work. First, you will examine purposes and questions.

Writing the Study Purpose and Research Question

Your study will always have a purpose, and usually it will have one or more research questions as well. It is not necessary to state both a purpose and a research question if they are essentially the same. The following principles provide guidance on developing the statement of purpose or research question.

Principle 1:   When you are not examining empirical relationships between variables, state a research purpose or question rather than a hypothesis.

When you are conducting either exploratory or descriptive research, you are not testing the relationship between variables empirically. With exploratory research, you might be exploring relationships among variables but you are not testing these relationships empirically. In other words, you are not measuring the variables in discrete fashion and examining their relationships statistically. In descriptive research, you are simply describing what is rather than whether one variable is a good predictor (or potential cause) of another variable. In both of these types of studies, you would state either the research purpose or the research question or both. Some examples of purposes and questions are as follows:

1. What is the pattern of service utilization for persons with developmental disabilities in Johnson County?
2. To what extent are the clients of Project Hope satisfied with the services they have received?
3. The purpose of this study is to describe the process that leads individuals to become homeless.
4. Are social work students more likely to describe the good human service manager in male-stereotyped terms than female-stereotyped terms?
5. The purpose of this study is to describe the roles that social workers play in the public school setting.

Principle 2:   When there is insufficient evidence to predict the direction of a relationship between variables, state a research question or purpose rather than a research hypothesis.

Sometimes when you have an explanatory purpose for a study, you will find that the literature, and other available evidence, does not provide sufficient guidance for you to predict the direction of the relationship between study variables.

For example, when York and Henley (1988) attempted to examine the relationship between gender and satisfaction with the bureaucratic form of organization, they found two contrary views on the subject in the literature and little empirical evidence that tested these two contrasting theories. One theory suggested that women would be more comfortable in bureaucratic organizations than would men, while the other theory suggested the opposite. In this situation, it would be wise to state either the purpose or the research question, such as, for example, *In social work, are females more likely than males to express satisfaction with the level of bureaucracy in their employing organizations?* This would be preferable to stating the hypothesis as, *There is a relationship between gender and satisfaction with bureaucracy among social workers.* The latter, however, is acceptable in some circles. This is known as a nondirectional hypothesis. However, it is not the optimal use of the concept of a study hypothesis in view of the nature of the role of the hypothesis in research.

Principle 3:   The statement of the research question or purpose should be specific to the task you are undertaking rather than something that is peripheral to it.

Your research purpose or question should give clear information on the specific nature of what you are doing. You might, for example, have encountered problems with how the social work role seems to be defined in a particular school system. You see a need for more clarity in the definition of that role. In the pursuit of this long-term goal, you might have decided to study the relationship between the teacher's knowledge of school social work as reflected in the literature, and the appropriateness of referrals of clients to the social worker in the school system. You would have developed tools to measure both knowledge of school social work and appropriateness of referrals. You would be wanting to know if teachers with higher scores for knowledge would have higher scores for appropriateness of referrals. Consider the following two ways to state the research purpose:

1. To define the role of social work in the school system.
2. To examine the relationship between teachers' knowledge of school social work and the appropriateness of their referrals to the school social worker.

Is alternative 2 obvious as the appropriate statement? It should be. Yet, one student wrote a paper on this subject and used alternative number 1 above as the statement of the purpose. The reader would expect a role definition to be the primary outcome of the study, but this was not the case.

Principle 4:   Your purpose should be to discover rather than to justify.

Perhaps at this stage of your learning, it is not necessary to state the obvious point that social work research is a process of discovery, not justification. You do not undertake research for the purpose of proving a point. Consequently, you would not say that the purpose of your study is, *To demonstrate that your agency has been effective in meeting client need.* You would not say that the purpose of your study is, *To challenge the criticism that social work has failed to be responsive to the needs of people with AIDS.* In both of these cases, it appears that you are trying to prove a point with your research study. This is inappropriate.

Writing the Research Hypothesis

The *research hypothesis* is a statement of the expected results of a research study on a given theme, based on theory or explanations derived from existing knowledge. The hypothesis should be supported by a knowledge base. You are not at liberty to state a prediction of the results of a study in the form of a hypothesis unless you have a knowledge base to support it. Thus, the hypothesis does not arrive merely from curiosity or a hunch.

The research hypothesis is distinguished from the *null hypothesis,* which is a statement that is true if the relationship between study variables in the research hypothesis can be explained by chance. For example, the research hypothesis, *Males will report higher salaries than females* would be stated in the null hypothesis form as, *There is no relationship between gender and salaries.*

The null hypothesis has an important role in traditional research methodology. When we apply statistics to data in order to test the research hypothesis, we are dealing with chance as one of the reasons for our configuration of data. The traditional researcher will state a null hypothesis and apply statistics to determine whether the null hypothesis should be rejected. If the null hypothesis is rejected, the research hypothesis is supported. However, the rejection of the null hypothesis does not provide proof of the truth of the hypothesis; it merely eliminates one of the alternative explanations for the data.

In this text, emphasis will be placed on the research hypothesis rather than the null hypothesis. You should remember, however, that if you wish to publish your work in certain journals, you may need to translate your research hypothesis into a null hypothesis in order to conform to the tradition.

Principle 1: The research hypothesis should name the study variables and identify the nature of the expected relationship between them.

Your research hypothesis should identify your study variables and indicate the nature of the relationship that you expect to find between them. For example, *There is a positive relationship between stress and burnout.* In this example, two variables have been identified, *stress* and *burnout.* The nature of the relationship has also been identified. This hypothesis indicates that a positive relationship is expected between these two variables, meaning that persons higher on one of them would be more likely than others to be higher on the other.

In the case of a variable measured at the nominal level, you cannot have either a positive or a negative relationship. Instead, you have to indicate how the groups or categories will differ from one another, as for example, *Males will report higher salaries than will females.* It would be inappropriate to say, *There is a positive relationship between gender and salary,* because a positive relationship would suggest an order to *both* variables. While salary has an order from lower to higher, gender is not ordered.

Principle 2:   The variables named in the hypothesis should be operationally defined.

The reader needs to know how the variables were measured. The operational definition should be relevant to the abstract definition of the concept reflected by the variable. The abstract definition of a variable provides the type of definition that we might find in the dictionary. It provides conceptual guidance about what we mean by the term. The operational definition specifies how we intend to measure that variable in our study. It is not necessary to specify the scale used in our study in our hypothesis, as long as we provide a clear operational definition of that variable in the research methodology section of the report. For example, we could say, *There is a positive relationship between self esteem and grades in school* rather than, *There is a positive relationship between scores on the Self-esteem Index and grades in school,* although either form would be acceptable. With the former, of course, you would be specifying in your report the specific scale you were using to measure self-esteem and you would specify how you were collecting information on school grades.

Principle 3:   You should be careful to specify the variables that you are directly measuring in your study rather than other concepts that might be inferred from them.

This principle may sound a little familiar in view of the previous suggestion about being specific in the statement of your purpose. The same advice holds for the hypothesis. For example, the number of days of training on computers is not the same thing as computer literacy. If you are testing someone's computer literacy, you should use this term in your hypothesis (e.g., *There is a positive relationship between computer literacy and willingness to use computers in practice*). But if you are measuring days of training, you should refer to days of training in your hypothesis (e.g., *There is a positive relationship between days of computer training and willingness to use computers in practice*).

Principle 4:   If two groups are being compared, both groups should be identified in the hypothesis.

Examine the following hypothesis:

> *Older social work students will be more anxious about taking a research course.*

They will be more anxious than whom? It may seem to go without saying that we are going to compare older students with younger students, but this is not acceptable. Remember that a statement of hypothesis is a very precise statement and does not follow normally from everyday language. The reader needs to know precisely what you intend to do. Thus, we would say,

> *Older students will be more likely than younger students to express anxiety about taking a research course.*

Principle 5:   Hypotheses should be free of terms that are not directly relevant to the variables being measured.

It is tempting to put a lot of unnecessary language in the hypothesis of a research study. For example, suppose a researcher were studying the relationship between self-esteem and the use of drugs among adolescents. Both self-esteem and the use of drugs would be measured by appropriate scales. Suppose this researcher had learned from the literature that an adolescent's willingness to use drugs was theorized to be related to self-esteem because the drug culture is the only social group available to some adolescents who are socially inept (which tends to lower one's self-esteem). Their only admission requirement is the willingness to use drugs. Thus, they choose the drug-oriented social group rather than have no group at all. Examine the following two ways to state the hypothesis:

> *Because some adolescents have no other social group to which to turn for social interaction, they use drugs so they will be accepted by the drug-oriented group.*

> *Among early adolescents, there is a negative relationship between self-esteem and the use of drugs.*

Is the distinction clear? With regard to the first statement, ask yourself the following: How is "having no other group to which to turn" being measured in this study? How is "being accepted by the drug-oriented group" being measured? As you will recall, there is no provision for the measurement of these variables in this study. This study only measured self-esteem and the use of drugs. Thus, the second statement is appropriate and the first is not.

Principle 6:   When the scope of the study is restricted to one population, you should specify that population in your hypothesis.

When your literature review suggests that your hypothesis applies to a specific population, such as children or military personnel or abused wives, you should specify the population in your hypothesis. The key is the literature review. If your literature review is focused on one population as the place where the particular theories or concepts apply, you should specify that population in your hypothesis. For example, you might have conducted a literature review about stress among social work students. If your literature review revealed no distinctions between social work students and others, you would not need to specify social work students as your population. However, most likely you would have focused on knowledge about students and about social workers, and inferred that knowledge logically to social work students such that you had the basis for predicting the outcome of a study regarding stress among social work students. Thus, you might state the hypothesis as follows: *Among social work students, there is a positive relationship between social support and stress.*

In another example, you might have conducted a study of salaries among social workers with the expectation that males would report higher salaries than females even when position level was taken into consideration. In this situation, you would state the hypothesis as, *Among social workers, males will report higher salaries than females even when position level is taken into consideration.* If you had selected the New Jersey Chapter of the National Association of Social Workers as the study population from which your sample was to be drawn, it would not be necessary to identify the New Jersey Chapter of NASW in your hypothesis unless your literature review had suggested that social workers in New Jersey would be different from social workers in other states. Most likely, your literature review would not have suggested that. You might have selected New Jersey as a matter of convenience. In this case, it would not be necessary to name the specific population from which the sample was selected in the hypothesis; that information would be included elsewhere in your paper.

Principle 7:   The statement of the hypothesis should match the means used to measure study variables.

A common problem is for the researcher to measure a variable in a continuous fashion but to state the hypothesis as though the variable is a dichotomy. For example, if you measure social support with a scale with scores that can range from a low of 0 to a high of 20, you would not state your hypothesis as though you were dichotomizing your study participants into the categories of support and nonsupport. For example, you would not say, *Social work students who have social support will have lower stress than will social work students who do not have social support.* Instead, you would say, *Among social work students, there is a positive relationship between social support and stress.*

Also, it is wise to avoid using such phrases as, *Persons who are high on X will be high on Y.* You do not normally restrict your analysis to persons only on one end of a scale. Instead, you should say, *There is a positive relationship between X and Y.* The latter statement includes all persons, not just those who are high on the scale.

Writing the Title of the Research Article

The title to the research article should convey meaningful information to the prospective reader of the report. It will give the reader an idea of what is being investigated in the article. One should not have to read the report in order to find this out.

Principle 1:   The title should be concise, yet meaningful.

If your title is concise, yet meaningful, it will convey the essential information needed by the prospective reader and will do so in the fewest words necessary for that purpose. You can be too cumbersome, leaving the reader a little impatient or confused, or too vague, leaving the reader in the dark. For example, consider the situation of a study to examine the effectiveness of school social work in reducing risk factors associated with high school students dropping out of school. Consider the shortcomings of the following title: "School Social Work: Are We There Yet?" You may have quickly noticed that this title tells you only one thing, that the article is about school social work, but it does not tell you that it reports on the effectiveness of school social work. It does not tell you that it deals with school dropouts among high school students. In fact, it could be a broad essay on the role of social work in the school system. But that is not the case. Thus, this title would convey little information useful to the prospective reader. Now, consider the following two ways to write the title for this study:

1. A Study of the Effectiveness of School Social Work in the Reduction of School Absenteeism, the Reduction of Disciplinary Episodes, the Improvement of Grades, and the Improvement of Self-Esteem Among a Group of 12 High School Students at Walker High School Identified as Being at High Risk for Dropping Out of School.
2. A Study of the Effectiveness of School Social Work in the Reduction of Dropout Risk Factors for High School Students.

The second title conveys the essential information for the prospective reader but does so with fewer words. While it is true that the first title conveys more information, it gives information not essential for the title of the report. Although the titles of dissertations are often stated in the form of the first version above, the second would be more appropriate for most titles, especially those submitted for publication.

Principle 2:   The title should identify the types of variables in the study, as well as the study population.

The last title mentioned above identifies risk factors as the dependent variable, school social work as the independent variable, and high school students as the population. It was not necessary to name each dependent variable because there were several. Instead, the variables were grouped in the general category of dropout risk factors. In many cases, you will have only two or three variables and will find it appropriate to name each variable rather than its general category. In fact, this is precisely what you should do when you have only a few variables.

Principle 3:   The title should identify what was studied rather than the results.

It would have been inappropriate to state the above title as *School Social Work is Effective in the Reduction of Dropout Risk Factors for High School Students.* This states the results. It may be tempting to state the results, especially if they are favorable, but you should remember that you are writing a research report, not an article for a newspaper.

The reason you should refrain from stating the results in your title is that research results are considered to be tentative in their support of a study conclusion. You should present your findings in the spirit of that tentativeness and invite the reader to consider various limitations of your study in drawing conclusions about the nature of your topic.

References

Pyrczak, F. & Bruce, R. R. (1992). *Writing Empirical Research Reports.* Los Angeles: Pyrczak Publishing.

Chapter **10**

Using Standardized Instruments for Measuring Study Variables

Standardized instruments are scales developed by experts in the field, usually copyrighted and published. These scales require permission for reprinting in your work. In other words, you could not reprint the scale in its entirety in your own published article without such permission. If it is a highly commercial instrument such as the MMPI, you will find that it can only be obtained by purchasing copies of the instrument from the copyright holder. You will not find an entire copy of such a test in a book or journal article.

There are many advantages to using established instruments. They were developed by experts in the field who have a keen understanding of the phenomenon being measured. The typical social work researcher has neither the time nor the expertise to engage in this level of instrument development. Furthermore, those who have published instruments have typically tested them for reliability and validity.

In this chapter, you will be given a set of principles to guide your efforts in selecting a standardized instrument for your research. You will also be given descriptions of a dozen selected instruments that appear in a two-volume set by Fischer and Corcoran (1994). I selected these instruments because I have found them to be most frequently used by social work students in their research projects.

Principle 1: Select an instrument that clearly measures your study variables as you have defined them.
Your first step in the process of measurement is the development of an abstract definition of the variable you wish to measure. There are various ways to define such concepts as anxiety, stress, self-concept, and so forth. You should be clear on your own definition before you seek a measurement device.

Avoid selecting a standardized instrument that does not do a good job of measuring what you want to measure. Often, you will find your treatment objectives with your client do not lend themselves to measurement by existing instruments. It is better that you develop your own scale that really measures client progress according to your objectives than to select something that is ill-suited for this purpose, or measures a secondary objective rather than the primary one. Do not make the mistake of selecting an established instrument simply because it is available and will require no work to adapt.

Take the example of the concept of stress. What does it mean? Would you say that stress is defined by the number of environmental demands made upon a person, such as being a full-time student, a part-time employee, a mother, *and* a caretaker for an elderly relative? You might tend to say that a person who was carrying all these roles would be stressed. You could, therefore, define stress as the number of roles that place significant demands on a person. You would measure it by listing such roles and asking the respondent to indicate the number of such roles or the extent to which each one demands time or energy, and so forth.

But you might ask yourself, why am I concerned with the concept of stress? Perhaps it is because stressful situations cause people to experience psychological tension, which can be unhealthy. Thus, maybe you should define stress as psychological tension rather than environmental circumstances. If so, you would ask yourself, *How is psychological tension manifested?* You might respond by thinking of such words as "tense" or "uptight" or "anxious." In this case, you would be seeking a different type of scale than if you had defined this concept as presented in the previous paragraph.

Principle 2: Select an instrument that is appropriate for your study sample.
Some scales have been developed for adults rather than children. If you are administering a scale to children, be sure to obtain a scale that is appropriate. The education level is also important. If you are dealing with persons with a third-grade reading level, you should not select an instrument that was designed for college-educated people.

You should also be mindful of the feasibility of administering a certain instrument. The instruments in the work by Fischer and Corcoran (1994) were selected partly because of their ease of administration. They are short scales that take only a few minutes to complete. Complicated scales such as the MMPI and the Myers-Briggs Type Indicator take much longer to administer and may not be feasible for your situation.

Published instruments typically have been tested for reliability and validity, but they have not been tested with your study sample. Because they have stood the test of reliability and/or validity in other contexts, you normally can assume that they will be appropriate for your situation, but you should consider the audiences for whom the selected scale was developed and with whom it was tested. For example, you might suspect that incarcerated sex offenders, who are the subjects of your treatment program, would be more likely to express a social desirability bias than would a group of college students upon whom a certain scale of sexual attitudes had been validated. Persons in prison may have a vested interest in looking better than they are.

Principle 3: Select an instrument that is sensitive to the kinds of changes you can reasonably expect.
If you are engaging in evaluative research, you will seek instruments to measure client progress. Consider the extent to which a given behavior is amenable to change when you

seek an instrument. For example, you might find that locus of control, in its general form, does not change very much over small periods of time, but health locus of control is more amenable to change. Thus, you would seek a health locus of control scale rather than a general locus of control scale if health locus of control is what you are trying to change.

You should also consider whether a given scale is sensitive to the level of changes you could reasonably expect to achieve during the treatment period. This is especially important for short-term interventions. How much can you expect your client's level of depression to change with four treatment sessions? Does your selected scale tend to be sensitive enough to pick up on this level of change? A scale with a narrow range of possible scores may not be suitable.

Principle 4:   Select an instrument with adequate reliability and validity.

The extent to which you need a scale that has been tested for reliability and validity will vary with the situation. If you plan to publish your work, you will need to pay a lot of attention to this question. If you have reason to be concerned with reliability and validity with your particular study subjects, you will need to pay special attention to this question. Of course, the more a scale has been tested, the better. But you might find a relatively untested scale that seems highly appropriate for your study, and another scale that is less appropriate but that has been tested extensively. Normally you should give more priority to appropriateness than to reliability and validity, providing that there are no obvious problems with the latter.

You should remember from your examinations of these issues that reliability refers to the consistency of an instrument, while validity refers to its accuracy. An instrument must be reliable in order to be valid, but it could potentially be reliable without being valid. In other words, an instrument could be consistently inaccurate.

You will see reference to different types of reliability and validity in your examination of reports on clinical scales such as the one by Fischer and Corcoran (1994). Some of these types of reliability and validity are reviewed in the following paragraphs.

Internal consistency refers to the extent to which the items on the scale correlate with one another. Thus, if John has a higher score than Mary on item 3, he is likely to have a higher score than Mary on item 9. This provides evidence that the items on the instrument are measuring the same thing. There are several formulas for ascertaining the level of internal consistency of an instrument. These include Cronback's alpha, the Kuder-Richardson formula, and the Spearman-Brown formula. Generally speaking, if you see a coefficient of .70 or higher for such measures, you have adequate evidence of internal consistency. However, there is no clear rule for judging the adequacy of internal consistency.

Test-retest reliability refers to the consistency of an instrument when it is administered more than one time to the same study subjects. If Sue receives a higher score for depression than Martha in the first week in May, we would expect her to receive a higher score than Martha at the end of May (assuming that these persons are randomly drawn from a population). If this pattern persists for a study sample, we will find a high correlation between the scores on this depression scale at time one and time two. This would provide evidence of the test-retest reliability of the instrument. Correlations of .70 and higher are normally considered adequate.

Criterion validity refers to whether the scores on the scale correlate with other variables with which they would be expected to correlate. Forms of criterion validity include *predictive validity* (whether scores on this scale predict some future event) and *concurrent* *validity* (whether scores on this instrument correlate with other means of measuring the same thing). Graduate Record Examination scores, for example, are supposed to predict grades in graduate school. Are GRE scores correlated with graduate school grades? If so, we have evidence of predictive validity. If you and I both develop scales designed to measure depression, the scores of the same group of persons on both of these scales should be highly correlated. This would be evidence of concurrent validity.

Construct validity refers to whether an instrument operates in the manner that would be predicted theoretically. For example, we would expect that marital happiness and a desire to get a divorce would be negatively associated. Thus, we would expect to find that marital happiness scores for persons seriously thinking of divorce would be lower than for persons who were not giving this alternative serious thought. Such a finding would be evidence for construct validity.

Construct validity also deals with the precision of the instrument in measuring what it is supposed to measure. We would expect that scores on the XYZ Test of Research Knowledge would correlate with IQ scores, but we would not expect this correlation to be higher than a correlation of scores on the XYZ Test with scores on another test of research knowledge. The latter would suggest that the XYZ Test is doing a better job of measuring someone's intelligence than their knowledge of research. An important test of construct validity comes from the study of the correlation of scores on a given instrument and scores on an instrument designed to measure the social desirability bias. Social scales designed to be self-administered are vulnerable to the social desirability bias because we might respond to questions on the basis of what we consider to be socially desirable rather than what we really feel or believe. If scores on the ABC Scale of Self-Esteem are found to correlate significantly with scores on a scale of social desirability, we have evidence to question the construct validity of the ABC Scale.

Principle 5:   Carefully adhere to the instructions for administering the instrument.
Reproduce the scale in the same form as it was designed and be sure you administer it properly. If it is designed to be administered by a clinician rather than being self-administered, be sure to do that. If any deviations are essential in your situation, be sure to report them in your article so the reader can assess the limitations imposed by these changes.

Consider the circumstances under which the study subject will respond and the implications of those circumstances for reliability and validity. If your client is asked to take an instrument repeatedly while at home, try to get him or her to do it under uniform circumstances, such as immediately before going to bed, or right after dinner.

Principle 6:   Obtain the study subject's informed consent to respond to the scale.
Informed consent is an important ethical consideration in social research. You should provide the opportunity for the study subject to refrain from participating in your study. You should inform the subject of the way the information will be used. If you are administering the instrument to a group of persons, it is usually feasible to guarantee the subject's anonymity. If not, you can at least guarantee that the information will be kept confidential.

When you employ the one-group pretest-posttest design (and some of the other evaluation designs), you will need to administer the instrument before and after treatment for the same persons. The pretest score for each client will need to be matched with that client's posttest score when you analyze the data. Thus, you will need a mechanism for identifying the individual. But you can still maintain anonymity by a simple method of asking a few questions for identification purposes, questions the client could answer but not you or others who might be exposed to the forms filled out by the client. For example, you could ask how such questions as:

1. How many letters are in your mother's maiden name?
2. How many siblings does your father have?
3. What is the last number in your social security number?

Each of the responses is in the form of a number. The combination of these numbers would constitute the identification number for the client. You would need to ask these questions on both the pretest and posttest instruments so you can match the two.

Principle 7:   Pilot test the instrument.

Even though your chosen instrument will be one that has been tested on other people, you may be surprised at the response you get from your study subjects. If you have the opportunity, you should pilot test the instrument with persons similar to those in your study sample.

While the instrument has been tested for reliability or validity, it has not been tested with your study subjects. You may find that a depression scale is valid with people in general but not with your one client you are studying through a single-subject design. In fact, I have had students whose clients received low scores on a depression scale even though they were clearly depressed. Obviously this scale was not valid as a measurement device for depression for this one person. Sometimes people respond to a scale according to the way they think is socially desirable rather than the way they really feel. The fact that a given scale is not valid for a given person does not mean it is not valid overall. Scales can only be expected to be valid with large numbers of people in general. Each scale has a certain amount of measurement error. This is one of the limitations we must live with.

Principle 8:   Be careful about the way the instrument is to be scored.

Most instruments will contain items that are worded in opposite directions. This means that certain items must be reverse-scored so that all items operate in the same direction. For example, you might find the following items on a depression scale:

I feel blue.

      Always   Frequently   Seldom   Never

I feel hopeful.

      Always   Frequently   Seldom   Never

A response of "Always" would result in the highest score for depression for the first item, but this same response to the second item would result in the lowest score for depression.

Thus, for the first item, *Always* would be coded as a 3, *Frequently* would be coded as a 2, *Seldom* would be coded as a 1, and *Never* would be coded as a 0. For the second item, the scoring would be reversed as follows: *Always* = 0; *Frequently* = 1; *Seldom* = 2; and *Never* = 3. With this scoring method, the client always gets the higher score if he or she gives a more depressed response.

Key Sources of Instruments for Social Workers

There are many useful sources for the selection of standardized measures of social and psychological phenomena. The ones most likely to be of use to the social worker are the following:

Fischer, J. & Corcoran, K. (1994). *Measures for clinical practice.* New York: Free Press. [This work is in two volumes. Volume I contains instruments for couples, families, and children. Volume II contains instruments for adults.]

Fredman, N. & Sherman, R. (1987). *Handbook of measurements for marriage and family therapy.* New York: Brunner/Mazel.

Hudson, W. W. (1982). *The clinical measurement package.* Chicago: Dorsey Press.

Nurius, P. S. & Hudson, W. W. (1993). *Human services practice, evaluation, and computers.* Pacific Grove, CA: Brooks/Cole.

Robinson, J. P., Shaver, P., & Wrightsman, L. S. (1991). *Measures of personality and social psychological attitudes.* San Diego, CA: Academic Press.

A key source for social workers is *The Clinical Measurement Package* by Walter Hudson (1982). This package was developed by a professor in a school of social work, especially for clinical applications for social workers. Each of these scales provides a five-point scale for response ranging from *Rarely or none of the time* to *Most or all of the time.* Each scale has 25 items with a range of possible scores from 0 to 100, which provides a convenient basis for interpreting scores. Each scale has been tested both for reliability and validity and found to be at least adequate for both. There are a total of nine scales in this package.

The most extensive source of instruments for social workers is *Measures for Clinical Practice,* by Fischer and Corcoran (1994). This book contains descriptions of many instruments that measure social variables ranging alphabetically from alcoholism to verbal aggressiveness. It is conveniently indexed by problem area, so you can look up a tool by reference to the kind of problem you are seeking to measure. Such problem areas include alcoholism, anger, anxiety, assertiveness, and so forth.

Each instrument is described with reference to its author, the purpose, a general description of what it looks like, norms, scoring, reliability, validity, primary reference, and availability. Each scale is also printed in the Fischer and Corcoran book.

References

Fischer, J. & Corcoran, K. (1994). *Measures for clinical practice.* New York: Free Press.

Fredman, N. & Sherman, R. (1987). *Handbook of measurements for marriage and family therapy.* New York: Brunner/Mazel.

Hudson, W. W. (1982). *The clinical measurement package.* Chicago: Dorsey Press.

Nurius, P. S. & Hudson, W. W. (1993). *Human services practice, evaluation, and computers.* Pacific Grove, CA: Brooks/Cole.

Robinson, J. P., Shaver, P., & Wrightsman, L. S. (1991). *Measures of personality and social psychological attitudes.* San Diego, CA: Academic Press.

Chapter *11*

Conducting a Mailed Survey

The social work researcher will often find a mailed survey to be the appropriate form for collecting study data. The mailed survey has the advantage of being one of the least expensive ways to collect data. You can obtain information on a relatively large number of people at a minimum cost, especially compared to an interview method of gathering information. The mailed survey also provides an optimal means of assuring the study subject's anonymity.

The mailed survey, however, has the disadvantage of failing to provide a mechanism for gathering information of a subtle nature, such as the meaning behind statements. The researcher does not have the opportunity to probe for subtle information that might lie behind the overt response if the mailed survey is employed. Consequently, the mailed survey is normally employed when quantitative methods of measurement are appropriate. However, the mailed survey can use open-ended questions that provide the respondent with the opportunity to respond in a unique fashion using their own words. Thus, some elements of the qualitative format can be employed in the mailed survey.

Before the social work researcher is ready to determine whether a mailed survey is most appropriate, he or she will have developed a knowledge base relevant to the study theme and will have articulated a study purpose, research question, or study hypothesis. The mailed survey is perhaps most appropriate for the descriptive study when information of a discrete form is needed from a large sample of persons and there is a limited budget. Examples include a survey of need for a program in a community or a survey of former clients to determine their level of satisfaction with the services they received. The measurement of public opinion is a very common use for the mailed survey, but it is not often employed by social work researchers.

Mailed surveys may be employed in both longitudinal research and cross-sectional studies. In the *cross-sectional study*, you collect data at only one point in time. When you employ the *longitudinal study*, you collect data at more than one point in time. Thus, the cross-sectional survey is more appropriate for descriptive research or for exploratory research than for explanatory research.

When you collect data at one point in time, you can easily describe social variables with precision (descriptive research) and you can explore relationships between variables in your attempt to develop hypotheses (exploratory research), but it is more difficult to examine causation (explanatory research) with this method of data collection. In the pursuit of causation, you could compute a correlation between the dependent variable and the independent variable, but the correlation will not tell you which variable is the cause and which is the effect. It will only tell you that these two variables are associated; thus, one may be the cause of the other but you do not know which is which with the correlation alone. Furthermore, you will remember that correlation is only one of the three factors that determine causation. You must also examine time order and alternative explanations if you are to fully examine causation.

Consider, for example, the association between job satisfaction and job performance. If you conducted a cross-sectional survey of the employees of an organization in which you collected data on job satisfaction and job performance, you could compute a correlation between these two variables. If you found a significant correlation, you might be tempted to assert that this correlation indicates that satisfaction is the cause of performance. But it might be that performance is the cause of satisfaction. It is also possible that the association between these variables is spurious, meaning that they are not causally linked.

You could address alternative explanations for the cause of performance, through an examination of other variables. For example, suppose females tended to be happier on their jobs than males and that they tended also to perform better. It may be that satisfied females are not more productive than unsatisfied females and that satisfied males are not more productive than unsatisfied males. In this case, the only reason satisfaction and performance are correlated is that females are more satisfied and more productive than males; thus, gender explains this relationship. If you controlled for gender in your examination of the relationship between satisfaction and performance, you would no longer find a significant correlation and you could rule out one of these variables as the cause of the other. This example illustrates the fact that the cross-sectional survey can be much more useful in ruling out causation than in confirming it.

Because the longitudinal survey collects information at more than one point in time, it provides the opportunity for considering time order in the examination of causation. For example, you could measure job satisfaction and job performance in January and again in February, and examine whether changes in performances were more likely to follow changes in satisfaction than vice versa. If changes in satisfaction tended to be followed by changes in performance, you would have one piece of evidence that satisfaction is the cause of performance. But if the reverse were true, you would have evidence that performance is the cause of satisfaction.

There are four major steps in conducting a mailed survey. First, you must clarify your study purpose and your research questions. For the explanatory or evaluative studies, you will also articulate your research hypotheses. This will guide everything else. Next, you select your study sample. Then you develop the research instrument. Finally, you administer the research instrument. After you collect your data, you will, of course, analyze that data, but that step will be dealt with in the next major section of this book.

Principle 1:   Do not encumber the survey questionnaire with items that are not consistent with the study questions or research hypothesis.

Perhaps it will seem to be obvious that the questionnaire should address the study purpose, but you may be surprised how often this principle is violated by the novice researcher. It is very tempting to start thinking of questions to ask on a questionnaire before you clarify the research questions that you wish answered. I have asked social work students why they had certain items on their research questionnaires and received the response "We were curious to know the answer to this question," even though the item did not fit into the research questions that had been articulated for their studies. Often, students will place certain questions on a questionnaire because they have often seen this question asked on other questionnaires and assumed that you were supposed to ask these questions. Sometimes a question will appear on a questionnaire because the information is in the general category of the research study, even though the student does not have a specific use for the data. These items are to be avoided. A good reason why you should avoid these encumbrances is articulated in Principle 8, keep the questionnaire as simple as possible.

Freedom from unnecessary items is especially important if the questionnaire is rather long, because a long questionnaire will have a lower rate of response. Thus, you should be very clear about each piece of information that you really need to collect in order to achieve your study purpose. However, if your purpose is somewhat exploratory in nature, you might find it acceptable to add a few items where you are not certain of their utility.

Consider the task of conducting a survey of the graduates of your social work program. You may be tempted to start this process by thinking of the questions that should be included in this survey. Perhaps this will seem like the perfectly logical place to start, but there is a flaw in this line of thinking. Pause for a moment and identify that flaw.

Okay, time's up. What is the flaw in this line of thinking? You should have noticed the fact that you need to identify the study purpose and the specific research questions that should be answered by this survey. Each item to be included on the questionnaire should be linked to this purpose and one of these research questions. For example, you might have started developing questions and found yourself asking "What was your selected concentration in your program of study? (a) Direct practice, (b) Administration, Policy, and Planning, (c) Other." The question you should be able to answer before entering this item on the questionnaire is "How will this information be used?" There are several purposes for such an item. You might want to compare your study respondents to your graduates to see if there is a difference. If fifty percent of your respondents were direct practice students and eighty percent of your graduates were direct practice students, you can see that these persons are underrepresented in your study sample. Another purpose for the inclusion of this item is to provide you with the opportunity to compare students according to concentration of study on certain other variables related to satisfaction with the program.

As you can see, there were some useful reasons for including this item. However, the task of identifying these purposes should take place before the articulation of the items to be included on the questionnaire. When this is not done, there is a high likelihood that unnecessary items will be included. Furthermore, there may be necessary items that were *not* included because you failed to clearly identify what you needed to know—something that is much easier said than done. It has been my observation that the temptation to frame questions before clarifying the needed information is quite strong—among both social work students and professionals in the field.

Returning to the task of surveying the graduates of your social work education program, what would be the major purpose? Would you seek information to help the faculty improve the program? Would you seek information to aid the school in achieving accountability with the university administration or the social work accrediting body? Perhaps you would identify both of these purposes. They are common purposes for a client satisfaction survey. However, there would be some difference in the information you would collect to achieve these two purposes. The first purpose is process-oriented, while the second is outcome-oriented. The school can learn how to improve by asking questions on the suitability of certain courses or components of the curriculum, and by soliciting recommendations on how to improve. The school can better achieve accountability with information on how effective former students feel the program was in their preparation for a professional career. The research questions in Exhibit 11.1 provide a good number of potential variables to be measured on a questionnaire. Some of these research questions contain reference to one vari-

---

EXHIBIT 11.1   Sample Research Questions

Within each purpose for the study, you should articulate research questions. Each research question must be addressed by one or more items on the questionnaire. Here are a few research questions you might want answered in a survey of graduates of a Master of Social Work (MSW) program:

1. Are program graduates employed in jobs consistent with the school's mission?

2. Are program graduates employed in jobs consistent with their chosen concentration or specialization?

3. To what extent do our graduates believe that their choice of specialization and concentration was the right choice for them?

4. How effective do our graduates believe our program to be overall in their preparation for a professional career?

5. How effective, in their professional career development, do our graduates believe our program to be in each of the major components of the program, such as human behavior in the social environment, social work practice, research, policy, and field instruction?

6. To what extent do our graduates believe our faculty are effective teachers?

7. How well has our program met the overall needs of our graduates?

    a. How well did it meet the graduates' need for professional identification?

    b. How well did it meet the graduates' need for obtaining employment after graduation?

    c. To what extent was class scheduling and so forth accessible to students?

    d. To what extent did our graduates receive helpful advice from the faculty regarding options in the curriculum, career development, and so forth?

8. Do responses to items addressing each research question in this study vary by the respondent's (a) gender, (b) race, (c) age, (d) concentration or specialization choice, (e) full-time or part-time status, or (f) year of graduation?

able, while the others refer to more than one variable that needs to be measured. The last question contains reference to eight variables that would need to be measured in the questionnaire. If you were conducting this study, you might want to add or eliminate questions.

Principle 2: Use the study purpose, research questions, or hypothesis to clarify whether you are seeking information on opinions, behaviors, knowledge, or something else.

If you are seeking knowledge on how AIDS is transmitted, you would construct an instrument with either True-False items or multiple choice items or other constructs that you are likely to find on a college test. You would not construct items with response categories such as *strongly agree* and *agree* and *disagree,* because the latter are related to opinions or attitudes rather than knowledge.

An opinion is a tendency to react favorably or unfavorably to a given idea. It implies a value position. Knowledge does not imply a value position; it refers to the accuracy of one's accumulation of information according to some standard of correct information. An attitude is a pattern of opinions around a certain theme. You might, for example, ask a set of opinion questions about the extent to which employees are satisfied with each of several aspects of the work life of the organization. This might include pay, working conditions, and supervision. Thus, you could have three opinion questions, one related to each. You could combine these items to form an attitude scale regarding "job satisfaction."

One of the most common variables measured in social work research is the psychological construct. These include such things as depression, anxiety, locus of control, extroversion, and so forth. The use of measures of psychological constructs requires attention to the questions of validity and reliability. Consequently, it is wise to thoroughly examine the available standardized measures of psychological constructs before attempting to create one for yourself. Guidance for the selection of such measures was given in chapter 10.

Principle 3: Use a probability sample if you are seeking to precisely describe a study population.

The nature of your research study will guide your identification of the study population. If your purpose is to describe this population with precision, you have two choices: include the entire population in your study, or select a probability (random) sample from that population. If you want to know the demographic characteristics of the members of your state's chapter of the National Association of Social Workers, you would be advised to select a random sample of persons from the membership list of that organization. This list, however, would not provide you with a random sample of all social workers in your state, because some social workers do not belong to this organization. If you wanted to describe the clients of your agency, you could include all of them unless their number was too great for this to be feasible.

To describe a study population with precision means that you wish to be able to know certain characteristics of that population within a small margin of error. For example, you may want to know the percentage of your agency's former clients who would recommend your agency to others. You may want to know the percentage of your present clients who are living in single-parent households. A school of social work may need to know the proportion of applicants for their graduate program who wish to pursue a career in human service administration. In each of these examples, the necessity is to describe with precision.

If a school of social work operates on the assumption that one-third of their applicants wish to pursue human service administration and the fact is that this figure is actually only five percent, the school is likely to engage in poor course scheduling.

There are two major ways to draw a simple random sample. You can organize a list of the population and draw names using a table of random numbers or you can use the systematic random sampling method. The procedures for the *systematic random sampling* method are as shown in Exhibit 11.2.

EXHIBIT 11.2   Procedure for Systematic Random Sampling

1. Secure a simple list of all persons in the study population, such as an alphabetical list. Avoid lists that place a certain kind of person in a given position, such as having every fifth person be someone who is unemployed.

2. Determine the sampling interval. The sampling interval is the interval between persons to be selected on this list. If you have a sampling interval of 5, this means that you will select every fifth person on your list. You determine the sampling interval by dividing the number in the population by the number to be selected for the study sample. If your population is 500 and you wish to select 100 persons from that list, your sampling interval would be 5 (500 / 100 = 5).

3. Identify the first person for the sample by identifying those who fall in the first sampling interval and by selecting one person at random from that group. You can use a random method by drawing a number (e.g., from 1 to 5 if the interval is 5) from a hat, rolling a die, or a similar method.

4. Determine the second person to be included in the sample by selecting the person who falls exactly one sampling interval beyond the first person selected. Then select the remainder of the sample by continuing to select the person who falls at the next sampling interval. For example, if you had randomly selected person number 3 from the first sampling interval of 5, the second person selected would be person number 8 on the list, while the next person would be person number 13, and so forth.

You can safely generalize from a random sample to its population. Therefore, there is an inherent advantage in the use of the random sample for a mailed survey. However, the employment of a random (probability) sample is less important if your purpose is to examine relationships between variables rather than describe the population. If male social workers receive higher salaries than female social workers, you will find the male advantage in most samples of social workers. However, you would not be able to describe the size of the male advantage with precision unless you were to employ a random sample.

If you are examining relationships between variables and you do not have a random sample, you should examine the issue of bias in sampling. A *sampling bias* is any characteristic of a sample that is believed to make it different from the study population in some important way. For example, a sample that included only the employees of women's organizations would likely be different from other human service agencies with regard to the distribution of salaries by gender. With this sample, you are not likely to discover a male advantage; therefore, you would obtain a distorted view of the relationship between gender and salary with this particular sample.

Principle 4:   Use multistage sampling when the study population is too complex for simple random sampling.

Multistage sampling includes more than one stage of drawing people for a study. If you wanted to draw a sample of social workers in one state, you would likely find that there is no convenient list of all such persons. You would probably not have the resources to travel to each county in the state and secure a list of all agencies that employ social workers and then secure a list of all social workers employed in those agencies. If you had the resources to do so, you could develop an optimal sample by selecting persons at random from that master list. However, the fact that you cannot do this does not mean that you have to abandon random sampling procedures. Instead, you could secure a list of all counties and draw a random sample of counties to be included in your study. This would constitute your first stage. Then you could secure a list of all human service agencies from these selected counties. In the second stage, you woud select a random sample of agencies from this list. Finally, you could secure a list of all social workers employed in these selected agencies and draw a random sample from this list. This would be your last stage.

The multistage sample is not as representative of the population as a simple random sample. There is an element of sampling error at each stage of sampling; therefore, the multistage sample will have more sampling error. *Sampling error* is the degree of difference between the sample and the population. All samples have some sampling error, in that there will be some difference from the population. However, the random sampling procedure provides us with the opportunity to estimate that error so we can better interpret our results.

Principle 5:   Use disproportional sampling if you need to compare groups where one group is very small.

Suppose you wished to conduct a mailed survey of all members of NASW for the purpose of comparing clinicians and supervisors on job satisfaction. Suppose there are 1,000 persons on this list identified as clinicians, and only 100 identified as clinical supervisors. If you selected a simple random sample of 10 percent of these persons, you would likely have about 100 clinical social workers and only 10 supervisors. Your supervisory sub-sample would be rather small. When a small sub-sample is divided into categories for the purpose of statistical analysis, problems can arise with the achievement of statistical significance.

In this situation, you could use disproportional sampling. With this approach, you divide the population into the relevant groups and you select a different proportion from each group. In the above example, you might select 10 percent of the clinical social workers but 50 percent of the supervisors. In this situation, you would have 100 clinical social workers and 50 supervisors. It is not necessary for the two groups to be equal in numbers in order for you to do a comparison.

Principle 6:   The cover letter should motivate participation without encouraging a biased response.

The mailed survey questionnaire will be accompanied by a cover letter that tells the prospective respondent about the study. The letter should motivate participation. Knowing the purpose and sponsorship of the survey will normally motivate the respondent to complete the questionnaire, especially if this information is something with which the respondent can identify.

On the other hand, the cover letter should not state the research hypothesis or give information on what the researcher expects to find from the results. For example, if a cover letter to social workers indicated that males and females were going to be compared on their sex-role biases about management, some respondents would become concerned with achieving a socially desirable response. They might not want to be caught expressing a sexual bias and would become especially alert to language that might be testing such biases.

It is important that the cover letter be brief. Most people can be motivated with simple statements about purpose, sponsorship, and so forth. An extensive letter will be a turnoff to some people and could cause them to trash the questionnaire.

McMurtry (1993, pp. 279–280) summarized the tips for writing the cover letter as follows:

1. Give the exact date of the mailing of the questionnaire.
2. Identify the researcher and institutional affiliation, preferably on official, printed stationery that is unique to the project or organization.
3. Explain the research project sufficiently to allow the respondent to understand its general purpose, but not in such detail as to be confusing or discouraging.
4. Explain the significance of the study in terms of its potential benefit to policy or practice.
5. Convey to the respondent the importance of participation in the study.
6. Explain how the responses are to be used and how confidentiality will be maintained.
7. Instruct the respondent on how to return the completed form.
8. Identify the person to contact with questions or concerns about the survey.

Principle 7: Use standardized instruments where feasible.
In the previous chapter, you were guided through the process of selecting and using standardized instruments for measuring study variables. The advantage of such instruments is that they have been carefully designed by persons with more time and expertise in such matters than you might have. Furthermore, they have typically been subjected to tests of reliability and validity.

Simple questions are easily constructed by the novice researcher. It is not difficult to compose questions about the respondents gender, age, and willingness to volunteer for agency work. But the measurement of psychological constructs (e.g., depression, anxiety, attitudes toward the elderly, marital satisfaction) is a different matter. If you must develop your own psychological constructs, you should address the issue of either reliability or validity. Ideally, you should address both, but there are numerous published scales that fail to address both. Thus, if you address one of these issues in one test, you will normally be on acceptable grounds. One such method would be the examination of internal consistency. For example, you could examine whether there was an acceptable pattern of correlations among the items on the scale.

Principle 8: Keep the questionnaire as simple and brief as possible.
Persons in your study sample are less likely to choose to participate if your questionnaire is too long or cumbersome in its instructions. How simple you need to make it will vary with the nature of your sample. If you employ a sample from the general public, you must be very simple in your wording of items and your instructions. Samples of highly educated people require less simplicity, but the length of the questionnaire will be an important con-

sideration. Normally you should restrict your questionnaire to an instrument that will take no more than 20 minutes to complete. Longer questionnaires are feasible if you have a highly motivated audience. Motivation will vary with the extent to which the respondent identifies with either the sponsor or the issues being addressed.

You should employ a print type that is rather small but easy to read. Smaller print allows you to place more items on the questionnaire without giving the appearance that the questionnaire is too long. However, really small print will be a disadvantage. Type point sizes of 9 and 10 are suggested. This is approximately the size of the print in this text. You should print the questionnaire on the front and back of the page, both to reduce the weight of the questionnaire and to avoid the appearance of being too long.

You should arrange the items on your questionnaire so there is not a lot of empty space on the page because this wastes paper and gives the appearance of a longer questionnaire. For example, examine the following two ways to arrange the same question:

What is your gender? _____ Male _____ Female

What is your gender?

_____ Male

_____ Female

The first one does not take up as much room on the page from top to bottom, leaving more space for additional questions on the same page. However, you also want to avoid giving the appearance of a cluttered questionnaire, or placing items in ways that might be missed. It is usually not a good idea to place two questions on the same line, such as the following:

7. What is your gender? _____ Male _____ Female 8. What is your age? _____

Avoid the use of initials or jargon in your questionnaire items unless they are quite well known to your study subjects. The pilot testing of your instrument will help show whether your wording is confusing to the respondents. When you construct an item, think carefully about how it might be read by some of your respondents. You might be surprised how some items can be interpreted in different ways.

Principle 9:   *Use the closed-ended question if you are aware of the normal pattern of responses to the question.*

Whether you employed closed-ended or open-ended questions will depend on the extent to which you can predict the typical responses to the questions. A closed-ended item is one that asks the respondent to select a category or to give a number such as age. Open-ended items leave it up to the respondent to answer in their own words. If you wanted to know the most important unmet needs of your fellow students, you could ask the question in either form, depending upon how much information you already had regarding the typical responses. If you have little information, you would provide a question such as *What are your most important unmet needs as a student in this social work program?* However, if you have already conducted discussion sessions with fellow students and have heard four needs repeated by many students, you might want to ask for your respondents to mark which of these needs is most important to them, or to rank-order these needs.

The closed-ended question will be easier to analyze when you receive your responses. You need only to enter the code for each response in your data set and you will be able to easily tabulate responses or ask the computer to calculate a correlation, or another measure of association, between this variable and another one. Open-ended questions require interpretation, which can be very time consuming.

Principle 10: Place demographic and controversial items toward the end of the questionnaire.

If you place demographic items at the beginning of the questionnaire, the respondent may be turned off by the thought that they are filling out some government form. This could reduce their motivation to complete the questionnaire. Controversial items can also reduce motivation because they provoke more emotions. If such items are toward the end of the questionnaire, the respondent will be more motivated because he or she will have already invested time in this task and will not want to abandon it after this investment.

It is better to begin the questionnaire with items that would seem interesting to respondents but would be noncontroversial. This approach gives respondents the feeling that they are participating in a worthwhile project. It is best that these first items be at the heart of what you have told the reader the questionnaire is all about in your cover letter. This improves the credibility of your questionnaire in the minds of respondents. You want respondents to get the feeling that the researcher knows what he or she is doing with this questionnaire.

Principle 11: Use transitional sentences if your questionnaire is complex.

You should gently guide the respondent through your questionnaire, especially if it is rather complex. Each major shift in focus should have a transitional sentence that guides the reader. For example, let's say you want to ask your agency's former clients four sets of questions regarding (1) the nature of the problem that brought them to the agency and the type of services they received, (2) how they were treated by the entire staff, (3) their evaluation of these services, and (4) their recommendations for improvement. If each of these categories had several questionnaire items, you should consider using transitional sentences such as "Now, we would like to know something about the way you were treated by our entire staff."

This approach keeps the respondent on track and reminded of the nature of what is being asked. You want to avoid giving the impression that your questionnaire is "all over the place" and doesn't seem to hang together.

Principle 12: Avoid common errors in questionnaire item construction.

There are two fundamental principles of item construction that may need your review. The first is that response categories should be *mutually exclusive*. This means that a given respondent cannot possibly fit into more than one category. Take, for example, the following item:

What is your age?

_____ 0–20   _____ 20–30   _____ 30 & above.

In the above classification, where does one fit who is 20 years of age? There are two categories for this person.

The second basic principle is that response categories must be *exhaustive*. An exhaustive listing of categories gives a category within which everyone will fit. For example, if you had age categories of 20–29 and 30–39 and 40 and above, you would have mutually exclusive categories, but you would not have exhaustive categories, because you have no place for someone who is below the age of 20.

Beyond these two fundamental principles are several things to avoid. You should avoid *double-barreled* questions. These questions contain two ideas or opinions in the same question, one of which may fit the respondent and the other may not—so what is the respondent to do? Here's an example: "Have you ever hit your child so hard it left a bruise, or witnessed someone else doing so?" How do you interpret a "yes" response? A respondent could have hit his child but not witnessed it elsewhere, or witnessed it but not hit his own child, or both. Even worse would be an opinion item with two different opinions in the same question. A respondent may agree with one but not the other.

You should also avoid negative items because respondents may miss the negative term and misinterpret the question. Rubin and Babbie (1993, p. 189) give an example from a survey which asked respondents to indicate whether several types of people should be prohibited from teaching in public schools. Groups such as the Ku Klux Klan, Communists, and so forth were listed with the response categories of "Yes" and "No." Answering "Yes" meant that you agreed that such persons should *not* be allowed to teach in the public schools. Yet, we are accustomed to responding with "yes" when we favor something, so it was pointed out that many people may have misread this item.

Principle 13:   *Pilot test your instrument before administering it to your sample.*
Some of the flaws mentioned above will become evident if you pilot test your questionnaire. A pilot test is an administration of the questionnaire to persons similar to your sample but not included in your sample, for the purpose of seeing how the instrument works. Ideally, you will obtain comments from the persons who participate in the pilot test. You can either ask for comments in the margins of the questionnaire or hold a discussion with them.

You only need a few people to participate in the pilot test, but the more people, the better the information. For example, from the pilot test you can see if persons mark two categories on an item when only one was supposed to be marked. You can ask if any of the items were confusing.

Persons who participate in the pilot test cannot be included in the sample for the study. However, you should select these persons on the basis that they are similar to the sample in education level or understanding of the concepts presented on the questionnaire. Your task is to simulate the actual experience of responding to the questionnaire.

Principle 14:   *Send follow-up correspondence to enhance your return rate.*
Response rate is a major issue in the mailed survey. Generally speaking, a response rate of 50 percent is considered acceptable for the publication of a study that employs a mailed sur-

vey. A response rate of 70 percent is considered exceptional. But there are published works with much lower response rates. The response rate that is acceptable for your study is not an easy fact to establish. The important thing to keep in mind is that the persons who did not respond may be different from the respondents, and this difference may render your sample data unrepresentative of the population from which the sample was selected.

You should ask yourself if there is any reason to believe that the nonrespondents are different from the respondents. Take this fact into consideration when you interpret your results.

Several procedures can help you obtain a good response rate. If you send out a mailed questionnaire without a follow-up letter, you can expect a much lower response rate than 50 percent. Each follow-up letter will generate additional responses. At a bare minimum, you should enclose a stamped, self-addressed envelope for response, and send one follow-up reminder to your respondents about 10 days after the questionnaire is sent out. A more sophisticated set of procedures has been developed by several researchers over the recent decades, as shown in Exhibit 11.3.

EXHIBIT 11.3   Mailed Survey Hints

The following procedures are considered an ideal approach to the mailed survey.

1. Send a brief cover letter along with the questionnaire and a stamped, self-addressed envelope for returning the questionnaire.

2. Send a postcard reminder about 10 days to 2 weeks after the first mailing. You can send this reminder to everyone on the original list, but if this is a really large number, you can employ the following technique for reducing costs:

    > Send a postcard in the original mailing and ask respondents to place their name on the postcard and mail it back when they place their questionnaire in the mail, but they should be instructed to mail the postcard separate from the questionnaire so that you will only know who has responded but not which questionnaire goes with which respondent. In this way, you will know who to exclude from the follow-up mailings.

3. About two weeks after the postcard reminder has been mailed out, send a modified cover letter with a second copy of the questionnaire. Some of the prospective respondents will have misplaced the first questionnaire.

References

McMurtry, S. L. (1993). Survey research. In *Social work research and evaluation,* R. M. Grinnell (Ed.). Itasca, IL.: F. E. Peacock.

Rubin, A. & Babbie, E. (1993). *Research methods for social work.* Pacific Grove: Brooks/Cole.

Chapter *12*

Writing the Methods, Results, and Conclusions for the Research Report

In this chapter, you will find practical advice on the preparation of the methods, results, and conclusions sections of the research article. Some of the principles included here were inspired by the book on writing research reports by Pyrczak and Bruce (1992). The present text, however, focuses on the needs of the social work student more so than the experienced writer of research articles.

Writing the Methods Section of the Research Report

In the methods section is information on the research study's design, instruments, data collection procedures, and sample. From this section of the report, the reader can assess the study's strengths and limitations.

Principle 1:   State the research question or study hypothesis if this was not sufficiently clarified in the introduction or literature review.
If you stated the research question or study hypothesis in the introduction and have not mentioned it again, it could be useful to restate it at the beginning of the methods section of the paper. The necessity for this increases with the complexity of your questions or hypotheses. You might find it useful to organize your methods section around your different study hypotheses if you have more than one. However, if you have only one rather simple hypothesis, you will not need to remind the reader of it in the methods section.

Principle 2:   The basic study design should be presented in sufficient detail to facilitate replication.

In this text, you have been given descriptions of several designs for evaluative research. These included the one-group pretest-posttest design, the comparison group design (non-equivalent control group), and the pretest-posttest control group design. These labels are useful in evaluative research for conveying to the reader the extent to which external influences on the client's behavior have been controlled in the study procedures. For example, you were informed that the one-group pretest-posttest design did not address maturation as a threat to internal validity.

If you are conducting descriptive or exploratory research, you will not find this classification system to be very useful. Instead, you might find it useful to report whether a cross-sectional survey or a longitudinal survey was employed. This classification system reveals whether data were collected at only one point in time or repeatedly.

While the provision of a correct label for the research design can facilitate communication with the reader, it is more useful for the report to include the specific procedures employed. For example, you could say that the one-group pretest-posttest design was employed, but it would be even more important to describe how this worked. For example, you could say *The study subjects were given the Generalized Contentment Scale before and after their participation in the treatment program.* In another example, you could say that "a cross-sectional survey" was employed, but it would be more useful for you to say, *The respondents' answers to the survey questions about salary, position level, and gender were statistically analyzed.*

Many traditional texts in research classify research designs into the categories of non-experimental, quasi-experimental, and experimental. I have found that this classification systems creates more problems than it solves for students of social work research. Furthermore, it is not necessary. If you can describe the design employed and you can identify its limitations, it means very little for you to be able to correctly place it into the category of quasi-experimental or experimental.

Principle 3:   Identify the instruments employed to measure study variables, and define the variables they were designed to measure.

You should provide an abstract definition of any complicated concept that is measured in your study. Such definitions would apply to concepts like self-esteem or extroversion, but not to variables such as gender or age. If you are employing a standard instrument that has been published, you will report what that scale was designed to measure. It is not sufficient to provide the name of the scale, even if the scale title has a commonly known concept such as depression or anxiety. There are various ways to define such concepts. You should specify how you are defining them in your study.

You should describe the format for the instrument and the kinds of response categories that are provided. For example, the Index of Family Relations contains twenty-five statements such as *My family gets on my nerves* and *I think my family is terrific.* Respondents are asked to indicate how often each statement is true and are given response categories on a five-point ordinal scale from *Rarely or none of the time,* to *Most or all of the time.*

You should also provide the possible range of scores and provide any information available regarding thresholds of functioning. In the case of the Index of Family Relations, scores can range from 0 and 100 with higher scores providing more evidence of family problems. Scores above 30 are considered to indicate a clinically significant problem.

Principle 4:   *If you employ a published scale, identify whether reliability and validity have been addressed, and refer to the source of the instrument.*
Published measures have normally been subjected to tests of reliability and/or validity. It is not necessary for you to describe in detail how this was addressed. At a minimum, you should indicate whether either the reliability and validity of the instrument have been tested and whether the results were favorable, and you should provide the source for this information.

If you wish, you can specify what types of reliability or validity were addressed, but you are cautioned not to rephrase statements in the published source unless you are familiar with the concepts being presented. I have often seen mistakes made by students who tried to describe such information when they didn't understand it. You could, of course, quote the material from that source.

The Generalized Contentment Scale can be found in Walter Hudson's *Clinical Measurement Package* (Hudson, 1982). The following is an example of how you could describe that scale:

> *The Generalized Contentment Scale is designed to measure nonpsychotic depression among adults. It focuses primarily upon the affective aspects of clinical depression. Scores can range from 0 to 100, with higher scores representing higher depression. Clients with scores higher than 30 are considered to have a clinically significant problem with depression. This scale has been tested for internal consistency and test-retest reliability with favorable results. In the category of validity, this scale has been found to correlate with several other measures of depression and has been found to effectively discriminate between persons known to be depressed through clinical observations and those not known for this problem (Hudson, 1982).*

Principle 5:   *If you employ a nonpublished scale, describe the instrument in detail and report on the ways that reliability and validity have been addressed.*
If you employ a published scale, you can refer the reader to the source of the scale for details about what it looks like and how reliability and validity have been established. If you develop one yourself or use one that has not been published, you face a greater burden for establishing its credibility.

Under these latter conditions, you should describe the scale with examples from it, or include the scale as an exhibit or appendix to your report. You should report how reliability and validity have been addressed. For example, if you computed a split-half correlation, you should report those results, including the correlation coefficient and the p value.

At a minimum, you should address face validity and internal consistency. Face validity is the weakest form of validity, but it is clearly better than no test of validity at all. You should develop a specific plan for testing face validity. This might entail selecting five persons known to have expertise on the subject of the scale and asking them to indicate whether this scale measures the thing it is supposed to measure. This could include a direct question about face validity (Yes or No) as well as comments about its weaknesses or recommendations for alteration. You should be clear how you plan to use the instrument, and the purpose it will serve.

Internal consistency is a simple matter to address because you do not have to collect any additional information. You simply examine the extent to which responses to the items seem to hang together. One of the primary methods for examining internal consistency is the split-half approach. With the split-half approach, you split the items on the scale (the ones that are supposed to be measuring the same variable) into two halves on some kind of random basis. A popular approach is the odd-even method, in which all odd-numbered items form one sub-scale and all even-numbered items form another sub-scale. Then you compute the correlation between these two sub-scales. You would expect a positive correlation that is rather high and statistically significant. If the correlation is weak, you would not have evidence that the various items on the scale are measuring the same thing.

Principle 6: Define the study population and the sampling method employed.

A study sample is a portion of a study population. The study population is that aggregate of persons to whom you wish to be able to generalize your results, however weak or strong might be your evidence for generalization. If your study purpose was to determine the extent to which the past clients of the Hopewell Family Counseling Center were satisfied with the services they received, your study population would likely be the former clients of the Hopewell Family Counseling Center. However, it is not likely that you would have the ability to include every past client in your study. Instead, you would select a sample of these persons, and you would hope that your sample was representative of the entire population.

In your report, you should define the study population and describe the methods you employed in selecting a sample. If you are well-versed in sampling terminology, you would give a label to your sample, such as convenience sample, probability sample, and so forth. If you describe how the sample was selected, you do not need to worry very much about the label to give it. The reader can draw proper conclusions about generalization without the necessity of a label, providing that sufficient information is given. Do *not* come up with your own terminology in labeling your sample, as for example, one student who decided to label his method a "slice-of-life sample."

A probability sample is one in which every member of the population had an equal chance of being selected for the sample. This is one label that is worth mentioning, because it says a lot about your ability to generalize your results to the population.

You should report on attrition from the sample. For example, if you mail a questionnaire to a random sample of 100 of the 300 persons who comprise the population of persons served by your agency in the past 10 years, you would also report on the proportion of persons who actually returned the questionnaire. If you asked each client to complete a satisfaction survey at the termination of service, you would report how many persons refrained from participation, and the reason why they refrained if that information is available.

When you have completed the description of the sample and the population, you will have given the reader a clear picture of who was included and excluded from the study sample. From that information, the reader can draw conclusions about the generalization of the study's results. For example, a study was conducted by Edleson and Syers (1991) of men who had been in a treatment program for males who had battered their mates. The following is a description of the study sample:

> *Over 500 men initially sought service during the study period. Of these persons, 340 completed intake interviews but only 153 completed the program. Of these persons, 70 could be located at the follow-up time period, which was 18 months after the completion of the program. These 70 cases constituted the study sample.*

With this description, the reader can draw conclusions about generalization. Can the results of this study be generalized to all men who batter, or all men who initially sought help from this program, or all men who completed this program, or all men who could be located at follow-up? You can draw your own conclusions, given a clear description.

Principle 7:   Describe the characteristics of the study sample.

The study sample should be described in sufficient detail to give the reader a general picture of what kinds of people were in the study. The particular variables to include will vary by the nature of the study, but you would normally report information on gender and age. Often, you will find it useful to report information on race or ethnic origin, income level, occupational status, and so forth. Of particular concern will be information on the nature of the problem being confronted in the study. For example, among the information given by Edleson and Syers (1991) in the above-mentioned study of men who batter was the following:

> *Those for whom data were available ranged in age from 18 to 56 years, with a mean of 33.75 (SD = 8.3). Fifty-one of the men were White, representing 72.9% of the sample. In addition there were 5 Black (7.1%), 1 Hispanic (1.4%) and 1 Asian man (1.4%).*
>
> *The average number of years of education reported by the men in this sample was 13.7 (SD = 2.2). The majority of the men (52.8%, n = 37) were reported employed full-time, whereas 22.8% (n = 16) stated they were unemployed at the time of intake....*
>
> *At the time of the intake into the treatment program, almost half of this sample (45.7%, n = 32) reported themselves married or living with their partners, and 50% (n = 35) of them were single, divorced, or separated. At the 18-month follow-up, however, only 21.4% (n = 15) of the men were reported to be married and living with their partners....*
>
> *More than one third of the men (35.7%) reported that they had been court ordered to treatment. Almost two thirds (61.4%, n = 43) reported having received mental health services at some point prior to intake, and 47.1% (n = 33) reported having been involved in some type of chemical-dependency treatment (Edleson & Syers, 1991, p. 229).*

Writing the Results Section of the Research Article

In the results section, information is presented on the results of the analysis of data in the pursuit of the study questions. Information on the sample's characteristics is normally placed in the methods section, but you might find it in the results section of some articles. The primary focus of the results section is on the information that was collected in the pursuit of an answer to the research question.

Principle 1: Organize the presentation of data around the research questions or study hypotheses.

If you have three research questions, you should present information regarding question 1 followed by question 2 and so forth. Your information should not move back and forth among the various study questions or research hypotheses. For example, suppose you administered pretests and posttests of (1) self-esteem, (2) self-confidence, and (3) knowledge about the consequences of drug use to a group of adolescents who were at high risk for substance abuse. Between the administrations of the pretests and posttests for these three variables, you have administered a program designed to reduce the risk factors. Thus, you have pretest scores for each of these three variables and you also have posttest scores for each.

In this example, you have three study hypotheses, one related to each of these variables. In this situation, you should *not* present the mean pretest score for self-esteem followed by the mean pretest score for self-confidence followed by the mean pretest score for knowledge, and then turn your attention to the presentation of the mean posttest scores in the same sequence. Instead, you should present the pretest and posttest scores as well as the test of statistical significance for the first hypothesis followed by the second, and the third.

Principle 2: Organize large amounts of data into tables, and refer only to the data highlights in the narrative.

It is quite boring for the reader to be presented with a myriad of details from your data analysis. This is a special problem for the descriptive study. Take, for example, the descriptive study of the characteristics and services of the clients of the neonatal intensive unit of a hospital reported by the author in another book (York, 1997). Data had been collected on the gestational age of the babies, the age of each parent, the education of the mother, the number of parents living with the child, the number of siblings, the method used to pay the hospital bills, the weight of the baby, the number of cases with each of six presenting problems, and the disposition of cases for each of these six presenting problems. Altogether, data were collected on 20 variables.

Consider the following way to begin the presentation of the results:

Only one baby had a gestational age of 25 weeks and this represented 2.2 percent of the total sample. Two babies had a gestational age of 26 weeks (4.4%) while four babies had a gestational age of 27 weeks. Twelve babies had a gestational age of 28 weeks (26.7% of the total) and seven babies had a gestational age of 29 weeks (15.5%). Of the remainder, two had a gestational age of 30 (4.4%), 4 had a gestational age of 31 (8.9%), 4 had a gestational age of 32 (8.9%), 6 had a gestational age of 33 (13.3%), and 3 had a gestational age of 34 (6.7%).

If you are not bored yet, just think how you would feel after being subjected to such a report on a total of 20 variables.

The solution to this problem is to organize these data into tables which the reader can review as he or she might wish. The narrative should refer only to the highlights. For example, the writer might point out that 62 percent of these families paid their hospital bills through the Medicaid program, indicating that they were in a low income category. Another fact of special interest was that 71 percent of these babies had a gestational age that was less than 32 weeks, which is a threshold for normal lung development.

Principle 3:   Present explanatory and evaluative results with statistical details in parentheses.

Data analysis for explanatory research entails testing a hypothesis or a set of hypotheses. Evaluative research is a particular type of explanatory research that is treated separately in this text, but it is similar in that you are testing a hypothesis. For this type of research, data results should be organized around the hypotheses that are being tested.

In the presentation of your data, you should provide three kinds of information as follows:

1. The descriptive statistics which reveal differences between groups or administrations of the instruments, where this is appropriate, such as the mean salaries by category, or mean pretest and posttest scores. With some statistical measures, however, this type of information will be lacking. For example, if you compute a correlation between scores on a self-esteem scale and number of absences from school, you will not be comparing groups. This information is distinguished from statistics that are used to describe the sample. The information discussed here refers specifically to the study hypotheses.
2. The statistical coefficient, or its equivalent, derived from the statistical measure employed (examples: $r = .31$; $t = 3.56$; $C = .58$; $X^2 = 2.96$). It is especially important to report the correlation coefficient where this type of test is employed, because this information reveals something about the strength of the relationship between the study variables.
3. The level of statistical significance achieved (i.e., the value of p). This can be reported in two forms. The traditional form is to report whether the level of significance (alpha level) established for testing the hypothesis was achieved. If you established the .05 level as your standard, you could report the p value as "$p < .05$" if your hypothesis was supported. If it was not supported, you could report either "$p > .05$" or "ns," which means "not significant." The newer form entails the presentation of the actual p value, such as "$p = .02$." In either case, this information should be given in parenthesis at the end of the sentence that presents the descriptive data about the hypothesis or states whether the hypothesis was supported.

Avoid such awkward terminology as "Significance was achieved at the $p < .05$ level." Expressions such as "$p < .05$" should be placed in parentheses.

The following are examples for the presentation of data results for explanatory and evaluative studies:

1. The mean pretest score for self-esteem was 9.7, while the mean posttest score was 14.2. This difference was statistically significant ($t = 2.6$; $p < .05$); thus, the hypothesis was supported.
2. The mean salary for males was $36,480, while the mean for females was $29,447. This difference was significant ($t = 3.1$; $p < .01$), providing support for the hypothesis that males would report higher salaries than females.

3. The first hypothesis (There is a positive relationship between self-esteem and number of days absent from school) was tested with the Pearson correlation coefficient. The results of this analysis failed to support the hypothesis ($r = .18$; $p = .34$).

Writing the Conclusions Section of the Article

In the conclusion section, sometimes referred to as the discussion section, the researcher summarizes the results and provides an image of how the results should be interpreted in light of the limitations of the study. In addition, it is customary for information to be presented on the direction of future research on the chosen theme.

Principle 1:   At the beginning of the conclusions section, restate the study purpose, question, or hypothesis, and summarize the evidence presented in its behalf.
The last part of the research article provides a synopsis of the study. The reader has been taken through a literature review, a description of the methodology, and the analysis of data. At the end, the reader may have missed a major point regarding the results of the study. For this reason, you need to provide a summary of the findings.

As an example, let's examine a study of the normative model of decision making. In this study, social workers were asked to think of a problem solving situation they had encountered in their work lives and to answer a set of questions designed to measure two major variables: (1) the extent to which the decision leader had adhered to the normative model in regard to the delegation of responsibility, and (2) the extent to which the respondent evaluated the decision outcome positively. The hypothesis was that those situations that had adhered to the model would have more positive outcomes. However, some potential intervening variables were also included.

The conclusions section of this article begins as follows:

> *Managers who employed the optimal level of decision participation according to the normative model were found to have achieved a better decision outcome than those who did not, but they achieved this outcome primarily because they had a positive decision climate and because those who adhered to the model were more likely to have employed a higher level of participation than those who did not. The contribution of the choice of an optimal level of participation seems to contribute rather little to decision outcome by itself. Further, the influence of the normative model seems to be greater at lower levels of participation (York, 1994, p. 157).*

In another example, social workers in rural and urban communities were compared on their perceptions of their communities with regard to a set of variables theorized to distinguish these two types of communities. The following is the beginning of the conclusions section:

> *The results of this study indicate that social workers in rural areas perceive their communities differently than do urban social workers. Rural communities are*

perceived as comparatively more informal in decision-making, slower in pace of life, more stable in lifestyle, more traditional in values, more likely to rely upon informal support systems, more likely to emphasize community acceptance over individuality, and less likely to place emphasis upon formal education as a necessity for achievement. However, these same social workers did not express differences, along the rural-urban continuum, with regard to emphasis upon role sets or the use of informal helping networks in their daily work. This is a surprising finding. If social workers perceive their communities differently, why do they not practice differently? (Denton, York, & Moran, 1988, p. 20)

Principle 2:   In the conclusions section, present only the highlights of the results rather than restating them in detail.

Notice that the above examples did not repeat the data given in the data analysis section, with means, or correlations, or p values, and so forth. That would be repetitious and would interfere with the major highlights of the study results. In this last part of the article, you want a clear focus on the highlights. There is seldom a need to mention specific pieces of data such as means or frequencies or correlations. You would, of course, indicate whether a given hypothesis was supported, and indicate what relationships were found between study variables, but repeating correlation coefficients and p values would be unnecessary. This information has been presented in the results section and the reader can refer back to this section if these details are of interest.

Principle 3:   Discuss the limitations of the study.

Help the reader place your study in perspective by noting the limitations of the study methodology, the key place to find limitations. Often, you will find that the sample selected for study can be generalized to a limited population because of the sampling methods employed. Another key place for the discovery of limitations is the study design. Did you conduct a cross-sectional survey where a longitudinal survey would have been better? What threats to internal validity were not addressed in your evaluative research design? Are these threats of special importance in your specific situation?

The selection of study variables and the means used to measure them is another candidate for the discovery of limitations. For example, a study was conducted by York, Denton, and Moran (1989) with the purpose of examining whether rural and urban social workers differed in their social work practice in accordance with theories about how the people of these communities differed in regard to norms of behavior. One expectation was that rural social workers would be more likely than their urban counterparts to make use of informal helping networks. Social workers in one state were asked to respond to several questions designed to measure various aspects of social work practice in addition to identifying the county of their work so that population variables could be used as measures of rurality. Social work practice was conceptualized according to roles, specialization among roles, and the use of informal helping networks. The major finding was that rural and urban social workers did not practice differently. But one limitation of this result was the way that social work practice was conceptualized and measured. Think of all the ways that one could characterize social work practice. It would seem that roles, specialization, and the use of informal helping networks would be among the various ways that it could be conceptualized, but there would be many other ways as well. Perhaps a study with social work practice conceptualized differently would have yielded different results.

You should be cautioned, however, not to take the "shotgun" approach to the overall task of identifying study limitations by automatically listing all the limitations of every aspect of your study. If you had the time, you can always find dozens of limitations of any study. But, instead, you should examine the ones of particular concern to your situation. For example, if you are conducting an evaluative study, you should examine the threats to internal validity that you believe logically should be of special concern in your study situation. If you were evaluating a one-year program designed to improve the parenting skills of adolescent mothers, you would need to be concerned with maturation as a threat to internal validity because it would be logical to expect new parents to improve their parenting skills with a year of experience in this role, even without an intervention. But if you had a client who had clearly been in a serious state of depression for a year, you would not expect this situation to change spontaneously in a mere month of time. Thus, if you were giving this person one month of treatment, you would not need to worry very much about maturation.

Principle 4:   Examine the implications of the study for social work and the directions for future research.

What should the results of your study mean for social work practice or social policy? Did your results provide reason for optimism regarding a particular treatment model? Did it suggest that a certain theory should be rethought because of your newly discovered limitations? Were your results ambiguous, suggesting nothing more than further research with different study samples or different methods of measurement? These are among the questions that you should pose for yourself as you discuss for the reader your views on the implications of your study results.

References

Corcoran, K. & Fischer, J. (1987). *Measures for clinical practice.* New York: Free Press.

Denton, R. T., York, R. O., & Moran, J. R. (1988). The social worker's view of the rural community: an empirical examination. *Human Services in the Rural Environment, 11* (3), 14–21.

Edelson, J. L. & Syers, M. (1991). The effects of group treatment for men who batter: An 18-month follow-up study. *Research on Social Work Practice, 1* (3), 227–243.

Hudson, W. W. (1982). *The clinical measurement package.* Chicago: Dorsey.

York, R. O. (1994). The influence of optimal decision participation upon decision outcome in human service organizations. *Journal of Social Service Research, 19* (1/2), 139–160.

York, R. O., Denton, R. T., & Moran, J. R. (1989). Rural and urban social work practice: Is there a difference? *Social Casework, 4* (70), 201–209.

Unit *III*

Analyzing Data in Social Work Research

In this section of the book, you will be given guidance in the statistical analysis of quantitative data. You will review concepts and learn how to answer the key questions in the selection of a statistics. You will be given a set of decision trees for selecting a statistic for your study and you will be given descriptions of your chosen statistical measure unless it falls out of the bounds of those described in this book. You will also be given information on using one particular statistical software package, SPSS for Windows, in the examination of the data for your study. You will also be given concrete guidance on the analysis of data for single-subject research designs. The objective of this section is to give you a means for selecting and using a statistical measure for your own study. This guide should be helpful for you in the future whenever you are confronted with a particular data analysis need.

Chapter *13*

Reviewing Basic Research Concepts Necessary for Data Analysis

In this chapter you will gain an understanding of how to organize data for statistical analysis. This understanding is essential to your task of selecting a particular statistical measure for the examination of your research question.

Objectives

There are several specific objectives for this learning experience. At the completion of this chapter, you should be able to:

1. Distinguish between description and explanation as general purposes of a research study which employs quantitative means of measuring variables.
2. Identify the hypothesis for a study.
3. Define the concept of "variable" and identify the variables in a given hypothesis.
4. Distinguish between the abstract and the operational definitions of a study variable.
5. Develop a scheme for coding data from a questionnaire for computer analysis.
6. Distinguish between descriptive and inferential statistics.
7. Distinguish between practical significance and statistical significance.
8. Identify the statistical concepts that provide guidance for determining practical significance and statistical significance.
9. Answer the five questions necessary for selecting a statistical measure.

If you believe that you already have achieved these objectives, you should consider moving on to the next chapter which helps you to select a statistical measure.

Reviewing the Research Process

In previous chapters, you have confronted many research concepts organized around the research process. Now, in preparation for data analysis, you will re-examine some of these concepts through the following themes:

> Developing the research question or study hypothesis
> Conceptualizing study variables
> Measuring study variables
> Using statistics to analyze data
> Interpreting results

Each of these themes will be briefly examined in the pages which follow.

Developing the Research Question or Study Hypothesis

The research literature generally classifies studies into three categories: descriptive, exploratory, and explanatory. Evaluative research is a fourth category, explanatory in nature, but singled out for special attention in the examination of social work research.

Exploratory research is designed for the purpose of developing theories or hypotheses on subjects where such are in short supply. For this reason, *qualitative* methods of measuring variables are often employed. Descriptive, explanatory, and evaluative research studies, however, typically use *quantitative* means of measuring variables. Quantitative studies use methods of measuring variables in which each study subject is measured discretely in either pre-determined categories or numbers.

This section of the book is designed to help you examine quantitative data. Therefore, we will deal with the research purposes of description, explanation, and evaluation. For example, you might want to know the number of your agency's clients with pre-school age children, or the proportion of your agency's clients whose income places them below the poverty level. In these cases, your purpose is description. You simply want to know what is the situation with a given set of people.

Another purpose is explanation. You might want to know why some clients fail to show up for their second therapy session after coming to the agency for an intake session. In this case, you might want to identify the variables that are associated with failing to show for the second interview. This could be done by comparing clients who fail to show with clients who do not fail to show on the basis of any number of variables such as age, presenting problem, income level, and so forth.

Another purpose is evaluation. You will often be in a situation in which you are expected to examine the extent to which social work services are effective in achieving their goals. Are clients less depressed after therapy than before? Are adolescent mothers better skilled as parents after they have completed a parent enhancement program?

One of the first tasks in the analysis of data in social work research is the determination of the research question or study hypothesis. The basic purpose you are pursuing will be your guide. A few questions have been illustrated above. One was the question *What is the proportion of our clients whose income is below the poverty line?* Another was *What are the variables that are most highly associated with failing to show up for a second clinic interview?*

Explanatory studies use the hypothesis as a conceptual tool. The hypothesis for a study is an educated guess of the outcome of the study. It is a statement of what you would find from your data if your theory were correct. A few examples are as follows:

Males will report higher salaries than females even when years of experience is controlled.

Employed social work students with a higher level of social support will experience less psychological stress than will employed social work students with lower levels of social support.

Clients of the Inpatient Mental Health Unit of the hospital will exhibit less depression after 20 days of treatment than before treatment began.

Conceptualizing Study Variables

A variable is an entity that can take on more than one value. In other words, a variable must vary! You cannot use gender as a variable in a study that includes only females because the concept of gender does not vary with this study sample.

In quantitative research, you distinguish between the abstract definition of a variable and the operational definition of it. The *abstract definition* is the kind of definition you might find in a dictionary (although a good study will have a definition that is more elaborate than that).

You must develop abstract definitions of your study variables before you can develop a means of measuring them. You might, for example, define stress as a condition characterized by feelings of psychological tension. You might find in the literature that writers often refer to stress as the experience of certain working conditions such as work overload and low levels of work autonomy. But this would be different from your definition, if you had defined stress in terms of a psychological condition rather than a set of environmental conditions. These environmental conditions may well be associated with psychological tension but they are not the same thing as psychological tension. Some people experience a great deal of psychological tension when they confront certain working conditions, while others who face the same conditions may not experience psychological tension.

Once you have defined your variable in abstract terms, you are ready for the operational definition of it. The *operational definition* of a variable is a statement of how the variable is to be measured in a particular study. With your definition of stress above, you are ready to seek instruments that measure psychological tension rather than instruments that measure working conditions.

Measuring Study Variables

One of your first tasks in the conceptual understanding of how to measure a variable is to distinguish between a variable, an attribute of a variable, and data. The concept of variable was defined above. An *attribute* of a variable is a particular value that a study entity (subject) can experience. Gender could be considered a variable, while the concepts of male and female would be attributes of that variable. Age could be a study variable and the number 37 could be one attribute of it because someone in the study could be 37 years old. Data, on the other hand, refers to the information collected for a particular study subject. This could include a particular subject's age, gender, score on the depression inventory, and so forth. The collective information for a variable would also be referred to as data. For example, the mean age for a given sample of graduate social work students might be 28.7.

After you have operationally defined your study variables, you will need to collect your data on those variables. This is normally done with some kind of survey instrument (e.g., questionnaire). You might, for example, ask the following questions:

What is your gender? _____ *Male* _____ *Female*

What is your age? _____ *years*

To what extent are you considering a career in some form of social work administration above the level of clinical supervisor?

_____ *To a very great extent*

_____ *To a great extent*

_____ *To some extent*

_____ *To a little extent*

_____ *To a very little extent*

_____ *Not at all*

After collection, data must be coded for entry into the computer for statistical analysis. You need to assign a number to each attribute of each variable. For example, you might code males as 0 and females as 1. You might code the highest level of interest in a career in social work administration as 5 with the next level a 4 and so on until you have the lowest level assigned the number 0. Age, on the other hand, can simply be entered into the computer in its natural form if it is collected in this fashion (as indicated above). However, it would be different if you had chosen to measure age with the following question:

Are you at least 30 years of age? ____ *Yes* ____ *No*

In this case, you would need to assign numbers for "No" and "Yes," probably 0 and 1.

Please don't forget that each study variable must be measured in your study. If you wish to examine whether stress is related to social support, locus of control, and employment status for social work students, you will need to collect data on four variables—*stress, support, locus of control,* and *employment status.* Furthermore, you will need to collect this information from social work students. However, if you only include social work students in your study sample, you will not have the concept of *student* as a variable because these study subjects do not vary on this entity. They are all students.

Using Statistics

Statistics are the means for analyzing data. There are two basic types of statistics. *Descriptive* statistics provide information on a given variable for a given set of study subjects. This could include the mean age of the subjects or the proportion who are female or the number who have a child under the age of 6. *Inferential* statistics provide you with the ability to infer from a sample of study subjects to a larger population. This is done with the assistance of probability theory, which provides guidance on the estimation of the likelihood of receiving a given set of data just by chance.

Inferential statistics generate a value for p (as in "p < .05"), which provides you with an estimate of the likelihood of finding your particular set of data results just by chance. The p value is presented as a fraction from .00 to 1.0, the latter representing 100 percent. Thus, a p value of .43 means that you would likely achieve your results 43 times in 100 by chance. In such a case, you would have little confidence that you had discovered a reality that can be generalized, and you would have good reason to suspect that a repeat of the same study with a different sample of people would generate a different result.

Among the commonly used descriptive statistics are frequency, mean, median, mode, and proportion. Among the frequently used inferential statistics are chi square, t test, Pearson correlation coefficient, and analysis of variance. The number of statistical measures, however, is enormous. In this book, you will be introduced to 16 such measures, in addition to descriptive statistics, but the total number of these measures is far greater than 16. In fact, a book by Gopal Kanji entitled *100 Statistical Tests* (1993) examines, you guessed it, exactly 100 such tests, and this review is not exhaustive.

Interpreting Results

In examining the results of your data analysis, you should be able to develop conclusions related to both practical significance and statistical significance. *Statistical significance* refers to the likelihood that your results could occur by chance.

Chance

Whenever you conduct a study using inferential statistics, you develop a hypothesis and you use your study data to test this hypothesis, but there are several rival hypotheses that might be true instead of your hypothesis. It may be that persons did not answer your questions honestly; thus, your data is worthless. It may be that the relationship between the two variables in your analysis represents a spurious (meaningless) relationship which can be rather fully explained by another variable not identified in your hypothesis.

The rival hypothesis that is addressed by inferential statistics is chance. It could be that you obtained your results just by the luck of the draw, and if you repeated your study you would obtain different results. The likelihood of obtaining results similar to your own is represented by the letter p.

The p value obtained from statistical analysis tells you the fraction that corresponds to the number of times in 100 that your results would be expected to occur by chance. As illustrated in the previous section, a p value of .27 means that your results could occur by chance 27 times in 100. The p value that is the accepted standard in social science studies

P is negatively stated - # of times by chance

is .05, or 5 times in 100. If your results would be expected to occur by chance less than 5 times in 100, you can say that your hypothesis was supported, unless, of course, you had decided to set a different standard for statistical significance. In published research, you will see the designation "p < .05" to represent this level of statistical significance. In some cases, you might see "p < .01" which means that we would expect this finding to occur by chance less than 1 time in 100. You might also see the designation "p = .03". In this case, the actual p value is being presented rather than it being designated in more general terms such as "p < .05". Both of these forms of presentation are acceptable.

Practical Significance

Practical significance is a matter of judgment. It answers the question, *How noteworthy are my results?* How much of a relationship between two variables is necessary for you to conclude that your results are something to pay a lot of attention to? If males and females report a different average salary, how much of a difference is necessary for you to get excited about the potential problem exhibited by this condition? How much better off must our clients be at the end of treatment than before treatment for you to feel that the intervention has truly succeeded?

Coefficients.   One place to seek guidance for practical significance lies in the examination of the coefficient depicting the strength of the relationship between the study variables. Some of these coefficients include the phi coefficient, the contingency coefficient, the Pearson correlation coefficient, and the Spearman rank order coefficient of correlation. Coefficients like these represent the strength of the relationship between variables. They typically range from a low of 0, representing no relationship, to 1.0 which represents a perfect relationship between the variables. The stronger the relationship, the higher is the value of the coefficient. The question of whether a given value of the coefficient represents practical significance is a matter of judgment.

Interpreting the phi Coefficient.   In one of the previous chapters, you were given a practical illustration of how to interpret the value of the phi coefficient. I will briefly review that lesson here. Suppose that you wish to compare a treated group of clients to a group of persons with the same problem who were not treated. You have measured recovery for each group so that each person can be classified in two ways: (1) the group they are in, and (2) whether or not they achieved recovery from the problem. Examine the following hypothetical data.

	Group	
Recovery	*Treatment*	*Non-treatment*
Yes	40 (80%)	40 (50%)
No	10 (20%)	40 (50%)
Total	50 (100%)	80 (100%)

From these data, you can see that 80 percent of the treated clients recovered, compared to 50 percent of those who did not receive treatment. If you assume that your treatment group is comparable to your nontreatment group with regard to potential for recovery on their own, you can conclude that the treatment made a difference for 30 percent of those treated. This is the difference between 80 percent (.80) and 50 percent (.50). In other words, the treatment made a difference for 30 persons out of 100 because 80 percent recovered and you would have expected 50 percent to have recovered without treatment. If you convert this 30 percent figure to a fraction, you have the value of 0.30. You will find this figure (.30) to be a good estimate of the value of the phi coefficient when the formula is applied to these data. This is one way to make practical sense out of a coefficient value such as those you will see from the data analysis.

ASSIGNMENT 13-A

1. Which of the following types of research employs the hypothesis as a tool?

    a. Descriptive   **b.** Explanatory

2. For which of the following types of research is the concept of statistical significance especially relevant?

    a. Descriptive   **b.** Explanatory   **c.** Exploratory

3. Develop a research hypothesis regarding a study you would like to undertake. (Don't use one that has been articulated in this book.)

    More males than females will mow lawns.

4. Which of the following tasks comes first in the research process?

    a. The operational definition of the study variables.

    ✔ **b.** The abstract definition of the study variables.

5. Which of the following is more subjective?

    ✔ **a.** Practical significance.

    b. Statistical significance.

Notes:_____

_____

_____

6. Suppose you have examined the relationship between the study subjects' scores for stress and their scores for support, and have discovered a correlation of 0.45 with a p value of .02.

What would be your guide for determining statistical significance?

$p \not= .02$

What would be your guide for determining practical significance?

correlation of 0.45

Five Questions You Must Answer in Order to Select a Statistical Measure

In the next chapter, you will be given a set of decision trees to use in determining the particular statistical measure to use for analyzing your data. You have reviewed, in this chapter, several basic research concepts that you must understand in order to be prepared for data analysis. Once you have determined your research questions and have collected your data, you will be prepared to select statistical measures for data analysis.

In this section of the present chapter, you will examine five questions which must be answered before you are ready to use the decision trees in the next chapter to select a statistical measure. These questions are:

1. What specific research question or study hypothesis is currently being analyzed?
2. How many variables are in this specific research question or study hypothesis?
3. Which variable is dependent and which is independent?
4. At what level is each variable measured?
5. Are the data drawn from independent samples?

If you are already prepared to accomplish these tasks with your hypothesis, you should consider going on to the next chapter in which you will be given a guide for the selection of the particular statistic that would be appropriate for your hypothesis or question.

Question 1. What is the specific research question or study hypothesis?
You may have several research questions in a given study which you will need to analyze one by one. In one study, for example, the following research questions were analyzed:

1. Are salaries different for male and females in social work?
2. Are males more likely than females to be employed in management positions?
3. Is gender related to salary when position level is taken into consideration?

If you were conducting this study, you should be careful not to become confused in responding to the other questions in this section of the chapter by lumping all these questions together. Instead, you would statistically analyze each of these questions separately. For example, when answering the question, *How many variables are in this analysis?* you would take these questions one by one rather than count all the variables for all questions.

Question 2. How many variables are in this specific analysis?
The first question in the salary study mentioned above identified two variables—gender and salary. The second question identified the variables of gender and position, while the third identified three variables, gender, salary, and position. There are a total of three variables in this study, but only one of the research questions includes all of these variables. Thus, the answer to the present question for the first research question above would be two variables (gender and salary) and this same answer would be given for number of variables in the second question (gender and position), while the third research question is the only one with all three variables (gender, salary, and position).

When you are asked for the number of variables, you are being called upon to designate the number of variables for which you wish to apply a statistic. In a purely descriptive study, you may have a great number of variables to employ in the description of a particular sample of persons, such as the clients of your agency. For example, you may want to know the proportion of your clients who are female and male, their mean income, the number of clients with a preschool age child, the average length of treatment for all clients, and the proportion whose bills are being paid by private insurance. This includes a total of five variables, but these variables will be analyzed separately because there are no questions in this analysis that pose a relationship between variables. If, however, you wished to know whether the average length of treatment was longer for those with private insurance than those without, you would be posing a question of a relationship between variables. In this case, there would be two variables in your analysis—length of treatment and type of payment.

You may have a study in which you have three hypotheses, each with one dependent variable and one or more independent variables. In this situation, you would examine each hypothesis independently. Thus, you would go through the decision tree separately for each hypothesis.

Remember that a variable must vary. You cannot employ gender as a variable in a study that contains only female respondents. You could not employ education as a variable if you simply asked whether the respondent had a college education and every single one had answered in the affirmative. If there was no further breakdown in education and all had answered in the same way, there would be no variance among study participants with regard to the concept of education; thus, there would be no variable to employ.

It is important to be able to distinguish between a variable and a category within a variable (an attribute of the variable). For example, the variable of gender has two categories but gender is only one variable. Likewise, the variable of position level may have the categories of direct practice, supervision, and administration. Again, this is only one variable. If you wanted to examine the relationship between gender and position level, you would be dealing with two variables. Consider the following hypotheses:

1. Males will report higher salaries than females even when years of experience is controlled;
2. Employed social work students with a higher level of social support will experience less psychological stress than will employed social work students with lower levels of social support;
3. Clients of the Inpatient Mental Health Unit of Memorial Hospital will exhibit less depression after 20 days of treatment than before treatment began.
4. Adolescent clients who use journal writing as a therapeutic aid will achieve higher self-esteem at the completion of three months of treatment than will adolescent clients who do not use journal writing.

What is the number of variables in each of these hypotheses? Let's look at the first one. The first one says that salary is different for males and females. Thus, salary is one variable. What about males and females? Are these two additional variables? The answer is No. These are categories of the variable. The variable is gender. Thus, we now have two variables. What about years of experience? Is it a variable as well? If we are to control for it, it must be a variable. Thus, we have a total of three variables in this hypothesis.

What about the second hypothesis? Two variables are identified here—social support and stress. You may have noted that this hypothesis is restricted to employed social work students. Many social work students are not employed, but they are being excluded from this analysis. Thus, employment status is not a variable in this analysis. There would be three variables in this analysis, however, if the hypothesis had been stated as, *Social work students with higher levels of social support will experience less psychological stress than social work students with lower levels of social support even when employment status is controlled.* In the latter case, it would be necessary to have measurements for all three variables—support, stress, and employment status—for the study subjects.

The third hypothesis above calls for you to measure depression at two points in time—before treatment and after treatment. Thus, you have two variables—depression before treatment and depression after treatment. This example, however, is a little tricky in view of the way in which this type of data is analyzed. Typically, before and after scores for a single group of clients are analyzed by taking the difference between the before and after scores for each client and then analyzing this individual score. Thus, one might prefer to conceive of this situation as generating only one variable. In this situation, however, I prefer to conceptualize it as two variables.

The fourth hypothesis calls for comparing a treated group and a nontreated group for self-esteem. Thus you have two variables: self-esteem and the group (treatment versus nontreatment).

Question 3. Which variable is dependent and which is independent?

In some cases, you only want to describe a single variable, such as the distribution of your clients into age categories or categories according to race or gender. In this situation, it would not be necessary to establish a hypothesis, and you would not need to distinguish between the dependent and the independent variables.

In other situations, however, you are attempting to use one or more variables to predict another variable in your attempt to determine what is the cause of the latter variable. For example, you may want to examine what causes clients discharged from an alcoholism treatment program to be re-admitted to the program within a short period of time. You could conceptualize a study that contains a sample of clients who were initially discharged from the program 24 months ago. Some of these clients have remained out of the program without apparent need for re-admission. Some of these persons may have been out of care for only one month before needing to be re-admitted, while others may have been out for six months or 12 months before being re-admitted to the program.

The research question is, *What distinguishes the persons who have remained out of treatment for longer periods of time from those who have needed re-admission within a comparatively short period of time?* In this situation, you are using the length of time a person was apparently free of need for re-admission as the dependent variable and we are asking, *What does this variable depend on?*

The dependent variable is the one that depends on another variable. That other variable is known as the **independent** variable. A question to ask in distinguishing between the two is which one is the cause and which one is the effect. The independent variable is the one you believe causes the dependent variable to be the way it is. For example, position level usually determines one's salary, or, at least, it is one of the things that we could use to predict a person's salary. People in higher positions usually make higher salaries than those in lower positions. But it would be strange to think that salary determined position, because one is not normally given a salary and then assigned a position level according to the level of salary that was negotiated. Thus, one's position level is determined first, then one determines which salary suits that position level. In this case, the position level is the independent variable and salary is the dependent variable.

Another way to look at this issue is to imagine whether changes in one variable are more likely to precede changes in the other variable than vice versa. For example, does religious denomination influence income or is it income that influences religious denomination? Imagine a group of people having changes in both religious denomination and income over a period of several years. Is it more likely that Baptists would change to the Episcopalian denomination after an increase in income level, or that persons would experience a major increase in income after changing from the Baptist to the Episcopalian Church? If you believed the former to be more likely, you would treat income as the independent variable and denomination as the dependent variable. If you believed that denomination caused (or predicted) income, you would treat denomination as independent and income as the dependent variable.

In this attempt to distinguish between the dependent and independent variables, the word "cause" has been employed. Please do not make the mistake of assuming that a relationship between two variables means that one is truly the cause of the other. The establishment of such a relationship is only one of the conditions necessary for the determination of causation.

The distinction between the dependent variable and the independent variable is not always necessary in the selection of a statistical measure. It is not necessary, for example, in the use of the Pearson correlation coefficient, which presents information on the strength of the relationship between two variables measured at the interval level. The discovery of a significant correlation between number of family visits for a hospital patient and the level of depression of the patient provides partial empirical support for the argument that one of these variables is the cause of the other. But this statistical test does not tell you which is the cause of the other.

In fact, in the information presented in this book, the only time you must distinguish between the dependent and independent variables is when you have three or more variables in your analysis. Theoretically, of course, you should be able to distinguish between the dependent and independent variables in your hypothesis, but this is often not necessary in the selection of a statistical measure.

Consider the following hypothesis:

Full-time social work students who are employed will experience more psychological stress than will full-time social work students who are not employed.

First, how many variables are in this analysis? This hypothesis states there is a relationship between employment and stress; thus, there are two variables. Which variable is the independent variable? In other words, which variable is believed to be the cause of the other? Is stress the cause of employment? This does not seem logical, because people do not normally become employed as a result of achieving an increase in stress. Does being employed while one is a full-time student cause one to be stressed? This seems the more logical choice; thus, employment is the independent variable and stress is the dependent variable. Being a student is simply a condition of the sample. It is not a variable in this study. All persons in the study are students.

In the above example, you have only two variables; thus, you do not need to distinguish between the dependent and independent variables in the choice of a statistical measure. However, you should be able to do this in order to present your analysis in a theoretically logical manner. In the examples below, I will focus on hypotheses that have three or more variables.

Example 1.   Consider this example: *Males will report higher salaries than females even when years of experience is controlled.* I have already identified that this hypothesis has three variables. Which of these is the dependent variable? Is gender dependent on salary or position level? In other words, does one acquire a gender because of the salary he or she has attained or does one's gender change as a result of a change in salary? Obviously not! Thus, we would not designate gender as the dependent variable. Does position level depend upon salary or is it the other way around? Do we first decide that Barbara will be given a major raise in pay and then determine that this means she must be given a higher position in the organization? Or, do we determine that Barbara will be given higher pay because she has been promoted to a higher position? The answer should be obvious. Salary is the dependent variable. It is dependent on both gender and position level. In other words, one of the reasons that John has a higher salary than Barbara is that he has a different gender. This, of course, does not sound good because one's gender should not determine one's pay. But studies have shown differences in salary between men and women. Another reason that John has higher pay is that he is in a higher position in the organization.

Control Variable.   The independent variable is the variable that the dependent variable is dependent on. Thus, there are two independent variables in this hypothesis—position level and gender. Sometimes you will consider the idea of the control variable. One form of a control variable is known as the "intervening variable." You can use a variable as a control variable by either measuring it and including it in your hypothesis, or you can control for the effects of a given variable by restricting your analysis to only those persons who have a certain characteristic. In the above example, the control variable is position level. A control variable is normally treated as another independent variable in the analysis of data.

Example 2.   Consider another example: *Employed social work students with higher levels of social support will experience less psychological stress than will employed social work students with lower levels of social support.* This analysis is being restricted to employed social work students and has only two variables. The dependent variable is stress and the independent variable is social support. In other words, I am saying that persons have lower stress because they have higher support.

I could change this hypothesis as follows: *Social work students with higher levels of social support will have less psychological stress than will social work students with lower levels of support even when employment status is controlled.* In this case, employment status is being included. This hypothesis, therefore, has stress as the dependent variable and both employment status and support as independent variables.

Question 4. At what level is each variable measured?

There are four levels of measurement: nominal, ordinal, interval, and ratio. Some statistical measures can be employed for data that are measured at only one of these levels, and most statistics are best suited for only one of these levels even if they can be used for more than one. These four levels are organized into a hierarchy, with nominal at the lowest level and ratio at the highest. A higher level variable can be treated as a variable measured at a lower level with no problems in the assumptions made by the proper statistic. The reverse, however, is not true. One cannot treat a lower level variable as a higher level variable without violating some of the assumptions associated with the calculation of the proper statistic. Because there are no statistics in this guide that are reserved for ratio data, variables that are measured at this level are treated the same as if they were interval.

Nominal Variable.   A **nominal** variable is one that classifies subjects into categories such as male and female. With nominal data, there is no ordering in values of the categories. For example, males are not higher or lower than females. Likewise, *Republicans, Democrats,* and *Independents* are not in categories that are numerically ordered in any meaningful way.

A nominal variable must have at least two categories, and the categories must be distinct, mutually exclusive, and exhaustive of all categories that could fall within the bounds of the variable. For example, the above classification of political party affiliation should have a category called *Other* because there may be subjects (e.g. Libertarians, Socialists, etc.) in a study that would not fall into any of the three enumerated affiliations.

Ordinal Variables.   The second category in our hierarchy is **ordinal**. An ordinal variable not only classifies observations, but also ranks them from high to low, or most to least, and so forth. In nominal measurement, you can say that one category of the variable is different from another, but with an ordinal variable, you can say that one category is higher or lower than another. An example of a variable measured at the ordinal level is as follows:

How much do you agree with the statement "Most people can be trusted?"

_____ *Strongly Agree*

_____ *Agree*

_____ *Neither Agree nor Disagree*

_____ *Disagree*

_____ *Strongly Disagree*

With ordinal data, however, you cannot say that the distance between each category is equal to the distance between each of the other intervals. For example, you cannot say that the distance between Strongly Agree and Agree is the same as the distance between Agree and the next category below. For this reason, ordinal variables ideally should not be treated as interval even though this violation of the principle of levels of measurement is frequently found in published research. Some researchers are willing to treat these distances as equal even though they realize that this practice weakens their research procedures. In fact, some scholars have even argued that the distinction between ordinal and interval data is not very important (see, for example, Labovitz, 1970).

Interval Variable.   With **interval** data, however, you can say that the distance between categories is equal. An example would be degrees on a thermometer. You can say that each degree is equal to each of the other degrees. The highest level of measurement is **ratio.** With ratio data, the intervals are measured with reference to a fixed zero point; thus, there can be no negative value on this kind of variable. Examples would be age and height, because one cannot have negative age or negative height. A major advantage of the ratio variable is that a value of 100 is twice the value of 50. In the examination of statistical measures in this book, however, there will be no distinction between the interval and ratio scales. This is because there is no reason for this distinction on the statistical measures examined in this book. Thus, I will treat a ratio variable as interval and simplify the task for the reader.

Examples.   Let's examine a few examples regarding level of measurement, starting with the first hypothesis presented as an example in the previous section:

Males will report higher salaries than females even when years of experience is controlled.

In this example, suppose the data were drawn from the following items on a questionnaire:

What is your gender? _____ *Male* _____ *Female*

What is your annual salary? $_____

How many years of professional experience have you had? _____ years

At what level is gender measured—nominal, ordinal, or interval? You will note that the study subjects have two categories into which to put themselves. These categories are not ordered into a hierarchy. Thus, this variable is measured at the nominal level.

What about salary? Subjects are being asked to record their salary in dollars rather than in some kind of salary categories. Each dollar is equal to each other dollar. Thus, you can say that this variable is measured at the interval level (it is actually measured at the ratio level, but remember that I am not making the distinction between interval and ratio levels of measurement).

On the other hand, suppose you had asked the salary question in this format:

What is your annual salary?

_____ *0–$19,999*

_____ *$20,000–$29,999*

_____ *$30,000–$39,999*

_____ *$40,000 and above*

In this case, you are asking subjects to place themselves in a category rather than give a specific dollar figure. These categories are ordered; thus, you would say that income in this example is measured at the ordinal level.

What about years of experience? Yes, it too is measured at the interval level because you are asking people to give a number that represents the years of their experience. Each year is equal to each other year.

Special Case: Dichotomous Variable. The **dichotomous** variable presents a special case. A dichotomous variable is one that has only two categories. Examples include gender, whether one passed or failed an examination, and so forth. A dichotomous variable can usually be treated as interval because the issue of equality in the difference between categories is not relevant in view of the fact that there is only one interval in a dichotomous variable. Thus, a statistic that can be applied only to interval variables can often be used with the dichotomous variable. A dichotomous variable can also be treated as ordinal.

One should not, however, treat a dichotomous variable as ordinal or interval unless it is the only way to obtain the information you need. It is not the normal way to treat a dichotomous variable. By its nature, a dichotomous variable is nominal because it has only two categories. Thus, it should be treated as nominal under normal circumstances. In fact, the only use of this trick that will be explored in this book is the use of a dichotomous variable as an independent variable when you employ multiple regression analysis. More on this later.

Question 5. Are the data drawn from independent samples?

In order for the data representing two different variables under study to be drawn independently, it is necessary that the values (categories) for the variables be drawn in such a manner that you would not have reason to believe the two sets of data are related. Take, for example, a study in which you have measured people with reference to a variable, such as the mean ages of males and females in a sample. In this case, the ages of the two groups are drawn from different people—some males and some females. Thus, you can say that the data for these samples (males and females) were drawn independently. Likewise, you may want to explore whether there is a relationship between gender and political party affiliation. If you constructed a table with female Republicans in one cell, female Democrats in another cell, male Republicans in a third cell, and male Democrats in a fourth cell, you would have independent samples, because the persons in each cell are different. One cannot be both a female Republican and a female Democrat.

On the other hand, if data for the same variable are drawn from the same subject at two points in time, you have what is known as **related samples.** For example, a pretest and posttest measurement of one's level of depression is not drawn in an independent manner, because you are taking two depression scores from the same person. Another example of related samples would be the case of the examination of matched pairs of subjects. You may want to examine salaries of males and females while controlling for whether or not the subjects are employed in management positions. One way to do this would be to develop a sample of matched pairs of males and females in which each pair had a similar position.

Let's examine the following two hypotheses:

1. Clients of the Inpatient Mental Health Unit of Memorial Hospital will exhibit less depression after 20 days of treatment than before treatment.
2. Adolescent clients who use journal writing as a therapeutic aid will achieve higher self-esteem at the completion of three months of treatment than will adolescent clients who do not use journal writing.

Are the data for the first hypothesis drawn from related or independent samples? This hypothesis suggests that patients will be measured on depression at two points in time and the two measurements will be compared in order to determine if the level of depression is better after treatment than before. In this case, the data are drawn from related samples. The pretest-posttest comparison of clients is perhaps the most typical case where the data are drawn from related samples.

What about the second hypothesis? You are going to compare a group of clients who used journal writing with a group of clients who did not use this therapeutic aid. In this case, you are drawing data from independent samples.

References

Kanji, G. (1993). *100 Statistical Tests.* Newbury Park, CA: Sage Publications.

Labovitz, S. (1970). The assignment of numbers to rank order categories, *American Sociological Review, 35,* 515–524.

ASSIGNMENT 13-B

In this assignment, you will examine a hypothetical study of graduate social work students that were posed the questions shown in Exhibit 13.1 (p. 278). Refer to that exhibit in developing your responses to the following questions.

1. Suppose you wished to describe this sample in regard to age and gender. For each research question, how many variables would you have? _____

2. Consider the following hypothesis: *Male students will report more years of experience than will female students.*

   a. How many variables are in this analysis? _____

   b. At what level is each variable measured?

   _____

   _____

   _____

   c. What is the dependent variable?

   _____

   d. What is/are the independent variable(s)?

   _____

   e. Are these data drawn from independent samples?

   _____

3. Consider the following research question: *Is there a relationship between years of experience and chosen specialization in graduate school?*

   a. How many variables are in this analysis? _____

   b. At what level is each variable measured?

   _____

   _____

   _____

_____

c. What is the dependent variable?

_____

d. What is/are the independent variable(s)?

_____

e. Are these data drawn from independent samples?

_____

4. Consider the following hypothesis: *There is a positive relationship between age and number of stressful life events experienced in the past year.*

    a. How many variables are in this analysis? _____

    b. At what level is each variable measured?

_____

_____

_____

    c. What is the dependent variable?

_____

    d. What is/are the independent variable(s)?

_____

    e. Are these data drawn from independent samples?

_____

5. Examine the following research question: *Is there a relationship between gender and choice of a specialization in graduate school?*

    a. How many variables are in this analysis? _____

    b. At what level is each variable measured?

_____

_____

_____

c. What is the dependent variable?

_____

d. What is/are the independent variable(s)?

_____

e. Are these data drawn from independent samples?

_____

_____

EXHIBIT 13.1   Questionnaire

1. What is your age?   _____ years

2. What is your gender?   _____ Male   _____ Female

3. What is your chosen specialization in graduate school?

   _____ Mental Health   _____ Family and Child

   _____ Health   _____ Other

4. To what extent are you satisfied with the MSW program?

   _____ To a very great extent.

   _____ To a great extent.

   _____ To some extent.

   _____ To a little extent.

   _____ Not at all.

5. How many years of social work experience did you have before entering the MSW program?

   _____ years.

6. Consider the following life events.

   a. Death of a spouse

   b. Divorce or marital separation

   c. Death of a close personal friend

   d. Being fired from a job

   e. Extended illness that incapacitated you for more than a few days

   How many of these events have you experienced in the past year? _____

Chapter *14*

Selecting a Statistical Measure for Your Study

In this chapter, you will examine a number of decision charts (trees) which you can use to select a statistical measure for examining your hypothesis. The goal of this chapter is to help you to identify an appropriate statistic for your research question or study hypothesis. For optimal use of this chapter, you should have a study hypothesis or research question. In addition, you should have developed a means of measuring each variable in your particular analysis, and you should be prepared to answer each of the following questions:

1. The number of variables in your analysis,
2. The level of measurement of each variable,
3. Which variable is the dependent variable and which variable(s) is the independent variable, and
4. Whether the data are drawn from related or independent samples.

If you are unable to answer any of the above questions, you will not be able to use the charts which follow. (See the previous chapters for assistance.)

The first chart is displayed in Exhibit 14.1. It assists you with the selection of another chart where you should be able to complete the task of identifying a statistical measure. For each chart, you should begin at the top and answer the question that is first posed. Then move down the chart depending on your answer to the question. At the end of your journey should be a statistical measure noted in all capitals.

However, you will note that some terminal points on these charts indicate there are no statistics in this book that apply. When you encounter this response, you should first consider whether your variables can be treated in another way. You will remember that a variable measured at the interval level can be treated as ordinal or nominal. Likewise, an ordinal variable can be treated as nominal. In special situations, a dichotomous nominal variable

ordinal - in rank ?
nominal - named ? only 2 options

can be treated as ordinal or interval. You may even find published research that treats ordinal level variables as interval. You may need to seek consultation on this matter. Another alternative is to consult additional books on statistics for the completion of your task of selecting a statistical measure.

   If you would like to have some practice examples for exploring the use of these decision trees, see below. If you're ready to use the decision trees with your own data, move on to the first chart in Exhibit 14.1.

Practice Examples for How to Use This Guide

In this section, a few practice examples will take you through the decision charts step by step.

Example A

Suppose you want to describe your sample in terms of age, gender, salary, years of experience, and level of interest in a career in administration using the following questions:

   What is your age? _____ years

   What is your gender? _____ Male _____ Female

   What is your annual salary? $ _____

   How many years of professional experience have you had? _____ years

   To what extent do you plan to pursue a career in an administrative position at some level higher than clinical supervisor?

   _____ *To a very great extent*   _____ *To a little extent*

   _____ *To a great extent*   _____ *To a very little extent*

   _____*To some extent*   _____ *Not at all*

Analysis of Example A

What statistical measure would be appropriate for each variable? The first variable in this example is age, which is measured at the interval level. You simply want to describe your sample in relation to age, so you have only one variable in this analysis. If you go to Exhibit 14.1 and answer the first question with the answer "Only one," you will be instructed to go to Exhibit 14.2. The first question from the chart in Exhibit 14.2 asks if you wish to describe your sample or determine whether the categories are significantly different. In your case, you wish to describe the sample in terms of age. If you move over to the answer "Describe the variable," you will encounter the question, "At what level is the variable measured?" Your answer is "Interval." You will see a set of answers that would be appropriate for your data including frequencies, percentages, mode, median, mean, range, and standard deviation.

Your second variable is gender, which is measured at the nominal level. Your options here, as given in Exhibit 14.2, are frequencies, percentages, and mode. Like age, years of experience and salary are measured at the interval level, so the options are the same for those as for age. The last question, however, is measured at the ordinal level; thus, the options are frequencies, percentages, mode, and median.

Example B

Suppose you want to know if the salaries of males and females are significantly different.

Analysis of Example B

In this example, you have two variables, one of which is measured at the nominal level (gender) while the other is measured at the interval level (salary). These data are drawn from independent samples. Salary is the dependent variable and gender is the independent variable.

If you consult the chart in Exhibit 14.1, you will respond that you have two variables. You will respond to the second question with the answer "One or more is interval." This will direct you to Exhibit 14.5.

Your response to the first question in Exhibit 14.5 will be "One interval and one nominal." You will answer that the nominal variable does not have more than two categories and that the data are not drawn from related samples (meaning that they are drawn from independent samples). This will take you to the answer "t test for independent samples" as your statistical measure.

Example C

The hypothesis is as follows: *Males will express a higher level of interest in a career in administration than will females.*

Analysis of Example C

In this case, you have two variables, one measured at the ordinal level and one at the nominal level. Exhibit 14.1, therefore, will direct you to Exhibit 14.4. You will respond to the first question in Exhibit 14.4 as follows: "One ordinal and one nominal." Your nominal variable has two categories, so your response to the next question would be, "Only two categories." The data are not drawn from related samples; therefore, your statistical measure would be the Mann-Whitney U test.

Example D

The hypothesis is as follows: *Males will report higher annual salaries than will females even when years of experience is controlled.*

Analysis of Example D

In this case, we have three variables: gender, salary, and years of experience. Salary and years of experience are both measured at the interval level and the data are drawn from independent samples. Salary is the dependent variable and the other two are independent variables. In other words, it is believed that gender and years of experience are two of the determinants of one's salary.

If you consult Exhibit 14.1, you will be instructed to go to Exhibit 14.6 because you have three or more variables. Your answer to the first question from Exhibit 14.6 (*Can the dependent variable be treated as interval?*) is "Yes," because your dependent variable is salary. The next question is whether all of your independent variables can be treated as interval. You will note that if your answer is "No," there are no tests in this book that apply.

In this example, you have a dichotomous nominal variable (gender) in addition to an interval variable (years of experience) that are both independent variables. You will see from your analysis that you have the possibility of using multiple regression analysis if you can treat all of the independent variables as interval. This is the situation in which it is okay, although not ideal, to treat a dichotomous nominal variable as interval, as explained in the previous chapter. Thus, your statistic is multiple regression analysis.

ASSIGNMENT 14-A

This assignment refers to the study described in Assignment 13-B. Return to that assignment for information in responding to the questions below.

1. Consider the following hypothesis presented in question 2 for Assignment 13-B:

   Male students will report more years of experience than will female students.

   What statistical measure would be appropriate for testing this hypothesis?

2. Consider the following hypothesis (question 3 from Assignment 13-B):

   There is a positive relationship between years of experience and satisfaction with the MSW program.

   What statistical measure would be appropriate for testing this hypothesis?

3. Consider the following hypothesis (question 4 from Assignment 13-B):

   There is a positive relationship between level of satisfaction with the MSW program and number of stressful life events experienced in the past year.

   What statistical measure would be appropriate for testing this hypothesis?

4. Consider the following hypothesis (described under question 5 from Assignment 13-B):

The number of visits from family members will be greater after community placement than before community placement.

What statistical measure would be appropriate for testing this hypothesis?

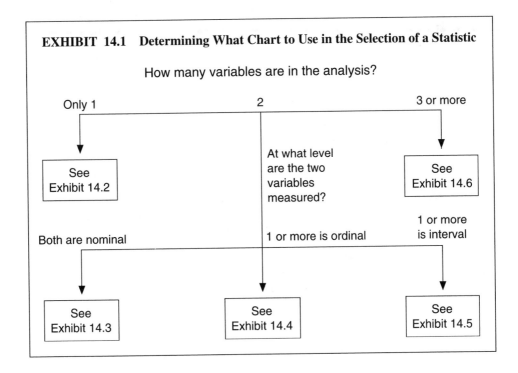

EXHIBIT 14.1   Determining What Chart to Use in the Selection of a Statistic

How many variables are in the analysis?

Only 1   2   3 or more

See Exhibit 14.2

At what level are the two variables measured?

See Exhibit 14.6

1 or more is interval

Both are nominal   1 or more is ordinal

See Exhibit 14.3   See Exhibit 14.4   See Exhibit 14.5

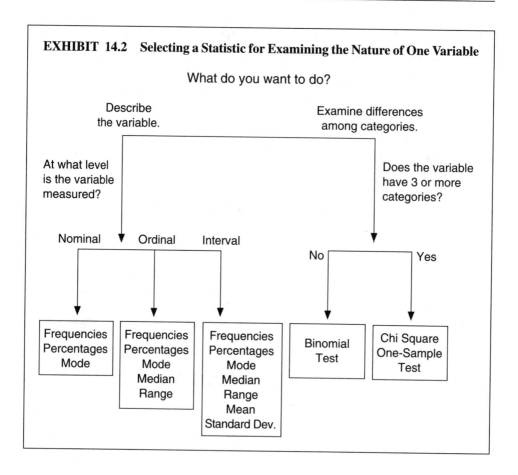

EXHIBIT 14.2   Selecting a Statistic for Examining the Nature of One Variable

EXHIBIT 14.3 **Selecting a Statistic for Examining the Relationship between Two Nominal Variables**

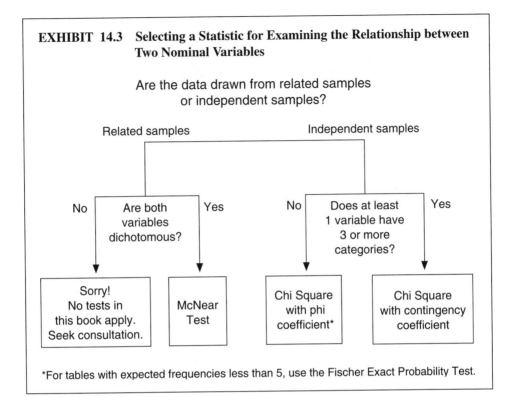

Are the data drawn from related samples
or independent samples?

Related samples

Independent samples

No | Are both variables dichotomous? | Yes

No | Does at least 1 variable have 3 or more categories? | Yes

Sorry! No tests in this book apply. Seek consultation.

McNear Test

Chi Square with phi coefficient*

Chi Square with contingency coefficient

*For tables with expected frequencies less than 5, use the Fischer Exact Probability Test.

EXHIBIT 14.4   Selecting a Statistic for Examining the Relationship between Two Variables Where At Least One Is Measured at the Ordinal Level

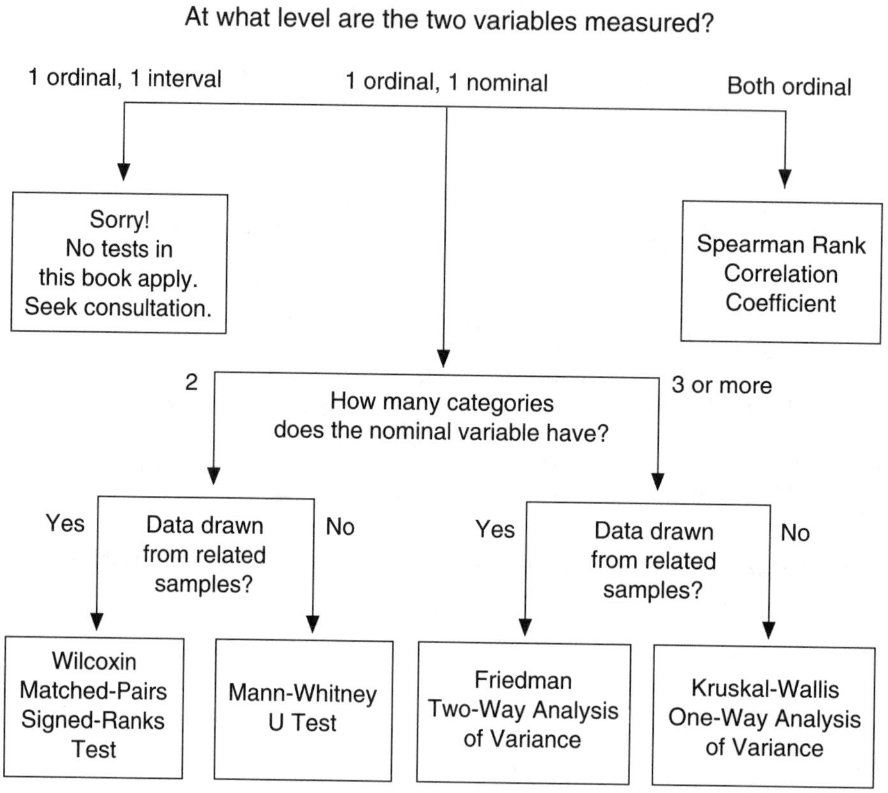

At what level are the two variables measured?

1 ordinal, 1 interval   1 ordinal, 1 nominal   Both ordinal

| Sorry!
No tests in
this book apply.
Seek consultation. | | Spearman Rank
Correlation
Coefficient |

2   3 or more

How many categories
does the nominal variable have?

Yes   Data drawn
from related
samples?   No   Yes   Data drawn
from related
samples?   No

| Wilcoxin
Matched-Pairs
Signed-Ranks
Test | Mann-Whitney
U Test | Friedman
Two-Way Analysis
of Variance | Kruskal-Wallis
One-Way Analysis
of Variance |

EXHIBIT 14.5 **Selecting a Statistic for Measuring the Relationship between Two Variables Where At Least One Is Measured at the Interval Level**

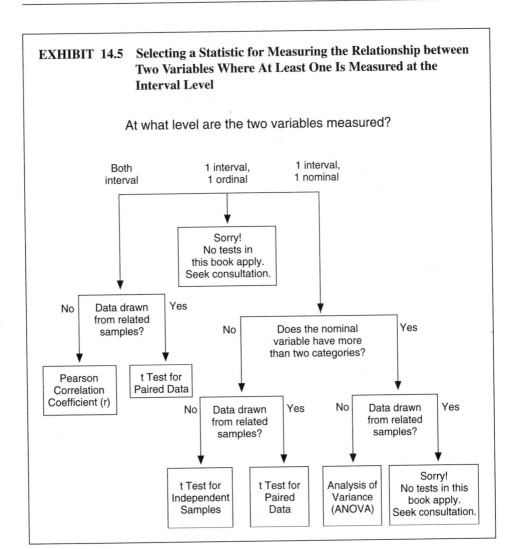

EXHIBIT 14.6 **Selecting a Statistic for Examining the Relationship between Three or More Variables**

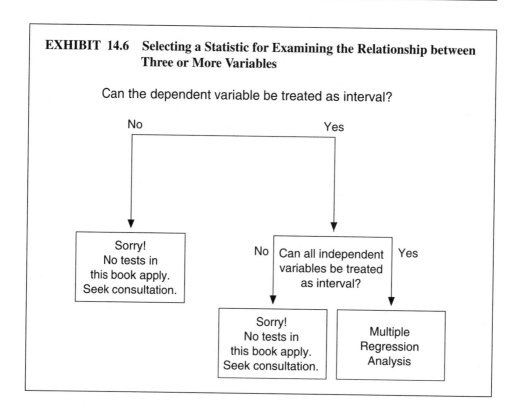

Chapter *15*

Data Analysis Using SPSS for Windows

SPSS is a type of computer software that can be used in the analysis of data using a wide variety of statistical measures. Most statistical measures are quite complicated to calculate by hand (using a calculator). Fortunately, that complex task can be greatly facilitated by the use of the computer. What would take you an hour to do with a calculator (assuming you know the statistical formula) might take the computer only three seconds to execute. There are a variety of computer software packages available which aid you in the statistical analysis of data. Each package is designed for a particular computer operating system. There are several editions of the SPSS software, one for the mainframe computer, one for DOS, and one for Windows. In this book, you will use the one for Windows. Note: At the end of this chapter is a Quick Reference for Using SPSS for Windows. Refer to it as needed when you are analyzing your data.

Objectives

At the completion of this chapter, you will be able to create a data file for your study using SPSS for Windows. This will entail naming variables, providing labels (such as "male" and "female") for the categories of certain variables, entering data on each study variable, and creating new variables using the existing variables. At the completion of this chapter, you will also be able to use your data file for analysis. You will be able, for example, to obtain a frequency count for gender, the mean age of study subjects, or a correlation between the variables *years of experience* and *salary*. You will learn how to obtain a printout of your analysis and to save your work on a disk for later use.

These objectives will be accomplished through the following topics to be covered in the pages which follow:

Data Files
Background Information
Getting Started with SPSS
Beginning Steps in Creating a New Data File
Giving Names and Labels to Study Variables
Entering Data
Saving your Data on a Disk for Later Use
Printing your Data File
Creating New Variables
Using a Sub-Sample of Cases
Opening an Existing Data File

You will be working with a data file consisting of information from 101 respondents to a survey presented to a random sample of the members of the National Association of Social Workers in North Carolina and Massachusettes in the spring of 1989. Exhibit 15.1 shows the questions they were asked. Exhibit 15.2 describes the thinking preference measurement. Look at those exhibits now so you will understand the nature of the data you'll be working with.

**EXHIBIT 15.1   Questions to NASW Members in North Carolina and
Massachusettes**

1. What is your age? _____ years **2.** Your gender? _____ Female _____ Male

3. How many years of experience have you had in the social work profession in all jobs?

_____ years

4. What is your position level?

_____ Direct service to individuals, families, or groups

_____ Case supervision (i.e., supervision of line staff)

_____ Management

_____ Other

5. What is the field in which you are employed?

(1) Health   (3) Family & Children's Services

(2) Mental Health   (4) Other

EXHIBIT 15.1 *Continued*

6. At the last time period for providing annual pay raises, did you receive a merit pay raise (i.e., pay raise based on performance, however that performance was measured) that was above the average merit pay raise offered to persons in your organization?

   _____ No _____ Yes _____ Uncertain _____ No merit pay raises were available

   [*Note:* For this study, those who did not answer Yes or No were presented as missing data.]

7. Indicate the statement that comes closest to the way you were rated by your immediate superior at your last periodic performance appraisal session.

   (1) Unsatisfactory.

   (2) Much below average for persons in your type position.

   (3) Somewhat below average for persons in your position.

   (4) About average for persons in your position.

   (5) Somewhat above average for persons in your position.

   (6) Much above average for persons in your position.

   (7) Superior.

   (8) Uncertain.

8. How would you rate your overall job performance (using the above scale)?

EXHIBIT 15.2   **An Explanation of How Thinking Preference Was Measured**

According to personality type theory, there are four dimensions of one's personality. One of these dimensions reveals the way we judge the information we perceive; there are two contrasting ways. One mode for examining the information we confront is the *thinking* mode, in which we apply logic and impersonal analysis. The other way of judging is by *feeling,* a process in which we employ personal values in coming to conclusions about the information we confront.

The most prominent means of measuring personality type is the Myers-Briggs Type Indicator. Another means is the Kiersey-Bates Temperament Sorter (Bates & Kiersey, 1978). The latter was used in the NASW study reported in this book. This instrument asks the respondent to select one of two responses to complete a sentence or respond to a question. For each question, one response is in the feeling mode and the other is in the thinking mode. There were twelve items measuring this dimension. One's score for thinking was determined by adding the number of thinking responses selected out of these 12 items. Thus, the highest score one could

Continued

EXHIBIT 15.2 *Continued*

receive for thinking was 12 and the lowest was 0. A score of 0 for thinking would mean, of course, that the individual had selected 12 feeling choices and no thinking choices. A score of 6 would mean that the individual had an equal number of thinking and feeling choices.

The feeling person values sentiment over logic, whereas the reverse is true for the thinking type. The feeling person is more interested in people than things and, thus, tends to be friendly, sociable, loyal, and tactful. Feeling people are stronger in the social arts than in executive ability and are not as comfortable when called upon to be brief, concise, and "businesslike" (Myers & Myers, 1980, p. 68). A good deal of the *feeling* preference is essential for persons whose jobs call for the development of a helping relationship. Persons with a preference for feeling are better at persuading staff to co-operate in implementing a plan than at designing the plan. In the design stage, they are best suited for forecasting how staff might feel about the changes being explored.

Persons with a preference for thinking value logic over sentiment and tend to focus more attention on things than people. They confront information with impersonal analysis and are impatient when sentiments interfere with rationality. Thus, they are stronger on justice than mercy, which is the opposite of what could be said of the feeling person. Persons with the thinking preference are independent minded and stronger in executive ability than the social arts. They don't mind standing alone on an issue, and thus are better able to tolerate the loneliness of being at the top of an organization than would their feeling counterpart.

The Thinking-Feeling preference is the only dimension on the Myers-Briggs Type Indicator in which there is a noteworthy difference between men and women. Approximately two-thirds of all women score as feeling persons, while only about forty percent of men show this preference (Myers & Myers, 1980).

References

Bates, M., & Kiersey, D. (1978). *Please understand me.* Del Mar, CA: Prometheus Nemesis Press.
Myers, I. B., & Myers, P. B. (1980). *Gifts differing.* Palo Alto, CA: Consulting Psychologists Press.

Data Files

A data file is the computer file that contains the data from your study. It will contain the names of the variables as well as the value for each variable for each study subject. For example, Exhibit 15.3 contains the data you will enter into the computer to develop the data file used in the basic illustration of how to use SPSS. Note from this exhibit that study subject number 1 was coded as 34 for the variable of **age** and 0 for the variable of **gender**. Person number 2 was 33 years old and was coded as 1 for gender. Also included in this file are the variables of years of experience (named "years" in the data file), work position ("position"), field of employment ("field"), whether or not the individual received a merit pay raise this year ("pay"), the study subject's performance rating from their supervisor ("superior"), the individual's rating of their performance ("self"), the state in which they reside ("state"), and their score on the thinking-feeling dimension of the Kiersey-Bates Temperament Sorter ("thinking").

EXHIBIT 15.3   Data on NASW Study Variables

	age	gender	years	position	field	pay	superior	self	state	thinking
001	34	0	13	1	1	–	7	7	0	–
002	33	1	5	3	3	1	–	5	0	10
003	40	1	15	3	3	0	6	5	0	7
004	35	0	15	3	4	–	–	6	0	9
005	29	1	3	1	2	0	–	5	0	7
006	29	0	5	1	3	0	5	4	0	7
007	46	1	11	2	3	0	5	4	0	7
008	35	0	11	1	3	–	5	5	0	4
009	35	0	6	1	2	0	5	5	0	–
010	43	0	16	2	3	0	7	7	0	–
011	39	0	10	1	4	–	6	6	0	7
012	38	0	10	1	2	1	6	5	0	6
013	34	1	6	1	2	0	5	7	0	2
014	35	0	12	1	3	–	5	5	0	2
015	30	0	5	1	2	0	5	5	0	1
016	30	0	6	1	3	–	4	5	0	7
017	44	0	21	1	3	0	6	7	0	–
018	44	1	22	3	2	–	7	7	0	8
019	49	1	26	3	4	0	5	5	0	10
020	49	1	20	1	3	–	7	6	0	4
021	51	1	30	4	1	0	4	6	0	7
022	63	1	34	3	3	0	4	4	0	11
023	34	1	2	1	4	–	6	5	0	11
024	25	0	3	1	3	–	4	6	0	7
025	37	0	15	1	2	–	7	7	0	5
026	36	1	3	1	2	–	6	6	0	6
027	34	0	9	1	2	0	7	6	0	6
028	–	0	21	2	1	1	5	5	0	12
029	51	1	30	1	3	–	6	6	0	3
030	40	0	9	1	1	1	6	6	0	–
031	52	0	20	4	2	–	7	7	0	6
032	45	1	24	4	3	–	–	6	0	12
033	33	0	9	4	2	1	6	5	0	4
034	48	0	25	1	2	–	6	7	0	9
035	42	0	19	3	2	–	5	5	0	10
036	40	1	15	3	2	–	7	7	0	10
037	26	0	2	4	2	–	–	5	0	–

Continued

EXHIBIT 15.3 *Continued*

	age	gender	years	position	field	pay	superior	self	state	thinking
038	56	0	34	1	2	–	5	5	0	9
039	24	0	2	1	3	–	6	6	0	2
040	47	0	15	3	2	1	7	7	0	11
041	48	1	6	1	2	–	5	5	0	6
042	52	1	29	2	4	1	6	7	0	10
043	37	0	13	3	3	1	–	4	0	–
044	33	1	8	4	2	1	6	7	0	6
045	39	1	15	4	2	1	6	5	0	3
046	59	0	18	1	2	1	6	6	0	8
047	38	0	4	1	2	–	–	4	0	2
048	41	1	16	4	3	–	7	6	0	–
049	45	0	25	4	3	1	6	5	0	8
050	41	1	13	3	2	1	6	6	0	4
051	54	0	15	4	–	–	7	7	0	10
052	30	0	2	1	4	–	–	–	0	4
053	42	0	4	2	2	–	7	6	0	8
054	58	0	3	4	–	–	6	6	0	–
055	55	1	30	4	3	1	7	6	0	1
056	40	0	10	2	2	–	7	6	1	7
057	58	0	37	1	2	0	7	5	1	6
058	36	0	9	1	4	–	5	5	1	8
059	36	0	9	1	2	1	6	7	1	–
060	27	0	3	1	3	–	–	5	1	–
061	42	1	15	3	4	–	–	6	1	12
062	41	0	16	3	1	1	6	6	1	9
063	35	1	11	2	2	1	7	6	1	10
064	62	0	20	2	2	–	4	5	1	2
065	39	0	7	3	4	1	7	6	1	6
066	40	1	10	2	2	1	5	4	1	7
067	26	0	3	1	1	0	5	6	1	4
068	38	0	4	1	1	1	5	6	1	4
069	42	0	15	3	2	1	6	6	1	9
070	59	0	35	1	2	–	–	6	1	7
071	33	0	8	1	3	0	4	4	1	7
072	34	0	8	1	1	–	5	5	1	5
073	–	–	–	4	–	–	–	–	1	–
074	25	0	5	1	3	–	6	4	1	–
075	42	0	20	2	1	–	6	4	1	10
076	37	0	10	1	2	1	6	6	1	1

EXHIBIT 15.3 *Continued*

	age	gender	years	position	field	pay	superior	self	state	thinking
077	47	1	2	1	2	–	6	6	1	0
078	53	1	25	1	3	1	5	5	1	–
079	44	0	22	3	1	1	5	4	1	9
080	54	0	30	2	2	0	6	6	1	1
081	56	1	28	3	2	–	–	4	1	10
082	27	0	1	1	3	–	6	5	1	9
083	38	0	12	3	1	1	6	4	1	2
084	71	0	26	1	1	–	–	5	1	–
085	44	0	15	3	3	–	7	7	1	11
086	43	0	14	4	4	–	7	7	1	8
087	43	1	4	1	2	–	–	6	1	–
088	47	0	15	2	4	–	7	7	1	2
089	27	0	3	1	2	–	5	5	1	5
090	27	0	3	1	2	–	6	6	1	7
091	35	0	12	1	3	–	7	7	1	3
092	25	0	2	1	2	–	5	4	1	4
093	34	1	3	1	2	1	6	6	1	5
094	46	0	10	1	3	–	5	5	1	7
095	45	0	22	4	4	1	6	6	1	8
096	40	0	15	3	4	–	7	6	1	7
097	51	0	5	1	2	–	7	7	1	–
098	40	0	15	3	2	–	7	6	1	–
099	59	1	12	3	1	1	7	5	1	6
100	49	0	12	1	3	0	5	7	1	7
101	38	0	11	2	2	–	5	6	1	–

Background Information

To use the SPSS software, you will need a computer with both the Windows operating system and the SPSS for Windows software. The instructions that follow operate on the assumption that you are basically familiar with the way computers work, and that you are familiar with the use of Windows-type systems which employ the mouse for providing instructions to the computer.

You will be given a set of options and you will choose among those options by moving to your choice with the mouse and clicking on that option. In some cases, this will lead you to another set of options, and you may have yet more options at that point. For example, when you are instructed to open a data file, you will be asked to click on the word **File** on the initial menu of options, then to click on the word **Open** from the next list of options, and then to click on the work **Data** from the next list. The fourth step in this process will be to click on the name of the file you wish to open, and then to click on the word **OK.** Here's how those instructions will look in this book:

(1) Click on **File**.
(2) Click on **Open**.
(3) Click on **Data**.
(4) Click on the desired file name.
(5) Click on **OK**.

The indented lines help illustrate the structure of the menus that you will be using. In this way, you will be reminded that the Data option is under the Open option which is under the File option from the opening window, which you access when you first load the SPSS software.

The above sequence of instructions illustrated the movement from one screen to another. Some instructions will call for you to do several things with the same screen. In those cases, the various instructions for actions within the same screen will be lined up beneath one another. To illustrate, let's examine the instructions for creating labels for variables repeated later in this chapter. The following are the instructions for giving the label of "female" for those study subjects who were coded as 0 for the variable of gender.

(1) Click on **Data**.
(2) Click on **Define Variable**.
(3) Enter the variable name of **gender** next to the space labelled **Variable Name**.
(4) Click on **Labels**.
(5) Click on the box labelled **Variable Label** and insert the word **gender**.
(6) Click on the box labelled **Value** and insert the number 0.
(7) Click on the box next to **Value Label** and insert the word **female**.
(8) Click on the word **Add**.

In this illustration, instructions number 5, 6, 7, and 8 were instructions for working with the same screen, whereas the previous instructions (1–4) would move you from one screen to another. You will be given more instructions on the above procedure for giving labels to variables. The purpose above was simply to illustrate how to read instructions and have a sense of where you are in the various computer screens that you will face.

Getting Started with SPSS

Your first task is to turn on the computer and access the Windows operating system. Very likely, you will get the Windows system when you turn on the computer. If not, you will need instructions on how to load this system into the computer's memory so you can use it.

Your next step is to load the SPSS software into memory. You do this by double clicking on the SPSS icon. You will see a computer screen that will display a number of windows for your use. You should direct your attention to the top bar, which contains a line of words designating your options. These options are as follows:

File Edit Data Transform Statistics Graphs Utilities Window Help

The above is the top line for the *initial menu* that you confront when you load the SPSS software into the computer's memory. In this chapter, we will often refer to the initial menu. These are two major options available to you when you first load the SPSS software:

1. You can create a new data file, or
2. You can use an existing data file.

Beginning Steps in Creating a New Data File

In the section which follows, you will be given instructions on the creation of a new data file. Data from the study of social workers in North Carolina and Massachusettes will be used in this illustration. In this exercise, you will do the following:

1. Give a name for each variable in the study,
2. Give labels for the categories for selected variables,
3. Enter the data for each of the study subjects,
4. Save the data on a computer disk, and
5. Print the data.

The study data from Exhibit 15.3 will be employed to illustrate how to use SPSS for Windows. This study contains ten variables as follows:

1. Age (Given in basic form rather than categories)
2. Gender (Female = 0; Male = 1)
3. Years (Designates the years of experience)
4. Position (Direct = 1; Supervisor = 2; Manager = 3; Other = 4)
5. Field (Health = 1; Mental Health = 2; Family & Child = 3; Other = 4)
6. Pay (0 = did not receive merit pay raise; 1 = did receive raise; blank = no such raises were given by the agency last year)
7. Superior (Rating by superior given on 7-point ordinal scale)
8. Self (Rating respondent gives self)
9. Thinking (Number of choices in the thinking category on the Thinking-feeling dimension of the Kiersey-Bates Temperament Sorter)
10. State (0 = NC; 1 = MA)

Step 1: Access Data Editor

Your first step in creating a new data file is to access the Data Editor window. This is the window with a grid of boxes with the word **var** at the top of each column of boxes. A portion of this grid is given below. This window is automatically displayed in the middle of the screen when you first load SPSS into memory. It is known in this chapter as the initial screen. At the top of the screen you will see the words **SPSS for Windows** followed by the line of options [File, Edit, Data, Transform, Statistics, Graphs, Utilities, Window, Help] followed by the word **Output** and then **Newdata**. The table (or grid) that will be displayed in the middle of the screen is the one where the names of variables and the data for each variable will be displayed. In part, it looks like the following:

	var	var	var
1			
2			

This Data Editor window is automatically accessed when you load SPSS into memory. Thus, you can simply begin the steps necessary for creating a new data file.

In this grid, the columns represent the variables and the rows represent the study subjects. The cells within this grid will contain the values for the given variable for the given study subject. In our example of the data from Exhibit 15.3, the first column will be the one designated for the variable of age, while the second column will contain information on the variable of gender, with females coded as 0 and males as 1.

In the example below, the first study subject is 34 years old and is a female (coded as 0). The second study subject is 33 years of age, and is a male (coded as 1).

	age	gender
1	34	0
2	33	1

Step 2: Define and Label Variables

Your second step is to **define the variables** and give **labels** to the categories for certain variables. In this example, there are 10 variables to define. Five of these variables (gender, position, field, pay, and state) need to have labels designated. The others do not need labels because the values for these variables are regular numbers which represent the true value for the variable rather than being a number used merely for coding purposes. For example, the variable of age is entered as the number of years rather than a category such as 0–19 or 20–29.

Naming the First Study Variable in the Example
Highlight the cell where the data is to be entered for the first variable. The first variable is **age** and will be entered in column 1. You highlight a cell by moving to that cell and you will see that it becomes darker than the others.

(1) Be sure the first cell in the first column is highlighted. If it is not, go to that cell and click on it so it becomes highlighted.

(2) With the designated cell highlighted, go to the word **Data** at the top of the screen and click on this word.

(3) Click on **Define Variable** from the next list of options. [You will obtain the Define Variable dialog box which contains places where you can designate the type of variable, label the categories to be assigned for each code (e.g., Female for 0 and Male for 1), and so forth.]

(4) Enter the name of the variable in the box next to **variable name**. Your first variable is **age**.

(5) Click on the word **OK** on the right side of the box.

You will be returned to Data Editor window from which you can follow the same procedures as above for defining your other variables. The second variable will require labels. This procedure will be illustrated in the next section. But you will first give a name to that variable with the same procedures as given above:

(1) Move to the second column (next to the one that is now labeled "age") and click on the first cell in that column so that it is highlighted.

(2) Click on **Data** from the Data Editor Window.

(3) Click on **Define Variable**.

(4) Name the second variable **gender** in the box labelled **Variable Name**.

Naming and Labeling the Variable Gender

The variable **gender** needs to have labels given to the coded values which will be inserted into the data file so that printouts will have the labels of "male" and "female" instead of 0 and 1. Labels for variables are given from the **Define Variable** dialog box as illustrated above. Thus, you must be there in order to execute the following instructions.

(1) Click on **Labels**.

(2) Click on **Variable Label**.

(3) Enter the name of the first variable to be given labels. This is the variable of **gender**.

(4) Click on the box next to **Value** and insert the number 0.

(5) Click on the box next to **Value Label** and insert the word **female**.

(6) Click on the word **Add**.

(7) Repeat steps 4, 5, and 6 for the category of male, designating the code as 1. In other words, execute the following steps:

Click on **Value** and enter the number 1.

Click on **Value Label** and enter the word **male**.

Click on **Add**.

You will now have the variable of gender labeled as 0 = female and 1 = male.

(8) Click on the word **Continue**. This will return you to the **Define Variable** box.

(9) From the Define Variable dialog box, click on **OK**. This will return you to the Data Editor Window where you can begin the process of defining the next variable. You still have the variables of years, position, field, pay, superior, self, thinking, and state to define.

Naming the Third Variable

The variable of **years** is numerical (like age); thus, it requires no labels for its values. It can be named in the same fashion as age without the option of giving labels as above.

(1) Go to the first cell in the third column and click on it.

(2) Click on **Data**.

(3) Click on **Define Variable**.

(4) Enter **years** in the box labeled **Variable Name**.

(5) Click on **OK**.

Defining **Position** *and Labeling Its Categories*

(1) With the fourth column highlighted from the Data Editor Window, click on **Data**.

(2) Click on **Define Variable**.

(3) Enter the name **position**.

(4) Click on **Labels**.

(5) In the box next to **Variable Label**, enter the name **Work Position**.

(6) Click on the box next to **Value** and enter the number 1.

(7) Click on the box next to **Value Label** and enter the label **direct**.

(8) Click on **Add**.

(9) Repeat 6, 7, and 8 for the next category as follows:

Click on the box next to **Value** and enter the number 2.

Click on the **Value Label** box and enter the label **supervisor**.

Click on **Add**.

(10) Repeat 6, 7, and 8 for the next category as follows:

Click on the box next to **Value** and enter the number 3.

Click on the **Value Label** box and enter the label **manager**.

Click on **Add**.

(11) Repeat 6, 7, and 8 for the next category as follows:

Click on the box next to **Value** and enter the number 4.

Click on the **Value Label** box and enter the label **other**.

Click on **Add**.

(12) Click on **Continue**.

(13) Click on **OK**.

Naming and Labeling Other Variables

Hopefully, you now have a basic idea of how this works. There are four additional variables to be defined, two of which need labels for the categories. The names of variables and the labels for the categories are given below.

Variable	Labels
field	1 = health
	2 = mental health
	3 = family & child
	4 = other
pay	0 = no
	1 = yes
superior	[no labels given]
self	[no labels given]
thinking	[no labels given]
state	0 = NC
	1 = MA

Entering Data

You will enter data from the Data Editor Window. This is the window that is presented to you when you first load the SPSS software into the computer's memory. After you have named your variables, you will have each variable name at the top of the columns of the table.

You will enter the data from Exhibit 15.3 as follows:

(1) Highlight the cell by moving the cursor to it or clicking on it.

(2) Enter the number for the first study subject.

(3) Hit the [Enter] key. This will move you to the cell for the next study subject for the same variable. In your case, the first variable is age. It is probably most convenient for you to enter the ages of all study subjects first.

(4) With the second cell under **age** highlighted, enter the age of the second study subject.

(5) Repeat the above procedures. Then move to the top of the column for the second variable and enter the value for the first study subject, then the second, and so forth.

If you are entering data directly from questionnaires, rather than a table or code sheet, you will probably find it more convenient to enter all the data from one study subject before moving to the next study subject.

Saving Your Data on a Disk for Later Use

You will normally want to save your data after you have created a data file. If you turn off the computer before you have saved your data, it will be lost! To save your data on a disk that is located in Disk Drive A, execute the following instructions:

(1) Insert a formatted disk in Disk Drive A.
(2) Click on **File** from the initial menu.
    (3) Click on **Save as**.
        (4) In the box beneath **File Name** insert the letter A and a colon and the name you wish to use for your file. [For example, if you were to give the name of **salary** to the file, you would insert **a:salary** in that box.]
    (5) Click on **OK**.

[You will be returned to the initial menu.]

Printing Your Data File

Before you can send your data to the printer, you should make sure the printer is turned on and has paper in it. You can print a copy of your data file through the following procedures:

(1) From the initial menu, click on **File**.
    (2) Click on **Print**.
        (3) Click on **OK**.
    [Your file will be printed and you will be returned to the initial menu.]

Creating New Variables

You can create new variables from ones that already exist in a data file. This process will be illustrated by the task of creating a new variable that divides the study subjects into only two categories for **position.** At present, they are in four categories—Direct, Supervisor, Manager, and Other. Suppose you wanted to compare managers with all others. While you could do this using the variable named *position* in the data file, your analysis will be simplified if you create a new variable. In the following instructions, you will create a new variable named **manager** that places each study subject into one of two categories. They will be coded 1 if they are a manager, or 0 if they are not. This means that persons currently coded 3 for **position** will be recoded 1 for **manager,** and all others will be recoded as 0 for this new variable. When you finish, you will still have the variable of **position** in your data file, but you will also have a new variable named **manager.**

(1) Click on **Transform** from the initial menu.

(2) Click on **Recode**.

(3) Click on the option **Into different variable**.

(4) Click on the variable of **position** which you will find in the box on the left of the screen where all variables in the data file will be listed.

(5) Click on the triangle figure [>] between the left and middle boxes on the screen. This will place the variable of **position** into the box labeled **Input variable→Output variable**.

(6) From the **Output Variable** box to the right of the screen, click on the box beneath the word **Name**. A blinking mark will appear to indicate that the computer is prepared to receive a name to be entered in this space.

(7) Enter the name of **manager** for the new variable.

(8) Click on the word **Change** which you will find beside the box in which you inserted the variable name.

(9) Click on **Old and New Values**.

(10) In the box labeled **Old Value** insert the number 1 in the box labeled **Value**.

(11) On the right side of the screen, you will find a box labeled **New Value**. Click on the little box labeled **Value** in this larger box.

(12) Insert the number 0 in this box labeled **Value**.

(13) Click on the word **Add** in the middle of the screen. This action will insert the designation **1→0** in the box labeled **Old→New**. This means that you have recorded the desire for persons coded as 1 for the old variable to be coded as 0 for the new one.

(14) Repeat steps 10–13 in order to recode subjects from 2 to 0. The first step is to click on the box labeled **Old Value** and insert the number 2 in this box. The next three steps repeat steps 11–13 for the transformation of those coded as 2 to 0.

(15) Click on the box labeled **Value** in the section labeled **New Value**.

(16) Insert the number 0 in this box.

(17) Click on the word **Add** in the middle of the screen. This action will insert the designation **2→0** in the box labeled **Old→New**.

This means that you have recorded the desire for persons coded as 2 for the old variable to be coded as 0 for the new one. Repeat steps 10–13 again so that those coded as 3 will be coded as 1.

(18) Click on **Value** beneath **Old Value** and insert the number 3.

(19) Click on **Value** beneath **New Value**.

(20) Insert the number 1 for new value.

(21) Click on the word **Add**.

(22) Repeat these steps so that those coded for 4 on the old variable will be coded as 0 for the new one.

(23) Click on **Continue** at the bottom of the screen. This will return you to the previous screen.

(24) Click on **OK**.

This final procedure will return you to the Data Editor screen where you can see that the new variable (manager) has been added next to the last variable in the old file. You can see that each subject has been given either the number 0 or 1 for this new variable.

Using a Sub-Sample of Cases

You can restrict your analysis to a sub-sample of cases. For example, suppose you wish to use the NASW study data to examine whether males and females differed on their preferences for thinking over feeling. You could undertake this analysis for only those persons from the state of Massachusetts by the procedure outlined below. (Remember that the study subjects from the state of Massachusetts were coded as 1, while those from North Carolina were coded as 0.)

(1) Click on **Data** from the initial menu.

(2) Click on **Select Cases**.

(3) Click on **If condition is satisfied**.

(4) Click on **if**.

(5) Click on **state,** the variable that contains the information on our basis for restricting our data.

(6) Click on the triangle figure next to the box at the top.

(7) Click on the equal sign in the keypad on the screen.

(8) Click on the number 1, which represents the code for the chosen state. You will see the instruction "state = 1." This means that you are asking the computer to restrict your analysis to those who are coded as 1 for the variable of state.

(9) Click on **Continue**.

(10) Click on **OK**. You will be returned to the initial menu, where you can enter your instructions for applying the independent samples t test to

the variables of gender and thinking with a sub-sample of study subjects from the state of Massachusetts. If you wish to complete this exercise, turn to the instructions for the independent samples t test in the next chapter.

To Return to the Full Data File

After you complete your analysis using only a sub-sample of cases, you may want to return to the full data file for more analysis. The following are your procedures.

    (1) Click on **Data**.

        (2) Click on **Select Cases**.

            (3) Click on **Reset**.

            (4) Click on **OK**.

Opening an Existing Data File

Once you have created a data file and saved it on your disk, you can later use that file for analysis. The procedures are as follows:

    (1) Click on **File** from the initial menu.

        (2) Click on **Open**.

            (3) Click on **Data**.

            (4) Highlight the desired file from the list and click on it.

            (5) Click on **OK**.

The desired file will be entered on your computer screen. You are now ready to use it. You can select statistics for computation and print out the results. You can also modify this file by adding or deleting variables or cases, and so forth. You can also create new variables from the ones that already exist.

Quick Reference For Using SPSS For Windows

Creating a New Data File

    (1) **File**

        (2) **New**

            (3) **Data**

Using an Existing Data File

    (1) **File**

        (2) **Open**

            (3) **Data**

            (4) [Select the file]

            (5) **OK**

Defining Variables When Labels are Not Needed

(1) **Data**

    (2) **Define Variable**

        (3) [Enter variable name]

        (4) **OK**

Defining Variables and Giving Labels

(1) **Data**

    (2) **Define Variable**

        (3) [Enter variable name]

        (4) **Labels**

            (5) **Value**

            (6) [Enter code for first category—e.g., 0 for female]

            (7) **Value Label**

            (8) [Enter label for persons with the above code—e.g. female]

            (9) **Add**

            (10) Repeat steps 5–9 for each additional category

            (11) **Continue**

    (12) **OK**

Saving Your File on a Disk in Drive A

(1) **File**

    (2) **Save as**

        (3) [Enter **a** and the file name—e.g., **a:myfile**]

        (4) **OK**

Printing Your Output	*Clearing the Output Window*
(1) **File**	(1) **Edit**
(2) **Print**	(2) **Select**
(3) **OK**	(3) **All**
	(4) **Edit**
	(5) **Clear**

Chapter 16

Selected Statistics with Illustrations Using SPSS for Windows

In this chapter, you will be given a description of 16 statistical measures that are common for social research, as well as several descriptive statistics. There are, of course, many more statistical measures than those presented here, and you may need to consult a text on statistics if your situation does not fit into the charts that are displayed in the previous chapter. Those charts helped you to identify the statistical measure that would be appropriate for you. This chapter will *explain* that choice.

At the end of each description, you will find the instructions for using SPSS for Windows for this analysis. You will also find an explanation of the computer printout that will result from this analysis. Many of the explanations will use variables from the NASW study described in Chapter 15. You may need to consult Exhibits 15.1 and 15.3 to clarify the nature of the data in the example.

Before taking this step in the research process, you will need to have collected your data, determined the hypothesis you are testing, and prepared your data for computer entry by determining how each value of each variable will be entered. You must have created the data file that contains the data for each variable, along with variable labels as needed. The process you will use in this chapter is as follows:

1. Find the particular statistical measure you wish to apply in analyzing your research question. These statistical measures are presented in alphabetical order.
2. Examine the explanation of that statistical measure to assure yourself that it is appropriate to your situation.
3. Follow the instructions for computing that statistic for your data.
4. Obtain a printout of that analysis.

5. Clear the contents of the output window for future use.

6. Examine the explanation of the printout to determine both practical significance and statistical significance.

The goal of this chapter is to help you to acquire an understanding of what your statistic will tell you, how to use the computer in applying this statistic, and how to read the printout from this analysis. As a result of this understanding, you should be able to avoid mistakes in using and interpreting data.

Objectives

At the completion of this chapter, you will be able to do the following:

1. Determine whether your chosen statistical measure is suitable for your hypothesis or research question.

2. Provide instructions to the computer for calculating any of 16 statistical measures included in this chapter, using SPSS for Windows.

3. Interpret the computer printout for any of these 16 statistical measures regarding both statistical significance and practical significance.

Outline of Measures Presented in this Chapter

The measures presented in this chapter are as follows:

> Analysis of variance—ANOVA (One-way)
> Binomial test
> Chi Square test for one sample
> Chi Square test for two independent samples
> Contingency coefficient
> Descriptive statistics (frequencies, proportions, mean, median, mode, standard deviation)
> Fischer exact probability test
> Kruskal-Wallis one-way analysis of variance
> McNear test for the significance of changes
> Mann-Whitney U test
> Multiple regression analysis
> Pearson correlation coefficient
> Phi coefficient
> Spearman rank correlation coefficient
> The t test for paired data
> The t test for independent samples
> Wilcoxon matched pairs signed ranks test

To facilitate your initial familiarity with these statistical measures, Assignment 16-A asks several specific questions for which you'll need to read the explanations of these statistical measures. At the end of this chapter is an assignment that asks you to undertake your own statistical analysis using the data from the NASW study presented in Chapter 15.

ASSIGNMENT 16-A

Note: The answers to the questions below require you to read the information that follows in this chapter about various statistical measures. Prepare your answers to these questions on a separate page.

1. For the NASW study, explain the frequency distribution for the variable of **position.**

2. For the NASW study, what is the mean age of respondents?

3. Examine the following hypothesis: *There is a relationship between gender and whether one received a merit pay raise.* The data for this hypothesis is contained in the explanation for one of the statistical measures in this chapter. Determine which statistic would be used to test this hypothesis and carefully read the explanation for this statistic. Provide a brief statement analyzing both the statistical and practical significance of the results.

4. Examine the following hypothesis: *Clients will be more likely to be below the threshold for depression after treatment than they were before treatment.* In this study, clients have been classified into two categories before treatment—below the threshold for depression and above the threshold for depression. After treatment, they were again classified into these two categories. Thus, for each client, we have information on their category before treatment and after treatment. Determine the statistical measure that should be used to test this hypothesis and read the explanation for that statistic in this chapter. Use the data from that explanation to provide a statement analyzing both the practical and statistical significance of these results.

Analysis of Variance—ANOVA (One Way)

The One-way Analysis of Variance (also known as ANOVA) is a method for determining whether the differences in mean scores of three or more groups are significantly different from one another. It assumes that the data for the dependent variable are normally distributed, drawn from independent samples, and measured at the interval level. This method of analysis yields an F score from which the p value can be determined (i.e., the probability that the differences in mean scores could be explained by chance).

Example

Suppose we wish to know if the average number of years of experience for social workers differs from one field of practice to another. We have classified our respondents into the categories of (1) *health,* (2) *mental health,* (3) *family and child,* and (4) *other* for field of practice. We have asked our respondents to indicate their years of social work experience. To examine our research question, we need to know the average years of experience for our respondents in each field of practice, and we need to know if these differences can easily be explained by chance (i.e., Are they statistically significant?).

The ANOVA procedure will produce an F score from which a p value can be derived. If the p value is less than .05, we can conclude that we could not discover differences in years of experience among four groups as large as the ones indicated by our data as often as 5 times in 100 just by chance. If the p value associated with the F value calculated for these data is determined to be greater than 0.05, we would conclude that the differences between groups are not statistically significant (i.e., they could be explained by chance too often for us to be confident that true differences do exist in these four groups).

Procedure

    (1) Click on **Statistics** from the initial menu.

      (2) Click on **Compare Means**.

        (3) Click on **One-way ANOVA**.

          (4) Click on **years** using our data file.

          (5) Click on the triangle figure next to **Dependent List**.

          (6) Click on **field**.

          (7) Click on the triangle figure beneath **Factor**.

          (8) Click on **Define Range**.

            (9) Click on **Minimum** and enter the number 1. This is our minimum value for the variable of **field**.

          (10) Click on **Maximum** and enter the number 4.

          (11) Click on **Continue**.

        (12) Click on **Options**.

          (13) Click on **Descriptive**.

          (14) Click on **Continue**.

        (15) Click on **OK**.

To Print Your Output	*To Clear the Output Window*
(1) **File**	(1) **Edit**
(2) **Print**	(2) **Select**
(3) **OK**	(3) **All**
	(4) **Edit**
	(5) **Clear**

Reading the ANOVA Printout

The printout for this procedure is shown in Exhibit 16.1. To examine practical significance, turn your attention to the average years of experience for each of the four groups of social workers. That information is contained under the column labelled **mean.** You can see that those in the field of *health* (Grp 1) had a mean number of years of experience of 15.07, while those in *mental health* (Grp 2) had a mean of 12.47, and those in *family and child* had a mean of 13.92. Those in the category of *other* had a mean of 13.92. But before you become serious about examining these differences, you need to know if these differences are statistically significant. That information is contained in the highlighted figure of .7959 under the column labeled "F Prob." This figure of .7959 is the value of p (i.e., p = .7959). In this case, the differences among these four categories were not statistically significant, because p is greater than .05.

EXHIBIT 16.1   Sample ANOVA Printout

Source	D.F	Sum of Squares	Mean Squares	F Ratio	F Prob.
Between Groups	3	85.3194	28.4398	.3407	**.7958**
Within Groups	94	7846.6806	83.4753		
Total	97	7932.0000			

Group	Count	Mean
Grp 1	13	15.0769
Grp 2	44	12.4773
Grp 3	28	13.9286
Grp 4	13	13.9231

Binomial Test

The binomial test is an appropriate statistical measure for determining whether the frequencies between two categories of a nominal variable are significantly different. For example, you might want to know whether the proportion of clients who selected family therapy over group therapy is significantly different from the 50–50 split you would expect to occur simply by chance. In order to employ this test, you must know, or be prepared to assume, what are the normal chances of persons to fall into the two groups. In many cases, you would expect approximately 50 percent of all persons to fall into one category and 50 percent into the other. For example, we know that approximately 50 percent of all persons are male and 50 percent are female. But we know that this is not the normal distribution of social workers by gender category, because we know there are more females than males.

In the example above in which clients were posed with only two choices, we know there was a 50 percent chance that they would select one option and a 50 percent chance that they would select the other. But this would not be the case if they had been offered a third option.

Example

Suppose you wish to know if the number of male and females differ significantly in the sample of social workers in the data file used as an example in this chapter. There are 69 females and 31 males. Is this difference significant?

Procedure

(1) Click on **Statistics** from the initial menu.

    (2) Click on **Non-parametric Tests**.

        (3) Click on **Binomial**.

            (4) Click on **gender** in the box of variable names.

            (5) Click on the triangle figure in the middle of the screen.

            (6) Click on **OK**.

To Print Your Output	*To Clear the Output Window*
(1) **File**	(1) **Edit**
(2) **Print**	(2) **Select**
(3) **OK**	(3) **All**
	(4) **Edit**
	(5) **Clear**

Reading the Binomial Test Printout

The printout from the data, in part, is shown in Exhibit 16.2. From these data, you can see that there were 69 persons coded 0 for gender (female, in this case) and 31 persons coded 1 for this variable (male). The p value is given as .0002, indicating that this distribution of persons is significantly different from a 50–50 split.

EXHIBIT 16.2   **Sample Binomial Test Printout**

Cases

$69 = 0$

$31 = 1$

—   Z Approximation

100 2-Tailed P = .0002

Chi Square One-Sample Test

The chi square one-sample test is an appropriate measure for examining whether the frequencies among three or more categories of a nominal variable are significantly different.

Example

For example, you might have the following data for hospital emergency room cases for child abuse:

Mon	Tues	Wed	Thur	Fri	Sat	Sun
11	13	9	6	8	5	6

You want to know whether there is any reason to believe that the day of the week has anything to do with the phenomenon of child abuse. The chi square one-sample test can help. It will tell you whether this distribution of cases could have occurred by chance. In other words, it will tell you whether these frequencies are significantly different from expected frequencies, the expected frequencies being those that would have occurred by chance. In our example, we have 7 days of the week and total of 58 cases. Thus, our expected frequency for each day of the week would be 8.29 rounded off to the nearest two decimal points ($58 / 7 = 8.2857$). If the distribution of frequencies for days of the week were something like 8, 9, 7, 8, 7, and so forth, it would probably not be statistically significant, because these differences from one day to the next are slight.

Procedure

The following procedure will instruct the computer to employ SPSS for Windows to calculate the chi square value to determine if the differences in the number of social workers (NASW study) in the four categories of field of practice are statistically significant. In our example, we have 13 persons in *health,* 44 persons in *mental health,* 28 persons in *child and family,* and 13 persons in the category of *other.* Are these differences significant?

    (1) Click on **Statistics** from the initial menu.

        (2) Click on **Nonparametric Tests**.

            (3) Click on **Chi-Square Test**.

                (4) Click on **field** (This is our chosen variable).

                (5) Click on the triangle figure in order to select this variable.

            (6) Click on **OK**.

To Print Your Output	*To Clear the Output Window*
(1) **File**	(1) **Edit**
(2) **Print**	(2) **Select**
(3) **OK**	(3) **All**
	(4) **Edit**
	(5) **Clear**

Reading the Printout of the Chi Square One-Sample Test

The printout from the above instructions will appear as shown in Exhibit 16.3. The Category column indicates the coding of the variable, while the Cases Observed column indicates the frequencies for each of the four categories of the variable. These frequencies can guide your determination of practical significance. Statistical significance is given under the heading Significance. In our case, that figure is given as .0000. This means that these differences are significant at a level below .0001. In situations where the computer printout has the value of .0000, you should not interpret the p value as an absolute 0. The designation of .0000 is given only because the computer does not give any more decimal places. You should report .0000 as "p < .0001."

EXHIBIT 16.3   Sample Chi Square One-Sample Test

	Category	Observed	Expected	Residual
Health	1	13	24.50	−11.50
Mental Health	2	44	24.50	19.50
Family & Child	3	28	24.50	3.50
Other	4	13	24.50	−11.50
Total		98		

Chi-Square	D.F	Significance
26.8163	3	.0000

Chi Square Test for Two Independent Samples

The chi square test for two independent samples is appropriate for determining if there is a significant relationship between two variables measured at the nominal level when the data are drawn from independent samples.

Data for this analysis are organized into tables with the subjects divided according to how they fell into the categories of the two variables. This distribution of frequencies into the cells of the table is compared to the distribution of frequencies that we would expect to find if there were no relationship between the two variables. This analysis yields a chi square value that is used to determine the level of statistical significance (i.e., the value of p) for the relationship. If the data in the table differ a great deal from a distribution that we would expect to find by chance, we will discover a p value that is low (less than 0.05) and we can determine that the relationship is statistically significant.

The chi square value, however, will not tell us the strength of the relationship between the two variables. It will only tell us whether the relationship is statistically significant. To examine the strength of the relationship, we must employ a measure of correlation such as phi coefficient (if the data for each of the two variables are dichotomous) or the contingency coefficient (if the data for one or both variables have more than two categories).

The value of chi square (and, thus, the level of statistical significance) is dependent on two things—the strength of the association (as determined by a measure of correlation) and the size of the sample. Larger coefficients of correlation yield greater levels of statistical significance, and larger sample sizes also yield greater levels of statistical significance.

Example

Exhibit 16.4 contains hypothetical data on the relationship between gender and job satisfaction. People were asked to identify their gender and whether or not they were satisfied with their present jobs. We can readily see that there is no relationship between gender and job satisfaction from these data, because the proportion of males with job satisfaction (two-thirds) is exactly the same as the proportion of females with job satisfaction (60 out of 90, or two-thirds). In this case, the actual frequencies are exactly the same as the expected frequencies. It is seldom, however, that we would find the proportion of two groups with a certain trait to be exactly the same. The chi square procedure is a method of examining just how different a given set of frequencies are from the proportions that we would expect by chance (the expected frequencies).

EXHIBIT 16.4   Sample Data for Hypothetical Study

Satisfied with Present Job	Gender		Total
	Male	Female	
Yes	40	60	100
No	20	30	50
Total	60	90	150

Warning

Chi square is not appropriate if 20 percent or more of the cells in the table have expected frequencies that are less than five. This often happens with small samples (less than 30). The SPSS software will give you information on the number of cells with expected frequencies less than five.

Expected frequencies are computed for a given cell in a table by multiplying the column total by the row total, then dividing that product by the total number in the sample. In the example above, the expected frequency for males who were satisfied would be calculated by multiplying 100 by 60 and by dividing that value by 150 ($100 \times 60 = 6000 / 150 = 40$). The expected frequency for this cell is 40.

For data in a 2×2 table (i.e., only 4 cells) as noted in the example, you can employ the Fischer Exact Probability Test if you find expected frequencies less than five. For tables with more than four cells, you should consult a text on statistics for use of the Yates Correction. When you ask for the **crosstabs** procedure with SPSS for Windows, the data from the Fischer test will be provided if there are too many cells with expected frequencies less than five.

Examining the Strength of the Relationship

The strength of the relationship between the two variables is the guide for determining practical significance. The chi square statistic will not give you this information. It will only be used in determining the p value, which is used to determine statistical significance

You may examine the strength of the relationship between the two variables by employing a measure of correlation for non-parametric data. For data in which both variables are dichotomous, you may employ the phi coefficient (explained later). For data in which one or more of the variables has more than two categories, you may employ the contingency coefficient (explained later).

Degrees of Freedom

If you are looking up the level of statistical significance in a statistical table when you have calculated the value of chi square, you will also need to determine the degrees of freedom for your data. The degrees of freedom for chi square are calculated by multiplying the number of rows in your table minus one, by the number of columns in your table minus one. For data in a 2 by 2 table with two dichotomous variables, the degrees of freedom is 1 (2 – 1 = 1, which multiplied by 2 – 1 will yield a value of 1). For data in a 2 by 3 table, the degrees of freedom would be calculated as follows:

$$(2 - 1)(3 - 1) = 2 \times 1 = 2$$

Procedure

Suppose we wish to know if males and females in our NASW study differ on whether they received a merit pay raise in the past year. The names we have given these variables are **gender** and **pay.**

   (1) Click on **Statistics** from the initial menu.

      (2) Click on **Summarize**.

         (3) Click on **Crosstabs**.

            (4) Click on one of the chosen variables. In our case, one is **gender**.

            (5) Click on the triangle figure next to the box labeled **Rows**.

            (6) Click on the second variable, **pay**.

            (7) Click on the triangle figure next to the box labeled **Columns**.

            (8) Click on **Statistics** at the bottom of the screen.

               (9) Click on each of the following options—

                  (a) **Chi-square**,

                  (b) **Contingency coefficient**, and

                  (c) **Phi and Cramer's V.**

              (10)Click on **Continue**.

         (11) Click on **OK**.

To Print Your Output	*To Clear the Output Window*
(1) **File**	(1) **Edit**
(2) **Print**	(2) **Select**
(3) **OK**	(3) **All**
	(4) **Edit**
	(5) **Clear**

Reading the Printout of the Chi Square Test

In our analysis of the relationship between **pay** and **gender,** we were seeking to learn whether males and females differed in receipt of a merit pay raise. A portion of the printout, using the NASW study, is presented in Exhibit 16.5.

From the table, we can see that the proportion of females who received a merit pay raise was about 60 percent (17 out of 28), and that this proportion was very similar to that for males (11 out of 16, or about 60 percent). These differences are very slight and not likely to be statistically significant. This lack of association between gender and pay raise is reflected in the very low phi coefficient of .00397, which is extremely close to 0, the figure that represents absolutely no relationship at all between two variables. Naturally, the p value will be very high, meaning that statistical significance was not achieved. This figure is given in the column labeled Approximate Significance. This figure is .97853 (i.e., p = .97853). The value of the chi square is given as .00072. While this figure is often quoted in published research, it has little meaning apart from the p value associated with it. It cannot be interpreted in the same manner as a phi coefficient, which can range from a low of 0 to a maximum of 1.0 and which represents the strength of the relationship between the variables.

EXHIBIT 16.5   **Sample Chi Square Printout for Two Independent Variables**

GENDER		*PAY*		
		No	*Yes*	*Total*
Female	0	11	17	28
Male	1	7	11	18
	Total	18	28	46

Chi Square	*Value*	*DF*	*Significance*
Pearson	.00072	1	.97853

Statistic	*Value*	*Approximate Significance*
Phi	.00397	.97853 *1
Cramer's V	.00397	.97853 *1
Contingency Coefficient	.00397	.97853 *1

Contingency Coefficient

The contingency coefficient (C) is a nonparametric measure of correlation for data measured at the nominal level. It is used in conjunction with chi square for data organized in tables with more than 4 cells (e.g., a 2 × 3 table, a 3 × 3 table, or a 3 × 4 table, etc.). The contingency coefficient will have a value of 0 if there is no correlation at all between the two variables, but the upper limit is not 1.0, as is the case of the Pearson correlation coefficient (r) for data measured at the interval level. The upper limit of the contingency coefficient will depend on the structure of the tables from which the data are drawn. Therefore, the value of the contingency coefficient cannot be compared to that of the Pearson r or other measures of correlation. But, as with other measures of correlation, the larger the value of the coefficient, the stronger the relationship between the variables.

The contingency coefficient can be computed easily if you have the value of chi square for your data. It is calculated by the following procedures: (1) add the value of chi square to the value of N (the number in the sample); (2) divide the value of chi square by the value obtained in the first step; (3) take the square root of the value obtained in step 2—this is the value of the contingency coefficient.

Instructions for using SPSS for Windows for calculating the contingency coefficient are the same as those presented for chi square. Like phi coefficient, the contingency coefficient is a measure of the strength of the relationship between two nominal variables. Statistical significance of the value of the contingency coefficient depends on the chi square statistic.

Descriptive Statistics

The most common descriptive statistics are frequency, proportion, mean, median, mode, and standard deviation. A *frequency* is the occurrence of something. If there are 34 females and 29 males in a study sample, the numbers 34 and 29 would be the frequency counts for each of these categories (attributes) of the variable of gender. A *proportion* is a percentage of the total. The *mean* is the average of all values in a data set. The *median* is the midpoint for all values if each value were to be lined up in numerical sequence. The *mode* is the value that occurs the most. The *standard deviation* tells us how much the values in a data set are similar to one another. The higher the standard deviation, the more variance there is in the values in a given data set.

Obtaining Frequencies and Proportions

Procedure

    (1) Click on **Statistics** from the initial menu.

        (2) Click on **Summarize**.

            (3) Click on **Frequencies**. You will obtain a dialogue box with the names of the variables displayed on the left. Your task is to move the chosen variables from the left box to the box toward the right which is labelled **Variables**.

(4) Click on a chosen variable so that it is highlighted.

(5) Click on the triangle figure in the middle. This will place the chosen variable in the Variable box.

(6) Repeat steps 4 and 5 for each chosen variable.

(7) Click on **OK**. Your frequency counts will appear in the Output Window.

Obtaining the Mean, Median, Mode, and Standard Deviation

Procedure

(1) Click on **Statistics** from the initial menu.

(2) Click on **Summarize**.

(3) Click on **Frequencies**.

(4) Click on the first variable to be analyzed. In our example from the NASW study, we will select **age** as the first variable.

(5) Click on the triangle figure in the middle of the screen.

(6) Repeat steps 3 and 4 for each variable in the analysis. In our example, we will select **years** as a second variable.

(7) Click on **Statistics** at the bottom of the screen.

(8) Click on **Mean,** then **Median,** then **Mode,** then **Std. deviation,** then **Minimum,** then **Maximum**.

(9) Click on **Continue**.

(10) Click on **Display Frequency Tables**. (This removes frequencies from the list of options)

(11) Click on **OK**.

To Print Your Output	*To Clear the Output Window*
(1) **File**	(1) **Edit**
(2) **Print**	(2) **Select**
(3) **OK**	(3) **All**
	(4) **Edit**
	(5) **Clear**

Reading the Printout on Frequencies

Exhibit 16.6 is the printout for the variable of **position.** From this printout, you can see that those persons who were labeled as "Direct" for position were coded as 1 in this data file and that there were 51 such persons in this data set. There were 13 persons who indicated that they were supervisors, 22 managers, 15 other, and this piece of information was missing for

---

EXHIBIT 16.6   Sample Frequencies Printout

POSITION

Value Label	Value	Frequency	Percent	Valid Percent	Cum Percent
Direct	1	51	50.0	50.5	50.5
Supervisor	2	13	12.7	12.9	63.4
Manager	3	22	21.6	21.8	85.1
Other	4	15	14.7	14.9	100.0
	.	1	1.0	Missing	
	Total	102	100.0	100.0	

---

1 person. The Percent column tells us that those labeled as Direct for position constituted 50 percent of all those in the study (including those with missing data). The Valid Percent column tells us that this group of 51 persons constituted 50.5 percent of those persons for whom data on this variable were collected. The valid percent does not include the one person for whom this information was missing.

Reading the Printout on the Mean, Median, Mode, and Standard Deviation

Exhibit 16.7 shows the printout you will obtain for the variables of **age** and **years** from the NASW study. From these data, you can see that the mean age is 41.3, while the median and mode are both 40. The standard deviation for age is 9.86. The youngest person in this sample was 24 years of age, while the oldest was 71. Information on age was included in the data file for 98 persons and was missing for 4 persons.

EXHIBIT 16.7   Sample Mean, Median, Mode, and Standard Deviation Printout

AGE

Mean	41.306	Median	40.000	Mode	40.000
Std. dev	9.860	Minimum	24.000	Maximum	71.000
Valid cases	98	Missing cases	4		

YEARS

Mean	13.340	Median	12.000	Mode	15.000
Std. dev	9.013	Minimum	1.000	Maximum	37.000
Valid cases	100	Missing cases	2		

Obtaining Bar Charts and Pie Charts

You can obtain a bar chart indicating the number of persons in each of several categories, or a pie chart which divides categories into slices of a pie. The graphs function is employed for this purpose. There are, of course, a wide range of ways to depict your data graphically. Only two will be presented in this section. Suppose we are using the NASW study and we wish to develop a bar chart that displays the number of persons in each of the different categories of the variable **position.** We can also divide the data into these same categories using the pie chart.

Using the Bar Chart to Display Subjects by Position

    (1) Click on **Graphs** from the initial menu.

       (2) Click on **bar**.

          (3) Click on **Define**.

             (4) Click on **position,** the chosen variable.

             (5) Click on the triangle next to **Category Axis**.

             (6) Click on **OK**.

Using the Pie Chart to Display Study Subjects by Position

    (1) Click on **Graphs** from the initial menu.

       (2) Click on **pie**.

          (3) Click on **Define**.

             (4) Click on **position,** the chosen variable.

             (5) Click on the triangle next to **Define Slices by**.

             (6) Click on **OK**.

To Print Your Output

    (1) **File**

       (2) **Print**

          (3) **OK**

To Discard the Graphics

    (1) Click on **discard**.

       (2) **Edit**

          (3) **Select**

             (4) **All**

       (5) **Edit**

          (6) **Clear**

Fischer Exact Probability Test

The Fisher exact probability test is used to examine a relationship between two dichotomous variables in situations where the data are drawn from independent samples. It is especially useful for data from small samples and may be used when chi square is not appropriate because of small expected frequencies in the cells of the table where such data are displayed.

The Fisher exact probability test will yield a value for p that can be used to determine if the difference between two variables is statistically significant. It may not be useful for large samples (i.e., over 25), because of the complications in its computation and because chi square would normally be appropriate for such samples.

Example

Suppose you wish to compare a treated group of clients with a group of persons who did not receive the treatment. We have classified each study subject according to two variables. They are coded as 0 if they were in the comparison group, or 1 if they were in the treated group. Each person is also classified according to whether or not they achieved recovery. They are coded as 0 if they did not achieve recovery, or 1 if they did achieve recovery. Our data file would look like Exhibit 16.8, with variable names at the top.

EXHIBIT 16.8   Sample Data for Hypothetical Study

	GROUP	*RECOVERY*		*GROUP*	*RECOVERY*
1	0	0	9	1	1
2	0	0	10	1	1
3	0	0	11	1	1
4	0	0	12	1	1
5	0	0	13	1	1
6	0	1	14	1	1
7	0	1	15	1	1
8	0	1	16	1	0

Procedure

The procedure for computing the Fischer test is the same as the chi square test for two independent samples. The Fischer test will be computed if there is an unacceptable number of expected frequencies that are less than five. You will need to enter the above data before using the following procedures.

    (1) Click on **Statistics** from the initial menu.

        (2) Click on **Summarize**.

            (3) Click on **Crosstabs**.

                (4) Click on one of the chosen variables. In our case, one is **group**.

(5) Click on the triangle figure next to the box labeled **Rows**.

(6) Click on the second variable, **recovery**.

(7) Click on the triangle figure next to the box labeled **Columns**.

(8) Click on **Statistics** at the bottom of the screen.

    (9) Click on each of the following options:

        (a) **Chi-square**,

        (b) **Contingency coefficient**, and

        (c) **Phi and Cramer's V**.

  (10) Click on **Continue**.

(11) Click on **OK**.

[Note: If there are expected frequencies less than 5, there will be a notation to this effect on the printout. In that case, you should not employ the chi square information, but rely on the information from the Fischer test instead.]

To Print Your Output	*To Clear the Output Window*
(1) **File**	(1) **Edit**
(2) **Print**	(2) **Select**
(3) **OK**	(3) **All**
	(4) **Edit**
	(5) **Clear**

Reading the Printout of the Fisher Exact Probability Test

The table displaying the data from our example will appear, in part, as shown in Exhibit 16.9. The printout for the Fischer test gives both one-tailed and two-tailed probabilities. If you have hypothesized a direction for the relationship between the two variables,

---

EXHIBIT 16.9   Sample Fisher Exact Probability Test Printout

	RECOVERY		*Row*
GROUP	No	Yes	Total
Comparison	5	3	8
Treatment	2	6	8
Column Total	7	9	16

Significance

Fischer's Exact Test:

    One-Tail   .15734

    Two-Tail   .31469

you would utilize the one-tailed probabilities. If not, you would refer to the two-tailed probabilities. In our case, we expect that the treatment group will be more likely to recover. Thus, the one-tail probabilities would be used (i.e., p = .15). (It is not necessary to carry decimal points out beyond two places.)

Kruskal-Wallis One-Way Analysis of Variance

The Kruskal-Wallis one-way analysis of variance is a statistical measure for determining if there is a significant relationship between a nominal variable with three or more categories and an ordinal variable, in situations where the data are drawn from independent samples.

EXHIBIT 16.10   Sample Data for Hypothetical Study

#	Group	Satisfy
1	1	4
2	3	4
3	1	3
4	2	5
5	1	4
6	2	4
7	3	5
8	2	3
9	1	5
10	2	3
11	2	3
12	3	2
13	3	3
14	1	4
15	1	5
16	2	4
17	3	3
18	1	4
19	2	5
20	3	3
21	2	4

For example, you may want to know if social workers, psychologists, and rehabilitation counselors employed in mental health centers differ significantly with regard to their level of job satisfaction as measured by a five-point ordinal scale.

The Kruskal-Wallis one-way analysis of variance yields a value for H, from which the p value can be derived. The H value is determined by the extent to which the persons in the groups were ranked similarly with regard to the dependent variable (e.g., job satisfaction). If they tend to be rather similar, then we conclude that these findings can easily be explained by chance; thus, the differences between groups are not statistically significant.

Example

The following are hypothetical data on 21 persons working in mental health centers. They are classified according to the variable of **group** and the variable of **satisfy.** For the variable of group, they are coded 1 if they are a social worker, 2 if they are a psychologist, or 3 if they are a rehabilitation counselor. Their values on satisfaction can range from a low of 1 to a high of 5. The data for 21 such hypothetical persons are presented in Exhibit 16.10.

Satisfaction (**satisfy**) is measured at the ordinal level; **group** is measured at the nominal level and has more than two categories. Our research question is whether there is a difference in level of satisfaction among three categories of personnel. Are social workers, for example, different from the others on level of satisfaction? The Kruskal-Wallis one-way analysis of variance uses a procedure whereby the above persons would be ranked according to their level of job satisfaction. Subjects identified as number 4 and 7 would be ranked among the top because they were among those who gave the highest possible rating to job satisfaction. Subject 12 would be at the bottom of the ranking because he or she gave a rating of 2 (the lowest of all subjects) to job satisfaction. The three groups would then be compared in relation to the extent to which they contained subjects with similar ranks.

Procedure

(1) Click on **Statistics**.

(2) Click on **Nonparametric Tests**.

(3) Click on **K Independent Samples**.

(4) Click on **satisfy**, the ordinal variable.

(5) Click on the triangle figure by the **Test Variable List** box.

(6) Click on **group**, the nominal variable.

(7) Click on the triangle figure by the **Grouping Variable** box.

(8) Click on **Define Range**.

(9) Click on **Minimum** and enter 1, the minimum value for this variable.

(10) Click on **Maximum** and enter 3, the maximum value for this variable.

(11) Click on **Continue**.

(12) Click on **OK**.

To Print Your Output	*To Clear the Output Window*
(1) **File**	(1) **Edit**
(2) **Print**	(2) **Select**
(3) **OK**	(3) **All**
	(4) **Edit**
	(5) **Clear**

Reading the Kruskal-Wallis Printout

The printout for the data in Exhibit 16.10 will, in part, appear as shown in Exhibit 16.11. These results indicate that social workers had the highest level of satisfaction and rehabilitation counselors had the lowest. The difference was close to being statistically significant, according to the normal standard (.05). The p value was .088 when corrections were made for ties, the figure that you should normally employ.

McNear Test for the Significance of Changes

The McNear test for the significance of changes is employed to analyze a relationship between two nominal variables that are dichotomous and drawn from related samples. A common example would be a Before and After study of persons who are dichotomized into high and low on the dependent variable. The question being addressed in such examples would be whether the proportion of persons who went from low to high during the pre-treatment and post-treatment periods is significantly greater than the proportion of persons who did the opposite—i.e., who went from high to low at these two points in time. The McNear test examines this question statistically and computes a chi square value for such data. From the chi square value, a p value can be determined as with other uses of the chi square statistic.

EXHIBIT 16.11   Sample Kruskal-Wallis Printout

Mean Rank	*Cases*		
13.71	7	GROUP = 1	Social Worker
11.88	8	GROUP = 2	Psychologists
6.67	6	GROUP = 3	Rehab. Counselors

			Corrected for ties		
Chi-Square	*D.F.*	*Significance*	*Chi Square*	*D.F.*	*Significance*
4.4250	2	.1094	4.8433	2	.0888

Example

Suppose you are treating persons with varying levels of depression and you are concerned with a particular threshold of depression at which time people are known to experience serious difficulty with the activities of daily living. The persons being treated are dichotomized into the categories of *high* if they are on or above this threshold or *low* if they are below it. You will give them a particular form of treatment and test their threshold level at a time before treatment and again after treatment. You have classified each person as 1 for low or 2 for high on two variables. Their level of depression before treatment will be entered as the variable **before,** while their level of depression after treatment will be labeled **after** in the data file. Exhibit 16.12 shows the data for these 40 hypothetical clients.

EXHIBIT 16.12   Sample Data for Hypothetical Study

client #	before	after	client #	before	after
1	1	2	21	2	2
2	1	2	22	2	2
3	1	2	23	2	2
4	1	1	24	2	1
5	1	2	25	2	1
6	1	1	26	2	1
7	1	1	27	2	1
8	1	1	28	2	1
9	1	1	29	2	1
10	1	1	30	2	1
11	1	1	31	2	1
12	1	1	32	2	1
13	1	1	33	2	1
14	1	1	34	2	1
15	1	1	35	2	1
16	1	1	36	2	1
17	2	2	37	2	1
18	2	2	38	2	1
19	2	2	39	2	1
20	2	2	40	2	1

Procedure

(1) Click on **Statistics**.

(2) Click on **Nonparametric Tests**.

    (3) Click on **2 Related Samples**.

      (4) Click on **before**, our first variable.

      (5) Click on **after**, our second variable.

      (6) Click on the triangle figure.

      (7) Click on **McNear**.

      (8) Click on **OK**.

To Print Your Output	*To Clear the Output Window*
(1) **File**	(1) **Edit**
(2) **Print**	(2) **Select**
(3) **OK**	(3) **All**
	(4) **Edit**
	(5) **Clear**

Reading the McNear Test Printout

The printout from the above example will appear, in part, as shown in Exhibit 16.13. From this table, you can see there were 17 persons who were at or above the depression threshold before treatment but below this threshold after treatment. The number who went from low to high was 5, a figure that is lower, as expected. The question is whether 5 and 17 are significantly different. The value of .0169 next to **2-Tailed P** gives us this information. This is the value of p in our case (i.e., p = .0169).

EXHIBIT 16.13   Sample McNear Test Printout

—McNear Test

		BEFORE			
		2.00	1.00	Cases 40	
AFTER	1.00	17	11		
	2.00	7	5	(Binomial)	
				2-Tailed P	.0169

Mann-Whitney U Test

The Mann-Whitney U test determines if there is a significant relationship between a dichotomous nominal variable and an ordinal variable, in situations where the data are drawn from independent samples. In other words, it will tell us whether two groups differ on their response to an ordinal variable. For example, it could be used to determine if adolescents and adults differed in their level of agreement (on a five-point ordinal scale) with the statement "Things are better today than in the past."

The Mann-Whitney U test calculates a value for U from which a p value can be derived. It calculates the U value by arranging all subjects in rank order according to their scores on the ordinal variable, and then examining the sequence with which these scores represent persons drawn from Group A and from Group B. Let's suppose, for example, that these sequences would be represented by a configuration such as that shown in Exhibit 16.14.

EXHIBIT 16.14   Sample Data for One Example

Subject No.	7	4	9	3	16	1	5	13	2	6	14
Ranked Score	2	3	4	7	8	9	10	12	13	14	15
Group	A	B	A	B	B	A	B	A	A	B	A

In this array of data, we can see that the two groups are represented in approximately the same sequence, with A followed by B, followed by A which is followed by B again, and so forth. There are only a few occasions in which the sequence deviates from this pattern. In this case, we cannot declare that the difference between the two groups is statistically significant, because such small deviations from this pattern can be explained by chance rather easily.

A more significant difference between groups would be represented by data such as that shown in Exhibit 16.15, in which a treated group (T) is compared to a comparison group (C) in regard to the level of life satisfaction on a 10-point ordinal scale.

EXHIBIT 16.15   Sample Data for Another Example

Subject No.	3	2	6	1	4	8	7	5
Ranked Score	2	3	4	5	6	8	9	10
Group	C	C	C	T	C	T	T	T

In the data in Exhibit 16.15, the three lowest persons on life satisfaction were in the comparison group that received no treatment, while the three persons highest on life satisfaction were in the treated group. Only one person in the comparison group was higher on life satisfaction than a person in the treated group.

Example for Analysis

Examine the following hypothetical data regarding treatment and life satisfaction. A group of 12 treated clients is compared to a group of 10 persons in a comparison group who did not receive the treatment. Each of these 22 study subjects is coded 1 for treatment group or 2 for comparison group for the variable **group.** Each person's score for life satisfaction is presented in the column for the variable labeled **score.**

EXHIBIT 16.16   Sample Data for Mann-Whitney Example

Sub. #	Group	Score
1	1	7
2	1	6
3	1	8
4	1	8
5	1	5
6	1	6
7	1	4
8	1	7
9	1	9
10	1	8
11	1	6
12	1	5
13	2	3
14	2	5
15	2	8
16	2	2
17	2	6
18	2	3
19	2	1
20	2	4
21	2	3
22	2	5

Procedure

(1) Click on **Statistics**.

(2) Click on **Nonparametric Tests**.

(3) Click on **2 Independent Samples**.

(4) Click on **score**, the ordinal variable in our example

(5) Click on the triangle next to **Test Variable List** box.

(6) Click on **group**, the nominal variable.

(7) Click on the triangle next to **Grouping Variable** box.

(8) Click on **Define Groups**.

(9) Click on **Group 1** box and enter 1, the coded value for one group (the treatment group was coded as 1).

(10) Click on **Group 2** box and enter 2, the coded value for the other group (the comparison group was coded as 2).

(11) Click on **Continue**.

(12) Click on **OK**.

To Print Your Output   *To Clear the Output Window*

(1) **File**   (1) **Edit**

    (2) **Print**   (2) **Select**

        (3) **OK**   (3) **All**

    (4) **Edit**

    (5) **Clear**

Reading the Mann-Whitney U Test Printout

The printout for our data, in part, will appear as shown in Exhibit 16.17. From this printout, you can see that the treatment group had the highest mean rank. The p value is given beneath the column **Corrected for ties.** In our case, p = .0057.

EXHIBIT 16.17   Sample Mann-Whitney U Test Printout

Mean Rank			*Cases*	
14.96			12	GROUP = 1.00 Treatment
7.35			10	GROUP = 2.00 Comparison
			—	
			22 Total	

		Exact		*Corrected for ties*	
U	W	2-Tailed P		Z	2-Tailed P
18.5	73.5	.0044		−2.7647	.0057

Multiple Regression Analysis

Multiple regression analysis is a method for determining the relationship between a dependent variable measured at the interval level and two or more independent variables measured at the interval level, in situations where the data are drawn from independent samples. With this statistical measure, you can determine if there is a relationship between a given independent variable and the dependent variable when the other independent variables are taken into consideration.

For example, it could tell you whether age is a predictor of salary (i.e., related to salary) when years of experience is controlled. Perhaps the relationship of years of experience and both salary and age are such that age is not a significant determinant of one's salary when years of experience is taken into consideration. In other words, older people make higher salaries only because they have more years of experience, not because age itself is a major determinant of salary.

Another benefit of multiple regression analysis is in determining the extent to which a set of independent variables fully explains the dependent variable. For example, suppose you want to examine the relationship between students' grades in junior high school and the number of special classes they attended on study technique. Some students attended no special classes, some attended one, others, two, three, and so forth, with some attending as many as twelve special classes. You may find, through a bivariate analysis of the relationship between classes attended and grades (measured according to numerical value such as 88, 73, 94, etc.), that there is a statistically significant relationship between these two variables. You may find, for example, that a Pearson correlation between these two variables is 0.35 and that this correlation for the given sample size is statistically significant ($p < 0.05$). But a correlation of 0.35 means that one variable explains only about 12 percent of the variance in the other variable, because when you obtain the square of the Pearson correlation coefficient, you find how much of one variable is explained by the other (the square of 0.35 is 0.1225). Thus, you find that attendance in these special classes does have a potential influence upon grades, but you also learn that there is a lot left unexplained about what influences grades. If your primary research question focuses on the latter, you will need to examine other variables.

A third benefit of multiple regression analysis is the determination of the amount of change in the dependent variable than is explained by a given independent variable when other variables are taken into consideration. For example, you could learn how much more salary a person makes with one additional year of experience when other variables are taken into consideration. Does the subject with one additional year of experience tend to make $600 more per year than the person with one year less of experience—or is the difference $1,000 per year, or something else?

The Problem of Multicollinearity

Multicollinearity refers to the situation in which some or all of the independent variables are very highly intercorrelated. Very high correlations between independent variables would be represented by correlation coefficients such as 0.80 or above. Multiple regression analysis is not appropriate in such cases. If age and years of experience, for example, had such a high correlation, you could not use both of these variables as independent variables in the analysis of the determinants of salary. A simple way to examine this issue is to compute the correlations among all independent variables and see if any are highly correlated. If so, you will need to eliminate one of any pairs with such high correlations.

The Special Case of the Dichotomous Variable

A dichotomous nominal variable can be employed as an independent variable in a multiple regression analysis, but it is not the ideal type of variable for which multiple regression analysis is designed. The reason that a dichotomous variable can be employed this way is that a dichotomous variable has only one interval between categories; thus, the issue of equality between intervals in the values of the variable is moot. In this situation, one of the categories of the variable should be assigned the value of 0 and the other, the value of 1. You will need to remember which category was arbitrarily assigned the higher value when you examine the output of the regression analysis so you will know how to interpret a negative sign for the parameter estimate given for the variable.

Example

Suppose we wish to know whether a social worker's score for thinking (over feeling) on the Kiersey Bates Temperament Sorter is related to gender or years of experience. We could, of course, examine the relationship between gender and thinking score and we could then examine the relationship between years of experience and thinking score. But suppose we want to know if gender predicts one's thinking score when years of experience is taken into consideration. Perhaps years of experience acts as an intervening variable and distorts the relationship between gender and thinking score. We can use the NASW study for this analysis. You will recall that each of these study subjects had recorded their gender, their years of experience, and their score for thinking. These variables were named **gender, years,** and **thinking,** respectively.

Procedure

    (1) Click on **Statistics** from the initial menu.

        (2) Click on **Regression**.

            (3) Click on **Linear**.

                (4) Click on **thinking**, the dependent variable.

                (5) Click on the triangle next to **Dependent** box.

                (6) Click on **years**, one of our independent variables.

                (7) Click on the triangle next to **Independent**.

                (8) Click on **gender**, another of our independent variables.

                (9) Click on the triangle next to **Independent**.

              (10) Click on **OK**.

To Print Your Output	*To Clear the Output Window*
(1) **File**	(1) **Edit**
(2) **Print**	(2) **Select**
(3) **OK**	(3) **All**
	(4) **Edit**
	(5) **Clear**

Reading the Multiple Regression Printout

In part, the printout for our data would appear as shown in Exhibit 16.18. In the examination of the output of a computer-assisted multiple regression analysis, there are several

---

EXHIBIT 16.18   Sample Multiple Regression Test Printout

Multiple R   .26612
R Square   .07082
Adjusted R Square   .04730

Variables in the Equation

Variable	B	SE B	Beta	T	Sig T
GENDER	.506	.695	.079	.728	.4689
YEARS	.08	.035	.244	2.244	.027
(Constant)	5.23	.61		8.48	.0000

---

items to notice. The first is the column providing the p value. This tells you whether the given independent variable was a significant predictor of the dependent variable when the other variables were statistically controlled.

The second item to notice is the **R square** value, which tells you how much of the variance in the dependent variable was explained by all the independent variables in the analysis. This is usually presented as R^2 and can vary from a value of 0 to a maximum of 1.0. An R^2 of 0 means that none of the variance in the dependent variable is explained by all the independent variables taken as a group. An R^2 of 0.50 means that 50 percent of the variance in the dependent variable is explained by all the independent variables, while an R^2 of 1.0 means that 100 percent of the variance in the dependent variable is explained. In examining this output, you should focus on the adjusted R^2 rather than the original R^2, because the adjusted R^2 adjusts for the number of variables in the analysis and presents a more accurate picture.

The third piece of data to notice is the parameter estimate, sometimes referred to by the lower case letter b. The value of b tells you how many units of change in the dependent variable are explained by one unit of change in the given independent variable, when the influence of the other independent variables is taken into consideration.

In our case, we wish to focus primarily on the R^2 value and the p value associated with each of two variables. First, in our case, the adjusted R^2 is only .04, meaning that only 4 percent of the variance in thinking scores was explained by both gender and years of experience. Thus, if we want to be able to fully understand what influences thinking score, we are apparently barking up the wrong tree. Our second focus is on the statistical significance of each independent variable as a predictor of the dependent variable. We obtain that information in the column labeled **Sig T**. This is where we find the p value. In our case, gender is not significant (p = .46) but years of experience is significant (p = .027). Now the question is whether it is the younger or the older persons who have the higher thinking score. If we examine the column labeled **B** we will see coefficients that are all positive. If the direction of the relationship between thinking and years had been negative, there would have been a negative sign next to the value of the B coefficient. In our case, that is not so. Thus, we can conclude that older persons have higher thinking scores than younger persons, and that this holds true even when gender is taken into consideration.

Pearson Correlation Coefficient

The Pearson correlation coefficient is useful for examining the relationship between two variables measured at the interval level, in situations where the data are drawn from independent samples. Sometimes referred to simply as the *correlation coefficient* or the Pearson r (always designated in the lower case), this measure will tell you the strength of the relationship between two interval variables as well as the direction of the relationship (i.e., negative or positive).

The product of this analysis will yield a value for r that can range from negative 1.0 to positive 1.0. A coefficient of 1.0 represents a perfect relationship between the two variables, while a coefficient of 0 represents no relationship at all. An r of 0.20 would represent a weak positive relationship between two variables, while a value of minus 0.20 would represent a weak negative relationship. A moderate positive relationship would be represented by r values that ranged from about 0.30 to about 0.50, although it should be noted that there is no hard and fast rule about what constitutes a "weak" relationship or a "moderate" relationship. Most people, however, would probably not argue with the designation of "strong" relationship for an r value of 0.70 or higher.

The r value can be employed in determining the value of p, or the probability that the observed relationship between the variables could be explained by chance. The value of p will be a function of two things—the size of r and the size of the sample. The higher the value of r, the greater the level of statistical significance. Also, the larger the sample, the greater the level of statistical significance. For example, a weak r of 0.18 would be statistically significant at the 0.05 level if the sample size were 120 or greater, but would not be significant with a sample less than 120. On the other hand, a strong r of 0.70 would not be significant if the sample size were smaller than 8, but would be significant at the 0.01 level if the sample size were 12 or greater.

The correlation coefficient can also be employed in determining the extent to which one variable explains the other, and conversely, just how much of the variable is left unexplained. This is determined by squaring the value of r, usually designated as r^2. A correlation of 0.50, for example, would have an r^2 value of 0.25, meaning that 25 percent of the variance in one of these variables is explained by the other variable. For practical purposes, you will be using an independent variable to predict the dependent variable. If 25 percent of the variance in the dependent variable is explained by the independent variable, this means that 75 percent of the variance is left unexplained. This is usually not an issue unless you are primarily interested in fully explaining the dependent variable rather than in determining if there is a relationship between the two variables.

Example

Suppose we wish to examine the relationship from our NASW study between thinking score and years of experience. Suppose we also wish to examine the relationship between thinking score and age. These three variables are given the labels of **age, thinking,** and **years** in our data file. We can instruct the computer to examine these two relationships in one set of instructions. Several variables can be examined at the same time, even though you are only interested in relationships between two of these variables per research question. In the instructions which follow, we will ask the computer to compute the Pearson correlation coefficients among three variables, which means that we will obtain a printout with the correlation

between thinking and years and between thinking and age; we will even see a correlation between age and years, even though we are not especially interested in that relationship.

Procedure

(1) Click on **Statistics**.

(2) Click on **Correlate**.

(3) Click on **Bivariate**.

(4) Click on **thinking**, one of our variables in our example.

(5) Click on the triangle next to **Variable**.

(6) Click on **age**, another of our variables.

(7) Repeat #5.

(8) Click on **years**, the third variable in our analysis.

(9) Repeat #5.

(10) Click on **OK**.

To Print Your Output	*To Clear the Output Window*
(1) **File**	(1) **Edit**
(2) **Print**	(2) **Select**
(3) **OK**	(3) **All**
	(4) **Edit**
	(5) **Clear**

Reading the Pearson Correlation Coefficient Printout

In part, the printout for our data will be as shown in Exhibit 16.19. In each set of figures,
the correlation coefficient is given first, followed by the number of persons in the analysis

---

EXHIBIT 16.19   Sample Pearson Correlation Coefficient Printout

	AGE	THINKING	YEARS
AGE	1.000	.1689	.7431
	(98)	(81)	(98)
	P = .	P = .132	P = .000
THINKING	.1689	1.000	.2541
	(81)	(82)	(82)
	p = .132	p = .	p = .021
YEARS	.7431	.2541	1.000
	(98)	(82)	(100)
	p = .000	p = .021	p = .

(given in parenthesis) and the p value. The first set of figures in the top left is the correlation of age with itself, which, of course, is meaningless. The second is the correlation of age with thinking. In this set of figures, you see a correlation coefficient of .1689. There were 81 persons in this analysis (those with missing data for either variable were dropped). The p value associated with the correlation coefficient for age and thinking is .132.

Phi Coefficient

Phi coefficient is a means for examining the relationship between two dichotomous variables in situations where the data are drawn from independent samples. The value of the coefficient can range from 0 to 1.0, the latter representing a perfect relationship between the two variables, and the coefficient of 0 representing no relationship between the variables. You can derive a phi value that is negative, but the negative sign is meaningless because you cannot have a positive or negative relationship between nominal variables. The negative sign is purely a function of how the data were arbitrarily placed in the cells of the table.

The interpretation of the value of the phi coefficient is somewhat similar to that of any coefficient of correlation, although you cannot make precise comparisons between such coefficients. A phi coefficient of 0.70 would indicate a strong relationship between the two variables, while a value of 0.30 or 0.40 might be best characterized as a moderate relationship. Phi coefficients below 0.30 would generally be characterized as weak relationships.

Like the Pearson correlation coefficient r, the phi coefficient can be used to determine the percent of the variance in one variable that is explained by the other variable. The procedure is the same for both—you square the value of the phi coefficient to obtain this information. Thus, a phi coefficient of 0.40 between gender and salary (as measure by the categories of High and Low) would mean that gender predicted 16 percent of the variance in salary ($0.40 \times 0.40 = 0.16$).

To determine if the phi coefficient is statistically significant, you must calculate chi square from the same data. Thus, chi square will tell you whether the relationship is significant and phi coefficient will tell you the strength of the relationship.

Phi coefficient can be easily calculated if you have the chi square value for a set of data. First, divide chi square by the number in the sample. Next, take the square root of that value. This is your value for phi coefficient.

For information on how to use SPSS for Windows for computing the value of phi coefficient, refer to the description of chi square for independent samples. You will need to compute the value of chi square in order to determine if your phi coefficient is statistically significant.

The Spearman Rank Correlation Coefficient

The Spearman rank correlation coefficient is appropriate for examining the relationship between two variables measured at the ordinal level, in situations in which the data are drawn from independent samples. The coefficient derived from this analysis can range from negative 1.0, representing a perfect negative correlation, to positive 1.0, representing a perfect positive relationship. Interpretation of the size of this coefficient is similar to that of other coefficients of correlation, although precise comparisons of the size of one coefficient to another are not appropriate.

The rank correlation coefficient is usually represented by the letters "rho" and sometimes by the letters "r_s" with the s in a subscript position; thus, the first designation is more convenient. The value of this correlation can be employed in determining the value of p. Thus, the value of rho will tell you the strength of the relationship, while the value of p will tell you whether this relationship is statistically significant.

Example

Suppose we wish to know if there is a positive correlation between the performance rating a social worker would have given himself or herself and the rating the person's organizational superior would award. We can use the data from the NASW study for our analysis. All study subjects were asked to give work performance ratings for themselves on a seven-point ordinal scale. They were also asked to indicate the rating their superior gave them at their last evaluation conference. The question is whether these two ratings are correlated. We would expect to find a high correlation between them.

Procedure

    (1) Click on **Statistics**.

        (2) Click on **Correlate**.

            (3) Click on **Bivariate**.

                (4) Click on **self**, one of our study variables.

                (5) Click on the triangle next to **Variables**.

                (6) Click on **superior**, our second study variable.

                (7) Repeat step 5.

                (8) Click on **Spearman**. This will select the Spearman correlation.

                (9) Click on **Pearson**. This will remove the Pearson correlation, which you do not need.

            (10) Click on **OK**.

To Print Your Output	*To Clear the Output Window*
(1) **File**	(1) **Edit**
(2) **Print**	(2) **Select**
(3) **OK**	(3) **All**
	(4) **Edit**
	(5) **Clear**

Reading the Spearman Printout

The printout for this analysis is rather similar to that for the Pearson correlation. For our example, the results will appear as shown in Exhibit 16.20. The first figure given is the corre-

---

EXHIBIT 16.20 **Sample Spearman Test Printout**

SUPERIOR .5798

N (86)

Sig .000

SELF

---

lation coefficient (.5798) between the variables of **superior** and **self.** The second figure is the number of persons in the analysis (N = 86). The final figure is the p value. In this case, p is designated as .000, and would be reported as "p < .001" rather than "p = .000."

t Test for Paired Data (Related Samples)

The t test for paired data is appropriate as a measure of the relationship between two variables measured at the interval level in situations where the data are drawn from related samples. It is often used in Before and After studies in which clients are given a measure of the dependent variable before treatment and again after treatment and the difference between their scores is examined to determine if the gain is statistically significant. The value of t can be employed in determining the value of p.

The t test for paired data is computed by subtracting the After score from the Before score to derive a *gain* score. The mean gain score is examined to determine if it is significantly different from 0, the value you would expect to find if treatment had no effect at all. It can be used with any type of paired data, not just the Before and After study.

Example with Matched Pairs of Study Subjects

This first example will involve matched pairs of study subjects rather than the before and after study (the one-group pretest-posttest research design), which will be illustrated in the second example. In our first example, suppose you want to examine whether two treatments for depression are significantly different in their effects. You have decided that whether or not a client has been previously hospitalized with depression is a major indicator of the severity of their problem and you want to control for this variable in your comparison of the two treatment models. Thus, you will select eight pairs of clients, with each pair being similar in terms of whether or not they had previously been hospitalized. The first column of Exhibit 16.21 shows the identification number for each of the eight pairs of clients. The second column indicates whether the pair consists of clients who were or were not previously hospitalized for depression. The third column contains the gain in functioning for the first person in the pair over a 3-month treatment period, as evidenced by a reduction in the client's depression level. Thus, a positive score in this column indicates progress with the problem of depression, reflected in the drop of points on the depression scale compared with the beginning of treatment. The fourth column contains the same information for the

EXHIBIT 16.21   Sample Data for Example Study

Pair #	Prior Hospitalization	First Person (Model A)	Second Person (Model B)	Difference (A–B)
1	yes	6	2	4
2	yes	8	4	4
3	yes	2	5	–3
4	yes	11	3	8
5	no	4	4	0
6	no	5	3	2
7	no	5	5	0
8	no	8	4	4

second person in the pair. The last column contains the difference in gain scores between the first person and the second person. In each pair, the first person received Treatment Model A and the second person received Treatment Model B.

These data reveal that in six of the eight pairs, the person with Treatment Model A received greater gain than the person with Model B. In one pair, the reverse was true, and one pair had similar gain scores. The question that emerges is whether these differences that favor Model A are statistically significant. The t test for paired data will tell you whether the mean for these gain scores was significantly greater than 0, the score that we would expect if the two treatments were identical in their effect.

The example of a Before and After study could be structured similarly. In that case, the pretest score for each client would be entered in one column and the posttest score for the same client would be entered in another column. The difference in scores from pretest to posttest would be entered in a third column, and a mean would be computed for these difference scores. The t test results would help us determine if the mean gain was significantly greater than 0.

Example Using the One-Group Pretest-Posttest Design

A common method of evaluating program effectiveness is to obtain scores from a group of clients before and after the introduction of an intervention designed to improve the behavior measured. The behavior could be depression, self-esteem, delinquency, marital conflict, absenteeism on the job, and so forth. The idea is to measure the rate of this behavior before intervention (pretest) for all persons given the particular treatment, then measure the same behavior using the same instrument after the treatment (posttest) to see if the mean score for the group after treatment is significantly better than the mean score for the group before the treatment.

A method of examining this data statistically is the one-sample t test. Each client's behavior is measured before intervention and after intervention. The pretest score is subtracted from the posttest score to derive a **gain** score for each subject. The statistical method involves computing a t score that indicates whether the mean **gain** score is significantly different from 0, which is the score expected if there is absolutely no relationship between intervention and gain in the target behavior. A method for calculating the t value using worksheets and a calculator is presented elsewhere in this text. This is one of the few tests for which this calculation is feasible without the computer. However, the computer will execute this procedure with much less trouble. Thus, if you have a computer with the proper software, you will be well advised to use it.

Exhibit 16.22 gives a set of data from a hypothetical study. In this study, the clients are given a self-esteem scale before and after treatment. The research question is whether the mean gain in self-esteem scores for these ten clients is significantly greater than a score of 0, the score that we would expect to find if the treatment had no effect whatsoever. The score for self-esteem before treatment is labeled before and the score for self-esteem after treatment is labeled after.

EXHIBIT 16.22   Sample Data for Example Problem

#	*before*	*after*
1	13	16
2	21	27
3	19	18
4	14	21
5	17	22
6	12	19
7	16	25
8	17	17
9	11	14
10	15	22

Procedure

    (1) Click on **Statistics**.

        (2) Click on **Compare Means**.

            (3) Click on **Paired-Samples T Test**.

                (4) Click on **before**, our first variable.

                (5) Click on **after**, our second variable.

                (6) Click on triangle figure.

                (7) Click on **OK**.

To Print Your Output

   (1) **File**

      (2) **Print**

         (3) **OK**

To Clear the Output Window

   (1) **Edit**

      (2) **Select**

         (3) **All**

   (4) **Edit**

      (5) **Clear**

Reading the Printout for the t Test for Paired Data

For the above data, the printout will appear as shown in Exhibit 16.23. You should direct your attention to two items:

1. The mean score for before was 15.5, while the mean score for after was 20.1, meaning that the average score after treatment was higher than the average score before treatment. The amount of this difference is a basis for determining practical significance. Is this degree of difference enough to declare the treatment successful?

    This information is displayed in the column labeled **Mean** at the top of the printout. The mean for after is given first, followed below by the mean for before.

2. The t value was 4.44 and the p value associated with this t value is .002. This could be reported as "p = .002" or as "p < .01".

    This information is displayed at the bottom of the printout under the column headed **2-Tail Sig.** This is in the lower section of the printout. Do not use the figure for **2-tail Sig** given at the top of the printout next to the **Corr** column.

    As with other printouts, there are several items that you can ignore. The items of information identified here are the critical ones you will need to use.

t Test for Independent Samples (Two Groups)

The t test for independent samples is used to examine the relationship between a dichotomous nominal variable and an interval variable in situations where the data are drawn from independent samples. In other words, it will tell whether the means of two groups are sig-

---

EXHIBIT 16.23 Sample Printout for t Test for Paired Data

Variable	Number of pairs	Corr	2-tail Sig	Mean	SD	SE of Mean
AFTER				20.10	4.06	1.286
	10	.614	.059			
BEFORE				15.50	3.13	

Mean	SD	SE of Mean	t-value	df	2-tail Sig
4.60	3.27	1.03	4.44	9	.002

nificantly different. From the value of t, you can determine the value of p from a statistical table or from the printout from the computer.

Example

Let's examine a research question from our NASW study. We have information on this group of social workers for both gender, and preference for thinking over feeling according to the Kiersey Bates Temperament Sorter. These two variables are labeled **gender** and **thinking** in our data file. The literature on personality type had revealed that males in the general population have a slightly greater tendency than females to favor thinking over feeling in their judgment of information. Approximately 60 percent of males have been found to favor thinking over feeling, as compared to approximately 40 percent of females. Thus, about 60 percent of females favor feeling over thinking, compared to about 40 percent of males. Our research question is whether in our study the mean score for thinking is greater for males than for females.

Procedure

   (1) Click on **Statistics**.

   (2) Click on **Compare Means**.

   (3) Click on **Independent-Samples T Test**.

   (4) Click on **Thinking,** our interval variable.

   (5) Click on the triangle figure next to **Test Variable**.

   (6) Click on **gender,** our nominal variable.

   (7) Click on the triangle next to **Grouping Variable**.

   (8) Click on **Define Groups**.

   (9) Click on **Group 1** box and enter the number 0, the code for those in one group for the variable of gender (females).

   (10) Click on **Group 2** box and enter the number 1, the code for males.

   (11) Click on **Continue**.

   (12) Click on **OK**.

To Print Your Output	*To Clear the Output Window*
(1) **File**	(1) **Edit**
(2) **Print**	(2) **Select**
(3) **OK**	(3) **All**
	(4) **Edit**
	(5) **Clear**

Reading the Printout for the t Test for Independent Samples

The printout for the NASW study will appear as shown in Exhibit 16.24. The first column indicates that the interval variable is **thinking** and that the nominal variable has the labels of "fema" (only the first four letters are allowed for this printout) and "male." The second column tells us that there were 54 females and 28 males in our analysis. The mean score of 6.27 for females, and 6.96 for males is given in the next column. This tells us that the mean score for thinking for males in our sample was higher than that for females, as expected.

EXHIBIT 16.24   Printout of t Test for Independent Samples

Variable	Number of Cases	Mean	SD	SE of Mean
THINKING				
fema	54	6.27	2.86	.39
male	28	6.96	3.36	.63

Mean difference = −.6865

Levene's Test for Equality of Variances: F = .658 p = .420

t-test for Equality of Means   95%

Variances	t-value	df	2-Tail Sig	SE of Diff	CI for Diff
Equal	−.97	80	.335	.708	(−2.096, .723)
Unequal	−.92	47.7	.362	.745	(−2.185, .812)

The next question is whether this difference in mean scores for males and females is statistically significant. The p value is given in the column labeled **2-Tail Sig** in the lower half of the printout. However, you will see that there are two p values in this column, one for equal variances (first line) and another for unequal variances (second line). To determine which line to use, you should examine the p value associated with Levene's Test, which is given in the middle of the printout. If the p for Levene's Test is higher than .05, use the equal variances p value; if it is less than .05, use the unequal variances p value. In our case, the p value was given as .42 which is clearly above .05; we should use the line that is labeled "equal variances." Thus, our p value for this study is .335.

Wilcoxon Matched Pairs Signed Ranks Test

The Wilcoxon matched-pairs signed-ranks test is a means for examining the relationship between a dichotomous nominal variable and an ordinal variable in situations where the data are drawn from related samples. It could be used in a Before and After study (One

Group Pretest-Posttest Design) in which the data on the client's behavior (dependent variable) is measured at the ordinal level. The results of the Wilcoxon test will yield a value either for T (not to be confused with lower case t in the t test) for small samples, or a value of z, for larger samples. These values can be employed in determining the value of p (the extent to which the differences between the two pairs of data could be explained by chance).

Example

Suppose you wanted to test the effectiveness of a program of shared housing for the elderly in which dependent elderly persons without an adequate housing arrangement were matched with independent elderly persons with adequate housing arrangements who needed companionship. Services are offered to such couples at the beginning of the shared housing arrangement so typical adjustment problems could be overcome and the arrangement could meet with success. You will measure the effectiveness of this program by giving the participants a life satisfaction scale which asks people to indicate the level of their general life satisfaction on an eight-point ordinal scale. Exhibit 16.25 has data for this hypothetical study.

EXHIBIT 16.25   Sample Data for Hypothetical Study

Client #	Life Satisfaction Score	
	Before Treatment	*After Treatment*
1	3	6
2	5	5
3	4	7
4	3	8
5	4	5
6	2	6
7	3	6
8	4	3
9	5	6

The Wilcoxon test would examine the ranks of the differences in scores from the pretest and posttest periods to determine if the differences can be explained by chance.

Suppose we have named one variable **before** (the before-treatment score) and the other variable **after** (the after-treatment score).

Procedure

    (1) Click on **Statistics**.

        (2) Click on **Nonparametric Tests**.

(3) Click on **Two Related Samples**.

(4) Click on **before**, our first variable.

(5) Click on **after**, our second variable.

(6) Click on the triangle figure.

(7) Click on **OK**.

To Print Your Output	*To Clear the Output Window*
(1) **File**	(1) **Edit**
(2) **Print**	(2) **Select**
(3) **OK**	(3) **All**
	(4) **Edit**
	(5) **Clear**

Reading the Wilcoxon Printout

The printout from this example would appear as shown in Exhibit 16.26. The first line of information tells us there were 7 subjects for whom the **before** score was less than the **after** score, the direction that was expected in our data. There was one person who had an **after** score that was less than the **before** score, and one person whose scores were the same both times (i.e., both variables equal). The designation LT means "less than," GT means "greater than," and EQ means "equal to."

EXHIBIT 16.26   Sample Wilcoxon Test Printout

Mean Rank	*Cases*	
4.86	7	—Ranks (BEFORE LT AFTER)
2.00	1	—Ranks (BEFORE GT AFTER)
	1	—Ties (BEFORE EQ AFTER)
	9	Total
Z = −2.2404	2-Tailed	P = .0251

Statistical significance is presented as the value for **2-Tailed P.** In our case, p = .0251.

ASSIGNMENT 16-B

1. Use the data from the NASW study to test the following hypothesis.

   Males will provide higher self-ratings of work performance than will females.

2. Use the data from the NASW study to analyze the following questions.

   a. Is there is a relationship between field of practice and preference for thinking over feeling as measured by the Kiersey Bates Temperament Sorter?

   b. Is there is a relationship between state of the respondent and preference for thinking over feeling as measured by the Kiersey Bates Temperament Sorter?

   Provide a report on your test of these hypotheses.

Chapter *17*

Analyzing Data in Evaluative Research

In this chapter, you will receive step-by-step guidance on how to analyze data in evaluative research. Data analysis for both group research designs and single-subject research designs will be included. You will be given a set of decision trees for your guidance in selecting a particular approach to statistical analysis. You will also be given instructions on how to apply that approach, or where to seek guidance in doing so.

Group research designs are employed when you have a group of clients receiving a common intervention directed toward a common treatment objective. There is also a common means of measuring the dependent variable when you employ the group research design. It is not necessary, however, that each client receive the designated intervention together in a group. This type of research design, for example, could be employed for all clients of the Hampton Mental Health Center with a diagnosis of depression receiving cognitive therapy and measured on the Beck Depression Inventory before and after treatment.

With the group research design, there can be more than one practitioner who is offering the treatment as long as the treatment is the same. Whether there is one or more than one practitioner, it is important that the treatment be carefully defined and described so that one can better understand what it was that did or did not work in the improvement of the client's functioning. With this type of design, there can also be more than one treatment objective, and more than one means of measurement, provided all clients are administered each measurement device. For example, you could test the effectiveness of cognitive therapy in the reduction of depression and the improvement of self-esteem using one instrument for depression and one for self-esteem. In this situation, you would normally analyze the data separately for each dependent variable.

The single-subject research design is employed with a single client who is measured repeatedly on the same dependent variable (and measurement device) over a period of time which includes the treatment period and usually includes a baseline period before treatment began. There can be more than one dependent variable and more than one measurement tool, but only one client for each analysis. There can be more than one client who is administered a common treatment with a common means of measuring progress when the single-subject design is employed, as long as the analysis of data is done separately for each client.

Before you employ the information in this chapter you should have completed the following tasks:

1. Definition and analysis of the client's target problem.
2. Selection of one or more treatment objectives.
3. Selection of the clients for treatment.
4. Selection of one or more means for measuring client progress.
5. Selection of a research design.

Your next step is to examine the decision trees which will guide your determination of an approach to statistical analysis. The next section will guide you if you are employing one of the single-subject designs. Then you will see information on the various group designs.

Data Analysis for Single-Subject Research Designs

Before you employ the instructions in this chapter, you should have administered an intervention for a specific client and you should have collected data on the client's target behavior repeatedly. You should have placed these repeated measures of client condition on a chart for visual inspection and data analysis.

There are several research designs for single-subject data. The decision trees which follow this section make reference to the B design, the modified AB design, and the AB design.

B Design

The B design is one in which the client's behavior is charted during intervention but no baseline recordings (pretreatment) of the client's behavior are available. In this situation, the only option presented in this chapter is to examine the extent to which the line depicting the client's behavior during the treatment period constitutes a slope, in the favorable direction, that is significantly different from a straight line (which would represent no progress at all).

Modified AB Design

The modified AB design is the label given to the situation in which you have a few pretreatment recordings but not enough recordings to constitute a trend. One might argue that even two or three recordings can represent a trend, but I argue that you need a minimum of four baseline recordings in order to declare that you have trend data and can employ the procedures of the AB single-subject design. In situations in which you have fewer than four baseline recordings, you are instructed to use your few pretreatment recordings to draw a straight line throughout the treatment period and to employ the binomial test in determining whether the number of treatment recordings that are on the favorable side of the trend line are significantly greater than the number that are not.

AB Design

With the AB design, you have a minimum of four baseline recordings. You use these recordings to draw a trend line throughout the treatment period on your chart. If the trend line is slanted, you use the binomial test to determine if the number of treatment recordings on the favorable side of the trend line is greater than the number that are not. If the trend line is relatively level, you employ the standard deviation approach, in which you determine if the mean of treatment recordings is at least two standard deviations better than the mean of the baseline. The procedures employed for the AB design can be adapted for use with the BA design, the BC design, the ABA design, or the ABAB design.

BA Design

With the BA design, you have no pretreatment recordings of client behavior, but you do have repeated recordings of client behavior during the period of time that follows treatment, in addition to repeated measures of client behavior during the treatment period. In this situation, you can compare the treatment phase (phase B) with the follow-up period (phase A) in the same way that the baseline (phase A) would be compared with the treatment (phase B) when the AB design is employed. In this situation, you wish to know whether the B phase is significantly better than the A phase, just as when you employ the AB design.

ABA Design

When you employ the ABA design, you will continue to record client behavior during a follow-up period (the second A phase, or the second baseline). In this situation, you would combine the instructions for the AB design and the BA design. Your first step is to employ the procedures for the AB design in the comparison of the first A phase with the B phase. Then you would compare the B phase with the second A phase to see if the client's condition was better during the treatment phase than the follow-up phase.

ABAB Design

When you employ the ABAB design, you will be collecting repeated measures of the target behavior during a baseline period followed by a treatment period which is followed by a second baseline period and, finally, a second treatment period. You can employ the procedures for the AB design for examining the first two phases followed by a comparison of the first B and the second A (as you would with the BA design) followed by the comparison of the second A and the second B.

BC Design

With the BC design, you are comparing two treatments for the same client without any baseline data. This means that you begin treating the client and repeatedly measuring progress on the target behavior and you change the treatment. With this design, you are comparing the second treatment (C phase) with the first treatment (B phase) to see if there is any significant difference. Thus, you would employ the same procedures as you would for the AB design. However, because you have no baseline of measurements before treatment began, you have no basis for addressing maturation as a threat to internal validity.

Using Exhibits 17.1 and 17.2

Your next step is to select an approach to statistical analysis by using the decision trees offered in Exhibit 17.1 and 17.2. You should begin with Exhibit 17.1. When you have reached a terminal point you will be referred to a note which will further explain what you should do with your data.

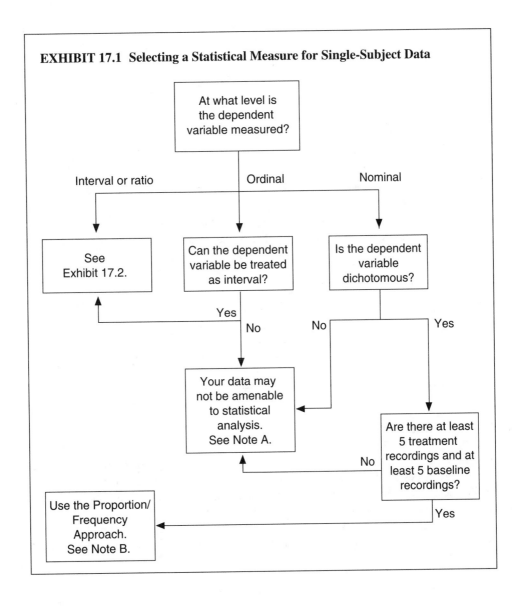

EXHIBIT 17.1 Selecting a Statistical Measure for Single-Subject Data

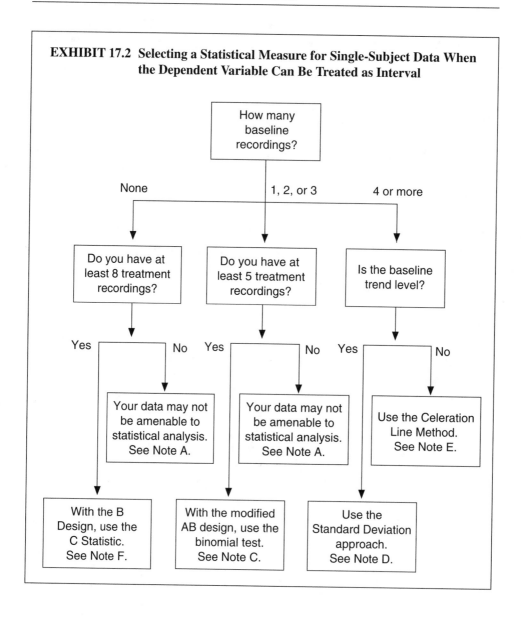

EXHIBIT 17.2 Selecting a Statistical Measure for Single-Subject Data When the Dependent Variable Can Be Treated as Interval

Notes for Data Analysis for Single-Subject Designs

The following notes refer to the two decision trees for the analysis of single-subject data. These trees are designed for use with the B and AB designs, but the same principles will apply to other designs as well. For example, if you used the BC design, you could treat the B phase as the baseline and the C phase for the treatment phase and employ the tree in this manner.

Remember that you need to exercise your professional judgment about the extent to which your recordings of the client's behavior is a reasonable depiction of the client's target behavior. If your client's scores on a depression scale do not match very well with clinical observations, you should not use these recordings in the statistical analysis of your data. If the trend in these scores during the baseline is not a trend that logically can be projected into the future, you cannot use this trend for the statistical analysis of your data. Also, remember that the issue of autocorrelation is relevant to the employment of the binomial test and the standard deviation. You can test for autocorrelation. If your data are autocorrelated, you can either (a) throw out the data, (b) ignore the issue of autocorrelation (This would not be appropriate if you wished to publish your study), or (c) employ a method of transforming your autocorrelated data to a form that can be more amenable to statistical analysis.

Note A: Data That May Not Be Amenable to Statistical Analysis

Your situation may not be amenable to statistical analysis. There are several terminal points on the decision trees which lead to this note where statistical analysis is problematic. For example, you cannot achieve statistical significance with only four treatment recordings when you apply a particular form of the binomial test (the one that assumes a 50–50 split in the baseline) even if all four treatment recordings are favorable. Another example can be found with the use of the C statistic. When you use the C statistic to calculate a Z score, you will need at least eight treatment recordings. Otherwise, your data are not amenable to statistical analysis. If it is impossible for you to achieve statistical analysis with the configuration of data at your disposal, you are advised to consider your data to be unsuitable for statistical analysis. Reporting that you had failed to achieve statistical significance in these situations would be slightly misleading, even though it would be a true statement. Instead, it is better to report that your data were not suitable to statistical analysis. An alternative would be for you to consult an expert who might be able to guide you toward a suitable form of statistical analysis for your data.

Note B: Data Analysis for the Proportion/Frequency Method

You have a dichotomous dependent variable, at least five baseline recordings, and at least five treatment recordings. When you have a dichotomous dependent variable (i.e., measured in only two categories), you should determine the proportion of favorable recordings during the baseline period and employ this figure in the application of the binomial test (See Appendix B). You should normally have at least five baseline recordings and five treatment recordings in this situation. If not, you should seek consultation because your data may not be amenable to statistical analysis. The steps in your procedures are:

1. Record the measurements of the client's behavior during both the baseline and the treatment periods on a chart.
2. Draw a line that separates the favorable side of the chart from the unfavorable side of the chart. Determine the proportion of recordings during the baseline period that are on the favorable side of the line.

   For example, suppose that the favorable side of the line is the answer "No" to the question, *Did Johnny clean his room today?* You will likely have some days with the answer "No" and some days with the answer "Yes." What is the proportion of baseline recordings that are Yes? If there is only one day out of five with the answer "Yes," the answer to this question is 20 percent. See the following example.

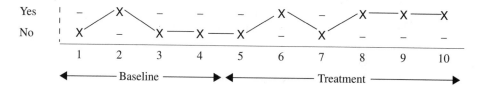

Before moving to the next step, count the total number of treatment recordings and the number of favorable treatment recordings.

3. Consult Appendix B, which presents some of the data on the binomial test. Use the data line in that table that comes closest to your proportion of favorable recordings for the baseline but which is not lower than your proportion. For example, if 20 percent of your recordings are favorable, you would go to one of the lines that depict a .25 proportion of favorable recordings in the baseline. If .15 of your baseline recordings are on the favorable side, you would also select .25 on the table because it is greater than your proportion, even though .10 is closer to your data than is .25.

4. Determine the proportion of favorable recordings during the treatment period. Check this proportion against the table of the binomial test to determine if you have achieved statistical significance.

In the example given above, the number of favorable baseline recordings is one out of five or 20 percent . The number of favorable treatment recordings is four out of five. According to Appendix B, you must have at least four out of five favorable treatment recordings in order to achieve statistical significance if your proportion of favorable baseline recordings is around 25 percent. Thus, these data have achieved statistical significance.

Note C: Data Analysis for the Modified AB Design

If you have fewer than four baseline recordings, you do not have sufficient data to establish a trend in the same manner that is done with the normal AB single subject design. You may call your design a modified AB single-subject design because it stands between the B design (with no baseline recordings at all) and the AB design (with enough baseline recordings to establish a trend). In your situation, you should use the baseline recordings to draw a trend line into the treatment period and apply the binomial test with the assumption of a 50–50 split in favorable and nonfavorable recordings in the baseline. You should determine the proper trend line by exercising your professional judgment about the scale used and the client you are serving.

If you have only one baseline recording, you can use this figure to draw your trend line, provided you are satisfied that this one score is a reasonable depiction of the client's pretreatment condition. If you have two or three treatment recordings, you might want to use the mean of these recordings, provided they tend to be reasonable representations of the client's fluctuations in functioning on the dependent variable. You should seek information supporting the assumption that your chosen score for the baseline is a reasonable depiction of the client's pretreatment condition. You *cannot* use the method for data analysis depicted below if you have reason to believe that the client's pretreatment condition was progressing before treatment. In that situation, you will need enough data to draw a trend line for the analysis of your data, because you wish to know what difference your treatment is making in the client's condition. If it is already improving, you will need to depict that improved trend on your chart when you enter your treatment recordings. Your procedures are as follows:

1. Record the baseline measurements of the client's behavior as well as the treatment measurements on a chart.
2. Draw a line through the treatment period on the chart which represents the trend line established from the baseline data.
3. Determine the number of favorable recordings during the treatment period.

The following is an example of data for scores for self-esteem in which higher scores represent higher self-esteem. There are three baseline recordings as follows: 22, 23, and 20. The mean of these scores is 21.66. The clinician has decided that a score of 22 is a reasonable depiction of the client's level of pretreatment functioning. There are six treatment recordings as follows: 21, 22, 24, 23, 25, and 26.

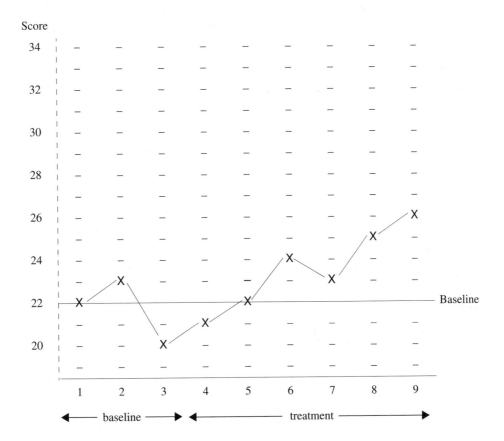

4. Determine statistical significance with the following information:

   a. If you have fewer than five total recordings during the treatment period, your data are not amenable to statistical analysis with this statistical measure.

   b. If you have five or more treatment recordings, you will achieve statistical significance if all treatment recordings are on the favorable side of the trend line.

   c. If you have seven treatment recordings, your data will approach statistical significance (i.e., p = .06) if six of these recordings are favorable.

   d. If you have eight or more treatment recordings, your data will achieve statistical significance if all but one recording is on the favorable side of the trend line.

   e. If you have ten or more treatment recordings, your data will achieve statistical significance if all but two of these treatment recordings are on the favorable side of the trend line.

In the example given above, there are six treatment recordings. The first two recordings (21 and 22) failed to reach the favorable side of the trend line which had been established at 22. Thus, there were four favorable recordings (24, 23, 25, and 26) out of six. According to the data above, these data did not achieve statistical significance. Because the last four recordings were favorable, this is a situation in which statistical significance might have been achieved if the treatment period had been extended. With ten treatment recordings, you can achieve statistical significance when two recordings are not favorable.

Note D: Using the Standard Deviation Approach

If you have at least four baseline recordings and a level trend in these data you can employ the standard deviation approach providing that you are satisfied that these recordings are a reasonable depiction of the client's pretreatment functioning.* With this approach, you will calculate the mean and standard deviation for the baseline recordings as well as the mean for treatment recordings. You will then determine the figure that represents two standard deviations better than the baseline trend by multiplying the standard deviation by 2 and adding this figure to the baseline mean. You will compare this figure to the treatment mean to see if the latter is better. If so, you can declare statistical significance at the .05 level. Your procedures are as follows:

1. Record the baseline measurements of the client's behavior as well as the treatment measurements on a chart.

2. Calculate the mean and the standard deviation of baseline recordings (see Appendix C for instructions.)

3. Draw a line through the treatment period on the chart that represents the mean of baseline recordings.

4. Calculate the figure that represents two standard deviations better than the baseline mean. In other words, multiply the standard deviation of baseline recordings by two and add this value to the baseline mean.

---

*The issue of autocorrelation is relevant to this approach, because the standard deviation makes the assumption that the data are drawn from independent samples. You can test for autocorrelation with SPSS for windows.

5. Draw a second line through the treatment period on the chart that represents two standard deviations better than the baseline mean.
6. Calculate the mean of treatment recordings. Compare this figure to the figure that represents two standard deviations better than the mean of baseline recordings. If the treatment mean is superior to the figure that represents two standard deviations better than the baseline mean, you can declare that you have statistical significance at the .05 level (i.e., p < .05).

Example: In the example below, the client is measured on self-esteem five times during the baseline and five times during the treatment period. Higher scores represent better self-esteem. The objective is to improve self-esteem. The client's scores for the baseline are 12, 16, 11, 14, 12. The mean of these scores is 13 and the standard deviation is 1.78. Two standard deviations above the mean would be a score of 16.56 (13 + 1.78 + 1.78 = 16.56). The treatment recordings are 14, 17, 21, 22, 20. The mean of treatment recordings is 18.8 which is higher than 16.56; thus, these data are statistically significant (p < .05).

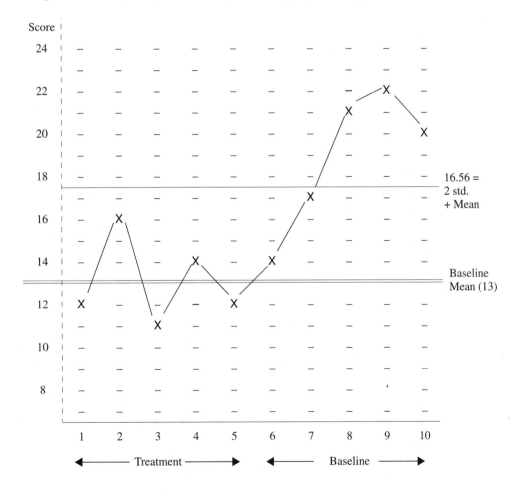

Note E: Using the Celeration Line Approach for Sloped Data

If you have at least four baseline recordings and a nonlevel trend, you can use the celeration line approach. With this approach, you drawn a line that represents the baseline trend and you extend this line throughout the treatment period. You calculate the number of treatment recordings that are better than this trend line and the number that are not. You apply the binomial test with the assumption of a 50–50 split in the baseline recordings. The binomial test will assist you in determining the probability that your split between superior and non-superior treatment recordings could occur by chance. Your procedures are as follows:

1. Record the baseline measurements of the client's behavior as well as the treatment measurements on a chart.
2. Separate the baseline period into two halves. If you have four baseline measurements, recordings number one and two would be the first half of the baseline while recordings number three and four would be the second half. Calculate the mean of each half and place a dot that represents that mean in the respective half that is mid-way of that half of the baseline. See the illustration below.
3. Place a ruler on the chart which connects these two baseline dots and draw a line into the treatment period. This line represents a projection of the baseline trend into the treatment period.
4. Determine the number of treatment recordings that are on the favorable side of this trend line. The binomial test which assumes a 50–50 split in the baseline can be employed to determine statistical significance (See Appendix B). The following will serve as a general guide:
   a. If you have fewer than five total recordings during the treatment period, your data is not amenable to statistical analysis with this statistical measure.
   b. If you have five or more treatment recordings, you will achieve statistical significance if all treatment recordings are on the favorable side of the trend line.
   c. If you have seven treatment recordings, your data will approach statistical significance (i.e., $p = .06$) if six of these recordings are favorable.
   d. If you have eight or more treatment recordings, your data will achieve statistical significance if all but one recording is on the favorable side of the trend line.
   e. If you have ten or more treatment recordings, your data will achieve statistical significance if all but two of these treatment recordings are on the favorable side of the trend line.

Example

In the data shown on p. 359, the client has been measured on self-esteem five times during the baseline with scores of 12, 12, 14, 15, and 16 respectively. The baseline is divided in half. Because there is an odd number of recordings for the baseline, the middle recording (14) is the dividing line and this recording is counted in both halves. Thus, the mean of the first half of the baseline is 12.66 ($12 + 12 + 14 = 38 / 3 = 12.66$), while the mean of the second half is 15 ($14 + 15 + 16 = 45 / 3 = 15$). Dots are placed at 12.66 for the first half and 15 for the second half and a ruler is placed on the chart connecting these two dots. A line is drawn and extended into the treatment period. The treatment recordings are 17, 20, 21, 21 and 24, respectively. The recordings for week 6 and week 9 fail to be above the trend line.

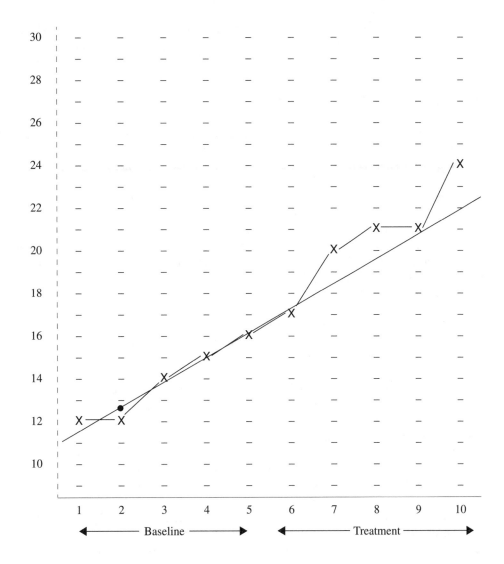

Only three of the five treatment recordings are better than the trend line. When you have five treatment recordings, all five must be superior to the trend line in order for the data to be statistically significant. In our case, this is not true.

Note F: Data Analysis for the B Single-Subject Design

If you have no baseline recordings but you have at least eight treatment recordings, you can employ the C statistic for determining whether the slope of the line for the treatment data is significantly different from a horizontal line which would represent no gain in functioning. Instructions for calculating the C statistic and the Z score are given in Appendix E. If the Z score is greater than 1.64, you can declare statistical significance at the .05 level. The issue of autocorrelation is relevant to your data because the Z statistic assumes that data are independent rather than being repeated measures of the same thing for the same person.

Data Analysis for Group Designs

This section presents guidance on analyzing data for several group designs for evaluating social work practice.

The first design is the *one-shot case study,* in which data are collected on client conditions after treatment is over. This design is rather weak and is seldom appropriate because it is only useful if there is a threshold of client behavior to which the post-treatment measurement can be compared. For example, you might have a group of alcoholics for treatment. You know that each person had a drinking problem before treatment. You could determine the number of persons who achieved a certain level of recovery and compare this figure to the number of clients who did not achieve this level of recovery. The binomial test would be useful in this situation. You could engage in treatment of spouse abusers, determining the number who maintained nonviolent behavior for a six-month follow up period, and compare those who succeeded with those who did not. If you had data that indicated that only one-fourth of spouse abusers recovered on their own (without treatment), you could perhaps assume that this proportion of your treated clients would have done so without treatment; this figure of one-fourth could be the threshold to which your post-treatment data could be compared.

The second design is the *one-group pretest-posttest design.* With this design, you administer the instrument for measuring client progress before treatment (pretest) and again after treatment (posttest) to each client. Your statistic is determined by the level of measurement of the dependent variable.

The *comparison group design* and the *basic experimental design* are similar in the approach you would take to data analysis. In both cases, you are comparing the progress of a treated group to a nontreated group. The statistic to employ would depend upon the level of measurement.

Your next step is to examine the decision trees given in Exhibit 17.3 if you are employing the one shot case study, Exhibit 17.4 if you are employing the one-group pretest-posttest design, or Exhibit 17.5 if you are using a design that compares groups. After you have reached a terminal point, you will be referred to a note or to a particular statistical measure that is described in Chapter 16. You can return to that chapter for more explanation.

Note G: Comparing Successes with Failures (Binomial Test)

If you have a dichotomous dependent variable and only post-treatment data, you can employ the binomial test to determine if the number of cases that had a successful outcome significantly outnumbered the cases without a successful outcome. Your dependent variable is measured in only two categories such as Yes or No or High or Low. In order to employ the approach described here, you will need some basis for predicting the outcome of the client's functioning in the absence of treatment. We do not often have such information. How do we know how many married couples would stop fighting without treatment, or how

EXHIBIT 17.3 Analyzing Data for the One-Shot Case Study

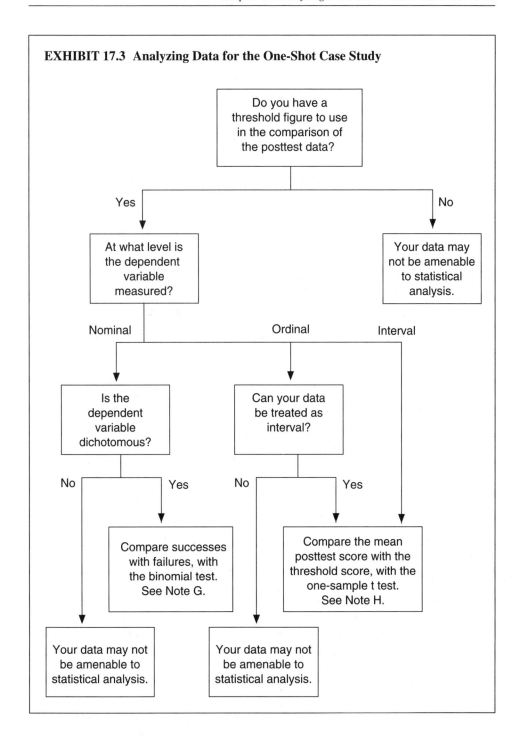

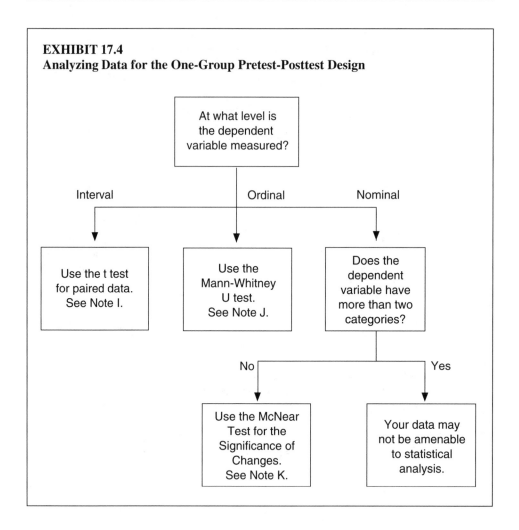

EXHIBIT 17.4
Analyzing Data for the One-Group Pretest-Posttest Design

At what level is the dependent variable measured?

Interval — Use the t test for paired data. See Note I.

Ordinal — Use the Mann-Whitney U test. See Note J.

Nominal — Does the dependent variable have more than two categories?

No — Use the McNear Test for the Significance of Changes. See Note K.

Yes — Your data may not be amenable to statistical analysis.

many troubled youth reduce their incidence of deviance without treatment, or how many alcoholics recover on their own with the normal help from family and friends that might be available? The longer our client has been in difficulty without improvement will be a clue to this endeavor. Recent changes in the client's environment will be another. An alcoholic is not likely to recover without treatment if he has been experiencing a drinking problem for five years unless there have been major changes in his environment that would impose higher motivation to recover, such as losing his job or his wife or being convicted of drinking while impaired. Often, this is when people go to a professional for help. When such events occur and you provide treatment, you are not in a good position to attribute recovery to the treatment rather than the other changes in the environment.

Perhaps you have found a study that discovered that twenty percent of alcoholics recover on their own after the first offense of a DWI. Suppose you have ten clients in a treat-

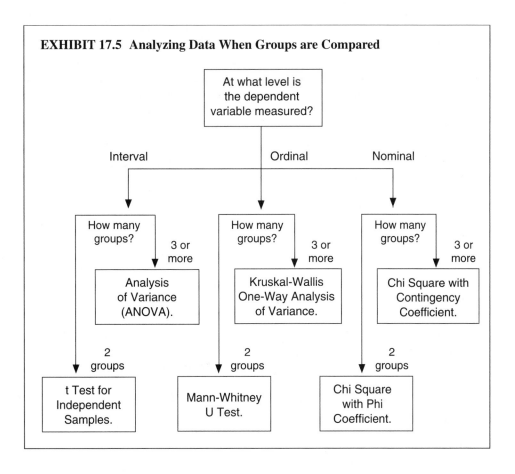

EXHIBIT 17.5 Analyzing Data When Groups are Compared

ment program for persons who have recently been convicted of their first DWI. If so, you could use this as the basis for predicting the outcome of the client's functioning in the absence of treatment. In this case, suppose that five out of ten of your clients achieved recovery. You would want to know if five out of ten is *significantly* better than two out of ten (twenty percent) because you would predict that two out of ten would have achieved recovery without treatment. Your procedures are as follows:

1. Determine the proportion of your clients who would be expected to achieve success, as you are measuring it in your study, in the absence of treatment. Clearly articulate the basis for this prediction. Test the face validity of this prediction by sharing it with experts in the field who are in a position to be objective about this question.
2. Determine the number of your clients who achieved success and the number who did not achieve success.
3. Consult Appendix B for determining statistical significance.

Note H: Comparing a Mean Posttest Score with a Threshold Score (One-Sample t Test)

If you have a dependent variable measured at the interval level and a threshold score to which it can be compared, you can employ the one-sample t test for determining if this mean posttest score is significantly different from the threshold score. For example, you may have established a score of 20 on a depression scale as the threshold for clinical depression and you have made the clinical observation that each client in the treated group was clinically depressed before treatment. You would administer the depression scale after treatment and compare it to the threshold score of 20 with the use of the one-sample t test.

It would have been preferable, however, if you had measured each client on this depression scale before treatment and after treatment so that you could compute a gain score for each client. This is the procedure described in Note I which is relevant to the one-group pretest-posttest research design. In that case, your mean gain score is compared to a score of 0 with a similar statistical procedure.

The steps in the employment of the one-sample t test for the one-shot case study are as follows:

1. Determine the threshold score to which the mean posttest score will be compared. Clarify the basis for selecting this threshold score. Test the face validity of your choice by sharing this decision with an expert in the field who is in a position to be objective about this question.
2. Collect data on the dependent variable from each client at the completion of treatment (posttest).
3. Refer to Appendix D for procedures on the determination of statistical significance.

Note I: Using the t Test for Paired Data with the One-Group Pretest-Posttest Design

If you have collected data on a group of clients before and after treatment using a tool that measures client conditions at the interval level, you can employ the t test for paired data in the determination of statistical significance. In this situation, you have administered the same scale to each client before treatment and after treatment. In the employment of the t test for paired data, you will calculate a gain score for each client and use the procedures of the t test to determine if the mean of these gain scores is significantly different from a score of 0, which would represent no gain in client functioning. The procedures are as follows:

1. Calculate the pretest score for each client and the posttest score for each client.
2. Refer to Appendix F for instructions on the use of the t test.

An alternative is to enter your data into a file using SPSS for Windows and employ the instructions for determining the value of t. See the previous instructions on using these procedures.

Note J: Using the Mann-Whitney U Test with the One-Group Pretest-Posttest Design

If you have collected data on a group of clients before and after treatment using a tool that measures client conditions at the ordinal level, you can employ the Mann-Whitney U Test in the determination of statistical significance. In this situation, you have administered the same scale to each client before treatment and after treatment. You will need to refer to the directions for employing SPSS for Windows in the use of the Mann-Whitney U Test.

Note K: Using the McNear Test with the One-Group Pretest-Posttest Design

If you have a dichotomous dependent variable and the One-Group Pretest-Posttest design, you can employ the McNear test for the significance of changes. In your situation, you have classified the client's behavior into only two categories, such as below or above a certain threshold of functioning. You are testing the hypothesis that the proportion of persons in a certain category will be significanly greater after treatment than before. You will need to refer to the directions for computing the McNear test in Chapter 16.

Questions to Be Considered in the Phases of Evaluative Research

Problem Formulation

1. What is the major problem confronting the client(s)?
2. Why is this problem important?
3. How is this problem defined?
4. What are the causes of this problem or the needs of persons experiencing it?
5. How can the intervention be described?
   a. Objectives
   b. Structure
   c. Content
   d. Personnel
6. How is the intervention justified?

Study Methodology

1. What is the study sample and the study population?
   a. How was the study sample selected?
   b. How is the study population defined?
2. What threats to internal validity are especially important in this situation?
3. What evaluative research design will be employed?
4. How well does this evaluation design address the important threats to internal validity?
5. What is the study hypothesis?

6. How will the dependent variables be defined and measured?
   a. What is the abstract definition of each dependent variable?
   b. How will each dependent variable be measured?
   c. What evidence suggests that these measurement devices are reliable or valid?
   d. What means of observation will be employed?

Data Analysis

1. How is the sample described in relation to basic characteristics?
2. What were the scores of the clients on each of the dependent variables at each administration of the tests?
3. Did the application of statistical tests provide evidence of the statistical significance of the results?

Conclusions

1. How can the results of this study be best summarized?
2. What are some of the limitations of this study in regard to research design, measurement, or sampling?
3. Was practical significance achieved?
4. What are the implications of these results for social work practice?

Appendix *B*

Determining Statistical Significance with the Binomial Test

1. Establish a trend line that projects the baseline data into the treatment period.

2. Determine the proportion of baseline recordings that were on the favorable side of the trend line. If you employ the celeration line with ordinal or interval data, you should assume a 50-50 split (i.e., 50 percent).

3. Determine the proportion of treatment recordings that were on the favorable side of the trend line.

4. Examine the data in the table (next page) in order to determine the level of statistical significance (p). For example, if you have a 50-50 split in the baseline and you have five treatment recordings and all five of these recordings are on the favorable side of the trend line, you will have achieved statistical significance at the normal standard of .05.

Determining Statistical Significance with the Binomial Test

If the proportion of favorable recordings in the baseline is this:	AND the number of treatment recordings is this:	You have statistical significance if the number of favorable recordings is this:
.50 (i.e. a 50-50 split)	4 or less	Not applicable
.50	5 or more	All must be favorable
.50	7	6 (p = .06)
.50	8 or more	All but 1 must be favorable
.50	10 or more	All but 2 must be favorable*
.25	3	Not applicable
.25	4 or more	All
.25	5 or more	All but 1
.25	6 or more	All but 2*
.10	4 or more	All but 1
.10	6 or more	At least one-half

*At higher numbers of treatment recordings, you can achieve statistical significance with a lower number of favorable treatment recordings. Consult a statistical text.

Unless otherwise noted, the statistical significance level for the one-tailed test is .05.

Appendix *C*

Calculating the Standard Deviation

Step 1: Calculating the Mean Score

The mean score is the sum of all scores divided by the number of scores in the sample (n). In the example given below, depression scores of 14, 23, 17, 15, 16, 11, 21, and 18 are used.

	S1 + S2 + S3.... = Sum / n =	Mean
EXAMPLE	14 + 23 + 17 + 15 + 16 + 11 + 21 + 18 = 135 / 8 =	16.88
YOUR DATA →		

Step 2: Calculating the Sum of Squares (SS)

The sum of squares is the sum of the squared deviations from the mean for each score. These procedures entail the subtracting of each score from the mean and the squaring of that figure by multiplying it by itself (Note: when a negative number is squared, it becomes a positive number). Each of these squared scores are summed and this figure represents the sum of squares.

EXAMPLE		YOUR DATA	
Score (x) – Mean (M) = x – M	$(x - M)^2$	Score (x) – Mean (M) = x – M	$(x - M)^2$
14 – 16.88 = –2.88	8.29		
23 – 16.88 = 37.45	37.45		

EXAMPLE		YOUR DATA	
Score (x) – Mean (M) = x – M	$(x - M)^2$	Score (x) – Mean (M) = x – M	$(x - M)^2$
17 – 16.88 = 0.12	0.14		
15 – 16.88 = –1.88	3.53		
16 – 16.88 = –0.88	0.77		
11 – 16.88 = –5.88	34.57		
21 – 16.88 = 4.12	16.97		
18 – 16.88 = 1.12	1.25		
SS = Sum of $(x - M)^2 \rightarrow$	102.97	SS = Sum of $(x - M)^2 \rightarrow$	

Step 3: Calculating the Standard Deviation (Std)

The standard deviation is the square root of the variance. The variance is the sum of squares (SS) divided by the number in the sample (n).

	SS / n = Variance	Square root of the variance is the standard deviation (Std)
EXAMPLE	102.97 / 8 = 12.87	3.59
YOUR DATA →		

Appendix D

Using the One-Sample t Test
for the One-Shot Case Study

The one-sample t test can be used to determine if the difference between a mean score and a threshold score is significantly different. This procedure can be used with the one-shot case study where the dependent variable is measured at the interval level. In the charts below, you will see an example in which the depression scores of a group of eight clients at the completion of treatment was compared to a threshold score of 20 which represents the cutoff point for clinical depression on this particular scale. Persons with scores above 20 are considered to be "clinically depressed." It was the judgment of the clinician and others that each of these eight clients was clinically depressed before treatment. The statistical question is whether the mean post-treatment score for these eight clients was significantly below a score of 20. Next to the example, you will find spaces to enter your data.

Step 1: Calculating the Mean Score

The mean score is the sum of all scores divided by the number of scores in the sample (n).

	S1 + S2 + S3.... = Sum / n =	Mean
EXAMPLE	14 + 23 + 17 + 15 + 16 + 11 + 21 + 18 = 135 / 8 =	16.88
YOUR DATA→		

Step 2: Calculating the Sum of Squares (SS)

The sum of squares is the sum of the squared deviations from the mean for each score. These procedures entail the subtracting of each score from the mean and the squaring of that figure by multiplying it by itself. Each of these squared scores are summed and this figure represents the sum of squares.

EXAMPLE		YOUR DATA	
Score (x) – Mean (M) = x – M	$(x – M)^2$	Score (x) – Mean (M) = x – M	$(x – M)^2$
14 – 16.88 = –2.88	8.29		
23 – 16.88 = 37.45	37.45		
17 – 16.88 = 0.12	0.14		
15 – 16.88 = –1.88	3.53		
16 – 16.88 = –0.88	0.77		
11 – 16.88 = –5.88	34.57		
21 – 16.88 = 4.12	16.97		
18 – 16.88 = 1.12	1.25		
SS = Sum of $(x – M)^2 \rightarrow$	102.97	SS = Sum of $(x – M)^2 \rightarrow$	

Step 3: Calculating the Standard Deviation (Std)

The standard deviation is the square root of the variance. The variance is the sum of squares (SS) divided by the number in the sample (n).

	SS / n = Variance	Square root of the variance is the standard deviation (Std)
EXAMPLE	102.97 / 8 = 12.87	3.59
YOUR DATA→		

Step 4: Calculating the Standard Error

The standard error is the standard deviation divided by the square root of n. In the example below, the square root of 8 (n) is 2.83.

	Standard deviation	divided by	Square root of n	equals	Standard error
EXAMPLE	3.59	/	2.83	=	1.27
YOUR DATA→		/		=	

Step 5: Calculating the Value of t

The value of t is calculated by computing the difference between the mean score of your clients and the threshold score to which it is being compared, and dividing that value by the standard error from step 4. In the example below, the mean score of 16.88 is compared to the threshold score of 20 to determine if there is a significant difference.

	Mean score – Threshold score = K	divided by	Standard error	equals	Value of t
EXAMPLE	16.88 – 20 = 3.12	/	1.27	=	2.45
YOUR DATA →					

Step 6: Determining Statistical Significance

When you are comparing a mean score on client functioning with a threshold score, you have a directional hypothesis because you are hypothesizing that the mean score is better than the threshold. Thus, you would employ the one-tailed t test for determining statistical significance. You can consult a statistical text with a table of t in order to determine statistical significance. A few values from such tables are presented here, all of which refer to significance at the .05 level.

If you have a sample of 5, your data are statistically significant if your t value is 2.13 or higher. Your data will be statistically significant with a sample of 10 if your t value is 1.83 or better, while a t value of 1.75 or higher is significant with a sample of 15 or more. With a sample of 20 or more, a t value of 1.72 is statistically significant. As you can see, the higher the number in your sample, the lower your t value must be in order to be statistically significant.

Determining Significant Improvement Using B Single-Subject Design

The following procedures are employed to determine if the slope of a trend line is significant. In other words, these procedures will tell you whether the line from your data has a slope (going up or down) that is significantly different from a horizontal line which would represent no gain in functioning. These procedures will assist you in calculating the value of Z which is significant at the .05 level (i.e., p < .05) if it is greater than 1.64. The steps below contain an example that illustrates how to calculate the data. There is a set of spaces for you to use for your data. The example contains the following set of scores given in proper time sequence: 68, 66, 64, 60, 56, 55, 53, 50, 46, 40. These figures start with 68 and end with 40. There is a trend that is going down in these scores for depression. The statistical question is whether this downward trend is *significantly* different from a horizontal line which would represent no growth at all.

Note: The formula for determining statistical significance that is incorporated into the instructions in this appendix was taken from the following source: Tropidi, T. (1994). *A Primer on Single-Subject Design.* Washington: NASW Press.

Step 1: Calculating the Mean for all Scores (M)

	Sum of all scores	divided by	number in sample (n)	equals	Mean (M)
EXAMPLE	68 + 66 + 64 + 60 + 56 + 55 + 53 + 50 + 46 + 40 = 558	/	10	=	55.8
YOUR DATA→					

Step 2a: Calculating the Value of SS(x)

The value of 2SS(x) represents the double of the squared deviations from the mean. Your first procedure in this step is to calculate the value of SS(x) by subtracting each score from the mean and squaring that figure and summing all of these squared deviations from the mean.

EXAMPLE		YOUR DATA	
Score (x) minus Mean (M) = x – M	$(x – M)^2$	Score (x) minus Mean (M) = x – M	$(x – M)^2$
68 – 55.8 = 12.2	148.84		
66 – 55.8 = 10.2	104.04		
64 – 55.8 = 8.2	67.24		
60 – 55.8 = 4.2	17.64		
56 – 55.8 = 0.2	.04		
55 – 55.8 = –0.8	.64		
53 – 55.8 = –2.8	7.84		
50 – 55.8 = –5.8	33.64		
46 – 55.8 = –9.8	96.04		
40 – 55.8 = –15.8	249.64		
Sum of $(x – M)^2$ equals SS(x) →	725.60	Sum of $(x – M)^2$ equals SS(x) →	

Step 2b: Calculating the Value of 2SS(x)
In this procedure, you double the value of SS(x) in order to obtain the value of 2SS(x).

EXAMPLE		YOUR DATA	
SS(x) times 2 =	2SS(x)	SS(x) times 2 =	2SS(x)
725.6 x 2 =	1451.2		

Step 3: Calculating D^2
In this step, you will subtract each score, beginning with the first score in the time sequence, from the next score in the sequence and you will calculate the square of that figure by multiplying it by itself. The sum of these squared deviations from subsequent scores is the value of D^2.

EXAMPLE		YOUR DATA	
Score (x) minus following score (f) equals x – f	$(x - f)^2$	Score (x) minus following score (f) equals x – f	$(x - f)^2$
68 – 66 = 2 66 – 64 = 2 64 – 60 = 4 60 – 56 = 4 56 – 55 = 1 55 – 53 = 2 53 – 50 = 3 50 – 46 = 4 46 – 40 = 6	4 4 16 16 1 4 9 16 36		
Sum of $(x - f)^2$ equals $D^2 \rightarrow$	106	Sum of $(x - f)^2$ equals $D^2 \rightarrow$	

Step 4: Calculating C

The C statistic is used in the calculation of Z. You compute C by subtracting D^2 from 1 and dividing that value by the value of 2SS(x) which you computed in step 2.

	1 minus D^2 divided by 2SS(x) equals	C
EXAMPLE	$1 - [106 / 1451.2] = 1 - 0.073 = C$	0.927
YOUR DATA		

Step 5: Calculating Sc

In this step, you calculate the standard error.

	n + 2 = E	(n + 1)(n – 1) = F	E / F = G	Square root of G equals Sc
EXAMPLE	10 + 2 = 12	11 × 9 = 99	12 / 99 = 0.1212	0.348
YOUR DATA				

Step 6: Calculating the Value of Z and Determining Statistical Significance

The value of Z is determined by dividing C by Sc.

	C divided by Sc = Z	Z
EXAMPLE	0.927 / 0.348 = Z	2.66
YOUR DATA		

If the value of Z for your data is greater than 1.64, you have achieved statistical significance at the 0.05 level (i.e., $p < .05$). This means that the slope in your data is significantly greater than the pattern of data that would represent a horizontal line. In other words, your client achieved a significant growth in functioning. However, because you did not have baseline data, you cannot rule out maturation as the cause of this growth.

Appendix *F*

Using the t Test for Paired Data with the One-Group Pretest-Posttest Design

If you are using the one-group pretest-posttest research design and have measured your dependent variable at the interval level, you may employ the t test for paired data in the examination of the significance of the difference between the pretest and posttest scores of your clients. The procedures for this approach entail calculating a difference score for each client, computing the mean difference score for the entire group, and applying the t test to determine if this mean difference score is significantly different from a score of 0, which would represent no gain at all. The procedure is similar to the procedure for the one-sample t test. In your case, the one sample of scores is the gain score and the threshold to which it is being compared is 0.

You can submit your data to SPSS for Windows in order to determine the value of t, or you can calculate the value of t using the charts in this appendix. This form of the t test is one of the simpler ones that can be reasonably done with charts, whereas most statistical procedures are more complicated and necessitate the use of the computer. However, it will take less time to determine the value of t with the computer if one is accessible.

Step 1: Calculating the Gain Score for Each Client and the Mean of All Gain Scores
The gain score for each client is the difference between the pretest and posttest score. Whether you subtract the pretest score from the posttest score or vice versa depends on whether you are attempting to increase or decrease these scores. If better functioning is displayed by higher scores, you would subtract the pretest score from the posttest score. For example, if your self-esteem score is 18 at pretest and 30 at posttest, you have achieved a gain of 12 points, assuming that higher scores represent higher self-esteem. If you subtract the pretest score of 18 from the posttest score of 30, you will have a difference score of 12.

However, if you are measuring depression, you would do the opposite—you would subtract the posttest score from the pretest score, assuming that lower scores on this scale represent lower depression. For example, if you have a pretest depression score of 34 and a posttest score of 21, you have achieved a gain of 13 points. In some cases, the gain score is negative, meaning that the client realized a loss in functioning during the treatment period. When you sum the gain scores, you will need to subtract the negative scores from the positive scores. For example, the scores of +10 and +15 and –5 result in a sum of 20 (10 + 15 = 25 – 5 = 20).

On the next page you can begin to enter your data. You will see an example that is given in one portion of each chart and you will have space for entering your data. The example is one in which depression scores were taken before and after treatment for a group of eight clients. Because lower scores are "better" for depression, the left part of the chart is completed. If higher scores had been better, the right side of the chart would have been used.

After you enter the pretest and posttest scores for each client and compute the gain, you will determine the mean gain score for all clients. This mean will be used in step 2.

	IF LOWER SCORES ARE BETTER		IF HIGHER SCORES ARE BETTER	
	Pretest Score minus Posttest Score	Gain Score	Posttest Score minus Pretest Score	Gain Score
EXAMPLE	30 – 15 = 28 – 26 = 20 – 22 = 29 – 24 = 36 – 32 = 24 – 25 = 28 – 20 = 27 – 14 =	15 2 –2 5 4 –1 8 13		
	Sum of Gain Scores →	44		
	Sum / n = Mean →	5.5		
YOUR DATA	Pretest Score minus Posttest Score	Gain Score	Posttest Score minus Pretest Score	Gain Score
	Sum of Gain Scores →		Sum of Gain Scores →	
	Sum / n = Mean →		Sum / n = Mean →	

Step 2: Calculating the Sum of Squares (SS)

The sum of squares is the sum of the squared deviations from the mean for each gain score. These procedures entail subtracting each gain score from the mean of gain scores and squaring that figure, (multiplying it by itself). You will notice that a negative score becomes a positive score when it is squared. Thus, the square of −7.5 is 56.25, the same as the square of 7.5. Each of these squared scores are summed and this figure represents the sum of squares.

EXAMPLE		YOUR DATA	
Score (x) − Mean (M) = x − M	$(x - M)^2$	Score (x) − Mean (M) = x − M	$(x - M)^2$
15 − 5.5 = 9.5 2 − 5.5 = −3.5 −2 − 5.5 = −7.5 5 − 5.5 = −0.5 4 − 5.5 = −1.5 −1 − 5.5 = −6.5 8 − 5.5 = 2.5 13 − 5.5 = 7.5	90.25 12.25 56.25 0.25 2.25 42.25 6.25 56.25		
SS = Sum of $(x - M)^2 \rightarrow$	266.00	SS = Sum of $(x - M)^2 \rightarrow$	

Step 3: Calculating the Standard Deviation (Std)

The standard deviation is the square root of the variance. The variance is the sum of squares (SS) divided by the number in the sample (n). (Most hand-held calculators have a square root key which you can press with a number in the display and you will obtain the square root of that number.)

	SS / n = Variance	Square root of the variance is the standard deviation (Std)
EXAMPLE	266 / 8 = 33.25	5.766
YOUR DATA →		

Step 4: Calculating the Standard Error

The standard error is the standard deviation divided by the square root of n. In the example below, the square root of 8 (n) is 2.83.

	Standard deviation	divided by	Square root of n	equals	Standard error
EXAMPLE	5.766	/	2.83	=	2.037
YOUR DATA →		/		=	

Step 5: Calculating the Value of t

The value of t is calculated by dividing the mean gain score by the standard error.

	Mean Gain Score / Standard Error =	Value of t
EXAMPLE	5.5 / 2.037 =	2.7
YOUR DATA →		

Step 6: Determining Statistical Significance

When you are comparing a mean of gain scores on client functioning with a value of 0 which would represent no gain, you have a directional hypothesis because you are hypothesizing that the mean score is significantly better than 0. Thus, you would employ the one-tailed t test for determining statistical significance. In the example given above, the t value of 2.7 is statistically significant ($p < .05$), as you will see from the explanation below.

You can consult a statistical text with a table of t in order to determine statistical significance. A few values from such tables are presented here, all of which refer to significance at the .05 level:

If you have a sample of 5, your data are statistically significant if your t value is 2.13 or higher. Your data will be statistically significant with a sample of 10 if your t value is 1.83 or better, while a t value of 1.75 or higher is significant with a sample of 15 or more. With a sample of 20 or more, a t value of 1.72 is statistically significant. As you can see, the higher the number in your sample, the lower your t value must be in order to be statistically significant.

Glossary

AB single-subject research design. A research design in which a single subject (client, group, organization, community) is measured on the dependent variable several times during a baseline period before treatment begins and is repeatedly measured on the dependent variable during the treatment period.

ABC single-subject research design. A research design in which a single subject is measured repeatedly during a baseline period (period A), given a certain treatment and repeatedly measured during this treatment period (period B), then given a changed treatment (period C), with the client continually measured on the dependent variable during this second treatment period.

Abstract Definition of a Study Variable. A definition of a variable that provides conceptual guidance on the boundaries considered fitting for the variable *for the present study.* It can be likened to a dictionary definition of the variable, although it is not required to encompass all territory that others might want to include, but only the conceptual territory that the researcher considers proper for the given study.

Analysis of variance (ANOVA). A statistic for determining whether the mean scores of three or more groups are significantly different.

Analytic induction. A method of qualitative inquiry that is designed to test, or refine, a hypothesis. The process begins with a tentative hypothesis and cases are studied in light of that hypothesis, with each case either confirming the hypothesis or suggesting a modification of it.

Assumption. A statement that is not being subjected to assessment in the present study, but which must be true in order for the study to provide an accurate inquiry into the research question being examined.

Attribute of a variable. A category or value that a variable can possess. For example, the variable of gender would have the attributes of male and female.

Average Deviation. The average of all deviations from the mean in an array of data. For example, the ages of 24, 26, 28, and 30 would have a mean of 27 (24 + 26 + 28 + 30 = 108 / 4 = 27) and an average deviation of 2 (3 + 1 + 1 + 3 = 8 / 4 = 2).

Bar chart.   A chart that depicts the frequencies for the various categories for a variable.

Bias.   A tendency toward inaccurate measurement in a given direction. For example, a person exhibiting a social desirability bias on a questionnaire would be inaccurately reflecting his or her true opinion in the direction of responses that are socially desirable.

Binomial Test.   A statistical measure for determining whether the frequencies between two categories of a variable are significantly different.

Coding.   The method of translating study subject responses into symbols that facilitate data analysis. For example, the category of female might be coded as 1 while the category of male might be coded as 0 for data analysis. A statement from an interview might be coded as "stress" because of its content.

Chi Square One Sample Test.   A statistic for determining whether the frequencies among three or more categories of a nominal variable are significantly different.

Data Analysis.   The third major phase of the research process whereby data are chanalyzed to address the research question.

Chi Square Test for Two Independent Samples.   A statistic for determining if there is a significant relationship between two variables measured at the nominal level when data are drawn from independent samples.

Content Validity.   The extent to which a measurement device covers the total content and meaning of the variable as it is defined for a given study.

Contingency Coefficient.   A statistical measure for determining the strength of the relationship between two nominal variables. It can be used in conjunction with chi square, the latter being a means for determining statistical significance.

Control Group.   A group of study subjects who do not receive the intervention.

Control Variable.   A variable that is held constant in the examination of a relationship between two other variables. For example, you could use position level as a control variable when examining the relationship between gender and salary, by comparing the salaries of male managers and female managers as well as male nonmanagers and female nonmanagers. In this way, the influence of position level on the relationship between gender and salary is controlled.

Construct Validity.   The extent to which a measure of a variable operates in the way it would have been predicted theoretically.

Cross-sectional study.   A study of one group of people at one point in time.

Descriptive Research.   Research that describes something with precision but does not attempt to explain it.

Descriptive Statistics.   Statistics that describe the characteristics of a study sample. Examples include the mean, median, mode, and standard deviation.

Dichotomous Variable.   A variable that has only two categories.

Causation.   The explanation of the reasons that events occur. In research, the concept of causation is treated cautiously because events typically have multiple causes and the pinpointing of causation is difficult.

Celeration line method of statistical analysis (for single-subject research).   A method of statistical analysis for single-subject research in which the baseline trend is not level—in other words, is either ascending or descending. The proportion of recordings of the dependent variable during the treatment period that fall on the favorable side of the trend line is compared to the same for the baseline period to see if the former is significantly greater than the latter. In most circumstances, if you have as many as six treatment recordings and all the treatment recordings are superior to the trend line, you will achieve statistical analysis; however, you should consult a statistical test to be sure.

Coefficient.   A figure representing the strength of the empirical relationship between variables. Various statistical tests employ the term "coefficient." For example, there is the phi coefficient, the contingency coefficient, the Pearson correlation coefficient, the Spearman rank correlation coefficient, and so forth. The values of such coefficients typically can range from 0 to 1.0.

Comparison group design.   A research design in which members of a group of treated clients are measured before and after the intervention and their gains in functioning are compared to the before and after measurements of a group that did not receive treatment. This design is also known as the non-equivalent control group design.

Conclusions.   The final major phase of the research process, in which conclusions are drawn about the data that were used to examine the research question.

Criterion validity.   A measurement device has criterion validity to the extent to which it corresponds to (correlates with) other criteria for observing the concept under study. For example, scholastic aptitude test scores should correlate with college grades if this test has criterion validity. A marital satisfaction scale should be able to predict divorce. One person's self-esteem scale should correlate with another person's self-esteem scale.

Cumulative frequency.   A frequency that includes all those in the present category (reference category) plus the frequency for all categories which come before the present one in the classification scheme.

Cumulative proportion.   A proportion that includes all those in the present category (reference category) plus the proportion for all categories that come before the present one in the classification scheme.

Deductive.   A process of inquiry that begins with theory and moves to observation for the purpose of testing theory.

Dependent variable.   The variable that is believed to depend on or be caused by another variable, the other variable being known as the "independent variable."

Direct observation.   A means of observation in qualitative research in which the researcher is directly observing the behavior of the study subjects.

Disconfirming evidence.   Evidence that is counter to a given explanation of things.

Efficiency Evaluation.   The evaluation of the ratio of inputs to outputs. Inputs are normally measured in regard to dollars, and outputs are normally measured as units of service. A comparison of the average cost per hour of counseling between two programs would be an example.

Empirical relationship. A relationship between variables that can be depicted through concrete measurement devices. An example would be the relationship between gender and salary.

Ethnography. The study of cultures in their natural settings through qualitative research methods.

Evaluative Research. Research used to evaluate whether an intervention achieved its objectives.

Experimental research design. The basic experimental design entails the assignment of persons to two groups on a random basis, one group being given the intervention (known as the experimental group) and the other group being excluded from treatment (the control group). Both groups of persons are measured on the dependent variable before treatment and again after treatment has been completed. The gain in functioning for the two groups is compared to see if the experimental group had a significantly greater gain than the control group. The basic experimental design is also known as the pretest-posttest control group design and is not the only design that is classified as experimental.

Explanatory Research. Research designed to explain something, usually by examining the relationships among a set of variables to see if one offers an explanation of another.

Exploratory Research. Research designed to develop knowledge about a relatively unknown phenomenon so that new theory can be developed or new insight can be acquired on the nature of it.

Exhaustive. Categories for a question on a questionnaire which include a category that fits each potential study subject.

Face validity. A measurement device has face validity if it appears to knowledgeable persons to be an accurate means of measuring the particular concept it is supposed to measure. This is the least objective of the various methods of assessing validity, but is often the only reasonable alternative for self-developed instruments.

Fischer Exact Probability Test. A statistic for determining whether there is a significant relationship between two nominal variables. This statistic is especially useful for small samples where chi square is not appropriate.

Frequency. The incidence of something, such as the number of females and males in a study sample. There could be, for example, a frequency of 24 females and 21 males in a given sample.

Generalization. The application of knowledge about one group of study subjects to another group of persons.

Grounded theory. A qualitative research methodology that is designed to develop theory through a highly inductive, but systematic, process of discovery. A major focus is on the observation of similarities and differences in social behavior across social situations.

History (as a threat to internal validity). When a client improves during the treatment period, it may be because of the treatment, or it may be because of a change in the client's environment, such as obtaining a job or getting a promotion. History as a threat to internal validity refers to changes in the client's environment that may be the cause of improvement. The comparison group design addresses history as a threat to internal validity because it is assumed that the two groups will be equivalent on history; thus, the superiority of the gain for the treatment group over the gain for the comparison group would be better attributed to the treatment than to history. The AB single-subject design, however, does not address this threat.

Hypothesis. A statement of the expected results of a research study on a given theme based on theory or explanations derived from existing knowledge. For example, one might hypothesize that males will report higher annual salaries than will females. This hypothesis would be based on knowledge of sexual discrimination.

Indirect observation. A means of observation (measurement) in qualitative research in which the researcher is examining products of behavior such as records or literature as a basis for developing theories or explanations about behavior.

Independent variable. The variable that is believed to cause the dependent variable to be the way it is.

Inductive. A process of inquiry that begins with observations from which theory or generalizations are derived.

Inferential Statistics. A body of statistical tests that are used to make inferences from a sample to a population.

Instrumentation. The means used in a study to measure variables.

Internal consistency. The tendency of items forming a common scale to operate the same way. For example, a self-esteem scale would have internal consistency to the extent that the items on the scale, when treated as separate variables, would be correlated with one another when given to a sample of study subjects. Thus, if John has a higher score than Tom on item 1 on this scale, he would probably have a higher score than Tom on item 2 on this scale as well. If this were *not* the general pattern for items on this scale, then it would *not* be considered to have internal consistency. This situation would suggest that the items on this scale are not measuring the same thing.

Internal Validity. The extent to which changes in the study subject (client) can be attributed to the intervention rather than something else. The key to the examination of internal validity is the research design.

Interval. A level of measurement in which subjects are given scores on a scale in which the intervals between each level are equal. For example, the temperature of 32 is 1 degree lower than the temperature of 33 which is 1 degree lower than the temperature of 34. This scale is measured in reference to degrees on the scale with each single degree being equal to each of the other degrees.

Interview. A personal encounter between persons in which one person is seeking information from another person. It can take place face-to-face or by way of another mode of personal interaction, such as the telephone.

Interview structure. The extent to which questions for study in an interview have been narrowed or specifically focused. The more specific the focus, the more the interview is structured. The extent to which questions are open-ended. More open questions have less structure.

Kruskal-Wallis One-Way Analysis of Variance. A statistical measure for determining if there is a significant relationship between a nominal variable with three or more categories and an ordinal variable in situations where the data are drawn from independent samples.

Levels of Measurement.   The hierarchy of measurement for study variables, each level of which provides a different level of sophistication in measurement, and is suitable for different statistical tests. The levels are nominal, ordinal, interval, and ratio, in that order from lowest to highest. A variable measured at a higher level can be treated as though it is measured at a lower level for statistical analysis purposes, if necessary. For example, a variable measured at the interval level can be treated as though it is measured at the ordinal level. However, we lose information when we do this, so it is not optimal.

Logic.   Whether something makes sense when subjected to careful analysis through the principles of good reasoning.

Longitudinal Study.   A study involving the collection of data at more than one point in time.

Maturation.   Sometimes people overcome their problems on their own through time and the normal process of growth. This is referred to as maturation, and is one of the most important threats to the internal validity of a research project. The comparison group design addresses maturation because it compares a treated group with an untreated group, the assumption being that the effects of maturation would probably be equal for the two groups; thus, the superiority of a treated group's improvement in functioning over the comparison group is normally better attributed to the treatment than to maturation. The AB single-subject design also addresses maturation because the baseline trend is assumed to be an indicator of the progression of maturation; thus, if the client's functioning during the treatment period is significantly better than the projected baseline trend, the client's growth can be better attributed to the treatment than to maturation.

McNear Test for the Significance of Changes.   A statistic for analyzing the relationship between two nominal variables that are dichotomous and drawn from related samples.

Mann-Whitney U Test.   A statistic for determining if there is a significant relationship between a dichotomous nominal variable and an ordinal variable, in situations where the data are drawn from independent samples.

Mean.   The average. The mean is calculated by summing the frequencies in a sample of data and dividing the sum by the number of people in the sample.

Median.   The mid point in an array of data laid out in numerical order. For example, examine the following numbers: 12, 15, 16, 19, 27, 28, 31. The median for this array of data is 19.

Methodology.   The second major phase of the research process whereby the study is designed in a manner that adequately addresses the research question.

Mode.   The most frequently observed value for a given variable.

Multiple Regression Analysis.   A statistic for determining if there is a significant relationship between a dependent variable measured at the interval level and three or more independent variables measured at the interval level, in situations where the data are drawn from independent samples.

Mutually Exclusive.   Categories for a research instrument that are not capable of overlap; a study subject could not possibly be placed into more than one category among those presented.

Needs Assessment.   A means for evaluating human need.

Negative relationship. A relationship between study variables in which *high* values on one variable tend to be associated with *low* values on the other variables. For example, we would expect to find a negative relationship between self esteem and depression, meaning that persons with higher self esteem scores would tend to have low scores for depression. Thus, if Paul has a higher score for self-esteem than does Jim, he is likely to have a lower score on depression than Jim.

Nominal. The lowest level of measurement. At the nominal level, the attributes of a variable are in categories that cannot be ranked low, medium, or high. Examples include gender, political party affiliation, and favorite color.

Nonequivalent Control Group Design. A research design in which a group of treated clients are compared to a group of nontreated people, in situations in which assignment to the groups was not made randomly. Also referred to as the **comparison group design.**

Nonprobability Sample. A sample that was not drawn randomly.

Observation. The measurement of something.

One group pretest-posttest research design. A research design in which members in a group of clients are tested on the dependent variable before treatment and again after treatment has been completed. The gain in functioning evidenced by these two tests serves as a measure of the effects of treatment.

Operational Definition of a Study Variable. A definition of a study variable that specifies how the variable will be measured in the present study.

Ordinal. The next level of measurement beyond nominal. Ordinal variables place subjects in categories that are ordered from low to high or most to least, and so forth. For example, the response categories of "agree," "undecided," and "disagree" place respondents in categories of agreement that are ordered from most to least.

p. The letter p is used to designate the estimate of the probability that a set of research data would occur by chance. The designation "p < .05" means that these particular data would occur by chance less than 5 times in 100. The designation "p < .01" indicates that this likelihood is less than 1 time in 100.

Participant observer. A role in research in which an individual is both a participant in a social process and a researcher of that process.

Pearson's correlation coefficient. A measure of the degree of relationship between two variables measured at the interval level. It is designated in research literature with the small letter r (e.g., r = .46). The value of this coefficient can range from a low of 0 to a high of 1.0, and it can be either negative or positive. In other words, possible values include –1.0, 0, and 1.0 and all possible values in between, such as –.21, –.58, –.94, .12, .33, .78, and so forth. Values close to 0 mean that there is little, if any, relationship between the variables.

Phi coefficient. A measure of the strength of the relationship between two variables measured at the nominal level. It can range from 0 to 1.0, but cannot be negative, because relationships between nominal variables can be neither negative nor positive (such variables having no order to their categories). For example, we could not speak of a negative relationship between gender and political party affiliation. To do so would suggest that the categories of these variables are ordered such that male is higher or lower than female.

Pie chart.   A circular chart that depicts the proportions of subjects (or entities) in each category for a variable.

Population.   The larger group from which the sample was selected.

Practical Significance.   The extent to which a given set of study findings are noteworthy.

Positive relationship.   A relationship between study variables in which high values on one variable tend to be associated with high values on the other variables (with low values on one being associated with low values on the other). For example, we would expect to find a positive relationship between IQ scores and college grades, meaning that persons with higher IQ scores would tend to have the higher grades, while persons with low IQ scores would tend to have the low grades. Thus, if Mary has a higher IQ than Bob, she is likely to have higher college grades than Bob.

Posttest.   A measurement of study subjects on the dependent variable after treatment has been completed.

Posttest-Only Control Group Design.   A research design in which a randomly assigned treated group is compared to a randomly assigned nontreated group after the completion of treatment.

Predispositions.   One's preconceived notions of reality. The explanations about our study subject which we take into our study process and which should be open to alteration by the results of our study.

Pretest.   A measurement of study subjects on the dependent variable before treatment begins.

Probability.   The likelihood of the occurrence of something that is not a certainty. Statistical tests are used to estimate probability, designated with the letter p.

Probability Sample.   A sample that was drawn at random from the specified study population.

Problem Formulation.   The first major phase of the research process in which the research question is developed and the research problem is analyzed.

Proportion.   The percentage of something, such as the percent of the sample that was female.

Purposive Sample.   A nonrandom sample that is drawn because of its special characteristics, such as being an expert on a subject or being a person known to have a certain problem.

Qualitative.   A means of observation (or measurement) that is flexible, such as an open-ended question on a questionnaire, or direct observation of behavior as it naturally occurs.

Quantitative.   A means of observation (or measurement) that is fixed, such as posing a question which places people in discrete categories (e.g., male or female) or gives them a number as a value for the response to the question (e.g. age).

Questionnaire.   A document that contains questions designed to measure study variables.

Range.   The distribution of scores from the lowest to the highest in an array of data.

Ratio.   The highest level of measurement. Variables measured at the ratio level have all the characteristics of variables measured at the interval level, with the addition that all scores on the scale are based on a fixed zero point. A practical way to remember this characteristic is to realize that variables measured at the ratio level cannot have negative values, because 0 is the lowest possible value. For example, a person cannot have negative weight, height, or age.

Random Sample.   A sample in which each person in the study population had an equal chance of being selected for the sample.

Reliability.   The consistency of a means of measurement. If a scale is reliable, persons will respond to it in a consistent fashion at different points in time.

Research design.   The protocol in evaluative research whereby study subjects are measured on the dependent variable and interventions are administered.

Sample.   A portion of a larger entity. In a research study, it pertains to the study subjects from whom data were collected.

Sampling Frame.   The list from which a sample is drawn.

Sampling Interval.   The standard distance between subjects selected for a sample from the sampling frame. If you select every fourth person starting with person number 2 on your list, your sampling interval would be four.

Scientific Inquiry.   A systematic process of inquiry that is designed to reduce the bias inherent in human observation through the application of both logic and objective measurement of social phenomena.

Single-subject research design (also known as single-system design).   A research design in which the study subject is treated as a single subject and data is collected on the dependent variable repeatedly for this one subject. While the single-subject design is typically used with a single client, it can also be employed with a single organization or community or group, provided that each is treated as a single unit for data analysis. For example, your dependent variable could be the weekly number of referrals to the hospital social work department.

Snowball Sample.   A nonprobability sample in which persons initially selected for a study sample are asked to identify others who would qualify for the study. These others are then included in the study sample.

Social survey.   A means of collecting information from people through questionnaires or interviews, in which the information to be collected is specified ahead of time and the questionnaire items for obtaining this information have been developed.

Spearman rank correlation coefficient.   A measure of the strength of the relationship between variables measured at the ordinal level. The value of this coefficient can range from 0 to 1.0 and can be either negative or positive.

Standard deviation.   A measure of variance for a distribution. It tells us how much the subjects in a particular sample are similar or different from one another.

Standard deviation method of statistical analysis for single-subject research.   A means of statistical analysis of single-subject research data when the trend during the baseline period is relatively level. Statistical significance is achieved if the mean for treatment recordings of the dependent variable is two standard deviations better than the mean for the baseline recordings.

Statistical Significance. The likelihood that a given set of study findings would be expected to occur by chance.

Statistical Test. A measure used to estimate the likelihood that a given set of study findings would be expected to occur by chance.

t test. A means of determining the statistical significance of data measured at the interval level for either two groups of subjects (t test for independent samples) or a single group of subjects measured at two points in time (t test for paired data). The formula for these two situations is not the same. When testing a directional hypothesis, a t value of 2.0 or greater is significant at the .05 (i.e., p< .05) level if the sample size is greater than 5. Slightly lower t values are significant (at the .05 level) with larger samples. Consult a statistical text with a table of t values for further information.

Testing (as a threat to internal validity). As a threat to internal validity, testing refers to the effect of being tested. One may develop a sensitivity to the administration of a pretest which may effect the posttest score. This is of special concern if the pretest and posttest deal with knowledge because one may remember items on the pretest when taking the posttest and may have been especially sensitive to this specific piece of information. Thus, it may be this sensitivity rather than the intervention that mostly effected the gain illustrated by the posttest. The comparison group and AB single-subject designs both address this threat. It is assumed that the comparison group would have the same reaction to the testing situation as the treatment group; thus, any differences between the two groups can be better attributed to the treatment than to the effects of testing. For the AB single-subject design, the baseline period establishes a trend that illustrates the effects of testing if there are any. Thus, the superiority of client functioning during the treatment period is better attributed to the intervention than to testing.

Test-retest reliability. To assess reliability using this method, subjects are measured on the scale at two points in time and the two scores for this same group of persons are correlated. High positive correlations indicate reliability, or consistency.

Theory. In the most simple terms, a theory is an attempt to explain something. Theories can be more or less formal and explicit or more or less sophisticated, but any attempt to explain is a theory, whether or not it is supported by scientific evidence.

Threats to internal validity. In evaluative research, a threat to internal validity is something that may be the reason for the client's change in behavior other than the intervention. For example, a change in the client's work situation may be the reason that he is no longer depressed; thus, the treatment may not have caused the improvement in functioning. There are a variety of threats to internal validity, also known as alternative explanations. Among these threats are maturation, history, and testing, which are defined elsewhere in this glossary. Some research designs do a better job of dealing with certain threats to internal validity than do other research designs. In general, experimental designs that randomly assign subjects to treatment and control (comparison) groups do a superior job of addressing the various threats to internal validity.

Treatment objectives. A statement of the nature of the gain in functioning that is expected for the client of a treatment program. It is a statement of a measured amount of progress toward the accomplishment of broad human goals.

Treatment period. A period of time during which the client is subjected to the intervention.

Validity. The extent to which a measurement device truly measures the thing it is supposed to measure. In other words, it refers to the accuracy of a means of measurement.

Variable. Something that varies in the present study. In other words, an entity that takes on more than one value. For example, the variable of gender would be divided into the categories of male and female. A concept is not a variable in a given study unless it is measured in that study and there is some variance in responses. The concept of gender could not be a variable in a study that included only females.

Variance. The extent to which numbers in a set of data are different from one another. The greater the difference from one number to another, the greater the variance. (The term "variance" in statistics has a special meaning. It is the square of the standard deviation.)

Wilcoxon Matched-Pairs Signed Ranks Test. A statistic for examining the relationship between a dichotomous nominal variable and an ordinal variable in situations where the data are drawn from related samples.

Index